Dear Reader,

In 2013 I travelled to Kalimantan, Borneo with my husband and children. Our primary objective was to visit Tanjung Puting National Park, one of the few places on earth where orangutans can still be seen in their native habitat. It turned out to be one of the most amazing experiences of my life and provided much of the inspiration for this book. Not only did I fall in love with those wonderful creatures, I fell in love with Borneo and its people.

Much of this book is drawn on our own adventure and experiences during that trip, and whilst I hope I've been able to pen a story that is entertaining for you as the reader, it's also my sincere hope that in my own small way I have succeeded in drawing some attention to the plight of the critically endangered orangutan and other species that are under immense pressure from the modern world.

Happy reading,

Melissa Kuipers

PS: I love getting feedback from my readers so don't forget to leave a review for this book on Amazon or Goodreads.

About the Author

Melissa Kuipers lives in Western Australia with her husband, their two children and a schizophrenic cat. Somehow in between being a wife and mother, a demanding full-time career and travel, Melissa still manages to find time to write.

Melissa also writes contemporary and western genre romance under the penname Tess McCallum, including the popular Molly Downs Outback Romance series.

If you want to know more about Melissa's (or Tess's) books and where she finds her inspiration, you'll find it all on her website: www.tessmccallum.com.

Books by this Author

Molly Downs Outback Romance Series:

    Different This Time (Book #1)

    One Time Thing (Book #2)

    Breaking Free (Book #3)

    Eight Seconds To Forever (Book #4)

Maelstrom

A Thousand Rivers (published under the penname Melissa Kuipers)

All my books are available in the Amazon stores worldwide

Want to know when my next book is available?

Be sure to sign up for my new release e-mail list at:
www.tessmccallum.com/subscribe

.

A
THOUSAND
RIVERS

Melissa Kuipers

Dedication

To Biruté Galdikas, for a lifetime dedicated to orangutan research
and conservation, and all those who have followed.
And of course, my family who were with me on this journey.

Contents

PROLOGUE   1

CHAPTER ONE   4

CHAPTER TWO   20

CHAPTER THREE   35

CHAPTER FOUR   44

CHAPTER FIVE   68

CHAPTER SIX   79

CHAPTER SEVEN   92

CHAPTER EIGHT   106

CHAPTER NINE   134

CHAPTER TEN   145

CHAPTER ELEVEN   173

CHAPTER TWELVE   205

CHAPTER THIRTEEN   219

CHAPTER FOURTEEN   244

CHAPTER FIFTEEN   269

CHAPTER SIXTEEN   273

CHAPTER SEVENTEEN   292

CHAPTER EIGHTEEN   297

EPILOGUE   304

PROLOGUE

The young ape nestled against her mother's side, clinging tightly to the soft orange hair that covered her body. Her mother reached around her, pulling leaves from the *Gagas* tree. The young leaves were sweet and moist and would go some way to assuaging her mother's hunger in the absence of the wild fruits she normally feasted on. But the meagre meal offered little in the way of nutrition and was barely enough to sustain the big primate. Her belly, once round and full was flat. Her breasts which should have been full of milk hung empty and her long limbs, normally strong and sinewy were thin and bony. She had little strength in the shrivelled muscles she depended on for climbing and feeding. Even her face was gaunt, the normally soft brown eyes now sunken beneath her hooded brow. The big primate was starving.

The infant shifted restlessly against her hip, moving onto her abdomen to suckle at one of the shrunken breasts. She would find little joy there as her mother's milk supply had slowed to a mere trickle and would shortly cease altogether unless food could be found. Without her mother's milk, the infant would not survive. She was too young to feed on her own and in any case, even the sweet young leaves were too hard for a weaning orangutan to digest.

Having picked clean the branches within her reach, the mother shifted her infant onto her back and swung her way slowly from branch to branch in search of more food. Finding none and her energy sapped, she settled in the fork of tree to rest. From here she could see right across the jungle canopy; a canopy that had once stretched endlessly towards the horizon.

But that was before the fires and before the people had come. Before the fires there had been plenty to eat and endless jungle in which to forage. Now it was almost all gone, replaced by the short trees with the spiky fronds and clusters of unfamiliar red berries.

Instinctively she knew that it was dangerous among the new trees. There was no protection to be had in their low foliage. Nowhere to hide from the people and the strange four legged creatures that often accompanied them. They moved more quickly than the creatures she was used to and made shrill noises when they called to each other. There were all sorts of strange noises now. When the people came they brought with them things that screamed so loudly at the trees they fell over, crashing to the jungle floor where the loud things screamed some more until the ancient trees split apart and were dragged from the forest floor like slain giants.

Fearful, the orangutan and all the other animals had retreated deeper into jungle where it was quiet but for the birds, the chattering macaques and the occasional snap of branches as the orangutans moved through the trees. It was a peaceful place. A safe place.

For a while she found peace there and had mated with the big male who sought her out. But then the people and their noise came again and this time there was nowhere else to go. Now even high up in her canopy nest in her shrinking patch of jungle, the strange noises reached her day and night. Even in the familiar embrace of the jungle she felt fear.

Trying to nurse again, the hungry infant cried out softly in frustration and distress. She clung tightly to a fistful of her mother's hair and suckled harder but it was no use. She cried out again. Her mother put a comforting hand to her baby's tiny body and pressed her lips against the small face. It wasn't what the infant needed but it was all that she could offer. She reached out, clutching some small branches with her feet and hands which she bent and twisted to form a crude nest. Then settling the infant into the crook of her arm she curled protectively around the small body and slept.

The sun hadn't yet broken the horizon when hunger and desperation enticed the orangutan from her nest. The infant, now quite listless, clung to her back as she moved silently through the trees until she reached the edge of the jungle. Deftly she climbed down to the ground, staying within the tree line so that she remained hidden among the foliage. Here she paused, gazing intently at the new place and lifting her nose to test the air. Finally she moved cautiously from the protective cover of the jungle, loping on all four limbs across a small clearing until she reached a group of the small trees with the red berries.

Standing up she leaned against the trunk and reached up to pick a clutch of berries. She sniffed them carefully and bringing them to her mouth she nibbled, testing the unfamiliar fruit. Finding the oily fruit to her liking she reached for more, greedily gulping down several handfuls. After months of little to eat other than leaves and green shoots she quickly picked the tree clean and overcoming her fear, moved deeper into the grove seeking more of the berries.

She was well into the grove when the shrill calls of the four-legged creatures reached her ears. Frantically she retreated towards the protection of the jungle. In the trees she was a skillful and graceful climber but on the ground her loping gait was far less efficient. She could not match the speed of the four legged creatures who came upon her in the narrow clearing. Snapping and snarling they surrounded her. She reared onto her legs, standing tall as she barred her teeth and hit out at the creatures, but her defence was ineffectual. The creatures rushed at her from every direction biting and pulling at her, trying to force her to the ground. Still on her mother's back the small infant, terrified and confused, desperately clawed her way higher until she was clinging to her mother's neck only just out of reach of the attackers.

Bloodied and weakening, the orangutan fought on. Her only chance lay in reaching the safety of the trees. Then over the commotion she heard a different sound and saw people running out of the grove. They stopped briefly, assessing the situation, then ran forward waving sticks and calling loudly to the attacking creatures. For the briefest of moments the attackers yielded. Sensing an opportunity the orangutan sprang away, making a desperate break for the jungle.

She had almost reached the tree line when she felt a sudden, sharp pain in her shoulder which sent her lurching to the ground. She tried to rise, pushing herself up from the ground. The pain in her shoulder was excruciating and with the limb now hanging uselessly at her side she stumbled forward again. Another sharp pain hit her in the back, bringing her down again but still she struggled towards the forest, frantic as one of the people advanced on her. He stopped close by, watching her struggles then pointed a stick at her. There was a loud noise and the old orangutan felt an impact to her chest that sent her reeling backwards onto the ground. She lay there unmoving but for her heaving chest. As death came upon her she stared up into the leafy canopy that had once been her home. Against the bright blue sky she saw the wind gently rustling the leaves and felt the breeze on her face. There was a clutch of her favourite fruit; she reached for it and savoured the sweet taste. As she ate she felt the infant suckling heartily at her breast and sighed deeply as her mother's milk flowed.

CHAPTER ONE

July 2013, Bali, Indonesia

Danni Pollard sighed and sat up on the beach towel stretching her long legs towards the sea. It was hot on the beach and as if to confirm it, she felt a bead of sweat slip down between her breasts. Definitely time to cool off. Rising to her feet she covered the few metres to the water's edge then waded in to mid-calf level, testing the water. It was cool on her heated body so she lingered in the shallows for a few minutes giving her body time to adjust before wading in a bit deeper then sinking down to her shoulders. She kicked off the sandy bottom and rolled onto her back, closing her eyes to the bright blue sky as she floated away from the shoreline.

The sound of children playing in the water, laughter and snatches of conversation drifted over the water to her. The small cove that housed Padang Padang Beach in Uluwatu was one of Bali's most popular tourist haunts and with August being high season it was crowded both in and out of the water. Not that Danni minded. She wasn't in the mood for reading despite the paperback novel she'd shoved into her beach bag and people watching was a good substitute to fill her time.

Treading water, Danni turned away from the beach and gazed towards the ocean. There were some small waves breaking not far out, good enough to provide a bit of fun for the tourists with their rented surfboards and kids playing on foam boogie boards but the experienced surfers were further around the point where there were bigger waves to be found. That's where her husband Rob was, off surfing with his mates. He was gone as he did every day after a quick, early breakfast; loading his surf board onto the purpose built carry rack hanging off the side of his rental scooter and then away. As long as the surf stayed up, Danni knew she wouldn't see him again until late in the afternoon.

The trip to Bali was one they'd made often, almost every year since university graduation, as it was for so many of their friends. Being only a three and a half hour flight from Perth many West Australian's regarded

Bali as their backyard. Aside from proximity, Bali was affordable. Accommodation, food and entertainment on the island were all cheap compared to Australia although if one had money to burn there were plenty of five star resorts, private spa retreats, up-market restaurants and boutique shops catering to the high end of the market.

Of course the real draw card of Bali was its unique Hindu culture and natural beauty. A mountainous interior surrounded by emerald green rice paddies, rainforests and a mixed coastline of high scenic cliffs, long stretches of sandy beaches and decent surf breaks.

From a tiny trickle of surfers, drop-outs and intrepid tourists that discovered Bali in the 1960's, the floodgates had opened. Over the succeeding decades the island had emerged as a one of the hottest tourist destinations in Asia, welcoming nearly three million visitors a year. In the ensuing frenzy of development many old-timers decried the loss of the real Bali and not without reason. With its abundance of resorts, hotels, guesthouses, shopping centres, restaurants and theme parks it was almost impossible to imagine the cluster of small villages and rice paddies that the old-timers remembered.

Danni and Rob both enjoyed their annual Bali pilgrimage, although for different reasons. Over the years they'd come to share their trip with a loose assortment of friends. For keen surfers like Rob and his mates, Bali's attraction began and ended with the various surf breaks around the island. On the rare occasion the Bali surf let them down the men consoled themselves with fishing or diving trips. Danni enjoyed just being able to relax and rejuvenate. Unless Rob woke her for early morning lovemaking, her days usually started with a late breakfast followed by a walk through town, maybe a few hours at the beach, reading in a hammock, a session at a spa, perhaps a little shopping or just hanging out with the other wives and girlfriends. The hardest decision of the day was where to eat but having been so many times, they had long ago narrowed their choices down to a few favourite haunts.

For the most part, the men did their thing and the women did theirs, the two groups not meeting up until late in the afternoon when happy hour kicked off at their favourite bar perched over the cliffs at Uluwatu.

A spray of water from a teenager paddling his surfboard nearby brought Danni out of her reverie and she slowly stroked her way back to the beach. Using a towel borrowed from the hotel she patted herself dry, donned her broad brimmed hat and wrapped a sarong around her waist. The sun was high in the sky now; time to find some shade. Although she smothered herself in protective sunscreen every morning before leaving her room, Danni needed to be careful; with her fair skin she tended to burn easily.

The popular Padang Padang beach was only a small patch of sand at the base of a grotto formed by jagged cliffs. Access to the beach was via a rough staircase hewn into a natural crevice in the cliff face. Only just wide enough for a single person, the steep stairway passed through a tunnel in the cliffs at one point. First time visitors always got a surprise on their first descent when they emerged from the tunnel to suddenly find themselves on the sandy expanse of beach.

Ever enterprising, local vendors had established a market of sorts right on the beach at the base of the grotto, a motley collection of bamboo, tin and canvas covered huts tucked into the shadow of the cliffs to take advantage of the almost all day shade. They traded in everything a beachgoer could possibly need. Cold drinks, food, boogie board and surfboard hire, t-shirts, hats, sunscreen, inflatable toys for the kids, jewellery and souvenirs. Eyeing the shady niche around the market, Danni decided to retreat for a cold drink and some lunch so after collecting her belongings she headed in that direction.

'Halo Danni,' a young Balinese man waved and walked out to meet her.

'Hi Made, how are you today?' Danni asked. As a regular visitor over the years, Danni had gotten to know a few of the locals like Made. He'd been running the family *warung* with his mum who did most of the cooking, right there on the beach for most of the last decade.

'I'm good but business is not so good. Very slow this week,' he lamented.

Danni gave him a sympathetic look and propped herself on one of the rough wooden benches flanking an equally rough table. Despite appearances it was actually quite a comfortable arrangement and from her position Danni had a good view of the beach.

Made handed Danni a laminated menu, written in English with corresponding photographs of each dish. It was like that just about everywhere in Bali, everything geared towards Western tourists. But as a regular customer, Danni already knew what she wanted and waved the menu away.

'I'll have my favourite please Made. *Nasi goreng* with chicken satay on the side.' The meal of fried rice and small chicken kebabs with peanut sauce was a Balinese staple. It was tasty, filling and just about everyone's favourite.

'You want coconut milk?' Made asked.

'Yes please.'

Made returned a few minutes later with a green coconut that he'd lopped the top off with his machete and dropped in a block of ice and a straw. Ever practical, he'd also sliced off the bottom of the husk so that the coconut would sit upright on the table. Danni smiled and sipped the cool, sweet liquid gratefully.

The meal was soon placed in front of her, a steaming aromatic mound of rice topped with a fried egg and several chicken sticks on the side. Danni knew that the meal was cooked simply in a wok over a charcoal brazier, the chicken grilled on a homemade wire rack on another. For such a simple meal it tasted delicious as always.

Made was right Danni thought, business was slow. It often amazed her, considering the number of people that crowded onto the beach at times that the vendors here often struggled to make a living. The food was always good and there weren't too many places in the world were you could sit right on the beach like this and enjoy good food at budget prices. But Danni knew that many tourists, so used to Western standard restaurants often found the rustic warungs with their ramshackle appearance rather intimidating and tended to steer clear of them, which was a shame really as they missed out on some wonderful local cuisine and genuine hospitality.

At that moment, as if to disprove her theory, Made seated a Western couple at the long table opposite Danni then scarpered off to fill their orders.

The woman caught Danni's eye and smiled, then offered her hand when Danni smiled back.

'Hi I'm Belinda, Bel for short, and this is Tim.'

Danni shook both their hands and introduced herself.

Bel laughed, 'Another Aussie. There are more of us here than there are back in Australia.'

Danni laughed. 'Yes it does seem like that at times. Bali has always been popular with Aussies and that popularity just continues to grow.'

'I take it you've been here a few times before then?' Tim asked.

'Yes, more times than I can count. Like many West Australians I came here on family holidays as a kid and have continued to come back almost every year since. Sometimes I think I should be more adventurous and go somewhere else but it's so relaxing here,' Danni shrugged.

'I know exactly what you mean,' said Bel. 'Between long, lazy breakfasts, massages on the beach, wandering from one cafe to another and cocktails at sunset Bali could turn me into a very relaxed, fat and happy person.'

Tim gave her a gently nudge. 'Who are you kidding? You'd soon get bored with that.'

Bel laughed. 'Yeah you're right.' Then turning to Danni she explained. 'I don't do nothing very well. One or two days lazing by the pool max before I need to be off doing something. Especially when I'm in a foreign country where there is so much to see.'

Danni could see that. Even in the short span of their conversation she'd developed the impression that Bel was a bit of human dynamo. The slender, auburn haired woman oozed energy. Tim came across a bit more laid back, a perfect foil for his energetic partner.

'So is this your first time in Bali?' Danni asked.

'No we've been once before but we've got some time up our sleeve before we head over Borneo to work so we thought we'd have a bit of a holiday and a look around.'

Danni was intrigued. 'You're going to work in Borneo? That sounds interesting. What is it you do?'

'I'm a builder and Bel's a teacher,' Tim explained. 'We've volunteered for an NGO working to improve the lives of some impoverished minority groups in Borneo.'

Danni was impressed. 'Wow, that's pretty generous of you.'

Tim shrugged modestly. 'Not really. Dropping in for a year to help out almost seems like a cop-out when you consider the hardships that some of these people face year in, year out.'

'Besides,' added Bel, 'we always feel like we get so much more out of it than we put in. When you spend so much time with people who have so little you very quickly learn about what really matters and what doesn't.'

'So you've done this sort of thing before?'

Bel nodded. 'I went to India with a girlfriend during university break one year. We'd planned to backpack around for a couple of months but we never made it out of Delhi. My friend knew someone who was volunteering at an orphanage over there so we dropped by with the intention of just saying hello and delivering a care package from home and the rest as they say is history. It was a real eye opener for a comfortably middle class girl from Perth.'

Tim took up the story. 'Anyway, I met Bel not long afterwards and she was so full of her experience at the orphanage that her enthusiasm rubbed off on me. As soon as Bel graduated, we headed back over there together and spent eighteen months at the orphanage; Bel teaching the kids to read and write English and me building and fixing whatever needed it whilst trying to pass on some of my skills to the boys there. Since then we've worked in Vietnam and Cambodia with time out back home in Australia in between.'

'You must have had some amazing experiences,' Danni commented. 'I'd love to hear more.'

'Yeah we've been lucky to be able to connect with so many people and to know that we've been able to make a difference to a few lives at least. We've also seen some amazing places and been able to experience different cultures on much deeper level than if we'd just been tourists,' agreed Tim.

'But it isn't always easy. It can be hard work and the living conditions are tough. Sometimes we get paid a local wage, other times we support ourselves from our savings. And there are plenty of days that you see things, experience things that just break your heart,' said Bel.

'So how do you find it within yourself to keep doing it?' Danni asked.

'The rewards are ultimately far bigger than the costs. I'll admit I've had days where I just didn't think I could go on and then something good happens and you know without a doubt that all the effort has been worthwhile.'

Made appeared with Bel and Tim's meals and they tucked in with gusto reminding Danni to finish her own meal which had been forgotten since the Australian couple's arrival. Danni liked both of them and was enjoying their company. Apart from having an interesting story to tell, they were friendly and outgoing and seemed to get on very well with each other.

'So Danni what do you do?' Tim asked.

'Oh nothing nearly as interesting as you two. I'm in marketing.'

'That sounds glamorous,' commented Bel.

'It can be. I work for a big company that handles a lot of large corporate clients with decent marketing budgets so there's lots of scope to be creative. On the flip side though there's a lot of pressure to keep coming up with fresh new ideas all the time.'

'Sounds competitive,' observed Tim.

'Extremely. There's plenty of new blood knocking at the door all the time and lots of marketing companies trying to win new accounts. Plus with the digital age there are so many new media options; internet, mobile apps, twitter, Facebook, bloggers to name a few, that it's getting harder and harder to know where to focus the marketing budget and effort.'

'But you like it?' Bel asked.

It was the first time anyone had actually ever asked Danni if she liked what she did and the question caught her a little by surprise. She paused, weighing her answer. 'Yes I do; for the most part anyway. Like you I have days where I wonder if it's all worthwhile but when a client really likes and appreciates my work and a campaign delivers real returns to the client it can be very satisfying. Certainly recharges the batteries.'

They finished eating but no one seemed in a hurry to leave and there were no other customers wanting the table so the three of them sat and chatted, cementing their new friendship. Danni didn't realise how much time had passed until her mobile phone started ringing. Hastily retrieving the phone from her beach bag she answered the call.

'Danni, its Emily. Where are you? None of the girls or I have seen you all day and I was getting a bit worried.' Emily was Danni's best friend and of the loose group of friends they were holidaying with in Bali, she was the only one of the women that Danni was close too.

Danni glanced at her watch and was surprised to see it was already well after three. 'Gracious Em, I lost track of the time. I'm still down at the beach.'

'All this time? You must be burnt to a crisp.'

Emily knew Danni and her fair skin well. 'No I've been sitting in the shade chatting with some new friends I've met.' Danni smiled over at Bel and Tim and mouthed an apology for the interruption.

'Right,' said Em. 'Well don't forget we're supposed to be meeting up with the guys at five. You'd better start getting your butt back here if we're going to be there on time.'

'Will do. I'll meet you in the lobby in an hour.'

'Okay. Feel free to invite your new friends if you like. I for one would be happy to have some new blood around rather than listening to the guys rehash their day on waves.'

Danni laughed and disconnected the call. The men did like to talk endlessly about the surfing, surfing and more surfing which often had their partners rolling their eyes at each other whilst they smiled indulgently at their husbands and tried to show some interest.

'Well guys, it's been lovely to meet you but I do need to get going. I'm meeting my husband and the rest of our group for sundowners at five.

You're welcome to join us if you like.'

'I'm up for it,' said Bel. 'What about you Tim?'

'Sure, why not?'

Danni was really pleased. The couple had been great company throughout the afternoon. 'Great. We'll be at the Blue Fin Bar at five. Do you know it?'

Bel shook her head.

'It's a great little bar perched on the cliffs overlooking the surf break at Uluwatu so it's a bit of surfies hangout as you can imagine, but it's very relaxed and one of the best places in Bali to watch the sunset. It's only a ten minute walk from here but it can be a bit hard to find so I'll draw you a mud map.'

Danni rummaged around in her bag and managed to find a pen and scrap paper on which she sketched out a map that she hoped was reasonably accurate. She also added her mobile phone number.

'Here you go. If you get lost give me a call and I'll come find you.'

Tim stuffed the map into his pocket and after waving goodbye to Made, they all headed towards the narrow staircase that would lead them off the beach. They waited their turn among the other beach goers before negotiating the stairs in single file. Despite being relatively fit, all three of them were breathless by the time they'd made the steep climb to the cliff top.

'No matter how many times I make that climb, it always leaves me out of breath,' commented Danni.

'You're not the only one,' laughed Bel. 'But have you seen the local ladies carrying huge blocks of ice on their heads down the stairs? Those blocks must weigh at least 15 kilos.' She shook her head in amazement.

'Yes I was astounded the first time I saw them and even now years later I still find it amazing. As tourists we tend to take our food and cold drinks for granted without ever really giving any thought to the logistics that go into it. Despite all the development the island has experienced, behind the scenes it's still a relatively unsophisticated place. '

'True,' agreed Tim. 'It's very evident the further you get from the mainstream tourist areas, not that many tourists seem to go much further afield.'

'I'm almost ashamed to admit that I fall into that category,' said Danni ruefully. 'In all the years I've been coming to Bali I haven't really got out and explored much of the island.'

Bel and Tim stared at her in amazement. 'You're kidding?'

'I'm afraid not.'

'Well we'll have to do something about that,' said Bel. 'Let's talk about it some more over drinks later on. Perhaps we can organise a few day trips.'

Considering it wasn't even on Danni's radar a few hours ago, the idea of getting out and about and doing a bit of exploring was actually rather appealing. 'Yes let's do that,' Danni agreed. 'But right now I need to get a move on. I'll see you at the Blue Fin in an hour or so.'

After walking back to the villa, Danni had a nice long shower, washing her hair and rinsing her skin clean of the inevitable traces of sunscreen, sea salt and sand from her day at the beach. After a half-hearted attempt at blow drying her long hair she gave up, sweeping it into a loose bun instead and slipping into a light cotton dress and a pair of sandals. All in nice time to meet her friends in the foyer.

'Well hello stranger,' greeted Emily with a grin, then turning to the other wives, 'Danni dumped us all in favour of some new friends she met today.'

Danni swatted her arm and laughed. 'And I'll just bet you were pacing the floor waiting for me.'

'Actually I have to confess I spent a very stress free day at the spa getting my nails done and an all over massage and exfoliation. After that I was so exhausted I had a nana nap.'

'So you didn't miss me after all,' said Danni.

'Not really,' admitted Emily, slipping her arm through Danni's as the group set off walking to the Blue Fin. 'Now tell me all about your new friends.'

As they walked, Danni filled her in on the details. 'They sound nice,' Emily observed, 'and obviously very committed.'

Danni sensed her friend was holding back. 'But?'

Emily gave her a wry smile. 'You know me too well. Okay...But are they a bit do-gooderish?'

Danni laughed. 'Do-gooderish? Is that even a word?'

Emily poked her in the ribs. 'Maybe not but you know what I mean.'

'Yes I do know what you mean,' said Danni seriously. 'I think what you're trying to say is are they wide-eyed idealists who think they can change the world and think less of those of us that don't?'

Emily nodded. 'Yep that's what I was trying to say.'

Danni shook her head. 'No I didn't get a sense of that from them at all. I think they are just two people who have the time and skills to be able to help give a few people less fortunate than themselves a leg up in the world and they just happen to care enough to want to do it. But I invited them to join us for happy hour so you'll get a chance to meet them shortly and judge for yourself.'

The conversation waned as the woman left the street and started along a narrow path threading its way between the simple concrete homes of the villagers, many of whom were now relaxing on their front steps or tending to their charcoal braziers. Cooking the evening meal outdoors was favoured by many Balinese as it gave them a chance to socialise and watch the children playing.

Danni smiled at some of the children and called greetings as she passed by to which the locals responded warmly. '*Selamat sore*', which meant good evening in Bahasa Indonesian. Over the years Danni had picked up a few Indonesian words but English was so widely spoken it was more out of courtesy than need.

After a few minutes the path led away from the houses and followed the cliff top for a short distance then over a wooden footbridge connecting the headland to a small rocky pinnacle that had broken away from the Uluwatu cliffs eons ago. Perched right on top and covering the small crown of the pinnacle entirely and to dramatic effect, was the Blue Fin Bar.

Apart from a roof over the bar and a small kitchen the Blue Fin was entirely open air, a solid wooden railing the only thing protecting patrons from a plunge into the pounding ocean below. With unobstructed views of the towering cliffs up and down the coastline and out across the Indian Ocean and the famous Uluwatu surf break, the Blue Fin's location was world class.

The bar itself was casual in both appearance and manner. Beer, usually Bintang the surprisingly good local brew, was served cold and in the bottle. For the ladies there were a few house wines and a long list of cocktails to choose from. The menu comprised of pretty standard Balinese fare, much the same as could be bought at most of the mid to low end restaurants throughout Bali, but it was usually tasty and of a good standard. But the truth was, the Blue Fin didn't need to be any more than it was. Its location, friendly staff and simple menu was what appealed to a loyal following of those in the know - surfers, ex-pats and Uluwatu regulars. It's location off the street and down a path that appeared to be nothing more than a village laneway kept the Blue Fin well off the radar of most tourists. Only occasionally did an accidental tourist stumble across the Blue Fin and they always left wondering how it was that the place wasn't more widely known.

As usual, the men were in a loose huddle on the deck of the Blue Fin. Having come direct from the surf they looked every inch the quintessential Aussie beach bums; windswept, salt encrusted hair, wrap-around sunglasses, loose singlets, board shorts and flip-flops. After a week in Bali they were all sporting decent tans and relaxed grins.

Rob spotted Danni as she walked across the footbridge and watched her make her way over to him with appreciative eyes, grunting with mixture of pride and proprietorship when he noticed a couple of young studs watching her also. He was used it. Danni was the sort of woman who turned heads; above average height, flawless skin, thick blond hair and hazel eyes that sparkled with intelligence. She jogged to keep herself in shape and had the kind of down to earth, happy disposition that appealed to just about everyone. And she was his; the smile that lit her face when their eyes met was for him alone and as usual, she never noticed the other men nor the possessive look that he threw them as he slid a welcoming arm around his wife's waist and dropped a quick kiss on her forehead.

'Hey babe. How's your day been?'

Danni shrugged. 'The same as usual, although I did meet a nice couple at beach and ended up spending a few hours chatting with them. What about you?'

'Great. The surf was really pumping today so I got some great rides. Unfortunately I also got dumped a few times and had a run in with the reef. Came off second best,' he said grimacing and gesturing towards his leg.

'Oh Rob!' exclaimed Danni looking at a nasty two-inch gash on the side of his calf. 'That looks awful.'

She bent down to give the wound closer inspection. 'It looks like it may need stitching and probably a good clean. A wound like that could easily become infected if you're not careful.'

Rob shrugged. 'Nah it'll be okay. The surf shop opposite the beach treated me out of their first aid kit and gave me some antiseptic cream to put on it.'

'Well I don't like the look of it just the same. I think it would be prudent to get a doctor to have a look at it.'

'I'll see how it goes,' said Rob noncommittally, which Danni took to mean that he had no intention of getting it seen too. She'd raise the subject again with him later in private.

Rob retrieved a drinks menu from the adjacent table and handed it to Danni. 'Choose your poison and I'll go get us drink.'

But as Danni was mulling over the cocktail list she heard someone call her name and looked up to see Bel and Tim approaching.

'Wow what an awesome location,' enthused Bel by way of greeting.

The women exchanged a quick kiss on the cheek. 'It sure is,' said Danni. 'You obviously found the place okay.'

'We did,' Tim confirmed. 'Your mud map was spot on although we did second guess ourselves a time or two. This place is well hidden.'

'Yes I've let you in on one of Bali's best kept secrets,' laughed Danni. 'Now first things first, let me introduce you to the rest of the group.'

Leading Bel and Tim over to the group, Danni introduced them then reeled off everyone's name. Tim exchanged handshakes with the men whilst Bel threw her hands up and laughed.

'I'm never going to remember everyone's name so please forgive me if I get it wrong,' she admitted.

Rob took orders from Danni, Bel and Tim and headed to the bar to get them a round of drinks whilst Tim drifted into conversation with the other men.

'Does Tim surf?' Danni asked Bel.

'Enough to hold his own, but he's not hard core.'

'Oh good, at least he's got something in common with the guys. They tend to become a bit obsessed about it when we're here in Bali,' said Danni. 'At home they're all pretty engrossed in their careers, which in Rob's case at least means long hours in the office and little time for play. The three weeks in Bali each year is the only real chance he gets to totally unwind.'

'It must be hard to find time together with two busy careers,' Bel commented.

'It certainly can be,' agreed Danni. 'Sometimes I feel like we're just ships passing in the night, particularly when I'm busy with a new campaign. By the time we've run errands and caught up with family and friends on the weekend we don't get much time together, just the two of us.'

'Try putting a couple of kids into the mix and see how hard it is,' commented Emily, having picked up the thread of conversation. 'Since our two munchkins came along Dave and I rarely get any time together and I think we both survive on about five hours sleep a night.'

'And you wouldn't be without them,' retorted Danni.

'True. I never regret for a minute having them,' agreed Emily emphatically. 'But it's so hard trying to juggle two full-time careers, raising kids and keeping house that I sometimes feel like I'm spending my life on a treadmill. Running hard and hoping like hell I don't fall and get spat out the back. Thank God for my parents who have the kids for two weeks each year so Dave and I can have this time away.'

'I hear the same thing from so many of my student's parents. The cost of living is getting higher and as a society generally, so too are our expectations. That adds up to a lot of pressure on the average family. I honestly I don't know how most families manage these days,' said Bel.

Emily nodded in agreement. 'The worst part is despite all the hard work and effort that Dave and I are putting in, I can't help but ask myself if we're doing the right thing. By trying to give the kids everything are we actually cheating them out of the most important thing - quality time with mum and dad?'

'That seems to be a dilemma of our time; one that so many families struggle with. Western society has become very materialistic with people judging each other and themselves based on what they have and who they are rather than their individual qualities. Along the way relationships with family and friends have suffered. We've become a society that is material rich, time and relationship poor. In contrast, Tim and I have spent a lot of time in third world countries where people struggle day to day just to put food in their bellies and keep a roof over their heads but they have very strong family and community relationships. To them, family is everything.'

'You can see that even here in Bali,' said Danni. 'Several generations of an extended family living and working together. It's quite common for women to take their children to work with them at the markets, a shop or warung; and if that's not possible then the children stay at home in the care of grandma, an aunt or older sibling.'

'Yes and in some parts of the world it goes even further where children are cared for by the whole village,' said Bel.

Rob returned with the drinks and Emily's husband Dave drifted over to join them. 'So what's got you girls looking so serious?' Dave asked.

'We were talking about the whole work and children issue and how hard it is to strike a balance,' answered Emily.

Dave took up the subject. 'Emily and I have been struggling with that for quite a while now. As a matter of fact, when we get home Emily is going to resign from her job and become a stay at home mum.'

'What!' exclaimed Danni. 'But you've worked so hard to establish your career.'

Emily sighed. 'It hasn't been an easy decision but I feel good about it now that we've made it.' She linked hands with her husband. 'We're fortunate that Dave has a good income and can support us but of course we'll have to tighten our belts somewhat and the house renovations will have to be put on hold for the time being. But I'm really looking forward to spending more time with Dave and the boys...and we haven't ruled out having another baby. As for my career, I'm hoping to be able to do some work from home. Not too much, but one or two steady clients would enable me to keep my skills up and stay in touch with the industry. Maybe I'll go back to work once the kids are in full-time school but I'll cross that bridge when I come to it.'

'Emily is a graphic artist,' Danni explained to Bel. 'That's how we met. I was working on a marketing campaign early on in my career and Emily's company did the artwork for the advertisements. She's very talented.'

'Well I'm sure you'll make it work,' said Bel. 'Who knows, stepping back from your career may actually be the start of a successful company of your own.'

'I agree Em. You can count on me to send some work your way,' Danni promised.

'Thanks girls, I appreciate the support but whatever happens I know I'm doing what's best for Dave, the kids and myself.' Dave hugged his wife to his side and they shared a loving smile. Watching them together, Danni couldn't help but envy the closeness and solidarity they obviously shared.

'Well mate,' Rob said lightly as he raised his beer towards Dave. 'Sounds like you're going to have the whole catastrophe going on.'

'Your time will come Rob,' Dave answered. 'Sooner or later there'll be the pitter-patter of little feet in your life.'

'Not for a bloody long time yet, if at all.'

'You two don't want to have children?' Emily asked, directing the question towards Danni. 'You're really good with our two.'

'I wouldn't say that we've categorically decided not to have kids, just that it's something we haven't put a timeframe on. I've always thought that it will happen when it happens.'

'The thing is when it comes to having kids I'm rather indifferent. If Danni decides she wants kids one day then I'm fine with that but if we never have kids it wouldn't bother me,' Rob added.

'And what about you and Tim?' Emily asked Bel. 'With all your travelling and volunteer work I imagine babies aren't on the agenda for a while.'

'Not for a while,' agreed Bel. 'But we definitely want to have two or three kids. For the time being I'm enjoying the time I spend with my students and the children we meet through our volunteer work. But as a teacher I'm quite fortunate in that when we do have children of our own, my work schedule is very family friendly.'

'So what sort of volunteer work do you do?' Rob asked with interest.

Bel gave Emily and the men a brief rundown of the projects they'd been involved in and how it had all started with the orphanage in India.

'So you're out to change the world then?' said Rob.

'I wish we could,' said Bel with a shake of her head. 'But that's not realistic. If we can just help change a few lives for the better we're happy. The thing is that breaking the cycle of poverty for even a few people can have a massive impact on those around them. For instance, often times an extended family will put everything they have into educating just one child because they know that if that child can eventually secure a decent job they will all benefit. As an adult that child will in turn provide financial support to the family; helping to educate his younger siblings and cousins, helping family members secure better jobs and generally just opening doors that would otherwise be closed to the family.'

'I get that,' said Dave. 'World Vision often make the point in their advertisements that sponsoring an impoverished child helps the whole family and sometimes an entire community. For example, ensuring a child has clean water to drink may mean having to sink a new well in their village which of course benefits everyone.'

'That's exactly what I'm talking about,' confirmed Bel.

'Bel and Tim are on their way to Borneo for their next project,' Danni commented.

'Did I hear my name mentioned?' Tim asked joining the group.

'You did. We were just hearing all about your work with the NGO's,' said Rob. 'So you're off to Borneo next?'

'We are indeed but we have a few weeks to enjoy a holiday and do some exploring before we start work and I must say this is a pretty good way to kick things off. That's got to be one of the best sunsets I've ever seen,' said Tim gesturing to the flaming orange sky. Then he raised his beer and proposed a toast. 'Here's to new friends and new adventures.'

CHAPTER TWO

The next morning Danni had a late breakfast sitting on the balcony of the villa restaurant as she usually did. Emily and Jade, one of the other wives had joined her to eat but had headed back to their rooms leaving Danni to linger over a cup of tea. It was a time of morning that she quite enjoyed. From the balcony she had a good view of the beach which was empty but for a local lady that came down to the beach every morning to collect the small tufts of seaweed that had washed up overnight. Danni assumed she would dry it to eat or sell at the local market.

As was his habit, Rob had left early to go surfing with the other men. Danni had tried to talk him into seeing a doctor about the gash on his leg, but he'd waved away her concerns and she knew her husband well enough to know that once his stubborn streak kicked in there was no changing his mind. He had made one concession though and applied some antiseptic cream that Danni had in her small travel first aid kit.

Danni was still sitting on the balcony when her mobile phone rang.

'Hello.'

'Hi Danni, its Belinda. Hope I'm not calling too early?'

'No not at all. Although I have to admit, even though it's well after nine I've only just finishing breakfast.'

'Cool. Listen the reason I'm calling is that Tim and I have hired scooters for the day so we can do a bit of sightseeing. Since you'd said yesterday you hadn't actually seen much of Bali outside the main tourist hotspots we wondered if you'd like to join us?'

Danni didn't have anything particular planned for the day other than meeting the other wives for lunch but getting away and doing something different for once sounded quite appealing.

'I'm supposed to be having lunch with the girls but I'm sure they won't mind if I give it a miss. So sure why not; I'd love to come.'

'Great. Where are you staying? We'll come by and pick you up in about an hour.'

Danni gave them directions to the villa and arranged the pick-up time then disconnected the call. The next call was to Emily to beg off the lunch outing.

'Are you sure you don't mind Em?'

'No not at all. Tell the truth if I wasn't feeling so lazy I might have come with you,' Emily responded. 'It can get a little bit same-same around here.'

'Then why don't you come? I'm sure Bel and Tim wouldn't mind.'

'I know they wouldn't but I really am just having an attack of the lazies. I never get time to myself at home what with Dave and the kids and work so I'm making the most of it whilst I can. I have a good book waiting to be read and there's a lounge by the pool with my name on it so my day is planned.'

Danni laughed. 'Well you've certainly earned it. Enjoy and I'll see you for sundowners at the Blue Fin this evening.'

'You have fun too and be careful on the scooter.'

Danni went back to her room and changed into three quarter length pants and enclosed shoes, a small safety precaution she took whenever she ventured out on a scooter. She was ready and waiting in the villa foyer when Bel and Tim arrived on a pair of scooters. Danni heard them laughing as they pulled up to the curb and they were still smiling when she walked out to greet them.

'Oh that's such good fun,' said Bel. 'I love the freedom of pottering around on scooters and mixing it with the locals.'

'As long as you don't mix it with the locals too much. There's plenty of holiday makers who have come to Bali, hired a scooter and ended up with a serious case of gravel rash or worse,' Danni warned. Scooters were ubiquitous to Bali and much of the rest of Asia. Cheap to buy and cheap to run they were the main form of transport on the island and it was not unusual to see whole families of three or four on a single scooter.

'Yeah I know. We're always careful,' Bel assured her. 'Now do you ride Danni? There are three of us and two scooters so we figured you could either ride pillion behind Tim or I can if you're happy to ride my scooter.'

'I'll take the second option if you don't mind. I've been riding scooters around Bali on and off for years so I'm quite confident on the things.' The vast majority of hire scooters were automatic and fairly low powered which was ideal for Bali's narrow roads, laneways and tracks. With a little practice, most people found them fairly easy to handle and Danni was the same. It was the busy roads and chaotic traffic that posed the biggest risk and in that respect Danni preferred to be in control of the scooter herself.

While Danni donned the spare helmet Tim handed her, Bel climbed onto the scooter behind him and got herself settled. Danni stowed her small bag in the compartment under the seat and climbed onto her scooter.

'So what's the plan?'

'Well Tim and I would like to visit the Uluwatu Temple and just poke around the peninsular for the afternoon, then maybe we could finish with a sunset dinner on the beach at Jimbaran Bay. Basically, wherever the road leads us, unless you've got any specific place you'd like to see.'

'Not really. I'm happy to wing it with you guys. Tell you the truth I'm looking forward to doing something a bit different for once. I'll have to check with Rob before I commit to dinner though.'

'Alright then, let's get going,' said Tim easing his scooter forward. Bel looked over her shoulder to check Danni was following along okay and gave her a thumbs up sign. They rode slowly around the steep and winding roads of Uluwatu. At first Danni focused her attention on handling the scooter and she was just beginning to relax when they arrived at the temple. They parked the scooters in the shade and went to the small kiosk to purchase their tickets which were handed over with a sarong each to wear; temple etiquette demanding that knees and most of the legs be covered.

'It's been so long since I've been here I'd forgotten about the sarongs,' laughed Danni. As they were tying the sarongs around their waists, a tall Balinese man wearing the official shirt of an Uluwatu temple guide approached. 'Good morning, my name is Wayan. It would be my pleasure to act as your guide for the temple.'

The three friends looked at each other and shrugged. 'Do we need a guide?' Tim asked.

'It is up to you of course,' answered Wayan. 'But perhaps your visit will be a little more interesting if you come to know some of the history and meaning of the temple.' Wayan named a price for his services and waited expectantly whilst the group conferred among themselves.

'Okay sure, why not,' said Tim, 'but you'll have to do better on the price my friend.' After some good natured haggling, a price was agreed but Wayan had some advice for them before they set off.

'The monkey's here at the temple can be a little aggressive and attracted to shiny things. Can I suggest that the ladies remove their jewellery and sunglasses and leave your bags with your scooters?' Seeing Danni and Bel exchange horrified looks, Wayan added, 'But don't worry, with me you will be safe. The monkey's know me and my stick and will not come near.'

The girls hastily removed their jewellery, shoving it into deep pockets, whilst Tim took their bags back the scooters and locked them in the under seat compartments.

'Okay this way please,' said Wayan once they were ready, leading them down a long, wide path into the temple grounds. There were long-tailed macaque monkeys scattered around the grounds, in trees and perched on top of the stone walls and rooftops, but thankfully they stayed clear of the group, no doubt wary of Wayan and his stick. Wayan led them passed some minor stone buildings and small gardens until they found themselves standing at the edge of the soaring Uluwatu cliffs, the Indian Ocean stretching endlessly before them. The famous Bali surf breaks rolled towards the shore, smashing violently against the unyielding limestone cliffs.

'Oh my, it's magnificent!' exclaimed Bel, eyes shining. 'No wonder it's regarded as one of Bali's must-see attractions.'

Wayan stood back whilst the three friends admired the view, then offered to take a photograph of them together which they readily accepted. Handing their camera's back, he explained. 'Okay so this temple is located on Bali's southernmost tip which contributes to the old Balinese name for this temple which is *Pura Luhur Uluwatu. Luhur* means 'something of divine origin', while *Uluwatu* is derived from *Ulu*, meaning 'lands end' and *watu* meaning 'rock'. So you can see, it is appropriately named. It is one of nine directional temples in Bali that protect the island from evil spirits.'

'How old is it Wayan?' Danni asked.

'Much of the temple complex was constructed in the eleventh century by a Javanese sage named *Empu Kuturan*. Sometime later another sage from East Java constructed the *padmasana* shrine at the inner sanctum of the temple complex,' said Wayan indicating to the tall, three tiered structure perched on the edge of the adjacent headland to the south. 'You will see the shrine, or *meru* as we call it, from the other side as we continue our tour of the complex.'

The trio followed Wayan away from the cliff top footpath along a network of paths fringed by terraces, solid walls and other structures, all constructed from dark grey coral stone. Eventually the pathway opened onto a large, paved courtyard, the far end of which was dominated by a tall archway adorned with an assortment of sculptured features and intricate engravings. It was flanked by statues that Danni recognized as Ganesha, the Hindu deity with the head of an elephant and the plump body of a human.

'We are now standing in the middle courtyard,' Wayan informed them. 'The archway that you can see is *kori agung*, or the Old Gate, which leads to the inner sanctum of the temple. The fierce, leering face engraved above the archway is a *Bhoma* head whose purpose is to deter malign influences from entering the sanctum. The sculpture above that, at the very top of the gateway, is *Kaman dalu*, the sacred vessel which holds ambrosia, the immortal elixir of life.'

'So does everything in the temple have a spiritual or symbolic meaning Wayan, or is some of it just decorative?' Danni asked.

'Yes, everything has a special meaning. For instance, you will also notice the upper sections of all three temple gates are shaped like wings; hence they are referred to as winged gates. They are styled to represent the Balinese version of the phoenix, the mythical Chinese firebird that represents the six celestial bodies of the sun, moon, sky, earth, wind and planets. Such winged gates are very rare in Bali and are considered to be an exotic influence. Around the complex there are also images of Mt Meru, the cosmic mountain at the centre of the Hindu-Buddhist universe. The three tiers of the *padmasana* shrine in the inner sanctum are a representation of Mt Meru, hence why it is known as *meru*.'

Tim ran his fingers lightly over the centuries old engravings. 'Those old stone masons and sculptors certainly knew their stuff. The workmanship is as good as you'd find anywhere and still in good condition.'

'Yes. You see the coral rock is very hard and durable. Much more so that the volcanic rock used to construct many of Bali's other temples. And also, the temple has undergone many restorations and additions throughout the centuries.'

'Wayan, can we have a look at the inner sanctum?'

'Unfortunately we cannot. The sanctum is only for those intending to pray. But we will go onto the terraces of the outer courtyard, where you will have a good view of the *meru*.' Wayan led them around to the outer courtyard, a series of attractive, grassed terraces. After pointing out several more sculptures he waited patiently whilst Danni, Tim and Bel snapped some photographs of the *meru* and lingered in the shade of several frangipani trees. Once they regrouped, Wayan showed them the temple amphitheatre and led them back to the cliff top pathway, where they had another fabulous view of the roaring ocean, the jagged cliffs and the triple-tiered *meru*, now some distance off, keeping sentry over Bali's southern peninsular.

'It is such an amazing view isn't it,' said Danni. 'These cliffs must be at least seventy or eighty metres high.'

'It sure is,' agreed Tim. 'Look at that ocean swell rolling in. Imagine the hammering these cliffs have had over the years.'

'The Balinese believe the cliffs are the petrified bark of *Dewi Danu*, the Goddess of the Waters and the symbol of fertility,' offered Wayan. 'She is one of the two supreme deities in Balinese Hindu tradition.'

'Who's the other supreme deity?' Bel asked.

'*Kang Ching Wie*, the Goddess of Prosperity.'

'The Balinese are extremely spiritual aren't they? There are Hindu temples all over the island, plus all the small family shrines outside homes and businesses. You can't walk a hundred metres without coming across one. Not to mention the daily offerings you see absolutely everywhere. They're so quaint. I'd love to know what the symbolism is behind the practice,' said Bel.

'Oh well that's something I can tell you,' said Danni. 'The little offerings are called *canang sari* and they're made two or three times a day. The baskets as you would have noticed, are made from a green or yellow leaf, usually banana palm leaf. They're just big enough to hold a small amount of rice, fruit, perhaps a little meat, fish or nuts and a flower or two. The offering is made to thank and praise the gods. Offerings are also made to appease the demons. Those ones usually consist of meat and alcohol. Making the offering is a daily ritual in just about every Balinese household, one that is taken very seriously because the essence of the offering is not so much the offering itself but the spirit in which it is made; with thankfulness, a loving attention to detail and self-sacrifice in that they take time and effort to prepare. The offerings are usually left at the entrance of homes or business or temples but you'll also find them on statues, road intersections to protect road users and all sorts of other places. There wouldn't be a guesthouse, hotel or resort in Bali that doesn't put out offerings each day, with the exception of the Javanese owned businesses which you can pick by the absence of an offering,' Danni added as an afterthought.

'Coming from a Catholic Christian background, I can see a similarity between the offerings and Catholics saying the rosary. Both are repeated acts of devotion,' observed Bel.

'That's probably a fair comparison,' Danni agreed. 'The Balinese make offerings constantly in a lot of different ways. Some are as simple as placing a flower on each step leading into a home. The flowers that you see adorning the statues of various gods everywhere you go aren't just for looks, they're actually very simple offerings to please and appease those gods. And have you noticed how some statues or shrines are draped in either black and white checked or yellow fabric? The black and white check symbolizes the dualism of life such as good and evil, brightness and darkness, men and women and so on; the yellow fabric aims to preserve purity and protect from bad intentions.'

'Well I think it's a lovely ritual and so uniquely Balinese. Tim and I've travelled extensively through India and Indochina where Hinduism is widely practiced but you don't see offerings so much there except at temples and special ceremonies.'

'The local squirrels and birds certainly appreciate them. You see them coming down from the trees to raid the offerings pretty regularly,' laughed Tim.

'The Balinese will go all out for special ceremonies and other important occasions and there are plenty of those; full moon celebrations, new moon, births, deaths, marriages, a child's six month birthday, temple birthdays, village cleansing ceremonies, harvest festivals and so on. There's even a celebration of all things metal. Once on a previous visit to Bali, Rob and I saw all the cars and scooters decorated with offerings and flowers which was really cute. But depending on the occasion, the offerings then can be quite elaborate and take many people many days to make. I've seen some really elaborate offerings being carried around on top of tall poles for temple ceremonies but I don't really know anything about them.'

'They are called *banten*,' Wayan offered. 'Very special offerings which must be constructed according to fixed patterns and motifs. The primary motive is the mountain—'

'—Like Mt Meru?' Danni chimed in.

'Yes but also Mt Agung which is the most sacred place in Bali. You see, the Balinese understand the difference between the gods, *Dewa* and *Dewi,* who reside high up in the mountains, and the demons, *bhutas*, that reside in the lower planes such as the shorelines of Bali. To symbolize the mountain, most *banten* are constructed in the shape of a cone. Also the colours of the *banten* are based on the pattern of colours of *Nawa Sanga* which is the Balinese concept of the nine cardinal directions. Food such as rice and meat are incorporated to symbolize the plant and animal worlds. In this way, the *banten* offering symbolizes the cosmic order of the world. Of course the tip of the cone is the most sacred part of the offering.'

'That's fascinating Wayan. Thank you for explaining it to us,' said Bel. 'And you too Danni. You've obviously learnt something of the Balinese culture in the years you've been coming here.'

'A little. You know the warung where we had lunch on the beach yesterday? Occasionally I've sat and helped Madi's mum make the little banana leaf baskets and she's explained it to me. By the way, you know you should never step on offerings that are placed on the ground otherwise you may have an encounter with a *Leyak,* a Balinese demon said to haunt graveyards and feed on human flesh. In human form they have long tongues and large fangs but they also have the power to change themselves into animals and fly.'

'Charming types,' said Tim with a grin.

Suddenly Bel shrieked and sprang away from cliff top guardrail.

'What the hell!' Tim dragged Bel into his arms as he searched for the source of her alarm. Experience was on Wayan's side, he'd obviously seen it all before, as he set about banging his stick on the solid cement balustrade and through the gaps between the spindles, sending a large male macaque into a reluctant retreat.

'Oh my god, he frightened the life out me,' said Bel giving a shaky laugh. 'I didn't even see him there. I just felt something grab me.'

'It's alright now miss,' said Wayan. 'He's a bad boy that one. Problem monkey.'

'No kidding. I swear he was trying to reach into my pocket.'

Tim stood by Bel, rubbing her back to comfort her and keeping a wary eye on the macaque who was now perched a safe distance away on the edge of cliff. 'I must say, he's quite a magnificent specimen.'

'Yes, he is number one monkey of the temple troop. A big fellow; favourite with the ladies,' said Wayan with a grin. 'Okay if you have you seen enough we will head back now.'

Once again the trio followed Wayan through the complex, both Bel and Danni taking care to stay close to Wayan and his monkey deterring stick, especially when he stopped briefly so they could watch two baby macaques playing with a straw broom that a cleaner had left behind. Finally he walked them back to the kiosk where Tim shook his hand and paid him, throwing in a decent tip.

'Thanks Wayan,' chorused the girls after removing their sarongs and heading to their scooters.

'I enjoyed that,' commented Danni. 'And I'm glad we decided to use Wayan. It was definitely a better experience with his input.'

'Yes it was, although that pick-pocketing monkey frightened ten years off my life,' answered Bel.

'Maybe it was *Leyak* in monkey form. You sure you didn't accidently step on an offering?' joked Tim.

Bel gave him a playful swat on the backside. 'Quite sure funny man, thank you for your concern.'

After consulting a map that Tim had tucked away in his bag, they all agreed to make a casual circumnavigation of the Bukit Peninsular, known affectionately by most regulars simply as Bukit or the Hill. Joined to the main island of Bali by only a narrow strip of land through Jimbaran Bay, the Hill was regarded as somewhat of a sleepy back-water, lagging a long way behind its famous northern neighbours of Kuta, Seminyak and Legian. Despite massive development elsewhere on the island, Uluwatu remained a ramshackle collection of local villages, warungs, home stays, guesthouses and small, affordable hotels and villas. And that was exactly how Uluwatu enthusiasts liked it because what it lacked in up-market tourist developments was more than made up for by being home to some of the best surf breaks in the world. Year round, wave chasing surfers spent weeks and months at a time riding the legendary breaks known as the Peak, Racetracks, Temple and Bombies, living comfortably on as little as twenty dollars a day.

At least that was the case for the western side of the peninsular which was occupied by Uluwatu. Nusa Dua, over on the eastern side couldn't be more different. The five star enclave was home to some of Bali's most exclusive, international resorts where the sky was the limit for those with money to burn and an inclination to do so. A gated community with twenty-four hour security, exclusive restaurants and shops, Bali's best golf course, expansive sandy beaches, raked clean of seaweed and other debris daily, lifeguard patrolled, shallow waters and a permitting system to limit hawkers, the Nusa Dua experience was like chalk and cheese to most of the rest of Bali.

Leaving the temple, the group rode slowly eastwards, hugging the coastline as much as possible, which meant leaving the main road around the peninsular in favour of narrow roads and laneways which networked through local villages, markets and the odd villa or warung. Occasionally, as the trio rounded a bend or crested a hill they were rewarded with more stunning views. They didn't rush, stopping for photographs and a quick chat or comment before they rode on. At one place, they parked the scooters and scrambled down a rough path to a long white expanse of beach sandwiched between the rocky cliffs and the Indian Ocean. Unlike the beaches of Uluwatu, this one was almost deserted but for local man fishing from a rocky headland and a woman combing the beach for flotsam and jetsam. Danni, Bel and Tim ambled along the sandy strip enjoying the cool sea breeze and paddling in the shallows. At the headland they searched the rocky pools and crevices for tiny crabs and watched as the fisherman reeled in a small fish, before turning back to retrace their steps. They hadn't ridden far from the beach when they rounded a tight bend leading into short, steep ascent so they were barely going more than walking pace when they spotted a strategically positioned café just over the crest of the hill.

Tim pulled off the narrow road onto the verge and waved Danni in alongside him. 'How about some lunch?' Bel called. 'We could try this place. It's certainly got a view.'

'Sounds good to me,' agreed Danni. The trio pulled further off the road and parked their scooters, then wandered into the café where they were quickly greeted and seated on a shady patio overlooking the ocean. They perused the menu, Danni opting for *gado-gado*, vegetables with peanut sauce, *tempeh goreng*, crunchy nutty deep fried fermented soybean pieces of which she was quite fond and fresh pineapple juice.

Whilst they waited for their meals to arrive Danni excused herself to call Rob, knowing the guys generally took a long break from surfing in the middle of the day to have lunch and rest, before hitting the waves again around mid-afternoon.

Rob answered on the third ring. 'Hey babe, how's it going?'

'Good. I'm out and about with Bel and Tim, scootering our way around Bukit. We're doing a bit of a circumnavigation.'

'Playing tourist eh?'

'Yes and really enjoying it. After all the times we've been coming to Bali, I've fallen into a bit of pattern of doing the same thing and going to the same places, so it's nice to be reminded of what else Bali has to offer. Speaking of which, Bel and Tim suggested dinner at Jimbaran Bay this evening. I know you like hanging out with our friends in Uluwatu, but in the spirit of doing something different I thought it would be nice to have dinner on the beach at Jimbaran.'

'Sure thing, but I might ask Dave and Emily to join us if you don't mind. They've only got a couple more days here before they head off to a fancy villa in Ubud for some romance before flying home to the kids.'

'I don't mind at all and I'm sure Bel and Tim won't either. I feel a bit guilty about taking off without Em today but she assured me she preferred to laze by the pool with a good book. I'll give her a call now to fill her in on our plans.'

'Okay and I'll let Dave know at this end. I presume we're meeting you there?'

'If you don't mind. If you skip the Blue Fin you could meet us there in time for sunset drinks on the beach. I'll give you a call as soon as we've found a table and let you know where to find us so check your phone for messages.'

'Okay babe, I'll see you then. Ride safe.'

'Always! Bye.'

After terminating her call with Rob, Danni rang Emily straight away and filled her in on their plans. 'Sounds like a lovely idea to me,' Emily enthused. 'I'm looking forward to it. By the way, how's your day going? Mine has been totally lazy and indulgent, just like I threatened.'

Danni laughed. 'I had no doubt you would make good on your threat. My day has been good so far, but I'll fill you in on everything tonight.'

'Fair enough. I've got to go anyway; I can see the waiter heading this way with a splendid looking mocktail and a prawn salad. Next week, I'll be back to vegemite sandwiches and eating leftovers off the kid's plates for lunch so I'm making the most of it here.'

Danni laughed again. Emily's self-depreciating humour and lack of airs and graces was one of the things Danni most liked about her. In her line of work Danni came up against a lot of people with over-inflated egos and cut-throat attitudes so meeting and working with Emily was a refreshing change. 'Make the most of it whilst you can I say. See you this evening.'

Danni was still grinning when she rejoined Bel and Tim, just as the waitress was bringing their meals to the table. 'Perfect timing,' commented Bel.

'Sorry, I didn't mean to take so long but it's all set for tonight. Rob, Emily and Dave are going to meet us at Jimbaran Bay in time for sundown drinks. I hope you don't mind Emily and Dave coming along too. They're heading off in a couple of day's time and I feel a bit guilty about leaving Em on her own yesterday and today, even though she swears she doesn't mind.'

'No problem,' Tim assured her. 'The more the merrier.'

The trio chatted happily over lunch and lingered over another round of cold drinks long after the waitress had cleared their empty plates, so it was well into the afternoon by the time they set off again to continue their circumnavigation of the peninsular. Within fifteen minutes they arrived at the tall gates marking the southern entrance of the Nusa Dua enclave, where a uniformed security guard waved them off the road into a bay where all incoming vehicles were undergoing a security check. Whilst they waited their turn, the trio watched with interest as every vehicle was quickly and efficiently searched by two or three guards; bonnets lifted, luggage compartments checked, every door opened for a quick inspection under the seats and the vehicle under body inspected with a mirror on the end of a long pole. Compared to the laid back, almost lackadaisical, atmosphere on the other side of the peninsular and elsewhere in Bali, it was rather a shock to witness, causing Danni and Bel to raise eyebrows at each other.

'I guess this is in response to the Bali bombings,' murmured Bel, referring to the October 2002 terrorist attacks on two Kuta nightclubs which killed 202 people including 88 Australians and left scores of others maimed and injured. Whilst the physical effects of the bombings were horrendous, the psychological impact on the hitherto carefree island, both tourists and locals, left an indelible and lingering shadow over the island. Determined to reclaim the previous carefree atmosphere of the island, support the Bali economy and locals, who were as much victims of the radical Islamist terrorist group as the western targets, tourists gradually returned to the island. Three years later, just as things appeared to be getting back to normal, a second series of bombings of warungs along the Jimbaran Bay beaches and the main square in Kuta left another twenty people dead and more than one hundred injured.

On the surface, Bali seemed to have moved on; tourists continued to flock to the island in ever increasing numbers and the economy galloped ahead at a rate of knots. But beneath the surface, the spectre of terrorism hung over the island like a dark cloud; regular terror threat alerts issued by both Indonesian and foreign governments and news reports of foiled terrorist plots meant it was never far from people's minds.

The Nusa Dua security checks were a sobering reminder of the dark side of Bali and Danni wasn't sure whether she felt safer or more frightened by them. In the comfortable familiarity of Uluwatu, the Bali bombings were never forgotten but it was easier to push them to the back of her mind. When their turn came, the under seat storage compartments on both scooters were given quick checks before the three friends, all now feeling rather subdued, were politely waved on through.

Aside from the security gate, the contrast between Nusa Dua and the rest of Bali was immediately and dramatically obvious as they rode along a wide tree-lined boulevard. Grand entrance ways adorned with contrastingly discreet name plates and meticulously manicured gardens announced the presence of some of the world's most recognized up-market hotel chains; the Grand Hyatt, Grand Mirage, the Westin, Conrad and St Regis to name a few. The immaculate greens of the Bali Golf &Country Club, dotted with gleaming white golf buggies and conservatively attired golfers looked almost austere.

They rode slowly along the main boulevard until Tim pulled off the road into a parking bay. 'I was looking for some public access to the beach but so far it looks like private access only through the private resorts.' Tim explained as Danni stopped beside him. He pulled out his map and studied it for a minute before pointing to a finger of land above Nusa Dua on the map. 'I think if we keep heading north into the Tanjung Benoa cape we'll have better luck.'

Within a kilometre or so, Tim's prediction proved correct when they found a small group of warungs and a water sports business just beyond Nusa Dua's northern gate. Leaving the scooters parked up, they wandered onto the beach and were immediately approached by a shirtless young man trying to sell them watersports activities. After several minutes of determined spruiking, he eventually gave up on them and left them alone.

'Anyone interested in walking back up the beach to Nusa Dua and having a sticky beak at the resorts?' Bel asked. 'Call me a glutton for punishment but I'm curious to see what I'm missing out on.'

'Me too,' agreed Danni.

'Just don't go getting any fancy idea's Bel,' warned Tim good-naturedly. 'I can't afford to keep you in champagne on my beer budget.'

'Don't worry honey, I'll just find myself some rich old dude instead. If only I'd brought my stiletto's. Apparently the older guys really go for babes in bikinis and high heels,' Bel quipped as she led the way along the beachfront pathway.

They spent the next hour or so wandering along the beachfront, marvelling without envy at the lagoon pools, swim-up bars, individual pergola's where pampered guests were being treated to beachside spa treatments, stylish restaurants and a bevy of uniformed staff waiting hand and foot on their well-heeled guests. The beach itself was clean and expansive but in Danni's opinion lacked the wow factor of Uluwatu's dramatic coves. Eventually they reached a small island, linked to the mainland by just the narrowest strip of land. A well-worn path led them to a modest shrine before branching off towards the rocky tip of the island where they stood and watched a group of fishermen standing in chest deep water on the edge of the rocky reef, casting out into the surf with their long fishing rods, apparently quite unintimidated by the waves breaking around them. It seemed awfully risky to Danni and she silently wished them luck before they began retracing their steps back the way they'd come. Back at the water sports place the shirtless spruiker had another shot at convincing them to hire a jet ski, have a go at paragliding or ride the flying fish and she almost felt sorry for him when his shoulders slumped in resignation. Poor guy probably worked on commission, so as she donned her helmet Danni was pleased to see him strike a deal with a young couple that had wandered along.

Tim studied his map again and suggested they ride a little further to the tip of the Tanjung Benoa cape, before heading over to Jimbaran Bay to finish their circumnavigation of Bukit in perfect time to find a dinner place and wait for the others to meet them for sundowners. So they did just that, stopping at another small temple right on the tip of the cape where they had an excellent view across the channel to the Benoa Harbor. They stayed for a while, watching the tourist boats returning from daytrips to nearby islands and the fishing boats heading out for the night at sea.

At Jimbaran Bay they rode up and down the beach side road a couple of times before deciding to give one of the restaurants in the small cluster at the southern end of the beach a try. It seemed that the menu's varied little from place to place, grilled seafood being the main cuisine, so in the end they made their choice based on what they felt was the best table they could find right out on the beach. At that time of the afternoon, the restaurants were filling up fast with tourists making sure they arrived in time to experience Jimbaran's famous sunsets.

After ordering a round of drinks, Danni called Rob to give him directions to the restaurant then sat back to soak up the view. The beach at Jimbaran Bay was one of Bali's finest, a long wide expanse of powdery white sand falling away gently into the clear waters of the bay. Like the neighbouring village of Uluwatu, Jimbaran was once a sleepy backwater with a motley collection of beachside warungs, a morning fish market and not much else until it was 'discovered' in the 1980's. Since then, several world class resorts and countless high-end villas had established themselves alongside the beach and in the ridges above the bay, earning it the nickname of the 'Beverley Hills of Bali' or 'Millionaires Row'. Nevertheless, Jimbaran still retained an innate charm and laid-back atmosphere, unlike the rather closeted enclave of Nusa Dua.

Danni was still sipping on her deliciously cool pina colada when Rob, Dave and Emily arrived. Spotting them as they stepped onto the beach, Danni stood and waved to get their attention.

'Hey babe, everyone. 'Rob greeted her with a kiss and shook Tim's hand across the table as he pulled out the chair beside Danni. 'I see you all survived the traffic okay.'

'Actually it wasn't too bad. They only busy section was coming across here from Tanjung Benoa as we copped a bit of peak hour traffic, at least what qualifies as peak here in Bali,' said Tim. 'How about you? No more surfing injuries?'

Rob grinned. 'No I learnt my lesson yesterday. Leg's still bloody tender though.'

A waiter was hovering so another round of drinks was ordered as the expanded group settled into conversation. Located just south of Bali's airport, Jimbaran was a great place for airplane spotting, the big passenger jets coming to land in an almost constant stream. Between chatter, they made a game of being the first to guess the airline company, Emily proving to have the superior eyesight as she consistently made out the logos on the tails before anyone else. The game lasted until the sun dipped towards the horizon in a flaming orange ball and it became too dark to make out anything but the blinking navigation lights.

The brilliant sunset signalled it was time to order, Rob and Danni choosing to share a seafood platter for two. A waitress lit some small candles on their table and several flaming torches around the dining area, which were reflected back off the water, magnifying the impact two-fold. The same was happening at other dining spots right along the beach, the small flames flickering like fireflies in the darkness and casting a romantic atmosphere over the entire bay. A soft breeze off the ocean chased away the last of the humidity and the smell of seafood grilling over smoky charcoal braziers wafted through the air and when Rob slipped an arm around her shoulders and pulled her close, Danni decided that the evening was a perfect end to a lovely day.

CHAPTER THREE

Over the next couple of days, the friendship between Danni, Bel and Tim and the wider group continued to grow. During their evening at Jimbaran Bay, plans had been made for Tim to join the boys surfing the following day whilst Bel would spend the day with the girls.

'Fellas, just promise me you'll go easy on me. I'm not as experienced a surfer as you guys.' Tim had cautioned.

'No problem,' Rob assured him. 'The tides up tomorrow morning and they're forecasting a relatively small swell so we'll hit the Peak, straight out from the cave where you met Danni yesterday. It gets a bit crowded but should be fairly mellow in those conditions. I'll get you set up with a long board and you'll have a blast.'

'Just keep him away from the reef and bring him back in one piece, that's all I ask,' said Bel.

'Don't worry, until my leg heals I'm playing it safe too,' said Rob, prompting Danni to make a mental note to have another look at the wound when they got back to their room later that night and when she did, she clucked her tongue in dismay. Still gaping open, the wound was dark red and angry looking and even in the dim light cast by the bedside lamp, Danni was convinced there were early signs of infection.

'Rob this looks bad to me. I really think you should see a doctor and be keeping it dry.'

'No it'll be fine.' But he couldn't help wincing when Danni gently prodded around the edges of the wound.

'I wouldn't be surprised if you've still got some coral grit in there. Why don't we try and chase up a doctor in the morning and get it treated, maybe get some antibiotics as well?'

Rob pulled his leg away from Danni's scrutiny. 'I'll admit it's a bit tender but not so much that I'm going to put myself in the hands of some dodgy

Indonesian doctor. Besides, I've set it all up for Tim to join me and the boys tomorrow. I can hardly not turn up.'

'Oh Rob, that's just silly. There are some very good medical clinics here in Bali and you know it. And Tim would understand perfectly; besides Dave would look after him.' Danni didn't bother to hide the exasperation in her voice. Sometimes her husband could be decidedly obtuse.

'Just leave it please Danni. I'm perfectly fine; it looks worse than it really is.'

'Well I can't force you to go, but I do think you're being silly.' Since there was no way Danni could physically drag her stubborn husband off to see a doctor, she had no choice but to concede the point, despite her misgivings. 'Have you got any of that antiseptic cream I gave you left?'

Rob nodded and went to his day pack to retrieve the cream whilst Danni rummaged around in the small first aid kit she travelled with and found a thin cotton bandage. After washing her hands thoroughly and gently cleaning the wound with a clean face cloth, soap and warm water and patting it dry, she applied a generous amount of antiseptic cream and wrapped the bandage around his calf. 'There you go. Best I can do for now and hopefully you'll have come to your senses by morning and will go see a doctor.'

Rob gave her a kiss and pulled her onto the bed to snuggle up beside him. 'Thanks babe. Stop being a worry wart.'

After the late night, Danni slept in the following morning and by the time she woke Rob had already left. Clearly, he hadn't changed his mind about seeing a doctor. She had a long shower then joined Emily and a couple of the other wives for a leisurely breakfast before walking to the nearby market to stock up on some fresh fruit. Still worried about Rob, she decided to walk on to the small village of Pecatu where there was a decent pharmacy. After explaining the situation to the pharmacist, she left with a supply of antiseptic cream, cleansing solution, dressings and the pharmacist's recommendation that her husband see a doctor ringing in her ears.

By the time she trekked back up the long hill to the villa, Danni had worked up a sweat and was longing for a cool drink. Back in her room, she donned her bathers, wrapped a sarong around her waist and headed for the pool where she found Emily and Bel lounging in the shade under a big umbrella. She plonked herself down on the end of Emily's sun lounge.

'Hi girls. Sorry I wasn't here to meet you Bel. I walked into the village to get some first aid supplies for Rob's leg and it took a bit longer than I anticipated.'

'No problem. Emily's been looking after me. Rob still in pain huh?'

Danni shrugged. 'Not that he'd admit it. But he refuses to see a doctor so maybe a bit of pain might bring him to his senses. I'm really worried that it's going to get infected, if it isn't already.'

'Men! They're all the same,' said Emily. 'Remember when Dave broke his finger on that fishing trip with Rob and some other mates several years back. He didn't want to spoil the trip and kept insisting it was okay so by the time he got it looked at a week later the bone had already started to mend and because he never got it set properly, his finger is now permanently crooked. Luckily it hasn't really affected him but the doctor told him he was very fortunate not to have permanent tendon or nerve damage. And he thinks having kids is the reason he's now grounded from boys trips!'

'All injuries worn as a badge of honour among men,' quipped Danni. 'Scars, crooked fingers and broken limbs to be compared and marvelled over with wondrous reverence and stories of derring-do.'

'But watch them turn into big babies when the dreaded man-flu hits,' added Emily, drawing laughs from the others.

Bel put her hands over her ears in mock horror. 'Time to change the subject girls. I'm starting to regret letting Tim go out with the boys today.'

'Oh you poor misguided woman,' said Danni with a grin and a sad shake of her head. 'Now, where's the waiter? I need a cool drink and a swim. I'm all hot and sweaty after my walk. '

The girls swam and chatted by the pool and when lunchtime rolled around they were feeling too lazy to walk anywhere so elected to eat in the villa restaurant on the balcony overlooking the ocean. Later they made use of the in-house spa, treating themselves to steam baths, massages and facials. By mid-afternoon they were so thoroughly relaxed all three of them dozed on the sun lounges by the pool where the attendant thoughtfully kept the big umbrella's adjusted to keep them shaded. It took some effort to rouse themselves to meet the men and the rest of their group for the usual sunset session, but their malaise quickly evaporated in the refreshing ocean breeze along the short cliff top walk to the Blue Fin and they arrived feeling bright and ready for an evening of socializing.

The boys looked happy and relaxed. 'Thank God you're in one piece Tim. After Rob's injury and Danni and Em filling my head with stories about Dave's broken finger, I was concerned,' Bel commented.

Rob and Dave adopted innocent expressions, but the effect was spoilt when Dave held up his crooked finger. 'Want to see?'

Everyone laughed as Emily playfully slapped her husband's hand. 'No she doesn't! Put it away. Geez you're incorrigible.' Which drew more chuckles from the group.

'Actually Tim handled the breaks really well,' complemented Rob. 'We all reckon he could tackle some of the more challenging breaks. I've been trying to talk him into joining us again tomorrow but so far he's resisted.'

Tim held his hands up, then groaned and dropped them back to his side. 'As much as I enjoyed myself, it's been awhile since I surfed regularly and after all the paddling today I doubt I'll be able to lift my board tomorrow let alone surf. Besides, Bel and I have a few errands to run tomorrow.'

Bel reached up and rubbed his shoulders in sympathy, drawing more groans from Tim. 'Poor love. We'll find time to get you a massage tomorrow and if you're extra nice to me, I might even give you one tonight.' Tim threw her a look that somehow managed to be sad and hopeful at the same time, causing Bel to sigh with resignation and exasperation. 'No fair! You know that hangdog expression works on me every time.'

That set the tone for the rest of the evening. Lots of banter, laughter and good-natured ribbing. After the Blue Fin, the entire group adjourned for dinner to a nearby restaurant where the food was good, the drinks were cold and a talented local guitar and vocal duo took their requests long into the night. It was a fitting send off for Emily and Dave's last evening with the group. Back at their villa, Danni cleaned and dressed Rob's wound before bed and it was only his continuing refusal to see a doctor that spoilt an otherwise thoroughly enjoyable evening.

The following day, Emily and Dave checked out of the villa around lunchtime. From there they were heading to a fancy private retreat, a couple of hours away in Ubud, where they were having a two night romantic getaway before returning home to Perth and the children. Dave squeezed in one final surf with the boys and Danni kept Emily company whilst she packed. Surprisingly, Rob returned to the villa with Dave, ostensibly to see their friends off but when he showered and changed and said he was taking his board to have it repaired, Danni sensed his leg was bothering him more than he was letting on. The repair his surfboard required was a minor chip and could easily have waited until he was home.

When the car they'd organized to transfer them to Ubud arrived, Dave loaded his and Emily's luggage whilst the two women hugged.

'Enjoy the next couple of days and have a safe trip home.'

'We will. I'm looking forward to having some time alone with Dave. He's had his fun and I'm totally relaxed and refreshed so it's a perfect way to finish off our trip. But I have to admit I'm missing the kids so it will be nice to get home,' conceded Emily.

'You'll be home before you know it.'

'Yes and probably wishing I was back here once I've been up to my elbows in dirty nappies and tripping over toys for a week,' Emily laughed.

'I doubt it. Besides, things will be a lot easier now you're going to be a stay at home mum.'

'True, although I'm still nervous about taking such a big step.' Emily bit her bottom lip anxiously, prompting Danni to give her friend another hug.

'Don't be Em. You're a great mum and a talented designer; you'll be successful in both even if you have to put your career on hold for a while. It's never easy to make big changes in your life and I admire you for having the guts to do so. Enjoy the extra time with the kids and Dave.'

'Thanks Danni. I appreciate the support.'

Dave came and put a hand on his wife's elbow signalling it was time to leave, then leaned over and gave Danni a farewell peck on the cheek. 'Come on girls, you'll have plenty of time to gas-bag when Danni and Rob get home in a couple of weeks.' And with that, they climbed in the waiting vehicle and waved as they were driven away, leaving Danni staring forlornly after them. Although they still had other friends with them in Bali, Danni was going to miss her best friend's company.

Rob threw a casual arm across her shoulders. 'C'mon babe, cheer up. You've still got Tammy, Jo and the other girls to hang out with. And Bel as well; you two seem to have really hit it off.'

Danni nodded. 'We have, but they're heading over to Borneo in a couple of days and I won't see them again until they return to Perth in a year's time. I wonder if they could meet us back here next year; the timing would be about right,' she mused.

'Well you'll have to ask them, but don't be surprised if they'll be anxious to get home after so long away,' Rob cautioned. 'Hey, why don't you come with me to drop my board off and we'll head into Kuta for some lunch and a change of scene?'

Danni smiled at the unexpected invitation. 'Sure, that would nice. But first let me put a new dressing on your leg since you pulled the old one off to go surfing,' she admonished.

'It would just come off in the water anyway. But yeah, let's go do it so we can get going.'

Danni rode pillion on the scooter behind Rob; his surfboard hanging off the side in the specially made holder until they dropped it off at the nearby surfboard repairer, then rode north to Kuta, Bali's main tourist precinct. As they drew closer the road became more and more congested and their progress slowed to a crawl. Kuta's development had far preceded any considered planning or forethought and despite recent improvements, its popularity continued to outstrip the available infrastructure. As a result was chaotic and crowded at the best of times and almost total mayhem during peak holiday season. Despite this, the one and a half kilometre strip of beach, the abundance of cheap accommodation, restaurants, pubs and nightclubs, shopping and its famous moniker continued to draw tourists in ever increasing numbers. Rob and Danni had learnt years ago to avoid the place for the most part, but every now and then, drawn by the better shopping, dining options and nightlife than Uluwatu offered; they braved the madness and ventured forth.

Rob persisted with the congestion right into downtown Kuta and then turned down a laneway towards the beach where he knew to find a designated parking area. It was usually pretty full but for a generous tip the attendants had a knack for finding space for another scooter. As soon as they parked, they were rushed by the notoriously persistent Kuta hawkers offering the usual tourist trinkets such as bracelets, singlet's, henna tattoos and massages. After four decades of dealing with predominantly western tourists the Kuta hawkers were master touts. Sad expressions, offers of 'special' prices, 'good luck' sales and plain old-fashioned persistence had conned plenty of Bali novices into paying overinflated prices for stuff they didn't really want. Just as they had a nose for picking out the Bali newbies, the hawkers quickly realized when they were dealing with more experienced tourists and tended not to waste too much of their time chasing an unlikely sale at 'local' prices. So after a few polite but firm refusals from both Rob and Danni in passable Bahasa Indonesian, they were left alone.

By mutual agreement they headed to a bar and grill they knew with a good international menu and a well-deserved reputation for serving the best steak in Bali at a reasonable price. After two weeks of eating almost exclusively Indonesian and Balinese cuisine, both Rob and Danni were ready for a change and thoroughly enjoyed their meals. Afterwards they wandered along Kuta's main shopping strip where brand names such as Billabong, Quick Silver and Reebok kept a shop front. Even though the prices and range were similar to what was available back home in Australia,

Rob bought himself a new t-shirt and some board shorts. Danni preferred the more boutique shopping on the adjacent beach road where she found some nice hair clips, a silver bangle and a couple of cute outfits for her four year old niece. Later they braved the touts and wandered through the central markets where Danni found a tiny 'I love Bali' t-shirt for her youngest niece. By mid-afternoon they'd had enough of the crowds, enough of endless honking horns from the gridlocked traffic and enough of the hawkers. They retreated into a Starbucks Coffee shop as much for the sanctuary as for the coffee and cake they treated themselves to. Fortified, they retrieved their scooter and joined the traffic chaos for a slow retreat back to Uluwatu. Rob collected his freshly repaired surfboard on the way back through and they returned to their villa just long enough to drop off the board and their shopping before heading over to the Blue Fin to meet the rest of the gang, including Bel and Tim who were now well entrenched in the sundown ritual.

'Hey guys. Where have you two been? We were surprised Rob wasn't hitting the waves with the boys this afternoon,' Bel said by way of greeting.

'He came back to the villa to see Emily and Dave off and then decided to play hooky whilst he got his board repaired, so we went up to Kuta for lunch and a bit of shopping. It was nice but the place is mad.'

'I know what you mean. The first time we came to Bali we headed straight to the famous Kuta. A few hours in we were wondering what all the fuss was about. Highly overrated in our opinion but to each their own I suppose. Obviously hundreds of thousands of visitors a year disagree with us.'

'Sorry to butt in girls, but I'm heading to bar. What are you having?' asked Tim.

Danni eyed the pina colada Bel was holding. 'Same as Bel thanks Tim.'

Whilst Tim was at the bar, Rob drifted off to chat with the men leaving Bel and Danni alone. 'So what did you and Tim get up to today?'

'Nothing special. We had a few errands to run, not the least of which was booking our flights to Borneo in three day's time. It was easier to wait until we got here to do it because the domestic Indonesian airlines don't have particularly reliable on-line booking systems, if at all. Anyway, all done now.'

'I know we've only known each other a few days but I'm going to miss you guys, especially now Emily's gone too.'

'Same Danni. Tim and I have really enjoyed your company and meeting everyone else. I know it's going to be quite awhile before we get home, but

I certainly hope we can catch up again once we're back in Perth.'

'Absolutely, and in the meantime I want you to keep me up-to-date with all your activities over there in Borneo. I'm really interested to hear about your volunteer work and the place in general.'

Bel looked thoughtful. 'Tim and I are going up to Sanur tomorrow to meet the guy that heads up the NGO we'll be working for. Why don't you come with us? It's a fairly casual meeting over lunch so I'm sure Rama wouldn't mind if you joined us. We can spend the rest of the day looking around and doing touristy things.'

'Sounds like fun, if you're sure I won't be in the way.'

'Absolutely sure,' said Bel firmly. 'So it's settled then. We'll swing by your villa and pick you up around nine.'

As with most nights, they dined with the rest of the group although neither Danni nor Rob were particularly hungry after their steak lunch and indulgent afternoon tea. Then Rob surprised Danni again by calling it a night much earlier than normal, all but confirming her suspicions that his leg was giving him trouble. She tackled him about it once they were back in their room and although he admitted his leg was now quite painful, he still refused to concede it needed medical attention, even after Danni pointed out the yellow crust that was now forming around the wound.

He spent a restless night, tossing and turning and disturbing Danni to the point that she eventually gave up trying to sleep and got up. She tiptoed around making herself a cup of tea from the complementary supplies in the room and went out onto their private balcony just as the sun was rising. The villa was very quiet since most of the guests were still sleeping. There were a few staff around, quietly going about their morning tasks; a young man sweeping the pathways free of leaves with a thatched broom, another carrying a room service tray to a room across the way. It struck Danni that it was a lovely time of day.

She heard some movement in the room then Rob stepped onto the balcony to join her. 'You're up early,' he murmured.

'I couldn't sleep with you tossing and turning beside me,' she explained without rancour.

Rob grimaced and reached across to give her shoulder a conciliatory rub. 'Sorry babe. My leg didn't appreciate being rubbed against the bed or the doona.'

Danni sighed heavily. 'Look Rob, I don't want to keep nagging you about it so I'm only going to say this one more time. You need to see a doctor.'

Rob pulled his hand away from her shoulder and adopted a defensive stance. 'Well I don't agree. As long as I don't knock it against something its fine, nothing a Panadol won't fix.'

'Rob, paracetamol will only mask the pain, it won't fix it.' Danni struggled to keep the frustration out of her voice. 'I don't understand why you're being so darn stubborn about this.'

'I'm being stubborn because I think you're overreacting and besides, I'm here to have a good time, not to waste my time trying to track down a decent doctor. Anyway, you just said you didn't want to nag so just let it go will you.'

Danni threw her hands up in frustration. 'Alright, I won't mention it again. You're big enough to make your own decisions.'

'That's right, I am,' said Rob, then realizing he'd sounded a bit harsh he leaned down and dropped a kiss on the top of Danni's head. 'But I know you're only concerned because you care about me and I appreciate it. I'd probably be on your case if the shoe was on the other foot.' I doubt it, I would have seen a doctor day's ago, thought Danni sourly but wisely she kept her thoughts to herself. Instead, she simply said, 'I guess so.'

Rob wandered back inside and donned his surf wear, cleaned his teeth and splashed some water on his face. Danni tried not to notice him rummaging around in their little first aid kit and downing a couple of Panadol, which was telling in itself because Rob rarely took anything. He snagged a couple of pieces of fresh fruit from the supplies Danni had purchased the previous morning, slung his daypack over his shoulder then returned to the balcony to retrieve his surfboard.

'I'm off then babe. Guess I'll see you this afternoon at Finny's as usual. What are you getting up to today?'

'I'm going up to Sanur for the day with Bel and Tim,' Danni answered, although Rob was already halfway out the door.

'Cool, have fun. See ya babe.' And with that he was gone.

CHAPTER FOUR

Bel and Tim collected Danni from the villa promptly at nine as arranged. As with their previous excursion, Bel rode pillion behind Tim whilst Danni rode the second scooter, following Tim as he guided them northwards. As they joined the main north-south road passing right through Kuta, the traffic congestion grew. Conscious of Danni following behind, Tim kept the pace slow and stuck to the outside lane and Bel regularly glanced behind to ensure Danni was keeping up. Once through the Kuta gridlock and passed the airport, the northbound traffic thinned considerably and they were able to relax and take in more of the surroundings.

Both sides of the busy roadway were lined with shops, office blocks, small warehouses and factories making handcrafted timber and rattan furniture, pots and garden ornaments, timber decked and palm frond covered pergolas, shrines, decorative carvings and ornately carved doors and doorways. It was all classic Balinese styling and probably the source of many of the items offered for sale by landscape and garden centres back home in Australia. Idly, Danni wondered how complicated it would be to buy a shipping container full of the stuff and send it back to Australia; she would love a house full of it, her very own piece of Bali right there in Perth. Lost in thought, she almost missed Tim slowing and had to brake hard to make the right hand turn towards the coast. Thankfully she hadn't been going very fast but it was a timely reminder to keep her focus on the road, lest she become another of Bali's road accident holiday statistics.

Away from the bypass road, it was immediately quieter as they shared the local road with fewer cars and scooters. A proliferation of signboards advertising guesthouses and boutique villas pointed down narrow village laneways, where they were tucked away among the modest local homes. Tourists strolled casually along tree-lined streets, comfortable and relaxed in the quiet atmosphere of Sanur. Slowly, they followed the lazy twisting, turning road, noting the growing abundance of warungs, restaurants, and small hole-in-the-wall shops known locally as *toko's*. When they reached a large statue in middle of a four-way intersection, Danni followed Tim's right hand turn into short, narrow street that took them to the beach. That was one thing about Bali; depending on whether you were on the east or west side of the island and travelling north or south, it was easy to find the beach by simply bearing left or right as appropriate.

They parked their scooters behind the beach beneath a stand of big, shady trees as directed by a parking attendant and looked around curiously. Nestled well back from the beach in the shade, was a large café crowded with tourists, all wearing standard beach attire of bathers, sarongs, hats and flip-flops. Business was not nearly as brisk for several cart vendors parked nearby or the canvas covered warungs set-up opposite.

'This is nice,' commented Bel. 'Different to Uluwatu and much quieter that Kuta; seems a bit more laid back.'

Danni nodded. 'Yes, Sanur does have reputation for being laid back. It's popular with more mature travellers and families with kids on account of having a nice beach and lots of cafes and restaurants without the rowdy pub and nightclub scene that Kuta thrives on.'

Whilst they were chatting, Danni and Bel absently moved away from the parking area for a better view of the beach, leaving Tim talking to the parking attendant. He joined them a few minutes later after the girls had already waved off several hawkers. 'Righto, I managed to get some directions from the parking attendant. There's good news and bad news I'm afraid. The good news is that I know where we're supposed to meet Rama; the bad news is that it's about two kilometres further up the beach. So either we have a long walk or we jump back on the scooters and find a closer place to park.'

Danni and Bel shrugged at each other. 'Well a long walk doesn't bother me,' said Danni. 'We've got plenty of time and we're supposed to be looking around and doing the touristy thing anyway.'

'And I could do with the exercise,' added Bel patting her stomach. 'Work off some of those yummy, sweet, sugar filled cocktails I've been drinking.'

Danni grinned. 'I know what you mean Bel. I always put on a kilo or two when I'm in Bali.'

'Okay so we're walking then,' said Tim, and with that they set off along the beach path, passed more warungs, passed massage huts and beachside stalls, covered only by a few sheets of tin, tarpaulins or canvas salvaged from old signs and banners, the faded photographs, logos and catch-phrases now draped crookedly and without prominence, over crude wooden or bamboo frames. Colourful outrigger canoes, the traditional fishing boat of the Balinese, were pulled up on the beach, their crab claw sails wrapped tidily around the cross beams that when in use, held the sail aloft above the short mast. Each canoe had a simple but decorative prow, usually resembling the long bill and gaping mouth of a marlin sailfish. Danni knew from her father, a keen sailor, that the double outrigger canoes were highly stable and manoeuvrable but to her, their appeal lay in the bright colours and simple design. They were quintessentially Balinese and neither she nor Bel could resist snapping off some photos off the canoes against the backdrop of golden sand and the shimmering Bali Sea. More photos were taken as they rounded a sand split and the Sanur Beach stretched endlessly before them with Mt Agung, Bali's sacred volcano, rising majestically in the distance.

'How beautiful. No wonder the Balinese believe Mt Agung is the abode of the Gods. It's like she's keeping watch over the island,' commented Danni. It wasn't the first time she had seen Mt Agung but from this angle, looming across the bay, she felt like she was seeing it for the first time. It was worth coming up to Sanur just for that, she thought.

They walked on, passing the carefully manicured gardens of several beachside resorts, occasionally pausing to look at the wares on offer at the tiny stalls although none of them were enticed into purchasing, despite the best efforts of the sellers. Bel and Tim couldn't see any point buying anything they would have to cart with them for the next twelve months and Danni had seen most of the souvenirs and trinkets before, since the same items were on offer all over the island. Eventually they came to a cluster of restaurants and cafes, with tables set up in the thick shade of several large fig trees right on the beach. Red lanterns and fairy lights were strung through the branches; at night it would be a delightful place to dine, but even now the shady nook was appealing.

'Anyone for a cold drink?' Tim suggested and when the girls both agreed they chose a table and seated themselves as a young waitress hurried over with menus. Feeling a little hungry, Danni ordered a fruity yogurt smoothie which turned out to be just perfect.

'This is lovely. I'm really liking Sanur,' commented Bel.

Danni agreed. 'Me too, but Rob would never stay up here. It's too far from his favourite surf breaks.'

'That's a shame,' Bel commiserated. 'But you're here for three weeks. Couldn't you at least talk him into a few nights up this way?'

Danni shook her head. 'I doubt it. He's not really into poking around doing touristy stuff so I think he'd be bored witless within a day or two. Plus he can be a stubborn sod when he wants to be. I've been trying to convince him to see a doctor about his leg but he flatly refuses.'

'Still no luck with that huh?'

'None I'm afraid. He tossed and turned all last night and was popping Panadol this morning so it's definitely bothering him, but I told him I wasn't going to keep nagging him about it so the ball's in his court now.'

'Fair enough. You can lead a horse to water but you can't make it drink,' Bel agreed.

After cooling off, they resumed their walk along the beach and although they found the remainder of the beach strip similar to what they had already seen, Danni enjoyed the rest of the walk. At about the two kilometre mark they located the restaurant where they would be meeting Rama for lunch but as they still had time to kill before then, they wandered a little further on until they came to a beachside market. Since it seemed to be a bit of a tourist and local market mix they poked around and when Danni spied some apricot sized fruit with shiny reddish-brown, scaly skin she was fascinated and held one up for Tim and Bel's scrutiny.

'Oh my God, look at this. It looks exactly like brown snakes skin.'

Bel ran her fingers across the skin. 'You're right, it does.'

Danni turned to the vendor who was watching them curiously. 'What is this fruit?'

'*Salak*. Also we call it snake fruit,' she replied in heavily accented English.

Danni nodded and repeated the new word '*Salak*,' concentrating on getting the pronunciation right.

The elderly women nodded and smiled approvingly. 'You want to try?'

'Yes please.'

The vendor deftly pinched the pointed tip off and pulled the skin away in one piece, then broke the fleshy inside open to reveal several creamy white segments. She handed it to Danni who took a segment then passed the rest on to Bel and Tim. The flesh was sweet with a hint of sourness and a crunchy texture similar to a slightly under ripe apple, and as Danni discovered, each segment contained a hard brown seed about the size of a marble. Although it left her with a slightly dry mouth, Danni enjoyed it and decided to buy some of the fruit to take back for Rob to try. Then the thought struck her that perhaps it wasn't a native fruit to Bali.

'Is this native to Bali?' Danni asked and then rephrased the question when the elderly lady looked puzzled. 'From Bali?'

The woman's expression cleared with understanding. 'Ya, ya, from Bali. You buy?' she asked expectantly.

Danni nodded and held up three fingers. 'Yes, three please.' Then grinned to herself when the vendor bagged three pieces of fruit and counted one, two, three, four, pointedly adding the fruit that had been sampled by the group. She named a price and Danni paid her without haggling. She couldn't be bothered haggling over two dollars' worth of fruit and figured the vendor needed the money more than she did. After Bel made a similar purchase, they gave the small temple adjacent to the market a casual look over, then Tim announced it was probably time they started heading back towards their meeting place.

Somehow they still managed to arrive fifteen minutes early, so they took a table and ordered some drinks whilst they waited for Rama to join them. When Bel and Tim talked between themselves about the upcoming meeting, Danni let her attention drift away towards the tourists wandering along the beach path, the middle-aged couple at the next table and a young family playing on the beach. Further out, at the very end of a long sand spit, a lone figure sat in a pergola. He sat cross-legged facing the ocean, his back to the beach, unmoving apart from his dark hair blowing in the ocean breeze. Danni sensed a stillness within him, his connection to the elements almost palpable. Realising she was staring, Danni looked away but her gaze kept wandering back to him so in the end she gave in and sat watching him. Only when he finally uncurled his legs and stood did she look away, guiltily, as if her eyes boring into his back had somehow disturbed his meditation.

Danni re-focused on her drink, fingering the droplets of condensation that had formed on the outside of the glass. She didn't raise her gaze until she felt another presence at the table and then nearly knocked her glass over when she found herself looking up at the very same man from the pergola. There was no doubt it was him. Despite the fact he'd since pulled on a t-shirt, she recognized his golden bronzed skin, his broad shoulders falling away to narrow hips and his shoulder length hair, slightly curly and tussled from the wind. From a distance she had assumed he was Balinese but now close up, Danni was mildly surprised to realise he was the product of mixed Balinese and Caucasian parentage, which explained why he was taller and more heavily built than the average Balinese man. His hair was a lighter brown too and although his face carried the finely defined lines of his Balinese heritage, it was slightly broader with a squarer chin. His almond shape eyes were warm and brown, sparkling with intelligence. Danni got another surprise when he spoke with an Australian accent, although his words were slightly more pronounced than the average Aussie.

'Tim, Belinda?' he inquired.

They both stood, Tim offering his hand which was accepted with a firm shake. 'That's us,' he confirmed. 'And of course, you must be Rama. It's great to finally meet you in person.'

Rama smiled warmly and offered his hand to Belinda, giving it a light shake. 'I'm glad to have you here. Judging from your previous experience and the conversations we've had over the phone, I think we'll work very well together over the next twelve months.' He glanced curiously at Danni, who had also risen to her feet but was standing back, not wanting to intrude on this first meeting.

'This is Danni Pollard, a friend of ours,' Bel explained. 'Since we were coming up from Uluwatu to Sanur for our meeting we decided to make a day of it and have a look around. I hope you don't mind if Danni joins us for lunch?'

Rama smiled warmly at Danni and offered his hand, just as he had with Bel. 'No not at all. You're most welcome Danni. Belinda and Tim, we've already been over the details of your assignment and how my organization operates so this is really just an informal get-to-know-you, a chance to meet in person. Once you start work in two week's time, I'll be there to meet you and get you settled in. Now please everyone, let's sit and order some lunch.'

As they took their seats Bel told Rama to call her Bel. 'Only my mother calls me Belinda, and usually only when I'm in trouble,' she said with a grin.

There was a pause in their conversation whilst they examined the menu and placed their orders, then Rama indicated to the shopping bags the girls had placed on the end of the table. 'I see you've brought some snake fruit.'

'Yes, we were quite fascinated by it,' Bel confirmed and Danni added, 'I've been coming to Bali regularly since I was a teenager but I've never seen it before, although the vendor assured us it was native to Bali.'

Rama nodded. 'It is indeed and you're right, it's fascinating fruit, quite apart from its appearance. It's actually the fruit of the *Salak* palm tree which is indigenous to Indonesia and Malaysia. The palm is short and has multiple stems covered in needle sharp spikes up to two inches long. The fruit grows in clusters at the base of the stems so the poor harvester has to be very careful when reaching in among the spines to retrieve it. There are a few varieties, one of which is very sweet and juicy and which the locals sometimes ferment into *Salak* wine. I'm surprised you haven't come across it before Danni; it is very popular with the locals. In fact, its popularity is growing further afield as it is now one of Indonesia's top fruit exports. I don't think you'll find it on grocer's shelves back in Australia just yet but don't be surprised if it turns up one day soon.'

'I didn't realize Bali had much of an export market,' Tim commented.

'They certainly do and it's growing. In recent years the government has been actively trying to diversify Bali's economy to reduce its reliance on tourism. The main focus has been on developing the financial sector and export markets. Apart from fruit, Bali now exports seafood, textiles, furniture, handcrafts and fashion items all over the world.'

'I'm not surprised the furniture and handcraft exports are doing well,' Danni said. 'The Balinese are really skilled craftsmen. I've collected a few nice woodcarvings and silver jewellery over the years. Mine are pretty modest but I've seen some truly amazing pieces on display. I once talked to a woodcarver in Ubud who was working on a really intricate, life-size carving. He told me it had taken him nearly a year to get that far and he still had another month or two to go before it would be complete. I'd love to have taken it home with me but it was outside my price range that's for sure. Not that I'd have anywhere to put something so big anyway.'

'No not the sort of thing you can put on the sideboard,' Bel agreed with a laugh.

Changing the subject, Rama turned to Danni. 'So I know Bel and Tim's backgrounds and I'm guessing they've given you some idea about what I do, so it's probably only fair that I ask what you do?'

'I work in marketing.'

'Ah I see. For yourself or a company?'

'A company. It's a very competitive industry so I prefer the security of working for a well-established company. Plus we have some really well-known corporate clients.' Danni mentioned a few names, drawing an appreciative whistle from Tim. 'Anyway, I couldn't hope to work on big accounts like that if I was out on my own.'

'So you don't like the small stuff?' Rama asked.

'Actually I do. I really enjoy the challenge of putting together campaigns for our smaller clients. There's usually more involvement from the owners, which can be both good and bad, but either way it's more personal than just dealing with corporate executives. Plus there's always less money to spend so I have to be really smart about how the marketing dollars are directed. But when a campaign comes together and is really successful, the impact on those small clients can be huge and that makes it all worthwhile. The reality is though, I would need a lot of clients like that to be able to make a decent living. Others have done it, gone out on their own and made a real go of it, but there's plenty who have tried and failed. At the moment I'm happy doing what I do so it's not something I've really considered.'

'Fair enough. Turning your back on paid employment and going out on your own is never an easy step. In my case, I think I always knew it was inevitable that I would eventually establish my own NGO but it was still a very difficult decision to make when the time came,' said Rama.

Their conversation was interrupted by the arrival of their meals and resumed on a less personal note when Rama asked Bel and Tim about their plans for the next couple of weeks.

'We've been in Bali for a week now, doing a bit of sightseeing, eating too much and just relaxing,' Bel explained. 'But yesterday we booked our tickets to Banjarmasin, which you mentioned was our liaison point. We're flying over in a couple of days and are planning to spend the time until we start work having a look around and getting a feel for the place.'

Rama nodded. 'That's not a bad idea. With your experience I'm quite confident you'll settle in quickly over there but it doesn't hurt to get a feel for the place, the people, the culture and the politics beforehand. I have a guy over there in Banjarmasin who acts as my driver when I'm there but he's also a very capable tourist guide. If you'd like, I could ask him to show you around. You'll find there is very little in the way of tourist infrastructure over there and English isn't widely spoken so it would be a lot easier for you to have some local knowledge.'

Bel and Tim looked at each other and nodded in agreement. 'I think we'll take you up on that Rama. Just let us know how to get in touch with him.'

'Actually he can be a little hard to get hold of, especially if he's up-country where the mobile telephone reception is a bit sketchy. I usually contact his wife and she gets him to ring me, so if you give me your flight details I'll arrange for him to meet you at the airport and show you the main attractions over a few days. Beyond that, you can make your own arrangements with him depending on what else you might like to see.'

'That sounds perfect,' said Bel happily.

'What about you Danni? What are you doing with yourself once Bel and Tim head off?'

'I'm actually over here with my husband and a loose group of friends. We've got another two weeks before we head home. My husband Rob is a mad keen surfer so Bali is something of an annual pilgrimage for him and his mates. What about you, do you surf Rama?'

'A bit. As you've no doubt guessed I have mixed heritage; an Australian father and a Balinese mother. My dad was one of the early visitors to Bali, an avid surfer, hippy and drop-out, who found his way to the island nearly forty years ago when it was little more than a handful of sleepy villages. He and his mates pioneered the surf breaks at Uluwatu, Padang Padang and Keramas. When the money ran out, he'd go home to Australia just long enough to save enough money to come back again. I think he was on his second trip to Bali when he met my mum, a village girl from Sanur. He married her on the third trip, something that back then was quite a social taboo, but they didn't care, they were madly in love and still are to this day. Anyway, having a Balinese wife suited dad fine in that it gave him every excuse to return to Bali for extended periods every year since, although once I came along he did have to knuckle down a bit work wise to provide for his family. Anyway cut a long story short, dad had me out on a surfboard as soon as I could swim. He got a lot my cousins surfing too, one of whom now runs a surf school on the beach just south of here. I don't get out very often these days due to work commitments but every now and then I manage to find the time. I was never as fanatical as my dad so I can live with that,' he finished with a shrug.

'Does your dad still surf?' Bel asked.

'He sure does. He's sixty-four now and still as fit as a fiddle.'

'It would have been amazing to experience Bali all those years ago. I bet he has some stories to tell,' commented Tim.

Rama grinned. 'He sure does. I think things were pretty wild back then. He's always lamenting the changes that Bali has seen since he first came here but then again, it was him and his mates who blazed the trail.'

Danni nodded. 'That seems to be a common sentiment among the old-timers but I wonder if the changes are really so bad. There are plenty of developing countries that would love to experience the sort of economic growth that Bali has.'

'That's true,' Rama conceded. 'But development always comes at a price and there are many who wonder if the price that Bali is paying in terms of loss of traditional lands, culture, environment and family life is worth it. Tell you what, if you guys are really interested, I could take you to meet my parents. They have a house not far from here where they spend most of the year now that dad has retired. Both mum and dad have interesting perspectives on Bali as it was and as it is now.'

'That would be great,' said Bel enthusiastically, glancing around at the others for confirmation. 'Are you sure they won't mind? As much as we'd love to meet them we don't want to intrude, especially at short notice.'

'I'm sure they won't mind. Dad loves telling stories about the good old days as he calls them and mum's used to drop-ins. I'll just ring ahead and make sure they're home though.'

After they finished lunch Rama rang his folks and warned them of their impending visit, then led them through a laneway to the main road running parallel to the beach a block back. Since they'd left their scooters at the southern end of the beach, it was decided that the best option was to grab a *bemo* back there to retrieve the scooters. Rama would then ride Danni's scooter, with her as pillion and Tim and Bel following to his parent's home. Spotting a *bemo* further down the street, Rama let out a loud whistle to attract the driver's attention, who raised a hand in acknowledgement and quickly jumped in the driver's seat, swinging the *bemo* around to pick them up.

Bemo's, usually a minivan or a small truck with wooden seating running down both sides of the tray, were the most common form of transport in Bali, used almost exclusively by locals because they were cheap. Mostly they followed standard routes, picking up and dropping off passengers wherever they pleased. The fares were a bit loose but generally depended on distance travelled. Tourists tended to avoid *bemo's* like the plague because the loose fare structure usually meant they got stung and drivers had a tendency to squeeze in as many passengers as they could pick up, so it wasn't uncommon to see twenty or so locals crammed into a minivan that only had seating for twelve. In villages like Sanur, *bemo's* usually just cruised up and down the main strip and just like the one Rama had flagged down for them, they were often pretty decrepit and barely roadworthy, having long since been retired off the longer routes. When Danni climbed into the battered, door-less minivan she was pleased to find an empty seat well away from the open doorway, although it was only a short lumbering five minute ride before Rama tapped the drivers shoulder and tossed him a few rupiah as they piled out of the van.

They walked back over to the beachside car park and retrieved their scooters. Rama seemed unfazed at the lack of a helmet and expertly guided the scooter through the streets with an ease borne of years of experience, with Danni propped on the seat behind him loosely holding onto his waist. After a few minutes, he turned into a narrow laneway, took another turn and then pulled to a halt outside a tall wooden gate. He tooted the horn and within a minute the gate was slid open from the inside by a teenage boy. Rama eased the scooter into the compound, followed by Tim as the boy closed the gate behind them.

The teenager stood by shyly shuffling his feet until Rama walked over and gave him a friendly slap on the shoulder. '*Selamat siang* Gede,' he said before introducing him to the visitors. 'This is my cousin's boy Gede. These are some friends of mine.' The three of them chorused greetings and received a shy smile and a mumbled *'Halo'* in return before the boy retreated into one of the buildings inside the compound.

Danni looked around curiously. The compound appeared to house several buildings, all contained within a high cement wall which was not unusual in Bali. Apart from the gated driveway entrance they'd come through, there was also pedestrian access through a decorative abhor, beside which stood a small family shrine bearing several offerings, a still burning incense stick and fresh frangipani flowers. Of the buildings, one stood higher than the others, with two residential stories above a ground level garage. Its façade was rendered cement, painted an attractive brown mocha colour. Unusually for local homes, both of the upper levels had large balconies, which Danni recognized as a western influence. As a concession to wet season rains there was a narrow, covered walkway running down the side of the house, supported by thick timber pillars, as were the upper level balconies. It was an attractive home, certainly what one would class as a villa, and bespoke of the relative wealth of the family living there. Of the other buildings, there was another large two story home of similar styling, but without a garage or upper balconies. The third building was more traditional, a single story cottage with a veranda running down one side and classic Balinese terracotta tiles on the roof. Although it was tidy and well maintained, it had obviously escaped the modernization the rest of the compound had undergone and remained in original condition.

Generous amounts of tropical plants of all types were planted throughout the compound and right along the perimeter wall, effectively softening what would have otherwise been a rather austere feature. Instead, it served to highlight the dense green, yellow, red and orange foliage. A raised pond stood in the centre of the front courtyard, the water trickling slowly over the sides into a surrounding collection moat to be re-circulated back into the pond. Several large frangipani trees shaded the courtyard, scattering their delicate yellow, white and pink flowers into the pond and across the pavers and filling the air with their sweet fragrance. It was a delightful garden; in fact, Danni was impressed with the entire compound which managed to achieve a tasteful balance between the traditional and the modern.

'Welcome to my family compound,' said Rama. 'Let me take you through to meet my parents and then I'll show you around.'

He led them down the side of the big house to the back of the building, onto a large patio and through an extra wide screened door, calling *'Ibu, pak,'* as he entered. Danni barely had time to take in the big, open room, the wide expanses of glass and the heavy timber rafters before a small Balinese women bustled into the room, flapping her hands energetically towards her son. 'Rama, come and give your *ibu* a hug,' she said even though she was on him before he had a chance take a step. Rama towered over his diminutive mother, so he had to lean down to envelope her in an affectionate hug, although remembering her manners, his mother quickly disentangled herself from him and turned to her guests.

'Hello and welcome. It is always nice to meet some of Rama's friends. Now please tell me your names,' she requested, smiling.

'Whoa there, slow down luv. There's no point doing the introductions twice.' The owner of the voice walked across the room towards them, his laconic pace quite the opposite to his wife's energetic entrance. He was tall like his son, fit looking and deeply tanned from years playing in the sun and the sea. Deep creases at the side of his mouth and crow's feet fanning from intelligent green eyes belied a man who laughed often, his thick blond locks streaked with grey, the only concession to advancing years. As she had with his mum, Danni took an instant liking to Rama's father.

'Pooh, pooh, you should hurry up and not keep our guests waiting,' his wife fired back cheekily, but her husband took not the slightest notice and Rama just grinned at the familiar byplay.

'Okay, now that you're both here let me introduce Tim, his wife Bel and their friend Danni,' he said pointing to them as he spoke. 'And as you've no doubt gathered, these are my parent Ngurah and Glen Thom.'

'Dad's one of your ilk Tim,' Rama offered as the men shook hands. 'A bricklayer by trade. Tim's a builder dad. He and Bel are heading over to Kalimantan to do some work for Helping Hands.'

'That's good. I'd give Rama a hand myself but I'm a bit past it these days. Slinging bricks and timber around is a young man's game.'

'You look fit enough to me,' protested Bel.

'That's because I had the good sense to give it away before I wore my body out,' he replied with grin.

'No that's because you are a lazy man. You want to lie in the sun and ride your waves and hang around here getting in my way,' Ngurah admonished fondly, without a hint of malice.

Glen chuckled. 'Never bothered you thirty-eight years ago when we met. As I recall you quite liked me hanging around.'

'Ah, I was young and silly,' said Ngurah dismissively and then turned her attention to her guests. 'Now, can I get you anything? A cold drink, tea, coffee?'

'Not for me thanks. We've not long had lunch,' said Danni.

'*Ibu*,' Rama butted in, 'I promised my friends a tour of the compound once we'd made the introductions. It won't take long then I'll bring them back. Tim, are you coming or staying here with dad?' Rama asked since the two men were already deep in conversation. When Tim indicated he was staying, Rama led the girls off the patio and across the garden to a small bricked temple where he paused. 'How much do you know about Balinese family life?'

Both girls shook their heads. 'Not much.'

'Okay, I'll give you the basics then. Traditionally, Balinese families live together with their extended family in a family compound. All compounds are designed in accordance with traditional laws and customs called *adat*, which dictates the orientation and layout of the compound and the buildings within, so although it's not always obvious to the inexperienced eye, one compound is much the same as another. They all have a perimeter wall, a central, covered pavilion for meetings and ceremonies and a family shrine such as this one here. Also within the compound, and usually quite centrally located, is another building for cooking and a storage room for keeping rice and other staples. Arranged around these are more buildings which serve as the living quarters for the family members and visitors, the number of buildings dependent on the available space and size and wealth of the family. In the past, most compounds also contained pens for raising pigs, chickens and a small garden for growing fruit and vegetables. To a large extent, most families were quite self-sufficient, they grew what they needed and bartered with other families and if cash was needed they might sell a pig or supplement their income by making things they could sell at the market such as chicken coops, woven mats etc. Out in the countryside this is still very much the way of life, but not so much in the more urbanised south where most people now have regular jobs.' Rama waved towards a gap in the low wall surrounding the small family temple. 'You're welcome to have a look if you'd like.'

The girls took Rama up on his offer and spent a few minutes looking at the lovely little temple. It was neat and tidy and obviously lovingly tended but just like the little cottage it appeared to be quite authentic to its original design. 'How old is it Rama?' Danni asked, curious.

'I'm not entirely sure,' he said with a shrug. 'I don't think anyone really knows. The compound has been in the family for many, many generations and there would have been a temple on that very spot since it was established, although it would have been added to and repaired over the years.'

When the girls finished looking at the temple, Rama skirted around the central pavilion and up alongside the second big house. As they passed the doorway, Danni noticed several pairs of flip-flops discarded by the door so out of respect to the occupants she only gave the building a cursory glance. Back towards the front of the compound he stopped by the veranda of the old cottage, giving Bel a chance to ask who lived in the compound.

'At the moment mum and dad live over in the big house but quite often they have extended family staying with them; some of my cousins or their offspring and family from Australia. My mum's sister, her husband, their oldest son and his family and Gede who you met earlier live in the other house. This old cottage was occupied by my grandma until she passed away last year. As you've probably noticed, the rest of the compound has been modernized but *nenek* preferred her cottage just the way it was. The plan is to renovate it a bit in the next few months and then my aunt and uncle will move in, giving my cousin and his family more space in the other house.'

'So who gets to live in the compound and who doesn't?' Danni asked. 'I assume not every extended family member can stay or you'd quickly run out of space.'

Rama grinned. 'By Australian standards maybe but by Balinese standards, it's not unusual for five or six families to live together in a compound, even two or more families in a house together. But to answer your question, traditionally a bride will go and live with the groom's family and they'll stay there until they can afford to set up a home of their own. Our family was a little different because mum was one of four girls. In Bali when parents have no sons, at least one of their daughters will have what is known as a *nyentana* marriage where the groom leaves his home and moves in with his bride's family. Effectively he is assumed into the brides' family to look after their property and continue the male lineage. So whilst two of my aunts went off to live with their groom's families, my other aunt had a *nyentana* marriage and brought her groom back here. Mum obviously married dad and moved to Australia but when in Bali, they also lived here in the family compound in a similar way to *nyentana*.'

'So if you marry will you bring your bride back here?' Bel asked.

'That's a possibility. Since mum and dad have permanently retired here in Bali it is my duty as the oldest son, in fact their only child, to care for them in their old age. In the Balinese culture our old people remain with their families until their deaths.' Rama straightened from his leaning post against the veranda. 'Better get a move on girls or my mum will come looking for us.'

Rama showed the girls the compound kitchen, explaining that

traditionally meals for everyone in the compound were prepared in the shared kitchen. 'Usually a big pot of rice and vegetables is cooked in the morning and everyone in the compound just comes in and helps themselves throughout the day. Protein like chicken, pork or fish is usually prepared and eaten fairly quickly for obvious reasons.'

Danni looked around intrigued. The kitchen was still fully stocked with several large pots, woks and the biggest mortar and pestle she'd ever seen rested against the outside wall. The stove was a big built-in charcoal burner that looked like it had been used quite recently. When she posed the question to Rama, he explained that although the updated homes now had their own kitchens for day to day cooking, the compound kitchen was still used for extended family gatherings and ceremonies when there were a lot of visitors to the compound. The final building was the old storeroom where rice and other dry goods were once stored. Nowadays it was used to store garden implements and other odds and sods.

As they headed back the main house, Rama explained that it had been built on the site of the original workshop and shed. 'It was used for that purpose up until about twenty years ago when the family construction business grew to a point that they moved the business off-site. There was a little room built in at one end of the shed which is where mum, dad and I used to stay when we were in Bali. Anyway, once the business moved it freed up the space here for mum and dad to build their retirement home. My aunt and uncles house was updated at the same time.'

They arrived back at the main house as Rama concluded his commentary; Ngurah waving them over to join herself, Glen and Tim on the patio. 'It's a lovely compound Ngurah, really nice,' complemented Danni. 'I love the way the old and the new has been blended together so well.'

'And I love the garden,' added Bel. 'Especially the frangipani trees; they're my absolute favourite.'

'Here we call them *Jepun* trees,' said Ngurah looking pleased. 'The Balinese have always considered the *Jepun* god's blessing on Balinese soil because the fallen flowers scattered across the ground make the land look and smell more beautiful.'

The girls grinned at each other. 'That's such a nice belief,' said Bel, echoing Danni's thoughts. 'The Balinese ability to find something spiritual in things that go unnoticed or are considered mundane at home is just so lovely.'

'In Australia we have a saying 'slow down and smell the roses'; I think the person that coined that phrase must have spent some time in Bali,'

Danni added.

'It is good advice,' agreed Ngurah.

'So what have you two been talking about all this time?' Bel asked, dropping onto the rattan lounge beside her husband who was still talking animatedly with Glen. Tim put a casual arm around her shoulders. 'Mr Thom was telling me about some of the changes he's seen in Bali over the years.'

'Sounds interesting. I'm curious to know when Bali really took off. I remember my mum singing along to Redgum's hit song 'I've been to Bali too' which I believe came out sometime during the eighties, so I figure Bali was already attracting plenty of tourists even back then.'

Glen laughed. 'Oh yes I remember that song. It was a bit of anthem for me and my mates for a time. Well I'll tell you Bel, by the eighties Bali was well and truly on the tourist map, had been for quite a while. Things really opened up for Bali in 1969 when the government built the international airport at Denpasar. Before that, you had to fly to Jakarta and then take a local flight to Bali, which wasn't easy or cheap. But after the airport opened you could fly direct to Bali which was a heck of a lot easier. Anyway, the government had this grand plan to turn Bali into a showcase for tourism in Indo, so they got some money from the World Bank or somewhere and started developing Nusa Dua with the intention of attracting cashed up tourists who would only take day trips into the interior and supposedly protect the cultural integrity of Bali, which even then was recognized as Bali's main attraction.

Well things didn't exactly go to plan. You see instead of big-spending tourists it was the young ones like me, with little money in their pocket who came to Bali. We certainly didn't have money to stay in those flash resorts down at Nusa Dua and we didn't want to. We loved the local people, loved interacting with them, even though back then hardly anyone spoke a word of English and we couldn't speak a word of Indo, but we soon learned enough to get by.' Bel, Tim and Danni hung on every word. Not only was it a fascinating insight, Glen had a knack for story-telling.

'So where did you stay?' Danni asked. 'I presume Kuta?'

Glen grinned. 'Ah now that's a story in itself. Back in those days, there weren't any hotels in Kuta except for a big government owned place that none of us could afford, so we used to just camp on the beach. The lucky ones had tents with mosquito netting but most of us just put up with the mozzies. We used to try and copy the thatched huts the locals made to rest under when they took a break from working in the rice paddies, so we'd scrounge up some bamboo and some palm leaves and knock up a bit of a roof to sleep under. They were pretty crude; a decent wind would blow them over but it was somewhere to stash our gear when we were out surfing. You could leave your stuff on the beach back then without it getting knocked off; the locals were as honest as the day was long and we didn't steal off each other. Anyway, our biggest problem was the lack of a crapper. None of us wanted to go on the beach since we were living on it and it was right out in the open, so we asked the locals if we could use theirs. Turns out they didn't have a toilet either but they soon figured out we'd be willing to pay them to use one, so a few enterprising fellas dug some holes and put a bit of thatched screening around them to give us a bit of privacy and voila, we had our toilets! Anyway that was about the start of it; the locals realizing they could make some money from us, so a lot of families starting renting their homes out to us. They'd go and squeeze in with another family or sleep in their kitchen or storerooms or wherever. From there on the locals starting building accommodation, shop houses and warungs to cater for us early travellers. It was all completely unplanned, it just happened. No one in the government took much notice and by the time they did it was too late. That's why Kuta is so chaotic to this day.'

'That's quite a story. Hard to imagine it now,' said Tim.

Glen was grinning broadly, enjoying his audience. 'Oh that's nothing. I've got a whole swag of stories. It was free and easy living back then, all quite innocent mind you, just chasing the waves, looking for great unknown breaks to surf and good times.'

'When did the tourists start arriving in big numbers?' Danni asked curiously.

'The numbers grew pretty steadily throughout the seventies. By the middle of the decade there were probably a hundred or so hotels in Kuta, a long way from what I'd first encountered. There were signs of strain even then but once the Indo government started allowing foreign aircraft to land in Bali in the early eighties, things went mental. You see, prior to that Garuda, the government owned airline, had a monopoly and that had kept airfares pretty high. Airfares became much cheaper once other airlines started flying in. Like a lot of my friends from those early years, I think we were a bit blind to what was going on because we were still a high on the paradise we'd first found in Bali. Certainly none of us envisioned the extent of where things were going. Besides that, we simply moved out of Kuta and left it the growing hoards. The surfing at Uluwatu and Bingin was much better anyway and the access was difficult enough to keep the faint-hearted away. You familiar with the Cave at Ulu?' he asked and waited for their confirmation before continuing. 'Well there were no steps down the grotto back then, just a crude bamboo ladder that we had to negotiate whilst carrying our boards, which was no easy feat I can tell you. There were more than a few boards dropped; rule was you never got below anyone on the ladder, lest they dropped their board on your head and kill you. On top of that, getting to and from our accommodation was a damned slug, uphill and down dale, seeing how there were no scooters back then and *bemo's* were few and far between. If we were feeling flush we used to pay the locals to carry our boards for us, and not just the young ones, the old-timers were good for a bob too. Then after all that effort just getting to the water, we had the long paddle out to the breaks. Kept us fit all right. And here's another thing, there weren't any warungs down the bottom then like there are now. Going up and down the ladder for a feed or a drink at lunchtime took way too much energy so the local woman used to come down with parcels of rice and fish or chicken wrapped up in banana leaves. Eventually they set up the warungs down there.'

'They're wonderful stories, Mr Thom. I wish my husband Rob was here; he'd love to hear them.'

'So where is he then lass?'

'He's probably on a wave at Uluwatu as we speak,' said Danni.

'Ah, a man after my own heart. Well Danni, next time you're up this way bring him by. I'm always happy to chat.'

'I'll be sure to do that,' said Danni, although she couldn't see a time when she'd be back in Sanur, at least not this trip. Maybe she could talk Rob into making a special trip.

'Mr and Mrs Thom, over lunch we were talking to Rama about Bali's development and he mentioned you both had some interesting views on that,' prompted Tim, looking at both Ngurah and Glen.

Glen shook his head ruefully. 'It's a bloody crying shame what's happened to Bali. It's being loved to death.'

Ngurah reached out and put a comforting hand on her husband's arm as she spoke. 'Bali's development has brought mixed blessings to the island and her people. Economically, Bali has benefited tremendously from tourism and foreigners who have come here and established businesses. There is much employment, many good jobs for our young people and compared to most of the rest of Indonesia, the Balinese enjoy a high standard of living. However, the impact on our landscape and environment has been devastating and I fear that our culture and traditional way of life is being severely tested. The last four decades has seen much of Bali's traditional lands swallowed up by developers. Either willingly or at the behest of government, families have moved off their land. Rice fields have been destroyed, family compounds bulldozed to make way for resorts and hotels, shopping centres, restaurants, convenience stores, others turned into fancy villa accommodation. Villages that once occupied only a small part of the landscape have expanded so much they have now blurred together into one big city and much of Bali's sacred landscape has been obliterated.'

'By the mid-eighties every man and his dog was jumping on the Bali bandwagon,' said Glen. 'The big men from Jakarta all wanted a piece of the action and foreign investors were pouring money into the place. Locals were being talked into sell their land, only to realize when it was too late that once the money was gone, their lands were gone and they had no skills other than farming, they'd sold themselves into a life of servitude. There were a few of the locals that did alright but most didn't. Fortunately I was able to help Ngurah's family, pass on some of my skills and give them a bit of a leg up, not that I had much myself. Financially, it was always a bit of a struggle splitting our time between Sydney and Bali.'

'Why didn't you just move permanently to Bali?' asked Bel.

'There were plenty of times I would have. My heart was always over here in Bali and of course Ngurah missed her family, but we had Rama to think about. Despite all the development that was going on, education and healthcare over here was rudimentary at best. Plus Ngurah wanted to do some courses herself—'

'Mum has an Arts Degree majoring in Social Policy, which considering she went to Australia with very basic English, a rudimentary education and worked part-time whilst raising me, is quite an achievement,' Rama said proudly and everyone agreed. The opinion Danni had already formed of a strong, determined woman was augmented with deep admiration.

'Anyway,' Glen continued. 'We realised we were in a better position to help ourselves and Ngurah's family by basing ourselves in Sydney.'

'And what of the families that sold their lands?' Danni asked.

'Bit of a mixed bag I'm afraid. There's a lot struggling to make ends meet and it seems to be a growing trend.'

'You see,' began Ngurah, 'Balinese society is traditionally agrarian, where people lived in their family compounds within small villages and worked to sustain themselves. Each village, each kampong much the same as the next and therefore, the lifestyle and wealth differential between families and individuals was almost imperceptible. Since marrying Glen, I have lived most of the last thirty-eight years in Australia, where there is much concern about the widening gap between the rich and the poor and all the issues that creates in a society; ambition, competition, stress, jealousy, resentment and dissatisfaction. We see that manifest itself in a rising crime rate and a breakdown of traditional family values.'

'You paint a rather negative picture of Australia,' said Danni feeling slightly offended.

Ngurah smiled warmly, 'Forgive me Danni, I don't mean to. Australia is a country of great achievement, opportunity and freedoms and I feel honoured to be able to call it my second home.'

'I think the point mum is getting to is that here in Bali, we're starting to see some of those same issues and emotions within our own society, where previously they weren't part of our psyche,' Rama explained.

Ngurah nodded and continued. 'There is much conflict creeping into our society now. Families are divided; many young ones want to sell the land, the elders want to hold onto it. Land has become very expensive now. The young ones are tempted by the money and the opportunities they see elsewhere and many have no wish to be a farmer. But the elders believe to sell the land is to sell their hearts. Villagers are arguing with each other. Those that sell are resented by those who stay.'

'Even Bali's famous rice terraces, the *sawahs*, so virulent they have been under continuous cultivation for 1200 years and are considered sacred are under threat,' added Rama.

Glen shifted in his seat and rubbed his chin, clearly agitated. 'There's just too much pressure on the environment. It's a small island with a fragile environment that's close to reaching breaking point. Public sanitation is a huge problem. Where's all the rubbish going? I'll tell you where; it's being discarded into open drains and into landfill sites, half of which are illegal, completely inappropriate or poorly contained. Sewerage treatment plants are overflowing and there have been countless cases of raw effluent being illegally dumped. Tourists talk about the dreaded Bali belly and being careful about what you eat and drink; well I reckon the biggest risk of picking up a bacterial infection is swimming off some of the beaches around the place. During the wet season you've got heavy rains flushing rubbish and sewerage out into the sea and its being washed back up onto the beaches. Kuta, that very same beach we wouldn't take a crap on all those years ago, becomes a trash strewn mess with filthy, murky water. The locals like to kid themselves and everyone else that it's all washed up from neighbouring islands and Java but that's just baloney. If they don't wake up to themselves soon there'll be nothing left of the beautiful landscape that attracted the tourists in the first place. You only have to look at what happened at Candi Dasa, up on the coast north of here. The locals raided the coral reef around the shoreline for building material for tourist accommodation. That exposed the beach to erosion and sent most of it washing out to sea. The government then came up with the bright idea of building a concrete sea wall to save the beach but it did little to help, so now as well as no beach there's a bloody great eye-sore of a sea wall. Tourists have been staying away in droves.'

'It's a grim picture you've painted,' said Tim sadly. 'I wonder how the north of the island will fare in years to come. Surely the government and the Balinese will learn the lessons of the past.'

Glen shrugged, looking far from convinced. 'I hope you're right Tim, but I wouldn't bet the house on it. The governments answer to easing the pressure on southern Bali is to build another international airport up north. At least they're considering it. The idea scares me to be honest. I've seen too much greed getting in the way of common sense so I wouldn't have a lot of faith in the government only allowing careful and controlled development.'

'I'd like to think dad is being overly cynical,' said Rama. 'Traditionally in Balinese culture people don't complain, they don't speak up. But that is changing, particularly among the younger generation. They're far better educated than previous generations, they're more worldly, more aware of social issues, more environmentally conscious and they're technology savvy. They're talking among themselves and they're on-line, using the internet and Facebook to protest and make statements against the continued exploitation of their traditional lands and culture. They want tourism, but they want sustainable tourism.'

'That's an admirable goal son, but I don't think that'll satisfy a government with dollar signs in its eyes.'

'I think the government is savvy enough to realize they have no choice. The world has changed dramatically over the last few decades. Bali has a lot more competition for the tourist dollar now there's a proliferation of budget airlines flying people cheaply all over the world. Countries like Vietnam, Thailand, Cambodia and Laos are attracting increasing numbers of tourists and they're much closer destinations for those flying from Europe. And after all, Bali doesn't have a monopoly on beautiful scenery, ancient temples and interesting culture. I think both the people of Bali and the government are waking up to the fact that they cannot allow the rampant land grab and the degradation of the environment to continue. You see, Bali's unique culture has always been its biggest draw card and it is irrevocably and intrinsically linked with the landscape; the rice fields, the ancient *sabuks* where farmers draw their irrigation waters from and sacred geographical locations such as Mt Agung and the crater lake at Mt Batur which is believed to be the abode of Dewi Danu, the Goddess of the Lake.'

'Yes, the three of us visited Uluwatu Temple recently and we learned from our guide how the temple features and physical features of the landscape are in fact earthly representations of the Hindu cosmic universe,' said Danni.

Rama looked surprised. 'Then you're a long way ahead of most visitors to our shores who come and go without ever learning much about the Balinese culture. They love and appreciate the aesthetic aspects of the temples, the festivals, the dances, the offerings and the traditional arts, but even among those who have been here many times it's surprising how little they know or understand.'

'Maybe educating tourists is another aspect of the tourist market that could have been done better,' commented Tim.

'Quite possibly, but most tourists don't come on holidays to be educated, they come to experience Bali, all of it in a week or ten days or however long they have. A temple visit in the morning, beach in the afternoon, a traditional dance after dinner, the rice terraces or Mt Batur the next day, a silversmith or batik workshop along the way. That's what the vast majority want and that's what they get.'

'Doesn't that imply, at least to some extent, that Bali's culture has been commercialized to meet tourist demand?' said Danni.

Rama inclined his head, 'To some extent yes. Many of our most sacred temples are overrun with tourists, many of whom are inappropriately attired, dances normally only performed at certain cycles of the Hindu calendar are being performed on request by hotels for the entertainment of their guests, sacred costumes and masks are being copied en-masse as souvenirs and the list goes on.'

'But surely that sort of thing is detrimental to the Balinese culture in the long term?' Bel protested.

'That's one view,' Rama admitted, 'but so far, in spite of the pressure from tourism I think it's holding up pretty well.'

'As an older Balinese,' Ngurah began, 'one who grew up on the island before tourism, of course I see changes, but like Rama I am confident that our culture is alive and well. Throughout the centuries we have been influenced by other cultures and we have survived and thrived by adapting those influences in a way that does not conflict with our Hindu beliefs. It is this ability to adapt that has made Bali's particular brand of Hinduism unique, even among other Hindu cultures. Despite its ancient origins ours is very much a living, evolving culture. A culture that is seclusive and inflexible is surely a culture that will wither and die as the world changes around them. I think we have proven already that despite the tourist onslaught, we can take advantage of the appeal of our culture without sacrificing our core values. In fact, it has been said by some scholars that the celebration of our culture by foreigners actually strengthens and fosters our culture through the proliferation of traditional dance, music, handcrafts and architecture. And even in this modern world, our young people are continuing to embrace our culture, they are proud of it and who they are.'

'Well I'm pleased to hear that Mrs Thom,' said Bel looking relieved. 'It would be truly awful to see Bali's culture suffer.'

'Absolutely! You know, I think I've learned more about Bali over the last few days that I have in all the years I've been coming here. I'm really starting to see it through new eyes. I'm so glad Rama brought us to meet you,' said Danni, smiling at Ngurah and Glen.

'You're most welcome Danni,' said Ngurah smiling back, then she stood and clapped her hands together. 'Now my young friends, let me get you some refreshments.'

Danni and Bel both insisted on helping and followed Ngurah into the kitchen where the three of them prepared a platter of fresh tropical fruit, a pot of sweet tea and a jug of freshly pressed pineapple juice and then carried it all out to the back patio where the men were still talking. Over afternoon tea, Glen entertained them all with more stories from the early years in Bali, alternately having his younger audience in fits of laughter and outright amazement. By the time they rose to leave it was late in the afternoon. As Ngurah and Glen walked them out to their scooters, Bel glanced at her watch with surprise.

'Oh my gosh, I can't believe we've monopolized so much of your time.'

Ngurah smiled warmly and squeezed her hand. 'It has been our pleasure. Glen and I have enjoyed everyone's company immensely. We want you all to come back and visit us anytime you are in Bali.'

'Tim and I would love that,' said Bel giving Ngurah a quick hug. Danni stepped forward and hugged the older woman as well. 'Me too. Hopefully next time I can bring my husband to meet you both.'

Whilst they donned their helmets and mounted the scooters, Glen slid the gate open for them and Ngurah went to stand at his side to wave the visitors off. As Tim and Rama eased the bikes into the laneway, Danni turned and gave them a happy wave. It had been a most delightful afternoon. Rama led them back to the heart of Sanur village and pulled off to the side of the road. 'This is my stop folks. Do you know your way back to the bypass road from here?'

'No problem,' answered Tim reaching across to shake Rama's hand. 'Thanks for this afternoon mate, we really enjoyed ourselves.'

'My pleasure. Don't forget to send me your flight details so I can make the arrangements with my man in Kalimantan and I'll see you in a couple of weeks' time. Danni, it was very nice to meet you. Enjoy the rest of your stay in Bali and do drop in and see mum and dad again if you get back up this way.'

'I certainly will. I'm glad I came along today, I've had a lovely time and it was nice to meet you also.' Danni offered her hand which Rama squeezed gently and then stepped onto the sidewalk. 'Ride safe,' he said as he waved them off.

CHAPTER FIVE

Unfortunately the long afternoon with Rama and his parents put the trio back on the road at peak hour so they had a slow return journey south. By the time Tim and Bel dropped Danni back at her villa it was well past sundowners hour at the Blue Fin. Realising Rob was probably worrying about her by now, she said a quick goodbye to Bel and Tim and hurried to her room, where much to her surprise she found Rob sprawled on the bed.

'Rob! What are you doing here? You never miss a session at the Blue Fin.' But even as the words came out, Danni realised her husband was not well. His eyes were dull and his forehead was glistening with sweat. She perched on the bed beside him and put a hand to his forehead, feeling the telltale heat of fever. Danni had expected Rob to be a bit annoyed with her for worrying him over being late and not calling, but her husband didn't seem to have noticed the time.

'I'm crook Danni,' he croaked through dry lips, looking up at her with doleful eyes.

'Oh honey, I can see that. How long have you been like this? Why didn't you ring me?'

'Got worse through the morning,' he said. 'I came back here and fell asleep but I just feel worse.'

Danni got up and retrieved a bottle of water and held it out to her husband. 'Here, drink this. I'm just going to check your leg okay?' Rob took a feeble sip of water and dropped his head back on the pillow and shut his eyes as Danni took the bottle from him. Turning her attention to his leg, as gently as she could she pulled off the crude dressing Rob had obviously applied after his morning surf and caught her breath. The wound had turned a deep, angry red but most worrisome was the sticky, yellow pus seeping from it. Hastily, she replaced the dressing.

'Rob your leg is infected and you've got a fever. You need to see a doctor now!' she said firmly, bracing herself for the argument she was sure would come, but to her surprise Rob just whispered 'Okay.'

'I'm going to reception to find out where to take you. Will you be okay on your own for a few minutes?'

Rob gave a slight nod so she bent down and dropped a kiss on his forehead then hurried to reception, where the helpful receptionist recommended she take Rob to the Sanglah Hospital in Denpasar and arranged a taxi for them whilst Danni went back to the room to get her husband, remembering at the last minute to grab his wallet and their travel insurance details. The taxi was waiting outside the foyer for them, the driver giving Danni a sympathetic look as Rob slumped in the back seat and Danni climbed in beside him. Rob appeared to sleep for most of the thirty minute drive to the hospital where the taxi driver helped Danni get Rob out of the taxi and into a chair in the outpatients waiting area. 'He be okay miss, good doctors here,' he reassured her as he left, waving off the tip Danni tried to give him.

The waiting room was quite crowded and once the triage nurse determined Rob's condition wasn't life threatening and had collected his personal details, she sent them back to the waiting area. Whilst Rob dozed beside her, Danni looked around curiously, noticing several other westerners also waiting for medical treatment. The waiting area was clean and the triage had been quick and efficient, much like any other hospital she supposed, feeling a little less nervous than she had been on the way over. Rob shifted restlessly at her side and she cuddled his arm reassuringly. 'Won't be long honey,' she said hoping she was right.

When Rob was eventually called they were ushered through to a cubicle in the accident and emergency ward, where another nurse took down Rob's medical history, checked his vitals and examined the wound on his leg. After making notes on the clipboard she assured them the doctor would be along shortly, pulled the curtain partway across to give them some privacy and left. Barely five minutes had passed when the nurse returned with the doctor in tow. He introduced himself, studied the nurse's notes, quizzed Rob about a few things and examined the wound under a bright overhead light.

'Well my friend, you certainly have a nasty infection,' he said with a shake of his head. 'But you already know this. We need to drain the wound, give it a good clean and put on a clean dressing. Also I will give you an injection of antibiotics to get them started but you will need to follow up with oral antibiotics okay.'

After giving Rob a local anaesthetic to numb the site, the doctor spent nearly half an hour cleaning and excising the wound with the help of the nurse. Danni kept her eyes averted through most of the procedure but even so, was stunned at how much pus and fluid was drained from the site. 'This should have been stitched,' the doctor commented as he applied the dressing. 'But too late now; you're going to have a nasty scar I'm afraid.' Rob just grunted; he was too sick to care and probably wouldn't have anyway.

It was late in the evening when they left the hospital, antibiotics in hand and instructions to return to the attached clinic each day for the next few days to have the wound cleaned and re-dressed. Furthermore, the doctor had been absolutely adamant that Rob was to keep the wound dry until it was healed over. In other words, no surfing!

By the time they returned to the villa and Danni had Rob settled into bed it was quite late and she was tired and hungry. She called room service and ordered a sandwich and set about tidying up the room whilst she waited; Rob having just dumped his stuff inside the door when he'd come home sick earlier in the day. The sandwich arrived just as she finished making herself a cup of tea and she took both out onto the patio, not bothering to turn the light on. The partial moon and garden lights around the villa cast an adequate glow to see by. As she sat munching on her picnic, Danni felt an inexplicable urge to cry; she supposed it was just a combination of tiredness, stress and the sudden letdown after such a lovely day out. Admonishing herself for being silly, she quickly finished her meal and headed for the shower. Five minutes later she slipped into bed beside Rob and was asleep as soon as her head hit the pillow.

The sky still wore the dull grey cloak of the pre-dawn when Danni woke. Rob appeared to be sleeping peacefully with none of the restlessness of the previous night. She reached over and felt his forehead; he was still warm but better than the clammy heat of the previous night. Pleased, she rose and padded to the bathroom then crawled back into bed and slept again. When she next awoke, the room was filled with bright morning sunshine and Rob was propped up against the bed head wide awake.

'Hey honey, you look a bit brighter,' she said smiling up at him.

'I am, but I still feel like I've been run over by a bus,' he answered.

'I'm not surprised; you had a nasty fever last night and your leg…' Danni didn't elaborate, her shudder spoke volumes. 'How's that feeling?'

'Tender but not too bad all things considered.'

Danni slipped out of bed and riffled through her handbag, looking for Rob's medication. Returning to the bed she handed him the tablet with a bottle of water. 'Do you think you could handle some breakfast? I can order room service.'

'Yeah, maybe just some toast.' Rob swung his legs off the bed and sat up. 'Think I'll have a shower. No, no, I can manage,' he said waving Danni's offer of help aside.

'Don't get your leg wet,' Danni reminded him.

'Hmm, guess I'll have to settle for a wash then.'

Whilst Rob was in the bathroom, Danni ordered their breakfast and arranged for housekeeping to come and put clean sheets on the bed. Rob emerged with his hair still dripping and a towel around his waist and sat down on the bed, clearly exhausted, so Danni found him some clean clothes and passed them to him. When breakfast arrived he insisted on sitting on the patio to eat but didn't argue after he'd eaten and Danni suggested he go back to the now freshly made-up bed. He was watching TV when she headed into the bathroom. Later on Danni went in search of the other wives in their group to fill them in on Rob's condition and found him asleep, TV still running, when she returned to the room. Flipping the TV off, she took a book out to the patio to read in the sunshine.

Rob dozed on and off for most of the day and by late afternoon the last vestiges of the fever had gone and he announced he was starting to feel human again. A couple of his mates dropped by to see how he was getting on and when they commiserated with him on the bad luck which was going to keep him out of the water for the rest of the trip, Danni bit her tongue. If Rob hadn't been so obstinate about getting medical treatment for his leg back in the beginning, it wouldn't have come to this!

Knowing Bel and Tim would be expecting to catch up at the Blue Fin for sundowners, Danni put in a quick call to Bel to tell her they wouldn't make it this evening.

'Oh Danni, I hope he's feeling better soon,' said Bel.

'He's already perked up a lot. I think he'll be back on deck by tomorrow although it may take a few days to get back to his old self,' answered Danni, feeling confident.

'Well I don't want to put any pressure on you Danni, but tomorrow is our last full day in Bali so I hope we can catch up before we fly out.'

'Yes we must. Even if Rob's not up for much, I'm sure we could meet you for lunch somewhere. I'm so going to miss you guys,' said Danni ruefully. 'I get along with the other women in our group quite well but I'm not particularly close friends with any of them to be honest. Really we've just been thrown together because of Rob's friendship with the boys.'

'I know what you mean,' sympathized Bel. 'Tim and I are going to miss your company too.'

'Not for long I'm sure. You guys have got this whole great adventure in front of you; you'll quickly forget all about me.'

'That's not true Danni. I think we're just at the beginning of great, long-term friendship. But you're right to an extent; the next twelve months are going to be very busy. I'm really getting excited now it's so close.'

'I can hear it in your voice,' said Danni laughing. 'Anyway, I better go. I'll give you a call in the morning to arrange something. Say hi to Tim. Bye.'

'Same, tell Rob we hope he's feeling better soon. Talk tomorrow.'

Danni was quite pleased when Rob suggested dinner in the villa restaurant as she already had a touch of cabin fever after spending the day around their room. They had their meal on the restaurant balcony as the sun was setting, just the two of them for once, chatting and laughing with each other. 'This is nice Rob. It's just occurred to me how rarely you and I do this sort of thing together, just us. Even at home, we tend to go out with friends.'

'I thought you liked going out with our friends.'

'I do, but I also like having time alone with you. It's just a pity you had to get sick to make it happen.'

'Ah, you know me Danni, romantic dinners, chocolates and flowers just aren't my thing,' he said reaching across the table to squeeze her hand. 'But you know I love you right?'

She smiled softly; for all Rob's faults he was a good man and she had never doubted his feelings for her. 'Of course I do Rob.' They gazed at each other for a few moments until Rob pulled his hand away and looked around self-consciously. 'Do you want coffee, dessert?' he asked.

'Hmm I wouldn't mind something sweet, but only if you're feeling up to it. I don't want you overdoing it.'

'I'm okay. Actually I'm feeling much better,' he answered. 'But listen Danni, I've been thinking we should call it quits and head home.'

'What! No Rob, we've still got two weeks left. With the antibiotics and getting your wound treated daily you'll be better in no time. Look how much better you feel already. Another day or two of rest and you'll be itching to get out and about again.'

'Yeah but you heard the doc, no surfing until the wound has healed and that's going to take several weeks at least. There's no point wasting our holiday sitting around doing nothing.'

'We won't be sitting around doing nothing,' protested Danni. 'There's more to Bali than just surf Rob. We could head up to Ubud or go over to Lembongan Island, maybe even go up north to Lovina; we've never been there and its years since we've really poked around Bali. The last few days with Bel and Tim have made me realize how much of a pattern we've slipped into in recent years just going to the same places and doing the same thing all the time.'

Rob didn't look too impressed with idea and said as much. 'C'mon Danni, doing that whole tourist thing just isn't me. You know that. Besides, I'd rather play it safe and have my leg treated back home by my own doctor.'

'You weren't too concerned about playing it safe a few days ago when I pleaded with you to go see a doctor.'

Rob held up his hands. 'Yeah, yeah, I know you told me so. I deserved that and I'll admit I was a bit foolish but I can't change things now. I'm sorry babe, I know you're disappointed but I really think it's for the best.' Clearly in Rob's mind the decision was made, regardless of what Danni wanted. Danni could feel an argument brewing but after the stress of the last twenty-four hours she didn't have the energy or inclination to pursue the issue further right now, so she clamped down further protests and decided to raise the subject again in the morning once they'd both had some time to sleep on it.

Tensions rose quickly the following morning when Rob announced he was going to ring the airline about changing their flights back to Perth. Clearly, he hadn't changed his mind overnight.

'Rob, we haven't finished discussing this. I really don't think there's any reason for us to rush home. We may as well be here in Bali as sitting at home doing nothing for the next couple of weeks,' reasoned Danni.

Rob ran a hand through his hair and sighed heavily. 'Danni we discussed this last night—'

'No we didn't discuss it. You announced it and assumed that it was a done deal,' corrected Danni. 'Well it's not as far as I'm concerned. This isn't just about you Rob, I get one break from work a year and I look forward to getting away. This is my holiday too.'

'I know that babe but I think we have to consider my medical treatment in all of this,' Rob cajoled.

'You can get perfectly adequate treatment here Rob. I was quite impressed with the doctor at the hospital. It's not like you've got a serious condition or anything. I imagine something like your injury is fairly straightforward.'

'I don't know Danni, you hear all sorts of horror stories about third world hospitals.'

'Bali isn't exactly third world Rob, developing yes, but not third world. I mean look around us,' she said, arms raised to emphasis the relative luxury of their villa. 'Frankly I think you're being overly critical.' Rob was annoyed, she could tell by the look on his face. 'Look, you're supposed to go over to the clinic today to have the dressing changed on your wound. Why don't you wait until then to make a decision? After all you were pretty out of it the other night when we were at the hospital.'

'All right,' said Rob grudgingly. Whether or not he was just buying time or genuinely committed to making a more informed decision about his treatment Danni wasn't too sure, but for now at least she had won a postponement.

A few hours later Rob presented at the clinic attached to the international wing of the hospital, where he received the same efficient treatment as the night before, but if he was expecting a western doctor he was disappointed. Apparently foreign doctors weren't permitted to practice in Indonesia, they were informed by another Australian in the waiting room at the clinic. Even so, the attending doctor seemed to know what he was doing and left Danni at least, with no doubts about his competency. Rob however, was not so convinced and said so as soon as they were in the taxi heading back to Uluwatu. When Danni accused him of being deliberately obtuse they fell into a tense silence which persisted all the way to the restaurant where they were meeting Bel and Tim for the last time.

'How're you feeling mate?' Tim asked, shaking Rob's hand as they sat down to join them.

'A lot better than I was forty-eight hours ago that's for sure,' Rob laughed. 'Bloody fever knocked the stuffing out of me. I'm still feeling a bit weak but otherwise okay.'

'Glad to hear it.'

As they were discussing Bel and Tim's plans and imminent departure, Rob announced his and Danni's plans to fly home, much to Danni's annoyance. As far as she was concerned the issue was far from settled and Rob had no right to say so, but Danni had no desire to bicker with him in front of her friends since it would be embarrassing to everyone present, although one look at her tight expression told Bel and Tim that something was up.

'Actually we haven't quite decided yet,' Danni corrected. 'Rob and I are at somewhat of an impasse on the issue. Rob's leg requires some ongoing treatment which he'd rather have at home, but I feel it can be managed quite well here and although there'll be no more surfing, we can still enjoy ourselves doing other things.'

To ease the tension, Rob reached across and grasped Danni's hand. 'Danni's obviously disappointed because it blows her annual holiday. Let's face it, who wouldn't rather be here in Bali than hanging around home? It's just an unfortunate situation all-round.'

Bel and Tim exchanged a quick look and wisely decided to change the subject. 'Yeah that's disappointing,' Tim said diplomatically. 'Hey by the way Rob, did Danni tell you about the folks we met up in Sanur the other day?'

Rob looked at Danni quizzically and shook his head. 'Sorry hon, with all that's been going on I clean forgot all about it.' And with that, the three of them filled Rob in on their Sanur adventure and related some of Glen Thom's stories about the old days in Bali. When the time came to bid farewell to Bel and Tim, the earlier tensions were forgotten. Danni had to wipe away a tear as she hugged both Bel and Tim.

'Let me know how you're getting on won't you?'

'We sure will,' Bel promised. 'I've got your email address and as soon as we can I'll drop you a line. I'm not sure how good the service is up there but Rama did tell us we'd have some internet access. Otherwise I'll resort to snail mail and write you a letter.'

'Travel safe,' Rob said shaking Tim's hand warmly and giving Bel a quick hug. 'We'll catch up when you're back in Perth.'

'Will do. Take care you guys,' said Tim, and with that both couples went their separate ways.

Danni and Rob had not long returned to their villa when Danni's phone rang; she was surprised to see Bel's caller ID come up on the display. 'Bel, didn't we just say goodbye?' she said laughing. 'What's up? Did you forget something?'

'No nothing like that. Actually Tim and I have been talking and we've had a bit of an idea. Why don't you come to Borneo with us? Rob's welcome to come too of course but I gather he's intent on going home?' Bel asked.

'Yes he is,' Danni managed to croak out as she sank onto the bed, Rob looking at her quizzically. 'Oh my gosh, I don't know Bel. I mean, this is just such a surprise. I just don't know.'

Bel laughed. 'I knew you'd be surprised. But look, we'd really love for you to join us. Tim's already been onto the travel agent to confirm there's a seat available on our flight so you could fly over with us tomorrow and spent the next two weeks with us doing the touristy thing. Then we'll put you on the plane back to Denpasar in time to catch your existing flight back to Perth.'

Danni's head was spinning. Did she want to go? Could she leave Rob on his own? She glanced at Rob who was still staring at her with a puzzled expression. 'Gee I don't know Bel. I mean, I appreciate the offer; I'm just not sure if I should. I really need to talk it over with Rob and give it some thought.'

'No problem,' Bel assured her. 'I'd be doing the same with Tim if it was me in your position. Have a chat and let me know. And you can assure Rob that Tim and I will look after you.'

'Okay thanks,' said Danni, still a bit shell-shocked. 'I'll talk to Rob and call you back in a little while.'

She hung up the phone and filled Rob in on the invitation. His reaction was lukewarm. 'I don't know Danni. I don't think it's a very good idea.'

'Well I'll admit it's rather out of the blue but I must admit, now the initial shock is wearing off, the idea does have some appeal,' said Danni cautiously. 'I don't want to go home just yet and let's be honest, you don't really need me to look after you do you?'

'Well no,' Rob admitted reluctantly, 'but Danni, what do you know about Borneo? Is it even safe?'

'I believe it is. Bel and Tim have talked to me about their plans quite a bit and I've never had any hint from them that the place was dangerous. Besides, I met the guy that heads up the NGO the other day, Rama Thom, remember we told you about meeting him and his parents in Sanur? Anyway, he definitely came across as trustworthy to me so I can't see him sending anyone into a dangerous area.'

'But still Danni…' Rob mumbled, unable to think of any real reason she shouldn't go.

'Well why not go Rob? It sounds like a great opportunity to see Borneo to me. Even the name inspires my curiosity. Even better, you could come with us.'

Rob shook his head. 'Hardly Danni, I reckon the health system over there would be even more backward than Bali.'

'Oh Rob, let's not go there again. I think you're being quite unfair on the doctors here.'

'Yeah well at the end of the day it's my leg,' Rob replied grumpily.

Danni sighed. His mind was made up and nothing she said was going to change it. Well that was his choice and now she had to make hers. 'You're right Rob, it is your leg and I have to respect that. But you know what, this is my annual holiday too and I don't want to go home just yet. If you won't stay here with me then I'm going to Borneo with Bel and Tim.'

Rob looked surprised and opened his mouth to say something then clamped it shut. It wasn't often Danni dug her heals in but when she did she could be just as stubborn as Rob himself. 'So that's it then, decision made. Just like that you're going to Borneo?'

Danni nodded, feeling the first tingle of nervous excitement in the pit of her stomach. 'Oh Rob,' she said throwing herself into his arms, 'be happy for me. This is a perfect solution even though I'd rather you were coming with me.'

Rob glanced down at his wife who was practically dancing on the spot in his arms. Pushing his misgivings aside he hugged her tightly then released her with a playful slap on the backside. 'Well alright then, if you're going you better start getting yourself organized.'

The rest of the afternoon passed in a blur. After ringing Bel back to confirm she was coming with them, Danni wrote down their flight details and took the scooter she and Rob had hired for the duration of their stay into Pecatu village to find a travel agency to book her flight. She exchanged some more money and purchased a duffel bag with wheels, so she could split hers and Rob's luggage, since they were currently sharing one big suitcase. Meanwhile Rob rang the airline to change his return ticket to Perth, securing a flight for early the following morning, and notified reception of their early departure. There were calls back and forth between Danni and Bel as they arranged the pick-up time and confirmed that Tim had been in touch with Rama to let their guide know they would have an extra person along.

Conscious of Rob not overdoing it, they skipped the sundown session at the Blue Fin but joined their friends later for dinner, where Rob announced their plans to quit Bali, explaining that he was heading home and Danni was off to Borneo with Bel and Tim. There were mixed reactions from the group who were understanding but also disappointed to see them go. Danni's plan to travel to Borneo raised a few eyebrows but there were also plenty of supporters who praised her for taking the initiate and making the best of a bad situation. A few of them even admitted to being a bit envious. Although their friends were keen to turn the evening into a farewell bash for them, Rob begged off fairly early, admitting he was still feeling the lingering effects of his illness and there was still packing to be done since they both had early flights the following morning, so in the end their departure was fairly low key.

Later than night, in the darkness of their room, they made love and held each other tightly. Lying there in the security of Rob's arms, Danni fought off some niggling doubts about the upcoming trip. Apart from a few brief work-related trips, Danni had never left Rob, although he had semi-regular boy's trips away. But this was different, this time it was Danni going off on her own, asserting her independence for what she realised was the first time in their eight year marriage. Somehow, instinctively she knew that things would never be the same again.

CHAPTER SIX

Rob left for the airport in a taxi just after dawn, leaving Danni to check out of the villa, settle their account and arrange the return of the scooter. She breakfasted alone since the rest of the wives were still sleeping and was ready and waiting in the foyer with her luggage when Bel and Tim arrived to collect her. Tim helped the driver load her new duffel bag into the back of the minivan and in minutes they were heading to the airport.

'I can't believe I'm really doing this,' said Danni, almost shaking with nerves which Bel and Tim soon allayed.

'Well I'm pleased that you are,' Bel told her. 'You'll have a great time.'

'Are you sure I'm not going to be in the way? You know, two's company and three's a crowd.'

'Of course not. We wouldn't have invited you to come along if we felt like that.'

'And I'm hardly going to complain about escorting two beautiful women around,' Tim added, earning him a grin from Danni.

'Well I want you to know that I appreciate the invitation. I certainly wouldn't have had the guts to go on my own and since Rob isn't interested...' Danni was still disappointed that Rob had chosen not come along but she pushed the thought aside. She was determined to have a good time, with or without him.

Bel gave her a sympathetic smile. 'You're not feeling guilty about coming without him are you?'

'No I'm not. It just feels a bit strange going off and doing my own thing. Rob and I have been together since we were at university so I haven't really ever done anything without him. But he goes away with his mates from time to time so I guess it's a bit of a role reversal for us.'

'Well good for you girl. It doesn't hurt to occasionally remind our guys not to take us for granted.'

'Hey, I heard that,' said Tim turning around from the front seat but when Bel poked her tongue out at him he just grinned back.

At the airport, they checked in for their flight and had about a half hour to wait until they were called to board. Since it wasn't possible to fly directly from Bali to Borneo, they flew to Surabaya, a city on the north-east coast of Java where they had another two hour wait for their connecting flight to Borneo. The travellers wandered around the small terminal to stretch their legs then found a typically ordinary airport café where they could sit and have some coffee whilst they waited for their flight to be called.

'So tell me about Borneo,' Danni said. 'I have to admit I really have no clue about the place other than images of wild jungles, head hunting tribes and villages full of poison dart blowing tribesmen wearing nothing but loin cloths.'

Bel laughed. 'I think you're probably about a hundred years too late for that.'

'Although,' added Tim seriously. 'From what I understand an element of the old Borneo still exists. Many Dayaks, who are the native people of Borneo, still live in villages and carry on traditional activities like cultivation, fishing, hunting and gathering, and many of the traditional skills such as canoe building, tool and basket making and so on are still very much alive. I'm hoping that we'll get a chance to visit one or two villages over the next couple of weeks before we start work.'

'Unfortunately though,' said Bel. 'Many Dayaks have been displaced over the last five decades as the jungles where they lived and made their homes for centuries are being ravaged at an alarming rate. In fact, our assignment with Rama's organization is working with Dayak villagers to help equip them with some of the skills and resources they need as they transition to a more modern world.'

'Surely the best option is to preserve their lands so they can continue to live as they always have. Can anything be done to save their homes?' Danni asked.

Tim sighed heavily, giving Danni a sad look. 'It's a complex issue and one that has vexed the United Nations, International aid agencies, NGO's and conservationists for years. Timber, especially rainforest timbers like Borneo produces, is an extremely valuable commodity and it's understandable that poor countries such as Indonesia and Malaysia, who control the western third of Borneo, see timber as a viable way of boosting their economies. The real crux of the issue is that there are very few controls around the industry. Forests are being clear felled at an alarming rate. I've seen estimates that the equivalent of three hundred soccer fields are being destroyed every hour which is mind-boggling. Both the Indonesian and Malaysian governments have come under increasing pressure over the last thirty years to preserve what jungle remains and both have made moves to do so, but to date it's been pretty ineffectual; corruption is rife and money in the wrong hands can readily buy timber concessions, even in designated reserves. And then there's the illegal timber industry to contend with as well, which some have estimated accounts for as much of seventy percent of Indonesia's logging.

The situation has really reached a crisis point now. Fifty years ago Borneo was blanketed with old growth rainforest. Now only the heart of Borneo, which is the inner third of the island, remains relatively untouched. In fact it's regarded as the only place in Southeast Asia where tropical rainforests can still be preserved on a grand scale.'

'Is it naïve to think the rainforests will regrow?' Danni asked.

Tim gave the question careful consideration before answering. 'They can but, and it's a very big but, only if conditions are extremely favourable. Rainforests have very complex ecosystems which makes them particularly vulnerable to even small changes in the environment. When large scale clearing has occurred, such as from fires and logging, the chances of natural regrowth occurring is very slim and even if it does occur it would take hundreds of years. Bel and I saw an example of this in Cambodia around the Angkor Wat temple complex. The forest there has been re-growing since the temples were abandoned in the fifteen century when the Khmer Empire fell. More than five hundred years later it's still not the same as the surrounding original forest. It's a similar story for forests in South America following the collapse of the Mayan and Aztec civilizations. Most experts believe it may take as long as one thousand years for a rainforest to recover to its original bio-mass. In contrast, temperate forests such as we have in the southern part of Australia can regenerate within a hundred years.'

Danni shook her head in amazement. 'I had no idea. So what happens to the land after logging?'

'Most of it has been turned over to cultivation. Rice, rubber and palm oil,' answered Bel.

'Palm oil! Isn't there a big stink about the palm oil industry?'

'There is, mostly because of the uncontrolled way in which the industry has developed. Palm oil is the world's second most widely produced edible oil. It's found in at least half the processed foods we eat – margarine, bread, biscuits, chips, deep fried foods and so on. But it's also widely used in things like cosmetics, toothpaste, soap and shampoo. So there's a huge demand for palm oil and a lot of companies and individuals want in on it. Right around Asia there has been a massive land grab on which to establish palm oil plantations but it's been particularly prevalent on the island of Borneo.

The industry is destroying forests even faster than the loggers. A common practice is to simply set fire to the forest, then the perpetrators move in and establish their plantations.'

'But surely it can't be that straightforward. It's not like you can hide a whole plantation!' exclaimed Danni.

'They don't need to. Once the forest is destroyed it's easy to convince a politician to release the land for cultivation, especially if you grease the right hands. The argument being that there's no use preserving something that is no longer there. Everyone knows what's going on but so far the governments of both Indonesia and Malaysia have proven fairly ineffectual at prosecuting the culprits so they continue to do it.'

'That's outrageous!' Danni was absolutely shocked.

'Yes it is,' agreed Tim. 'Apart from forcing the Dayaks off their lands, you can imagine how catastrophic the loss of habitat is to the wildlife.'

'The orangutans have suffered the most,' said Bel. 'The tropical lowlands preferred by the palm oil industry also happen to be the last remaining habitat of the world's orangutan population. Their numbers are declining at an alarming rate and there is a very real possibility of extinction. Wildlife and conservation groups, NGO's and academics right around the world have mobilized to try and save the orangutans but lack of funding and awareness are big hurdles. Whether or not they can do enough to save the orangutans history will have to bear out.'

'The whole situation sounds dreadful. Surely if consumers knew what was going on they'd stop buying products containing palm oil.'

Tim shook his head. 'Boycotting palm oil isn't the answer. Lots of other vegetable oils have serious social and environmental problems too and even if you wanted to avoid palm oil, good luck determining which products do or don't contain it. Like it not, we have to accept that palm oil production does have a place in the Indonesian and Malaysian economies. What's required is responsible production and responsible consumption of palm oil.

The industry has been working hard to clean up its reputation through government and self-regulation but there's a hell of a long way to go. Governments have to get serious about stopping further encroachment by the plantations on the rainforest. They need to get serious about investigating and prosecuting unscrupulous corporations and individuals, and they need to get serious about setting aside forest reserves and then not continuing to fiddle with the boundaries.

Western society isn't blameless in all of this either. Western food manufacturers, who are the biggest users of palm oil, have to accept some responsibility for what's been going on and going forward they need to understand their supply chain. Where is the oil coming from? Was it produced by an ethically responsible company both socially and environmentally? If manufacturers stopped buying oil off the dodgy producers, they'd very quickly put them out of business.'

'It all sounds so overwhelming,' said Danni. Her mind was reeling with everything she'd heard.

Bel reached across the table and gave her shoulder a comforting rub. 'It can be, but try not to let it tarnish how you feel about Borneo before you even get there. It never hurts to have some understanding of the social, political and environmental issues when you're going into a country for the first time, but ultimately it's your experiences on the ground that really matter.'

From Surabaya, the travellers flew northwards across the Java Sea to Banjarmasin, the capital of South Kalimantan province in Borneo. As their plane crossed the coastline, Danni and Bel who were seated closest to the window, both craned their necks for their first glimpse of Borneo. A vast carpet of green fields, several large rivers and a myriad of smaller waterways met their view. As the plane descended more details were revealed; roads, houses and even boats chugging up and down the river. Tantalizing glimpses of the island they had come to explore.

Then the city of Banjarmasin came into view. It didn't appear to be overly large, a few mid-rise buildings but no obvious signs of heavy industry that was often found on the outskirts of cities but Danni spotted what appeared to be a small port of sorts.

As the plane completed the landing manoeuvre and taxied towards the terminal, Bel clutched Danni's hand excitedly. 'This is it!' she squealed excitedly. 'We're actually here!'

Danni grinned, feeling every bit as excited as her friend. 'I'm still stuck on the fact that I'm even here. If you'd asked me a few days ago where I'd be right now I would have said lying on the beach in Bali.'

Since they were still in Indonesian territory there was no immigration clearance to contend with so after collecting their luggage the three friends exited the terminal building. As they stood blinking in the bright sunshine and trying to get their bearings a slim, well dressed Banjarese man stepped towards them.

'Hello, you must be Tim and Belinda?' he said in good, though heavily accented English, enthusiastically shaking Tim's hand. 'I am Yusuf. Rama asked me to be your guide here in Banjarmasin.'

'Pleased to meet you Yusuf,' said Tim. 'You come highly recommended by Rama. We're looking forward to having a good look around.' He gestured towards Danni. 'This is our friend Danielle.'

'Hi Yusuf, it's nice to meet you and please call me Danni.'

Yusuf smiled broadly again then scooped up the girl's luggage. 'This way please, I have a car.'

The three friends fell in behind Yusuf, noticing curious looks from the locals as they crossed the car park. Yusuf's car turned out to be a mini-van. It was old but in good condition, obviously the pride and joy of the owner. The girls piled in the back with their luggage, Tim riding shotgun up front beside Yusuf.

'It is about half an hour into the city,' said Yusuf. 'So you are all from Australia?'

'Yes, we're all from Perth in Western Australia,' answered Tim. 'What about yourself Yusuf. Are you local to Banjarmasin?'

'Yes, I have lived here all my life. It is a good place, the biggest city in South Kalimantan. During the time of the Kingdom of Banjar it was the most powerful city in all of southern Borneo. Even during the colonial period it was the capital for all of Dutch Borneo.'

'I didn't realise Borneo had been under Dutch rule,' said Danni.

'Yes, yes, for many years. The Dutch came here looking for spices in the early 1600's and established a trading centre. They convinced the ruling Sultanate of the time to supply them with pepper but there were many clashes with the local people. The British tried several times to push the Dutch out but they proved even less popular with the locals and eventually the Sultanate agreed to sign a treaty with the Dutch giving them a trade monopoly. In 1787 Banjarmasin officially became a Dutch protectorate, but things were very tense. You see, the Dutch were very heavy handed with the locals who felt they were being exploited and unfairly treated. So in 1859 there was a big uprising - the Banjar War. The fighting was very fierce and there were many local heroes, whom the Banjarese still revere today, but alas they were forced to surrender after the royal palace was completely destroyed and *Ratu Zaleha*, the last Banjarese Princess was captured by the Dutch. And so, Banjarmasin remained a Dutch colony until Indonesia won its independence in 1949.'

'Very interesting,' said Tim. 'How did Banjarmasin fair during the Second World War?'

'Ah, as the capital of Dutch Borneo, the city was naturally a target of the Japanese. Like the rest of Indonesia and our neighbouring countries, the city was occupied for several years. During that time the Japanese did much to destroy the economy and administration of the Dutch regime right across the region. We endured many hardships during that time but the occupation brought an end to Dutch rule in Indonesia. After the war, the Dutch were weaker and had little defence against the Indonesian National Revolution so perhaps the Japanese actually helped us,' finished Yusuf with a philosophical shrug.

The conversation lapsed as they drew closer to the city and the three friends took in their new surroundings. Danni was taken by the combination of modern buildings, rundown colonial buildings and haphazard markets that lined the roadway. The prevalence of mosques of all sizes and styles was instantly obvious and Danni was intrigued to see several businesses selling the domes and minarets.

They crossed over a bridge, Yusuf slowing the van to walking pace as he pushed his way through a local market that had spilled onto the road. Even from the confines of the van Danni could see vendors selling all manner of things; fruit and vegetables, clothes, plastic ware, carpets, mobile phones, hardware, even kitchen sinks, and like most Asian markets it was bustling with people on foot, on bicycles and rickshaws or *becaks* as Yusuf called them when he pointed them out.

Barely one hundred metres the other side of the market, Yusuf turned into the driveway of a rather tired looking, five story building. The pink façade was quite shabby, with faded, peeling and mould stained paint. Heavy metal grills covered the windows on all levels, the source of rusty orange stains down the walls, more telltale evidence of a building that had seen better days. Danni eyed the large sign above the driveway announcing it to be the Victoria Hotel, with some trepidation.

'So here we are. This is your hotel,' he said pulling into a car park at the rear of the hotel. It was only then that Danni realized the hotel was situated right beside a sizeable river and what she had mistaken for the front of the hotel was actually the rear. By the time she, Bel and Tim had alighted from the van Yusuf and a couple of porters that materialized from somewhere had already transferred their luggage inside.

Despite the drab façade of the building the interior décor was surprisingly modern, having obviously undergone a refurbishment in recent times, and with Yusuf acting as interpreter, check-in was quick and efficient. Never judge a book by its cover, a somewhat relieved Danni reminded herself.

'Okay,' said Yusuf. 'I will leave you now to settle in and have a rest, then later at five o'clock I will meet you here and we'll have a boat ride so you can see more of my city.'

'Sound good. We'll see you then,' said Tim.

The girls waved goodbye as they followed the porter into the elevator. They were pleased to find their rooms were located side by side on the third floor overlooking the river. Like the reception area, Danni's room was clean and modern but best of all was the small balcony from which she could see up and down the river. Wide and muddy brown, the river was lined with buildings, most of which appeared to be private homes. Unlike the million dollar McMansions that occupied the prime riverside locations back home, these homes were a ramshackle collection of corrugated iron, cement or timber buildings, in many cases perched right out over the river. Most of them looked rather dilapidated. Directly across from the hotel in a small park, there was an energetic soccer game going on and all the while boats of all shapes and sizes loaded with people or cargo chugged up and down the river.

'Great view isn't it?' said Bel from her adjoining balcony.

'It sure is. I've never seen anything quite like this before. Yusuf's boat trip should be very interesting.'

'Yes I'm looking forward to it,' agreed Bel. 'But right now I'm more looking forward to freshening up and having bit of a cat nap otherwise I'll be asleep on the boat. It's surprising how tiring sitting on a plane and waiting around airports can be.'

After freshening up and making herself a cup of tea from the complementary supplies in the room Danni gave Rob, who was by now back home in Perth, a quick call to let him know she'd arrived safely and bring him up-to-date.

'I haven't seen much of the place yet Rob, but what I've seen so far looks fascinating.'

'From what you've described it does sound interesting,' Rob answered. 'What about Belinda and Tim? How's everything going with them?'

'Great. They're good company and they're looking after me as promised.'

'Well that's good. I have to admit I was a bit concerned about you going off with them. It's not like you've known them for very long.'

'That's understandable,' Danni conceded. 'But you know how sometimes you just click with people you meet? That's how I feel about Bel and Tim. We hit it off right from the start.'

Danni thought she detected a slight undercurrent in Rob's tone and wondered if he was a bit miffed with her, perhaps not as okay with her heading off to Borneo as he'd made out back in Bali. Changing the subject, she asked about his leg.

'It's improving,' said Rob. 'I've not long been home from the doctors actually. He's keeping me on the antibiotics and I've got to go into the surgery daily to get the wound cleaned and dressed by the nurse but hopefully in a few days I can start doing that myself. The main thing is to keep the wound dry.'

'Is not too painful is it?'

'Not really, a little tender around the actual wound itself but other than that I'm feeling fine. There's no point me hanging around the house so I'm cutting my leave short and going back at work on Monday. I might take week or two off later in year and go on a fishing charter or something.' Danni got the distinct impression he was putting her on notice.

'I'm glad it's getting better. Did you call mum and dad for me to let them know what was happening?'

'Yeah. Like me, I must say they were a bit concerned about you going off on your own, especially somewhere so off the beaten track.'

'Well I hope you told them I was in good hands so they're not worrying unnecessarily about me. I'll give them a call myself in a few days just to let them know I'm alright but in the meantime can you please let them know I've phoned and everything is going well so far.'

'Okay I'll do it straight after our call,' Rob promised. 'Might even call around and see them tomorrow or the next day since I've got a few days before starting back at work.'

'Oh thanks Rob, I'd appreciate that. Now on that note I better wrap up this call. I don't want to run up a huge international phone bill.'

'No I suppose not. When will you ring again?'

'I'm not sure what the phone reception is going to be like over the next few days but I'll find some way of giving you a call, even if it's just a quick one,' Danni promised. 'So we'll talk soon. Love you.'

'You too. Bye.'

Yusuf was already waiting for them downstairs when they entered the reception area a few minutes before five. He was still beaming so happily that Danni couldn't help smiling herself. She couldn't ever remember meeting someone who seemed so happy.

'Hello. How is everything? Are your rooms good?'

'Yes excellent thanks Yusuf,' they assured him so that he smiled even more broadly.

'Okay come this way please. I have a boat ready.' He led them to a gate at the corner of the hotel grounds which was duly unlocked for them by a hotel staff member, then down a few steps to a small landing at the river's edge where a traditional longboat was waiting for them. The boatman who had been waiting in the stern stepped forward to help Danni and Bel on board then returned to the back of the boat to crank the primitive looking engine.

The long boat was constructed of thick timber planks, had several rows of seating and no roof of any type. From her balcony, Danni had seen similar boats moving along the river with seemingly impossibly large payloads of people or cargo, so they were obviously quite sturdy and stable. The propeller hung off a long shaft protruding a good six feet out the back of the boat and churned the water much like an egg beater.

Danni and Bel took the front row of seats with Tim and Yusuf sitting behind them and the boatman standing at the helm. As they headed off upriver, Yusuf provided some commentary.

'So, Banjarmasin is located at the junction of the Barito and Martapura Rivers. The entire city is built within the river delta. The city centre, where your hotel is located, is actually an island within the delta. As well as the rivers and the tributaries, there are also a great many man-made canals so daily life in Banjarmasin is very much linked to the waterways. That is why it is known as the River City. As we go along you will see that we use the waterways for everything – fishing, irrigation, transport, cleaning and playing.'

The long boat passed under a large traffic bridge and entered what looked like a commercial precinct. The riverbank was lined with large warehouses and tin sheds, some of which had seen better days. One boat was being piled high with sacks of onions, another with pineapples. Further along at what had to be a passenger terminal, people were crowding onto longboats somewhat bigger than the one Danni and her friends were currently in. Unlike their boat, the public passenger boats had roofs which were loaded with cargo. To Danni, they appeared dangerously overloaded and she was grateful they had their own longboat.

'As you can see,' said Yusuf, 'this is the main port for Banjarmasin. Shortly we will turn into the canals of a residential area. At this time of day you will see many people outside their homes washing and bathing and very many children swimming and playing. As Banjarmasin is off the main tourist trail, they do not see many western tourists so you will likely get lots of attention. Please do not be shy. If you wave back they will be very happy.'

As he finished speaking the boatman turned the boat into a narrow canal and immediately the scenery changed. Instead of the large warehouses on the river, the canal was lined almost wall to wall on both sides with corrugated iron homes. Most were built out over the water on stilts, connected by duckboards to a floating jetties, walkways and outhouses. Most of the homes looked very run down, decrepit almost, some sagging or leaning so precariously to one side they looked as if they could slide into the water at any time. Just as Yusuf had warned, there were people outside nearly every home washing clothes, bathing themselves or swimming.

Danni was still taking in the confronting state of the homes and trying not to think about the implications of the floating outhouses when it seemed as if the world suddenly went mad. Having spotted the three tourists in the boat, suddenly everyone was waving and calling out. Children ran down the rickety jetties, jumping, diving or somersaulting into the river; showing off as children do the world over. Word of the visitors seemed to ripple along the canal ahead of them. Children filled the water, many positioning themselves in the path of the boat and reaching up for high fives as they passed by; Danni, Bel and Tim happily obliging them. Ahead of them the water was so filled with swimming children, Danni was certain they would run over one of them. At one point she felt the boat slow and turned around just in time to see the boatman using a long bamboo pole to gently push hitchhiking children off the propeller shaft. Noticing Danni's worried look, he smiled broadly and gave her a reassuring thumbs up so she turned her attention back the locals, waving and smiling.

'Halo,' they called. 'Where you from?'

'Australia.'

'We love Australia,' they replied.

And so it went as they continued through the canals. Between waving and returning greetings Danni barely had time to take photos but obliged when many of the locals, both young and old, put their hands up to their faces as if they were holding a camera. After taking their photo, they laughed and gave her a thumbs up, very pleased to be captured on film.

Beside her and behind, Bel and Tim were equally busy waving, calling greetings and snapping away with their camera.

'Oh my god,' said Bel. 'I've never experienced anything like this in my life. I feel like a rockstar!'

Tim simply shook his head in amazement and Danni knew exactly how felt.

'To tell the truth, I feel a bit shell shocked,' said Danni. The three friends looked askance at each other then burst out laughing. 'Nobody back home is going to believe this.'

Things settled down somewhat once they left the narrow canals and returned to the wider river ways although the locals continued to wave and call greetings as they passed. The scenery changed dramatically as they cruised out into the countryside. Tall palm trees fringing the river swayed gently in the breeze and emerald green rice fields shimmered under the late afternoon sun. The standard of housing improved noticeably; unlike the canal homes these riverside dwellings were neatly constructed of timber, many with canoes tied up at the doorstep. They cruised by whole families paddling in their canoes, perhaps on their way to visit neighbours. Here and there a fisherman stood in his narrow canoe and cast a net wide in an impressive display of skill and balance. It was a fascinating glimpse of a lifestyle so very different from her own and Danni soaked it all in.

It was nearly dark when they returned to the hotel. They thanked the boatman and returned to their rooms just long enough to freshen up before meeting Yusuf again for dinner. A short walk from the hotel, Yusuf led them to a small restaurant that appeared to be the front room of someone's home. Danni could see children watching television in a back room and other adults moving about.

'You like Indonesian food?' Yusuf asked as the proprietor brought menus over to the table where they'd seated themselves.

Unlike Bali, there were no photographs or English translations on the menu so the three of them puzzled over menu until Yusuf took the initiative.

'Shall I just order for everyone? Some chicken, rice, vegetable?'

'Sounds good. I'm happy to try anything,' said Tim with Bel and Danni nodding in agreement.

The food came out relatively quickly and thankfully there was plenty of it; Danni, Bel and Tim not having eaten since their small meal on the plane coming over from Java.

'I'm starving,' said Tim, going in for a second helping. 'What is this Yusuf?' he asked pointing to a bowl of chicken pieces in a thin creamy sauce.

'Soto Banjar, a traditional food of Indonesia but slightly different here in Banjarmasin. Usually it is made with a meat; chicken, beef or even fish, fine noodles, potato, Indonesian spices, perhaps a little lime, all cooked in coconut milk. You flavour it to taste with sambal, this chilli sauce here,' he indicated.

'Well it's delicious,' Tim confirmed between mouthfuls.

'It all is,' agreed Danni. 'Yusuf, can I ask you about the canal homes we saw today?' Not wanting to sound critical, Danni searched for the right words. 'The people there don't look like they have much and some of the homes are pretty dilapidated. I guess what I'm asking is, are they getting by? What sort of a life do they have?'

Yusuf nodded in understanding. 'For most they have everything they need. To live by the water is a good thing. They have their homes, community and the waterways for food, washing, transport. Most consider it a good life. I too was raised on the canals and it was a happy life.'

'Well I must say,' added Belinda, 'they struck me as being the happiest, friendliest people I've ever come across.'

'Definitely,' agreed Danni. 'It was a fabulous experience Yusuf. Thank you for arranging it.'

Yusuf beamed his happy smile. 'Tomorrow morning you will like also. But we have a very early start; I will collect you at 4:30am to visit the floating markets.'

CHAPTER SEVEN

It was still dark when the small group quietly boarded the long boat at the front of the hotel again the next morning. Dannie recognized the boatman from the previous afternoon and smiled in greeting. After waiting for his passengers to take their seats, the boatman pushed away from the landing and turned his boat up river. In the darkness the river was black and indiscernible except for the lights reflected from the riverside buildings. The city was still sleeping; the only noise the chug-chug of the egg beater motor pushing their boat along.

They continued up river for an hour, gradually leaving the city behind. As the sun rose, the early morning chill was banished. The sky turned from black to blue then purple before turning on a spectacular orange sunrise, burnishing the river golden and casting a soft hue across the landscape and bringing the countryside to wakefulness. Sounds punctuated the early morning quietness; chatter drifted across the river like gentle murmurings, roosters crowed, an occasional dog barked and other boat engines mingled with theirs. Gradually around them people moved along the riverbanks, canoes were gently paddled along the river, fishermen set their nets, women and sleepy-eyed children washed in the river. Danni was absolutely enthralled by it all; a world so very different from the one she knew.

Sitting shoulder to shoulder beside her, Bel have her a gently nudge. 'God its beautiful isn't it?'

'It really is,' agreed Danni. 'It's so different from home where we're constantly rushing here, there and everywhere. We wake up to shrilling alarms, maybe race off to the gym, breakfast on the go before we head to our cars for the peak hour gridlock or the train and the usual commuter crush. Here they just seem to be in sync with nature; starting their day slowly with the sun. I'm almost jealous.'

'I know what you mean. Most third world countries are like that, particularly out in the countryside. Rushing and being dictated to by the clock is very much a Western disease. Tim and I always have difficulty adjusting when we come back to Australia after long stints working overseas.'

Danni laughed. 'I think I'll have trouble adjusting after just two weeks. After lazing around and sleeping late for the week Bali, this morning's early start was a bit of shock. I'd love a coffee.'

Ever attentive, Yusuf picked up on Danni's comment.

'You want a coffee, tea?' he asked.

The three travellers agreed in unison and after a quick word to the boatman, he turned course to a nearby pier.

'Okay, so we will have a drink and then it's ten more minutes to the floating market.'

They tied up at a rickety looking pier and after confirming their preferences Yusuf and the boatman disappeared ashore, leaving the travellers waiting in the boat watching an increasing number of canoes paddling by. One, a slightly larger canoe with a canvas canopy paddled alongside their boat and as it drew closer Danni was fascinated to realize it was a floating hawker selling fresh *pisang goreng*, or banana fritters. Perched towards the back of the canoe, the lady hawker had a complete mobile kitchen set up in front of her – bananas, a bucket with batter mix and a wok atop a charcoal brazier. Fast food made to order Borneo style. Noticing her curiosity, the vendor smiled and held up a fresh made offering in Danni's direction. Remembering they'd had no breakfast and suddenly feeing hungry, Danni smiled and waved her over to their boat.

The three friends grinned as the hawker quickly and efficiently prepared their order and after tasting the delicious sweet, hot morsels gave her appreciative thumbs up. The vendor smiled in return and waved, then paddled off. When Yusuf and the boatman returned with a tray of hot drinks all five of them enjoyed a very satisfying breakfast as they continued upstream.

As Yusuf had promised, barely ten minutes later they rounded a bend in the river and were greeted by the sight of a hundred or more canoes milling together for the floating market. Perched in canoes laden with produce, the majority of the gathering was ladies, some with small children and all adorned in colourful scarves and sarongs, some wearing *tangguy* traditional rattan farmer hats. It was a wonderfully colourful spectacle which captivated all three travellers.

Directing the boatman around the gathering Yusuf explained 'We will go behind the gathering so you are not taking photos into the sun and we can drift down among the market.'

'Thank you Yusuf,' exclaimed Danni, snapping off some photographs. 'This is wonderful.'

'How often do they hold the market?' Bel asked.

'Every day for over five hundred years,' answered Yusuf proudly.

'Wow, five hundred years!'

Yusuf nodded. 'Yes, this floating market *Pasar Terapung*, was established when land transport was very difficult so every day the farmers wives would bring their produce to this meeting place by canoe or *jukung* as we call them here. The buyers and traders come by boat to meet them. Even today transport by canoe is still considered easier and cheaper than land transport. So this is one of the most traditional markets in Asia.'

As they floated among the sellers, Danni was amazed at the variety of produce. There were all kinds of fruit and vegetable - bananas, coconut, oranges, rambutan, leafy greens, longan, cucumber and many others that she didn't recognize. There were vendors selling chicken, fish, sugar cane, banana leaves and woven mats.

'Look,' said Bel. 'There's the lady that sold us the *pisang goreng* earlier.' She waved to the lady who smiled and waved back.

'There's another lady over there selling donuts and one over there selling drinks,' gestured Tim.

'Well this is far more interesting than the supermarket at home,' commented Bel with a laugh.

'Have you noticed the paddling skills of the women?' said Tim. 'The way they handle those narrow canoes over the bumps and waves caused by the larger boats as they pass is truly amazing. Especially considering how laden down with produce some of them are. They certainly put my kayaking skills to shame.'

'Yusuf, what is the white paste some of the women are wearing on their faces?' Danni asked.

'Sandalwood paste, sometimes mixed with a little turmeric or ash. It is worn to treat blemishes and protect the skin.'

Neither sellers nor buyers seemed to mind their presence so they floated among the market for another hour, happily observing the trade until the gathering started to break up.

'I didn't actually notice a lot of trading,' commented Tim. 'It just looked like a big chin-wag session.'

Yusuf looked puzzled. 'What is chin-wag?'

'Chin-wag is what we Australian's call it when women get together and talk, talk, talk,' explained Tim giving the girls a cheeky grin.

'Ah I see,' Yusuf nodded in understanding. 'Yes many Banjar women also like to chin-wag.' Yusuf grinned as he tried out the new expression and then continued seriously. 'But in fact there was much trading today. Exchange of goods and bartering is the common business way here so that is why you would not have seen much monetary exchange. The bartering is very efficient and quiet so probably you did not notice.'

Now it was the three friends turn to nod in understanding.

Yusuf turned and spoke to the boatman, then back to the trio. 'The market is over now so we will head back to your hotel. Now it is daylight there is plenty for you to see on the way back so please enjoy the ride.'

Yusuf was right. There was plenty to see on the return journey. Long boats laden with household furniture, children paddling in canoes, fish farms, rice spread out to dry on floating pontoons, boat building yards, riverside shops selling everything from everyday house hold items to coffins and people just going about their daily lives. They stopped briefly at the pier to return their coffee cups, passed by a wholesale market where boats were being loaded with goods and the passenger boat terminal where an endless number of ferries were once again being overloaded with people and their possessions. Bel, Tim and Danni pointed out things to each other and soaked it all in but by the time they arrived back at the hotel, the hard wooden seats were becoming uncomfortable and all three were ready for a break.

Yusuf walked them into the hotel foyer where they made arrangements to meet up again for lunch in a couple of hours time. Conscious of giving Bel and Tim a bit of space, Danni said she'd do her own thing until then so the three of them parted company outside their rooms.

After the very early start and what Danni suspected was a touch of sensory overload, she was feeling rather fatigued and pleased to have a bit of break before the next round of sightseeing. After making herself a cup of instant coffee in her room and indulging in a nice long hot shower, she felt somewhat rejuvenated. When Danni's tummy grumbled, reminding her that the small breakfast of *pisang goreng* was many hours ago so she decided to head down to the hotel restaurant for some morning tea and more coffee. Along the way, she purchased a couple of postcards off the rack in reception and making sure she had a pen with her, headed into the restaurant with a plan to kill the next hour or so but had only just sat down at table overlooking the river when she heard her name.

'Danni?'

'Rama! What a surprise. What are you doing here?'

Rama grinned down at her. 'I have some business here in town and since I knew you guys were here I thought I'd drop by and see how everything was going. Yusuf told me where to find you.'

'Everything is going fabulous and Yusuf has been great. I'm so glad I came. Even if the rest of the trip is a letdown, I could not be disappointed.'

Rama smiled. 'Well hopefully you won't be let down. As a matter of fact, I'm heading into the hinterlands to the Meratus Mountain region tomorrow for a few days and I thought yourself, Tim and Bel might like to join me. It will be a good opportunity for you to visit a Dayak village and see some other things of interest.'

'Yes I'd love to come! I can't speak for Bel and Tim of course but I'm sure they'd be keen too.'

Rama looked around. 'Speaking of Bel and Tim, where are they?'

'Oh they're resting. We had a very early start for the floating market this morning so we're meeting up again in an hour or so. I was just about to order some coffee and a snack to try and bring my energy levels up. Would you like to join me?'

'Thanks, I could do with something myself,' said Rama taking the seat opposite and signalling the waiter over to take their order.

'So what did you think of the floating market?'

'I loved it. The women and their canoes, the produce, the colours and the scenery all kicked off with a beautiful sunrise, what wasn't to love!'

Rama smiled. 'The markets are always a big hit with visitors. At the moment Banjarmasin is off the mainstream tourist map but more intrepid travellers are finding their way here so word is starting to leak out. There may come a time when the floating market becomes a tourist spectacle like some in Vietnam's Mekong Delta or the Damnoen Saduak floating market in Thailand so be thankful that you got to see it as it is now.'

Danni nodded. 'We did a canal trip yesterday and that was amazing too. Those two attractions alone would be enough reason for many tourists to make the trip to Banjarmasin if only they knew.'

'You're right, but as you'll see over the next few days there is much more to attract the tourists. But right now, when most tourists think Borneo, they head over to the Malaysian side which is more heavily promoted and has better tourist infrastructure.'

Danni suddenly felt rather protective of this part of the world and its lovely people. 'I hate the thought of Banjarmasin becoming a tourist hotspot. I think it would rather spoil it. At the moment the people are so friendly and honest and open. Hoards of loud, cashed up, 'looking for a good time' tourists have a way of jading the locals after a while.'

'It does have its downside,' agreed Rama. 'But tourism also injects much needed money into the economy and provides people like Yusuf with an opportunity to make a decent living. It all comes down to balance and how the industry is managed. But despite the attractions, I don't think Banjarmasin will ever become a mainstream tourist destination, at least not for a very long time indeed. It simply doesn't have the tourist infrastructure and for that you need investors who at the moment would rather put their money into proven destinations like Bali.'

The waiter arrived with their coffee and some cake. Danni sipped her coffee with appreciation then studied the caramel coloured, thinly layered cake with interest before taking a bite, finding it delicate and sweet and moist.

'Oh yum, this is delicious.'

'It's *Lam* cake, once the food of kings but now very much loved by all Banjarese. My favourite is *Bingka Barandam*, a kind of cupcake soaked in sweet syrup.' Rama grinned, 'You may have noticed by now that the locals have a real sweet tooth.'

Danni smiled. 'Yes I have. We saw ladies at the floating market selling *pisang goreng* and donuts and other sweet goodies I'm not familiar with.'

'Banjarmasin is famous throughout Indonesia for its delicious cakes, known here as *kueh* or *wadai*. They make them with bananas, coconuts, condensed milk, sugar, rice, even chilli. Once a year to celebrate *Lebaran*, the end of the Ramadan fasting period, they have a huge cake fair along the riverfront opposite the Grand Mosque. The locals go all out with their traditional delicacies and other treats. The market opens mid-afternoon but nobody is allowed to eat until sunset, the official time of the break of fasting.'

'I'd love to see it,' said Danni.

'Unfortunately the month of Ramadan is not a good time to travel anywhere in Indonesia, with the exception of Hindu Bali. Traditionally people want to spend Ramadan with their families, resulting in an exodus of up to seven million city dwellers returning to their villages. Many restaurants close during this time and other services can be interrupted as the faithful become more diligent about observing the daily prayer times.'

'In Australia we hear every year of massive crowds of people around the world making annual pilgrimages for Ramadan but I've never really understood what it is other than being the Muslim holy month,' confessed Danni.

'Ramadan falls on the ninth month of the Muslim calendar *Hijrah* which is based on a lunar cycle of 29 or 30 days so the date varies from year to year. The exact date is calculated based on the sighting of the new moon. In Indonesia the government makes an official announcement so that the Muslim faithful know exactly when to start fasting for Ramadan and when to stop fasting.'

'So they fast for an entire month?'

Rama wavered. 'Yes and no. It's a bit more complicated than that. Fasting only applies during daylight hours but it is much more than just refraining from eating. During Ramadan, Muslims are expected to refrain from eating, drinking, smoking, marital relations and bad habits such as getting angry, lying or using bad language. They must also be more diligent in prayer, giving to charities and generally doing good deeds. This is all based on the belief that fasting heightens spirituality, develops self-control and compassion for the poor and needy who feel hungry and deprived every day.

Here's how it works. During the fast the faithful rise very early in the morning, usually well before sunrise, for *tahajud* prayers which must be performed after one has slept but before *subuh* or sunrise. After prayer, they can have a meal but it must be eaten before sunrise. To wake the faithful local mosques sound out the call to prayer and groups of young boys wander through the neighbourhoods banging drums and other noise makers yelling out *sahur, sahur* which means dawn.

After sunrise the faithful are permitted nothing else until sunset, once again signalled by the call to prayer or the banging of a drum. At this time, they can have a sweet drink or snack but a full meal isn't permitted until after *maghrib* sunset prayers. This meal is a usually very festive with lots of special food prepared to share with family and friends.

The prayer sessions themselves can be very long, well over an hour, during which time one must stand to read from the Quran and perform many cycles of standing, bowing, prostrating and sitting.'

Danni shook her head in amazement. 'That would take an incredible amount of self-discipline.'

'It certainly does and during the fast people are expected to keep up all their normal activities despite the lack of food, hydration and unusual sleep patterns. Generally though, most employers are very flexible during Ramadan.'

'And do all Muslims fast?'

'Fasting during Ramadan is obligatory for devout Muslims but for practical reasons there are exceptions such as children, menstruating, pregnant or breastfeeding women, the sick, the mentally ill and of course travellers such as yourself.'

'It's all very interesting. I've heard the call to prayer several times since arriving in Banjarmasin. Yesterday afternoon, last night and again this morning as we were going up the river.'

'The call to prayer occurs five times a day. The first just before sunrise, the second at midday, another in the afternoon, then at sunset and finally at night fall just as the light from the sun disappears. It all has to do with the sun so the exact times vary depending on where you are in the world and the seasons,' Rama explained. 'Does it bother you, the call to prayer?'

Danni shook her head. 'No not at all. Actually it sounds rather beautiful and exotic to me even though I don't understand the words or the customs of Islam. Coming from a predominantly Christian country it all seems quite strange to me.'

Rama nodded. 'That's understandable but at their hearts Islam and Christianity share many similar values. The five pillars of Islam have often been compared to the Ten Commandments in that both go to the core values of goodness, shaping ones moral code and having only one god. Remember also that Christians observe Lent which is the ritual of fasting for forty days in deference to the forty days that Jesus spent in the desert prior to his ministry. For most Christians it's nowhere near as extreme as Ramadan and each denomination has its own way of fasting. Catholics for instance tend to give up something they value for lent such as television, meat, chocolate or coffee. Importantly the basic purpose of both Ramadan and Lent are the same – to bring the believer closer to God, overcome challenges, develop compassion and do good deeds. Have you been to a Muslim country before?' Rama queried.

'I have but quite a few years ago. Rob and I did the whole backpacking thing during our university breaks. Mostly through Europe but our travels took us to Turkey for a while. I just don't remember finding the Islamic thing particularly interesting back then. I'm almost embarrassed to admit that I was probably more interested in ticking places of my must see list, partying with other backpackers and doing all the wild stuff like bungee jumping and abseiling.'

Rama looked amused. 'You bungee jumped?'

'Yeah, scared the bejeezus out of myself. Rob goaded me into it,' Danni laughed. 'But no amount of goading would get me to do it a second time.'

Danni took another sip of her coffee, looking thoughtful. 'You seem to know a lot about Islam Rama. If it's not too rude of me to ask, what is your religion?'

Rama smiled, shaking his head. 'Having lived and worked in a predominantly Muslim country for so long one can't help but learn about it. As for my religion, having a white Christian father and a Hindu mother, I guess I've always walked between those two faiths and now I find myself in a similar situation with Islam. In the truly devout sense I am neither Christian nor Hindu nor Muslim nor anything else in particular. However I still consider myself a spiritual being.' Rama shrugged, 'I guess I take a little something from all faiths. What about yourself?'

'Actually I'm a bit of fence sitter when it comes to religion,' Danni confessed. 'Mum and dad sent me and my brother to Catholic schools growing up but only because they offered affordable private education. We celebrated Christmas and Easter but that was as far as religious observance went in our household. Apart from attending compulsory school services I've only ever been to church for christenings, weddings and funerals. I must confess though that I am curious about the different faiths and beliefs.'

'This trip is bound to increase your cultural competency, as long as you approach it with an open and inquiring mind,' Rama commented, then seeing Danni's puzzled look he elaborated. 'Cultural competency is what we in the international sphere refer to as the ability to interact effectively with people from different cultures and backgrounds. It's a concept that's being widely taught in universities now as the world becomes more globalised.'

'Cultural awareness?' Danni quizzed.

'Awareness is just the first step. To be culturally competent you need to approach diversity respectfully and positively without discrimination or preconceptions and learn about different values, customs and beliefs so that you can communicate and interact effectively with people from different backgrounds. With the right attitude and spending time in a foreign country it's a process that generally develops naturally.'

Danni laughed self-consciously. 'Well I do seem to have a growing fascination with different cultures, particularly traditions, religion and mythology.'

'That's a good place to start,' Rama acknowledged. 'So you like mythology. Remind me to tell you the story of Ramayana, my namesake, one day.'

'Please do. I'd love to hear it,' said Danni enthusiastically, her curiosity piqued.

They finished their coffee, chatted some more and the rest of the hour flew by so when Danni spotted Bel, Tim and Yusuf in the foyer through the open doorway of the restaurant she got quite a surprise. When Bel looked her way, Danni waved to get her attention.

'Hey you guys, look who I found,' said Danni gesturing towards Rama with a grin.

'Rama! Great to see you.' Bel and Tim were as pleased as Danni was to have him there and Yusuf seemed just as happy.

'To what do we owe the pleasure?' Tim asked, shaking Rama's hand.

Rama went through the same explanation he'd given Danni an hour beforehand and just as she'd predicted, Bel and Tim were as enthusiastic as she was about Rama's offer to accompanying him on the Meratus Mountains trip.

'I expect we'll be away for two or three nights, so pack accordingly. The hotel here will be happy to store the rest of your luggage until your return and Yusuf will drive us of course.'

'It sounds perfect. Tim and I were both hoping to visit a Dayak village.'

Rama nodded. 'You'll have plenty of opportunities once you start work with Helping Hands but this visit will be a good introduction. Unfortunately right now, I have some more business to attend to so I will leave you in Yusuf's capable hands and see you again in the morning.'

After exchanging goodbyes, Rama set off on a scooter in one direction whilst the rest of them walked the short distance to the markets, Yusuf explaining that he had organized an afternoon tour of Banjarmasin.

'But first we will have some lunch here at the markets where you will have a chance to sample some traditional cuisine. Then I will take you through the market and you may ask me about whatever you see.'

'Sounds like a good plan Yusuf,' agreed Tim.

The markets were only a short block from the hotel, the same ones they had passed by when they arrived in town the previous day and just as they were then, they were bustling with activity. The *pasar*, which Yusuf explained was the local term for market, occupied a large double story building and several smaller adjacent buildings but there were also vendors occupying the sidewalks all around the perimeter, making it almost impossible walk along the sidewalk. Scooters, *becaks* and a few cars and small trucks were tightly parked in everywhere so that they had to weave and squeeze their way through. At a glance it all looked rather chaotic and random although Danni suspected everything was run with military precision, something Yusuf confirmed.

'Yusuf, do all the street vendors have a designated spot or do they just set-up wherever they can find space?' Danni asked.

'No, no. Very organised. Each vendor and stall holder has their own spot.'

Yusuf led them inside to an area of the market that was obviously the Banjar equivalent of a shopping centre food court, with several rows of food vendor stalls and a motley collection of wooden and plastic tables and chairs. Here deep inside the crowded market surrounded by charcoal braziers and hot woks the air was thick and steamy. Mindful of this Yusuf led the group to a table directly underneath some slow turning fans.

'Okay, so please have a look around and see what you wish to eat. I will help you to order,' he offered.

'Is it all safe to eat?' Danni asked. 'I don't want a dose of traveller's belly.'

'Definitely not!' agreed Bel. 'So what do think Yusuf?'

'Yes it is safe to eat but you must choose only food which looks fresh and is cooked when you order. Nothing that is already cooked; it's okay for locals but not tourists. But you choose then I will check it's okay.'

Satisfied, the trio wandered off in various directions to see what was on offer with Yusuf keeping a diligent eye on them. As soon as any of them showed any interest in something he was at their side interpreting, explaining the ingredients to them and Danni gathered, giving the vendor strict instructions regarding the preparation and cooking of their meals. No one was going to get an upset tummy on his watch.

Ever curious, Danni had a hard time choosing what to have and ended up with a selection of chargrilled chicken pieces, some delicious looking noodles and a dish of green spinach looking vegetables which Yusuf called river weed but Danni recognized as *kangkung*, which was popular on menus in Bali. Sautéed with garlic, shrimp paste and dried chilli it was one of her favourite dishes.

After lunch they wandered through the market. Everything the average household could want was available; plastic ware, clothing, shoes, hardware, tools and electronic goods. There were even vendors selling spare parts for motor scooters. But Danni was most interested in the fresh food market that seemed to have an endless variety of fruit, vegetables and nuts on offer and the wet market where fish, crabs, shrimp and eels were being sold live out of large tubs of water. Her favourite though, was the spice market where sacks and sacks of dried cinnamon, turmeric, pepper, chilli and many more, whole and ground, created a fusion of colour and intoxicating aromas. In comparison to the markets in Bali that Danni was familiar with, these markets were refreshingly free of gaudy souvenirs and persistent hawkers. In fact apart from some curious looks and shy smiles, the locals left them to explore the market from top to bottom in peace and it was mid-afternoon before they finally dragged themselves away.

'No matter how many Asian markets I've seen, I still find them endlessly fascinating,' Bel commented as they hit the street. 'I always see something I haven't seen before.'

'So where to now Yusuf?' Tim asked.

'We have the Wasaka Museum. It is housed in an old traditional Banjarese house and has a collection of artefacts from the Banjar Kingdom. Perhaps you will find this interesting? If you like, we can go there next.'

'I'm interested,' Bel confirmed.

'Okay Yusuf, lead the way,' said Tim.

'It is a long walk, maybe too far, better if we drive. So we must go back to the hotel for my car.'

'What if we take a *becak*?' Danni suggested looking at the twenty or so rickshaws lined up nearby.

'Yes let's do that,' agreed Bel. 'It will be fun and we'll see so much more than we will looking out of the windows of the van.'

Yusuf nodded. 'Okay, please give me one moment.'

After what appeared to be some spirited haggling, Yusuf waved them over to two *becaks* that were being extricated from the rest of the tightly parked bunch. Bel and Tim climbed onto one, Danni and Yusuf onto the other and they set off through the streets. Bel was right Danni decided, it was definitely more fun being pedalled around that sitting in the van and it gave her an opportunity to snap some photographs along the way.

'Oh look at that,' called Bel about fifteen minutes later, pointing and leaning out the side of her *becak* which was fifty metres ahead of Danni and Yusuf's ride.

Perched among palm and fruit trees on a large block of land, the Wasaka Museum was a substantial timber building and much larger than Danni had imagined. Built on high stilts to keep it above wet season flood levels, with a steep sloping roof that reared skywards over the centre of the building, timber roof shingles, slab sided walls and small windows it was an impressive structure.

'I'm surprised how big it is Yusuf. When you said the museum was housed in a traditional Banjarese house I pictured something about cottage size,' commented Danni.

'This is a genuine *Bubungan Tinggi* style traditional house, the most iconic of the twelve traditional Banjarese styles. The name *Bubungan Tinggi* means 'high ridge', due to the sharp pitch of the roof. During the time of the old Banjar kingdom, this style of house was the home of the royal family and the most important building of the royal palace complex. For this reason it became very popular throughout Kalimantan but the cost to build was very high, so *Bubungan Tinggi* was only for the rich. Even today, it is still expensive and the rich now prefer more modern styles. But many government buildings feature *Bubungan Tinggi* traits and the style remains culturally significant. *Bubungan Tinggi* traditional house is featured on the coat of arms of both South Kalimantan and Banjarmasin.'

The items on display in the museum were many and varied; traditional costumes, plates, jars and other antiques, though predictably Tim was most taken with the displays of swords and pistols from the Dutch VOC era. Finishing inside, Danni wandered behind the museum looking for a vantage point from which to photograph the building. Discovering a small pond and a lovely garden nook shaded by a large banyan tree, she sat down at the base of the tree to wait for Bel and Tim and by the time they emerged from the museum, she was well relaxed.

Re-grouping back at the *becaks*, Yusuf suggested a visit to the Sabilal Muhtadin Grand Mosque. 'It is a very special mosque, the second largest in Indonesia,' Yusuf explained.

'I'd like to see it,' said Danni. 'I think that's the one Rama mentioned to me earlier today. Yusuf, is that the mosque near where they have the cake fair at the end of Ramadan?'

'Yes, yes. That is the one,' Yusuf grinned delightedly although whether it was the thoughts of the cake fair or Danni's knowledge or a combination of both she couldn't tell.

Approaching from the Martapura riverfront, the mosque sat like a giant spaceship at the end of an impressive expanse of lawn and a long courtyard and feature pool. The complex consisted of a huge dome clad main plaza and several towers, one soaring forty-five metres into the air, topped with minarets of bronzed aluminium. The entire massive structure was clad in marble. It was modern and impressive and compared to downtown Banjarmasin with its rundown, faded concrete and rusty iron buildings, it was very unexpected.

'Yusuf, it's beautiful,' exclaimed Danni.

'Yes very impressive,' said Tim

Yusuf smiled broadly. 'It is the pride of Banjarmasin and our tribute to Islam. It's very beautiful inside. The wudu room, walls and the floor are all covered with porcelain. In the main plaza the entire floor is coated with ceramic. People come from all over to pray here. Sometimes as many as fifteen thousand people attend Friday night prayers.'

Tim whistled appreciatively.

'Yusuf, what's a *wudu* room?' Danni asked.

'*Wudu* is the ritual of cleansing oneself prior to formal prayer, or *salat*. Using water, you wash your face, your feet, arms and other exposed parts of the body. The Quran says 'For Allah loves those who turn to Him constantly and He loves those who keep themselves pure and clean'.'

'Ah so it's a symbolic cleansing. Interesting. I've learnt so much about the Islamic faith since being here. In fact,' said Danni turning to Bel and Tim, 'since meeting you guys I feel like a whole new world has opened up to me.'

'Glad to have been of assistance,' Tim joked.

'No seriously, over the last few days I've really become aware how sheltered my life is. I've travelled, been to Europe, Singapore, Bali. I honestly thought I was quite well travelled but I'm starting to realize there's a big difference between just going places and actually experiencing them. There's a big wide world out there that I know nothing about.'

'Sounds like you've caught the travel bug girl,' Bel gave her a knowing look.

Danni grinned back. 'I think you may be right and I've got you and Tim to blame!'

CHAPTER EIGHT

Danni stretched her legs across the seat and wriggled her bare toes appreciatively. With Rama riding up front beside Yusuf, Danni, Bel and Tim each had a row of seats to themselves in the back of Yusuf's mini-van and after three hours of travelling Danni was glad to have the room to stretch out. As arranged, Rama and Yusuf had collected the three friends from the hotel around mid-morning, a leisurely start time that had given them time to sleep in a little, enjoy a casual buffet breakfast from the hotel restaurant, pack and check out of their rooms since none of them could see any point paying for rooms they wouldn't be using. As Rama had suggested, Danni had packed a couple of changes of clothes and toiletries into a small overnight bag and left the rest of her luggage with the hotel to store until they returned in a few day's time. Noticing a computer with internet access for guest use in an alcove off the foyer, she'd sent Rob a quick email to let him know where she as heading and promising to call when she got back to Banjarmasin.

Sitting sideways on the seat in front of her, Bel yawned and giggled when she set Danni off with a yawn of her own.

'Getting restless back there?' Rama asked from the front seat.

'How much further?' Bel asked with a childlike whine.

'Yeah, when are we going to get there?' Danni added.

Rama grinned. 'Alright kids, time for a break.' He murmured something to Yusuf who slowed and pulled the van off the road outside a local warung when they came to the next village a short time later.

'We've still got an hour or two to go, so why don't we grab some lunch?' Rama suggested as everyone piled out of the van. The warung was large by local standards, with a thatched roof, open-sided dining pavilion and a detached kitchen. Oscillating fans whirred overhead, chasing away the midday heat and cooling the skin. A waitress led the group to a table large enough to accommodate them all and handed out the menus. After Rama explained that shared rice and noodles came with their meals, they each ordered a protein selection, Danni opting for the grilled fish and fresh juice. After placing her order she headed to the bathroom, finding an Asian squatter type toilet which Danni was starting to get used to but disliked nonetheless. Oh well, when in Rome...

The meal was lovely. Danni's grilled fish was served whole and once she gave up trying to eat it with the fork and spoon the waitress brought her and instead picked the flesh off with her fingers as Rama suggested, she enjoyed the succulent fish immensely. Likewise, Bel and Tim raved over their meals.

'The food is very good,' commented Tim. 'No wonder the place is crowded.'

'That's the secret when you're trying to find a good place to eat. Always look for the warung that's busy. If the locals are eating there you're just about guaranteed the food will be good. If the place is empty, avoid it,' advised Rama.

'Makes sense,' agreed Tim.

As they gathered by the vehicle after lunch, Danni noticed Yusuf quietly talking to Rama, who nodded then turned to rest of them. 'Folks, I'm going to need copies of your passports before we head on. There's a place near here that does photocopying so now is a good time to do it.'

The trio shared puzzled looks. 'What do you need them for?' Tim asked.

'We need to lodge your details with the local constabulary up the way,' Rama explained. Tim gave him a knowing look and gestured to Bel retrieve their passports from her bag. However, Danni wasn't satisfied. She felt there was more to it than Rama was saying.

'I don't get it. Why do you need to lodge our details?'

Rama sighed. Danni had a lot to learn about how things were done in Indonesia but he didn't want to explain it to her standing the street. 'Because they like to know who's in their region, especially visitors, so they can keep an eye out for them.'

Danni was still far from satisfied with the explanation but she could tell Rama didn't want to discuss it further so she pushed her qualms aside, dug out her passport and followed the others to a nearby shop where Rama organized the copies.

Back in the vehicle, Danni turned her attention to the passing countryside. The trip so far had passed mostly through urban areas and Danni suspected that despite the travel time, they hadn't actually gone very far from Banjarmasin. The traffic was heavy and their pace quite slow with a lot of stopping and starting. The locals seemed to have little regard for the road rules, if there were any, frequently travelling three cars abreast as if the line markings meant nothing, overtaking into oncoming traffic and failing to give way at intersections. Thankfully Yusuf seemed far more cautious than most of his fellow countrymen but he still had to share the road with them so for much of the first hour of the trip Danni had her heart in her mouth. Her travelling companions, all much more experienced than herself, seemed quite nonplussed by the chaotic traffic and eventually Danni decided it was probably best for her nerves to not watch the road at all.

But now they'd left the built up areas behind, the countryside became much more rural and as they left the lowlands behind and drove on into hillier terrain, rice fields gave way to rubber plantations, which Rama pointed out. The villages became smaller, further apart and noticeably poorer as they travelled on. A couple of times she noticed one or two men in the bush carrying nets and long poles and asked Rama what they were doing.

'Trapping birds,' he answered.

It was on the tip of her tongue to question him some more on the subject, but the slowing van diverted Danni's attention to a road block up ahead. There was no sign of any officialdom, just a tree branch placed across the road and some colourful buckets placed down the middle of the road, perhaps the Borneo equivalent of witches' hats. A group of men, some holding more buckets, seemed to be running the show. As Yusuf inched the van forward, one young man came to the window and after exchanging a few words, Yusuf reached into the console for some loose notes and tossed some rupiah into the bucket. The young man thanked him and signalled to his offsiders who quickly pulled the tree branch off the road and waved them through.

'What was that all about?' asked Bel.

'They're raising money to build a mosque,' Rama explained.

'You're kidding. So they just block the road and ask for money from motorists?'

Rama shrugged. 'It's not all that uncommon here in Kalimantan or Java.'

'What happens if you don't want to donate? Will they let you through?' Danni asked.

Again Rama shrugged. 'Everyone donates. They consider it an honour to contribute to a new mosque.'

'Hmm, well it's not like any fundraising effort I've ever seen,' said Danni. 'But that goes for a lot of what I've seen here in Borneo already.'

They drove on in silence for a while longer, Danni guessing they were getting close to their destination when the road narrowed and began to twist and turn through a steep sided valley. Heavily forested mountain pinnacles reared sharply all around them and after catching some glimpses of bare faced cliffs, Danni realised they were actually limestone karsts. Inevitably the road climbed higher, Yusuf's little van working hard to get over some of the steep inclines. To maximize power, he soon flipped off the air-conditioner and apologetically told his passengers to open their windows, which seemed to suit everyone just fine. Along with the breeze rushing through the windows came the smell of the jungle and at their slow pace, Danni felt like she could reach out and touch it. As the little van took them deeper into the ranges, excitement welled in the pit of her stomach.

'How big are the Meratus Mountains Rama?'

'Not overly big. They're quite low lying; the highest peak is just a little under two thousand metres above sea level. But geographically they're quite significant because the range runs in a north-south arc that almost bisects the South Kalimantan province. To the east the range slopes away to the coastal lowlands and to the west into the swampy basin formed by the Negara River. When we leave here in a couple of days, that's the direction we'll be heading.'

At what Danni assumed was the top of the range, they came upon a little settlement of timber and thatched huts clinging precariously to the steep mountain side on thin stilts. Banana palms, chilli bushes, papaya trees and other plants Danni didn't recognize were planted haphazardly around the place and chickens ranged freely picking at the ground as villagers went about their business or lay in hammocks in the shade beneath their stilted homes.

Yusuf stopped the van beside a bamboo pergola where several men were lounging. 'Wait here please,' said Rama, alighting from the vehicle with their passport copies in hand. Danni watched curiously as he handed over the copies and to her surprise, what appeared to be a small wad of rupiah. After a quick handshake, he returned to the van and they were on their way again. This time Danni's excitement was quelled by the realization that she'd just witnessed something a little bit shady.

Only a few short minutes later they descended into another valley and another village. The three friends craned their necks for a glimpse of the gurgling river lacing its way along the valley floor. 'Look there,' exclaimed Danni excitedly pointing to a hanging bridge across the river.

'Oh it's so pretty,' said Bel, referring to the entire scene, not just the bridge.

Rama grinned at them from the front seat, obviously please by their reactions. 'That's the Amandit River and you'll have plenty of time to enjoy it. We're here for a couple of nights,' he announced.

Bel clapped her hands together with glee. 'Fabulous. I can't wait to have a look around.'

'Just contain yourselves to this main area here for the time being,' Rama cautioned. 'I need to see the village head man first to ask permission before we go poking around too much. It's just a courtesy. Kind of like you wouldn't want strangers just wandering into your backyard at home. First up though, grab your bags and we'll organize our rooms.'

As instructed, they retrieved their bags and followed Rama across the hanging bridge over the river to a large double-storey building. It was located on its own, away from the village homes, surrounded by overgrown grass and hanging trees and judging by the peeling white paint and faded red shingles, it had seen better days.

'Welcome to the Loksado River Lodge,' said Rama. 'It's pretty basic I'm afraid but this is all there is.'

'This will be fine. Bel and I've stayed in far worse than this,' said Tim in his typically unflappable manner.

The three friends stood back and let Rama make the arrangements with the Dayak woman who met them inside the front door. There didn't appear to be any formal checking in procedure; she simply collected three keys from their hooks and led them onto a veranda at the rear of the lodge where she pointed out three rooms, handed the keys to Rama and left them to organize themselves.

'Casual,' commented Bel with a laugh.

Rama handed a key each to Tim and Danni, keeping one for himself. 'You'll find all the rooms are the same here. Get yourselves settled in and feel free to have a look around but only in this central area,' he reminded them. 'If you want a snack there's a little shop back over the bridge. In the meantime, I've got some business to do here so I'll meet you back here around six for dinner.'

The trio settled into their respective rooms which as Rama had warned them, were pretty basic; sparsely furnished with twin single beds, a small table, a wardrobe and a chair. There was no air conditioning, just a slow turning fan, but thankfully the mosquito netting across the windows looked to be intact. The bathroom housed a cold water shower and a dreaded squatter type toilet with big tub of water and a plastic scoop to manually flush. The beds had only a bottom sheet, a light blanket and a thin pillow but like the rest of the room, it all looked clean and when Danni stretched out on one of the beds she found it was surprisingly comfortable. Okay, she thought, it's a little below the standard she was accustomed too but she was no princess; it would do fine.

'Knock, knock,' called Bel, coming through the door Danni had left open. 'You okay with this?' she asked, concerned.

Danni grinned reassuringly at her friend. 'Perfectly fine.'

'Good. Listen, I'm dying to go for a walk and have a look around. You interested?'

'You bet. Just let me grab my camera.'

Outside, they found Tim leaning on the veranda railing peering curiously at a local couple who were manoeuvring a long pole up into the branches of a tree behind the lodge.

'What are they doing?' asked Danni.

'I'm not sure but if you look closely, there appears to be a bag of sorts hanging off the end of the pole.'

As they watched on, the man continued manoeuvring the pole and once satisfied with its position, gave it a vigorous shake. Danni strained to see until she had the bright idea to look through the zoom lens on her camera. 'It's an ants nest!' she exclaimed as she focused the camera. 'He's catching ants.' She passed the camera along to Bel, who in turn passed it to Tim so they could all get a closer look.

'I wonder what they do with them,' Danni mused.

'Ants and ant eggs are eaten in many Asian countries; considered a delicacy even. In Cambodia red ant larvae is a very special treat. I never got the chance to try it when we were over there but I heard it has a rich, creamy texture,' offered Tim.

At that point the ant collectors became aware of their audience and not to be rude, Danni gave them a friendly wave, then pointed into the tree foliage and brought her hand to her mouth to imitate eating. The woman smiled back and shook her head, then pointed to the river and wriggled her hand to imitate a swimming fish, then brought her hand to her mouth. Danni grinned and nodded in comprehension.

'It's for fish bait,' she said smugly, mystery solved. 'Who needs Bahasa

Indonesian?'

'Well done Danni,' said Bel.

The trio watched the ant collectors awhile longer until the man wielding the pole slapped his legs and jumped away from the tree, obviously under attack from angry ants. He persisted for another minute or two but gave it away under an unrelenting attack. Show over, the trio waved goodbye and set off across the river, stopping midway across the hanging bridge to admire the view. The river was clear and shallow, bubbling over boulders and river stones worn smooth over millennia. A few village homes were perched along the river bank, but only on the high side where the river curved gently through the valley. Beyond the valley, forested mountain peaks framed the horizon. Looking in the other direction, the river kept curling away until it was lost from sight in the narrowing valley, but not before it was crossed by another hanging bridge.

'It's magic isn't it?' said Bel to no one in particular. 'I think I'm in love with Borneo.'

'Me too,' agreed Danni. 'Just when I think surely I've seen the best, along comes another 'wow' moment.'

Unnoticed by the girls, Tim had moved further along the bridge and chose that moment to start rocking the hanging bridge for all he was worth, sending the startled girls scrambling for the steel cable, holding on for dear life. With two hands now safely on the cable, Bel shot Tim a fierce look. 'Tim! You're gonna cop it,' she threatened, which didn't faze him at all; instead he launched into another bout of rocking, drawing more squeals from the girls. Only when they were quite sure he was done did they dare to move along the bridge, keeping a wary eye on Tim and a cautionary hand on the cable. As they drew close to him, he planted his feet and made a show of threatening to rock the bridge again, sending the girls scrambling for the cable again. It was only when Tim flashed a sideways grin and wink, drawing giggles from the shadows beside the bridge uprights, that the girls realized they had an audience of several village children. Keeping up the game, as the girls got closer Tim put his hands up in defence and backed away as Bel advanced on him. Watching on, the children giggled some more, but when Bel turned and pretended to come after them instead, their giggles turned into delighted squeals and laughter as they ran away, retreating a safe distance. As they stepped off the bridge, Bel gave Tim and half-hearted slap on the arm then waved to the kids.

'Shall we walk up to the other hanging bridge?' Bel suggested.

'Yes let's do that. I'd like to get a photo looking back over the village,' said Danni. Although shorter, the other bridge was suspended higher over the river affording a good view back down the valley and over the village as Danni had hoped. After getting her photo, they retraced their steps to the lodge crossing, and then continued along the main village thoroughfare running parallel to the river. The village was oddly quiet, in fact apart from the ant collectors and children earlier, there didn't seem to be anyone else about, so mindful of Rama's instructions not to wander too far, they turned back after a few hundred metres and returned to the lodge where they dragged chairs out onto the back veranda outside their rooms and spent the next hour chatting whilst they waited for Rama.

Rama returned a little before six as promised, explaining when they inquired after Yusuf, that he was visiting with friends in the village. Once they got themselves organized, Rama led the group back over the river to a little warung that the three friends must have passed unnoticed during their afternoon walk. There were quite a few villagers around now, walking along the village street, talking with friends or sitting outside their homes, women squatting at the river's edge using the smooth boulders to wash and pound their washing against, children congregating to play, a lucky one or two on bicycles.

'This is a bit different. There was hardly a soul to be seen when we had a look around earlier,' Danni commented.

'They would have been out working in the fields or gathering in the forest,' explained Rama. 'Most of the villagers have a small plot of land that they farm but it can be up to several kilometres away so they stay in the field the entire day. You'll see some of that tomorrow.'

The warung Rama took them to seemed quite new. Although it was obviously the front room of someone's house, the building itself was of modern cement and tile construction, representing quite an investment for the owners. In fact, Danni had been rather surprised that most of the homes she'd seen during their walk were solid timber structures, which although small by western standards, were a substantial improvement over the tiny thatched huts they'd seen in many of the villages they'd driven through earlier in the day. Tim had obviously made the same observation Danni realized, when he commented that the village seemed quite well off by rural standards.

'Yes it is,' confirmed Rama. 'Unfortunately, it's in the minority. Most of the residents here in Loksado still depend largely on farming for a living but they've been able to generate some additional income by offering adventure based activities to school groups and the trickle of tourists that make their way up here. Plus it's a popular place with city dwellers who can afford to come up here for a short break. That's why the Lodge is here and a sealed road all the way. Many of the villages here in the Meratus Mountains don't have a road of any sort.'

'What sort of adventure based activities do they offer?'

'Hiking, abseiling, bamboo rafting, even caving; hiking and rafting being the most popular by far. There are still significant tracts of pristine, untouched jungle throughout the ranges, waterfalls, a hot spa or two and remote villages. It's even possible to hike to the top of Gunung Besar, the highest peak in the range. There are well-worn paths crisscrossing the ranges but it's very easy for an outsider to get lost so using a local guide from the village is essential. The technical stuff like abseiling and caving is run by experienced guides from the city with assistance from the locals.'

'I hope you've got some hiking and rafting planned for us Rama,' said Bel.

Rama grinned. 'I certainly have. Tomorrow's the day. Nothing too strenuous but it will give you a good taste of things.' He looked at Danni and winked, 'Sorry Danni, no bungee jumping.'

Danni grinned back, quite pleased that he had remembered her earlier confession. 'I'll try to contain my disappointment.'

They lapsed into silence whilst they ate their meals which Danni couldn't actually remember ordering. When she commented on it, Rama explained that it was a set menu which varied daily depending on the whims of the owner. 'You'll find that's the case more often than not once you get away from the mainstream areas.' Nevertheless, the meal of chicken and savoury rice was tasty and filling and no one had any cause for complaint. Since there was no reason to rush back to the Lodge, they lingered at the warung, sipping sweet tea and munching on a plate of fresh fruit the owner brought them.

Although reluctant to dampen the mood, Danni decided it was time to broach a subject that had been bothering her all afternoon. 'Rama, can I ask you about the passport incident today? I saw you give the man at the hut the copies and I think I also saw you give him some cash.'

Rama wasn't surprised by Danni's question; he'd expected her to raise the subject again at some point. But he took his time formulating his answer, in part because he was reluctant to burst Danni's innocence and in part because he was as much Indonesian as he was Australian and he felt it was only fair to try and put the countries failing into context.

'Yes you did see that,' he admitted, 'and I'm sorry you did. Such a payment is required by all visitors wishing to come to this region. Many tourists would never realize such a thing happens because their guide would take care of it without them ever knowing, especially if they've provided copies of their passports up front.'

'I don't get it,' said Danni, looking puzzled. 'Extortion? Pay up or don't come in?'

Rama grimaced. 'That's putting it a little strongly. Think of it as an admission fee; if you want to come here you pay for the privilege.'

'I wouldn't mind at all if the money was being collected for the good of the community, but those guys didn't look official to me. I bet the money is going straight into their pockets.'

'Some of it yes, but most of it will be passed up the line to anyone who has the ability to make or break your trip, both official and unofficial.'

'That's outrageous! If it's not extortion, it's corruption at the very least.'

'This is Indonesia' Rama said with a shrug. 'Things work very differently to what you are used to in Australia. Unfortunately in Indonesia corruption is widespread and occurs at all levels.' Realising Danni wasn't going to be mollified with that, Rama sighed heavily and continued.

'I appreciate it's difficult for you to understand coming from your background but the issue of corruption isn't unique to Indonesia. It is rampant in many parts of the world and for many, many millions of people less fortunate than yourself, corruption is something they deal with almost daily. They may not like it, but they accept that it occurs. For instance, each week at home you probably put aside a certain sum of money for your living expenses such as rent, food and electricity. If you live in a society tainted by corruption, depending on your circumstances, you would most likely also include an added expense for corruption, or as some prefer to think of it, as a payment for favour.'

Danni nodded slowly. 'Of course I have heard about corruption but only at a higher level such as bribes to government officials. But I had no idea that it occurs at all levels of society, even among the poorest of the poor.' She shook her head in disgust. 'How do they pay?'

'That', said Rama 'is the part of the problem. Millions can't pay and because they can't pay they're effectively locked out of many opportunities that could improve their lives. Take Yusuf for instance. Every time he brings tourists out here, he has to pay. If he was unable to pay officials to ensure his clients unhindered and enjoyable access to the area then he would quickly be out of business. I'm sure like most Indonesian's he dislikes intensely having to make those payments but he accepts that he must.'

'So if the system can't be changed where does that leave the poorest people who can't afford to participate?'

Rama sighed heavily. 'It's not that the system can't be changed. It can change and if equality, opportunity and prosperity for all is to ever be achieved in this country, it must change. But the problem requires cultural change at all levels and for that to happen we first need to acknowledge that corruption exists, secondly create a will for change and then a framework to drive it through and ensure that it remains permanently eradicated. There are signs that this process has started but we have to be realistic. Change won't occur overnight. In fact it may take several generations.

Up until a couple of decades ago corruption was the elephant in the room. Seen but never spoken about. First world nations tended to view it as a political problem rather than an economic one so it was a problem to be navigated around rather than solved.'

'So what happened a couple of decades ago the change their view?' asked Danni.

'Globalisation. When large international companies and mining conglomerates began investing in third world countries the scale of the corruption became too big to ignore. For instance, when you have government officials in a position to skim fifteen to thirty percent off the top of a $15 billion dollar arms deal that's $4.5 billion that is diverted from investment in a nations development such as in basic infrastructure, health and education. It becomes difficult for the world to ignore certain individuals acquiring enormous unexplained wealth whilst the people they are supposed to serve and protect continue to languish in abject poverty'.

'Like former Philippine President Ferdinand Marcos,' said Danni.

'And Indonesia's former President Suharto,' added Bel.

'Yes just like them,' agreed Rama. 'But for every one that you know of there are thousands of officials who remain under the radar. Corruption takes many forms – outright corrupt payments, bribery and nepotism – and it exists at all levels of government being local, provisional and central. It also occurs in institutions such as the police, customs, the attorney general's office and the judiciary.'

Tim nodded in agreement. 'As an example it is widely reputed among western holidaymakers in Bali that if you get caught riding a scooter around without a valid international licence, you can buy your way out of trouble with an on the spot 'fine' to the police officer. Of course this is only hearsay but...' he trailed off with a shrug.

'Westerners especially have to realise that that although corruption has been allowed to flourish in Indonesia due to decades of impunity, the kind of behaviour you mentioned Tim perpetuates the problem and they become equally culpable. In fact one might argue that they are even more culpable than the corrupt police involved,' said Rama.

'How so?' asked Bel.

'Because it's not a level playing field. One of the biggest issues with corruption in Indonesia is that many public services such as the police are inadequately funded. Public officers are very poorly paid and some seek to supplement their income through questionable means such as demanding payment from subordinates in return for a promotion or simply to keep their job. Other examples include demanding payment for simply carrying out the job they're employed to do in a timely and efficient manner, such as releasing goods from the waterfront or sending a work crew out to repair a broken telephone line. Many tourists experience this when they arrive at the airport in Denpasar. They have a choice between a long wait in the understaffed immigration line or paying for a fast track clearance.

It's not that these people are necessarily bad or greedy. They simply see it as an extension of their meagre salaries. In fact, it's almost expected of them. For them it is often the difference between being able to keep a roof over their heads, put food on the table or pay for their children's education. On the flip side you have a scooter riding tourist who for the sake of convenience or a bit of fun would rather pay a corrupt US$25 fine, what is to them a rather immaterial amount, than abide by the law.'

'Hmm I see what you mean,' said Danni feeling somewhat overawed by the scale of the problem. 'So how do you stamp it out?'

'One step at a time,' answered Rama. 'It requires commitment from both the Indonesian government and the international community. It is not enough to say that corruption will not be tolerated anymore. They must also walk the walk and we are seeing progress in this regard, albeit slow progress.

When he came to power in 2004, the current Indonesian President Susilo Bambang Yudhoyono promised to root out corruption from the top down. There has been some success and recently we learned that about half of local government officials, mayors and governors in Indonesia have been charged with corruption. Within his own Democratic Party there have been several high profile corruption scandals. But even seven years into his presidency Yudhoyono publicly stated that overcoming corruption still remained Indonesia's biggest challenge. There are those that say he should have and could have done more but history will have to be the judge of that.

Catching and charging corrupt officials is one thing but there must also be an environment that takes away the temptation. Improving pay and conditions for both government and non-government employees is an important step and in this regard there is a very long way to go.

Outside Indonesia we have much needed and growing support from first world governments, the World Bank, the International Monetary Fund and other large financial institutions. The financial aid packages or money they lend comes with significant obligations on how it is used and accounted for in a fully transparent manner. There are now numerous examples of major assistance packages being pulled because the donor wasn't satisfied with the way funds were being spent or contracts awarded so corrupt countries are starting to get the message.

International anti-corruption laws have also improved significantly. The OECD and United Nations Conventions Against Corruption place certain obligations on the countries that sign up and the introduction or strengthening of anti-corruption legislation such as the UK Foreign Bribery Act serves as a further deterrent against corrupt conduct by private companies or individuals.'

'It all sounds like things are moving in the right direction,' said Tim, 'but how effective is it?'

'Of course it would be naive to think that these initiatives will solve the problem of corruption but they do help immensely. Certainly without them, we have no chance. Perhaps the biggest weapon in the anti-corruption arsenal is awareness and a growing intolerance for corrupt behaviour. It's one thing for organisations like Transparency International and whistleblowers to expose corrupt behaviour but ultimately it is up to stockholders, other stakeholders and society in general to stand up and voice their disapproval loud and clear.'

'Like the Nestlé baby formula scandal,' suggested Danni. 'If you recall Nestlé were accused of aggressively marketing their baby formula products in developing countries. They flooded health facilities and maternity wards with free or low cost supplies of formula and sold mothers on the idea that baby formula was better for their babies than breastfeeding. They were also accused of providing gifts and sponsorship to local health workers to promote their baby formula. After leaving hospital many parents found they couldn't afford the product at market price but by then many mothers had stopped lactating so reverting to breastfeeding wasn't an option. Nestlé were accused of contributing to the unnecessary suffering and deaths of hundreds of babies in those third world countries. An ongoing boycott of Nestlé products by consumers has spread right around the world and has probably cost the company billions of dollars in lost revenue. That whole episode is now studied in universities by just about every marketing and business student as an example of how unethical behaviour can have enormous and ongoing ramifications.'

The rest of the group nodded in agreement. 'That is the sort of thing that I am talking about,' agreed Rama.

'Okay, but in the meantime what can be done to help the poor?' asked Danni.

'That's where organisations such as mine can assist. There are literally thousands of not-for-profit organisations operating in Indonesia, each with its own manifesto. Some focus on providing emergency aid in crisis situations such as the Indian Ocean Tsunami or the Bali bombings. Others specialise in the delivery of basic services such as education, health, food, shelter, clean water etc. There are some that focus on child services, family planning, conservation, sustainable agriculture, animal welfare or the development of infrastructure such as roads and bridges. The list is endless really and of course some are more effective than others. In any case as long as the government fails, for whatever reason, to provide these basic services to its citizens, NGO's will endeavour to fill the void.'

'But by filling the void, aren't NGO's somehow enabling government to abdicate their responsibilities?' Danni philosophised.

'That is an argument that many commentators have made. It's true that primary responsibility for the welfare of its citizens and environment should rest with the government and in an ideal world this would be the case. However, that's not the world millions living in poverty occupy,' said Rama sadly. 'Perhaps the question you should be asking is not so much about the dependency of governments on NGO's but of the recipients,' he prompted.

Taking up the baton, Danni said 'Okay I'll bite...'

'Well,' began Rama, 'creating a dependency environment is a valid concern and not just with third world NGO's. Even in a modern, flourishing country like Australia there's the phenomenon referred to as the welfare society where long term welfare recipients become unwilling or unable to break the dependency cycle.'

Danni, Tim and Bel murmured in agreement. The issue was always a hot topic in Australian politics.

Rama continued. 'There was certainly a time when charity organisations were reactive, focusing on meeting immediate needs such as feeding as many starving people as they could manage. It's an admirable goal but in the long term it's not sustainable. Nowadays the focus is on empowering individuals and communities to help themselves. We do this first by meeting their most pressing needs such as food, shelter, healthcare and clean water. Then we equip them with the skills, education, financial and emotional support they need to improve their lives in a meaningful and permanent way. Remember these are individuals who have suffered enormous hardships and want nothing more than to improve their lot in life. Given an opportunity they grab it with both hands and run with it. '

Danni's mind was whirring. 'God this is a frustrating country. On the one hand there's so much about it that I love, on the other things like this that I hate.'

'It's a lot to take in Danni. Don't try to process it all at once,' advised Rama. 'Very few things in this world are black or white and I have a hunch that as you see more of the country and its people your feelings will land firmly on the love side of the scale. After all you can still love something or someone without necessarily loving everything about them.'

***

Despite the revelations of the night before and the lack of creature comforts in her room, Danni slept soundly until the cock-a-doodle-doo of a village rooster woke her just after dawn. It was already warm; at least enough to be able to convince herself the cold shower she rushed through was refreshing. She wrapped her long hair in the towel as she dressed, bathers beneath her clothes as Rama had recommended, then stepped outside onto the veranda to enjoy the morning air as she brushed her hair. She had just about brushed her hair dry and was staring absently through the trees across the little creek at the back of the lodge when she heard Rama's voice behind her.

'You have beautiful hair Danni. I didn't realize it was so long; it's the first time I've seen it down.'

The brush stilled in her hand as she turned to face Rama. 'Thank you.' Rama was regarding her frankly, as if the complement was nothing more than a casual observation, but Danni felt awkward nonetheless. As a married woman she wasn't used to receiving complements from attractive, single men. 'Actually at this length it can be a pain to manage and I keep threatening to go short but I just can't bring myself to cut it.'

'That would be a shame.'

'Have you been out?' Danni asked, reaching for a less personal topic.

'Yes, the early morning when everything is still and quiet is a good time for meditation and little yoga.'

'Outside?'

'That's my preference. I find it more challenging to focus my mind, in spite of the distractions that mother nature presents; the wind on my face, a bug buzzing near my ear, a river gurgling, the sweet smell of frangipani's, the sun on my back.'

'Oh. And the yoga?'

Rama cocked his head. 'Always the inquisitive Danni.'

Danni flushed, feeling her cheeks turn bright red. 'Sorry, I didn't mean to pry.'

Rama grinned. 'You're not, I was just teasing. In its true form yoga is practiced in the pursuit of physical, mental and spiritual well-being. I'm afraid that like most westerners, I practice yoga simply for physical exercise.'

'I watched you meditating in Sanur before we met. You were on the gazebo out on the sand spit.' Danni blurted and then mentally kicked herself. She didn't add that the sight of him had made her catch her breath.

'A favourite spot when I'm in Sanur,' was all he said although Danni saw surprise flicker in his eyes.

'How often is that?' Danni cringed. 'Sorry, there I go prying again. Don't answer; it's none of my business.'

Rama grinned again. 'It's alright Danni. A perfectly reasonable question for new friends getting to know each other. Apart from my family being there, Sanur is where I keep the main office for my organization so I'm there a fair bit. I have a small flat above the office which is where I notionally call home.' He paused, 'Now my turn to ask a question.'

'That's only fair,' conceded Danni.

'Is that your natural hair colour or do you dye it?'

'Rama!'

Rama threw his head back and laughed. 'Gotcha again Danni.' And with that he headed back to his room leaving her staring open mouthed behind him.

***

Once everyone assembled for breakfast, Rama led them back across the river which was sparkling in the morning sunshine. From the bridge, Danni noticed some activity on the river bank and stopped to watch a man lugging some long bamboo poles to the water's edge where another man appeared to be strapping them together.

'That's our bamboo rafts they're building,' said Rama over her shoulder.

'Really!'

'Yep, once they've put them together they'll take them down the river to rendezvous with us after our hike.'

'Oh I'm really looking forward to today. I can't wait to get started.'

Rama grinned. Danni's genuine enthusiasm about everything was something he really liked about her. 'Breakfast first.'

They ate breakfast at the little shop opposite the bridge from the lodge. With barely four square metres of floor space and most of it jam-packed with stock, there was hardly any room for customers to enter. Danni and Bel sat on a wooden bench and ate their *pisang goreng* at the counter, whilst the guys ate theirs standing outside. Before they left the female proprietor handed Rama some brown paper parcels which he popped into his daypack. 'Our lunch,' he explained and after ensuring everyone had bottled water with them, he led them off along the main track beside the river. They soon left the village and river behind, passing by farm plots planted with banana palms, papaya, tomatoes, chilli and cucumber. They waved to the few farmers they saw tending their plots and hiked on. Eventually the track swung back towards the river which they crossed via another hanging bridge and on the other side, the two wheel track they'd been following narrowed.

'I guess that's the extent of the road,' commented Tim.

It was also the extent of the farm plots. They were now walking through thick jungle, although there was evidence of past clearing alongside the track. After an hour or so the jungle thinned and they entered a clearing dominated by a massive building.

'That has to be a longhouse surely?' exclaimed Bel excitedly, which Rama confirmed with a nod of his head.

At least thirty metres long and fifteen to twenty metres wide, the longhouse was much larger than Danni had imagined. Raised off the ground on timber stilts, the thatched walls stopped about a metre below roof level, presumably to allow plenty of ventilation, as would the large, shuttered windows.

'Is it still in use?' Bel asked.

'Not in the traditional sense when everyone in the village lived together in the longhouse. Nowadays, most villagers live in their own separate houses but the longhouse still remains the heart of the village and a place for gatherings, ceremonies and celebrations and sometimes village guests will stay in the longhouse.'

Noticing some activity in the yard beside the longhouse, Danni walked over for a closer look although she stayed well back not wanting to intrude. The rest of the group followed her over. 'It's okay, you can go closer,' said Rama. 'They won't mind you looking.' Danni watched with interest as the couple spread out a large tarpaulin on the ground and poured several large baskets of nuts onto it, which they spread into a thin layer, the purpose obviously to dry them in the sun.

'They're candlenuts,' Rama explained. 'The villagers gather them from the forest around here. What they don't eat themselves they sell at the markets.'

'How long does it take to dry them?' Danni asked.

'Depending on the weather, three to four days, sometimes longer. It's important that they're dried properly so the nuts can be ground down and used in recipes as a thickening agent or to add flavour. Many, many Dayak recipes include candlenuts in this way.'

Leaving the longhouse behind, the group walked on a short distance to the village. A handful of timber cottages were loosely arranged along a central thoroughfare; an uneven, hard-packed track dissected by an open ditch to catch and direct the rainfall away from the village. Smoke hung in the air trapped beneath the thick jungle canopy and chickens pecked at the ground. Villagers, many engaged on a variety of activities outside their homes, glanced curiously at the visitors but looked away shyly whenever any of their group caught their eye.

Rama broke away from the group to speak briefly with a villager. 'I need to find the *kepala kampung*, the village headman, to ask his permission for us to have a look around,' he explained when he rejoined them. They followed him further into the village until he located a group of men sitting on a raised bamboo platform at the top of the thoroughfare. 'I won't be a moment.'

Danni watched as Rama approached the men and after chatting casually for several minutes, he reached into his daypack and produced a couple of packets of cigarettes which he handed to the long-haired elder whom she guessed was the head man. There were smiles all round and some more chit-chat before Rama took his leave and rejoined Danni, Bel and Tim who were watching a young girl cracking candlenut shells open with a rock. She couldn't be more than six or seven years old Danni thought, but she worked with an efficiency borne of long experience.

'Okay, we have permission to look around now and visit their waterfall further down the trail.'

They wandered around the village with Rama stopping and explaining the various activities they came across. At one home, they watched fascinated as a young mother sat weaving thinly split palm fronds into a large basket. Despite the toddler sitting on her lap, her fingers moved rapidly so the basked took shape in front of the onlookers. There was nothing crude about her work; the basket was tightly woven into perfect shape and dyed fronds incorporated to form a delicate pattern.

'Rama, will you please tell her that her basketwork is the finest handiwork I've ever seen,' Danni asked. Rama translated for her and the young woman accepted the complement with a shy smile.

'She probably learnt her craft sitting on her own mother's lap just like her baby is,' commented Bel.

They moved along. There were several groups of women and children cracking candlenuts with rocks and hammers but the friends were most fascinated by one man who was working on his veranda processing cinnamon. As they watched, the villager used a sharp knife to dissect a large, thin piece of cinnamon into narrow strips which he set aside to dry. As he worked, Rama explained the process.

'Cinnamon is one of the main sources of income for the village. Here they call it *kayu manis,* which means sweet wood. The large piece of cinnamon he has there is actually the inner bark of the cinnamon tree. To harvest it they scrape off the outer bark then beat the branch or trunk all over with a heavy wooden club or the back of an axe. That loosens the inner bark to a point where they can prise it away from the woody portion of the tree. Once it's harvested, the cinnamon has to be processed immediately, whilst it's still moist, as he is doing now.'

'When do they roll it into quills?' Danni asked.

'They don't. The strips curl into quills naturally as they dry, a process that takes about four to six hours in good conditions.'

'Doesn't the harvesting kill the cinnamon tree? I mean essentially they're ring-barking the tree,' Tim commented.

'Yes they are but they don't leave the tree to die and in fact, this is the part of cinnamon cultivation that I find most interesting. Have you ever done some tree pruning at home and noticed how some trees will later sprout new growth where the tree was cut, and in many cases they'll actually sprout multiple new branches?'

'Yes, my parents have a several old WA peppermint trees in their backyard and dad is always complaining that every time he prunes back a branch they re-sprout five or six new branches in its place,' said Danni.

'Well the cinnamon trees are exactly the same and the growers use that to their advantage. Once a young tree is established they cut it off at ground level, which prompts up to a dozen new shoots. After a few years they'll take their first harvest from the tree, then cut it back to stump level, over the years they repeat the whole process again and again and each time the stump produces more and more shoots. With careful management of his plantation, a grower will always have some trees in the re-growth stage and others ready for harvest.'

'That's ingenious,' said Tim, echoing everyone's thoughts.

'Could we try a little cinnamon?' Bel asked.

Rama leaned down and spoke to villager, who smiled at his audience and gestured to a nearby stack of dried cinnamon quills. Bel retrieved a quill from the pile and brought it to her nose, inhaling deeply. 'Mmm, it's intense. Much stronger than the stuff we get in the supermarket at home.' She passed the quill around to the others to smell and when Danni broke a piece off and popped it into her mouth, it prompted another round of tasting. 'Wonderful.'

They said goodbye to the cinnamon worker and continued their circuit of the small village until they were back where they started from.

'Rama, how much of the forest are the Dayaks allowed to hunt, gather and cultivate?' Tim asked. 'It seems to me there must be a fairly delicate balance.'

'Absolutely. Just like the Australian Aborigines, the Meratus Dayaks consider the forest their motherland. For centuries they've lived in harmony with nature, using their local wisdom to manage and sustain the forest based on a three tiered system of land usage. The first is the restricted area, known as *katuan larangan*, where cultivation and farming is forbidden. Only resin and honey collection is permitted in this zone. The second zone is the communal forest, *katuan adat*, which belongs to the village administration and is partly open to agriculture. Villagers are allowed to farm crops and establish tree plantations such as rubber and cinnamon, and cut down trees for houses and firewood, with the exception of large trees with honeybees and resin. Finally there is *katuan karamat*, the sacred forest zone, which is reserved especially for spiritual and cultural reasons such as ancestral burial grounds. But just like the Aborigines, the Dayaks are facing a constant battle to hold onto their traditional lands against a growing demand for mining, timber and large scale commercial cropping. They've seen their traditional land holdings shrink; in some cases they've been re-allocated land many miles from their home village and often in quite inaccessible areas. They've been forced to abandon more traditional rice farming in favour of less labour intensive or land hungry crops. It's a situation which has forced a change to the Dayaks way of life and is one of the primary reasons they've had to look for other ways to supplement their traditional income streams. Unfortunately it's the same story all over Borneo, not just here in the Meratus Mountains.'

'It's the same story all over the third world,' observed Tim dryly. 'Unfortunately so called progress comes at a very high price for the hapless traditional land owners and peasant farmers.'

'Sadly that is the case,' said Rama sadly. 'Seen enough everyone? There's a small waterfall not far from here. We'll be there in nice time for a swim and our picnic lunch.'

Tim gave Rama a friendly slap on the shoulder. 'Sounds good to me. Lead the way my man.'

They headed out on another well-worn jungle path, walking in silence, each of them lost in thought. At one point they passed a husband and wife heading towards the village, both carrying a heavy, woven pannier full of candlenuts on their backs. They murmured polite greetings as they passed and hurried on to the village with the morning's harvest.

Danni enjoyed hiking through the jungle. Apart from the footfalls of her party, all was quiet. Sunlight trickled through the canopy, the light playing on the leaves creating a kaleidoscope of green, yellow, red and orange. Occasionally, she caught sight of a lizard scurrying across the leaf litter or a bird flitting from branch to branch. Here and there, she saw orchids clinging to the trunks of the trees, their delicate flowers almost incongruous in the shadowy understory. It was completely different to the hot, dry eucalypt forests Danni was used to back home in Perth, yet somehow she found the jungle comforting, felt embraced almost, by the giant buttress trees and dank warm air. When they stepped out of the jungle and into the small clearing at the waterfall, she felt an inexplicable sense of loss that left her momentarily disorientated.

'Are you okay Danni?' Rama asked, noticing Danni's hesitation when the others had rushed over to admire the small cascade.

'Yes, I'm fine…I just had the strangest feeling.' She shrugged, not sure just how to explain it, or even if she could. But when Rama looked at her quizzically, she felt compelled to try. 'It was like the jungle was embracing me, as if I was part of it. Except I wasn't quite me, just a mass of senses; sight, smell, hearing.' She laughed self-consciously. 'Sorry, I'm not making sense am I? Maybe there was something in the cinnamon…'

'Actually you could be right Danni. Herbalists and traditional doctors have believed for thousands of years that cinnamon induces a heightened sense of contentment and modern day scientists are well down the road to proving it improves brain function. Think about how the sweet smell of warm cinnamon buns brings on a feeling of well-being like nothing else.'

'Great, so I'm having a cinnamon high,' said Danni drily, causing Rama to chuckle appreciatively.

'The cinnamon you tried back there in the village would have come off the tree less than twenty-four hours ago. Being so fresh, it's a lot stronger than what you're used to,' said Rama.

'Hey what are you two doing?' called Bel. 'Come and have a swim.'

Rama and Danni dropped their daypacks on a big boulder at the edge of the plunge pool where Bel and Tim were already swimming. The waterfall wasn't overly high, perhaps only fifteen metres or so, but the water tumbled steadily over a series of smooth granite boulders before splashing into the crystal clear pool at the bottom. Gentle and inviting now, Danni had no doubt after heavy rains it would be a raging torrent. Danni stripped of her clothes and sandals, gingerly treading over the stony bank to the water's edge where she dipped in a toe and quickly withdrew it. The water was distinctly chilly. A few metres over, Rama slipped off one of the big boulders, straight into the water and with a few efficient strokes he joined Bel and Tim treading water in the middle of the pool.

'C'mon Danni. Don't be a sissy,' called Bel and was rewarded with Danni poking her tongue out at her. Bracing herself, Danni stepped into the water and slowly inched her way deeper until finally, feeling a little self-conscious, she pushed off the bottom and glided over to her friends. Within a minute her body adjusted to the cool water and she began to relax and enjoy her surroundings. She breath-stroked her way over to the cascades, moving under the falling water so it pounded down on her neck and shoulders like a natural spa. She felt around with her feet and found a small ledge and by pushing back against the granite rock face, was able to stand and retain her balance beneath the force of the water. Bel swam over to join her so Danni inched along the ledge to make room for her friend beside her.

'This is nice,' said Bel.

'It's lovely. You're so lucky to be staying here in Borneo for a year. I'm sure you'll get to do a lot more of this sort of thing.'

'Maybe, although I guess that all depends where Rama sends us.'

'Don't you know where you're going yet?'

'We do. We'll be based in a Dayak village on a tributary off the Mahakam River out from Samarinda, the capital of East Kalimantan. Pretty remote from what I can gather; we'll fly from Banjarmasin to Samarinda and from there it will take us a full day by river boat to reach.'

'Well it may not be like this but no doubt there'll be plenty to see, if you can get away that is. Do you get time off?'

'We do, but you've seen enough to know how difficult it can be to get around once you get away from the major centres. And depending on how things are going and what we're doing, you don't always want to just take off for more than a day or two. In our experience, you tend to live and breathe the volunteer work to a large extent and it's not easy to just switch off. Rama told Tim these few days he's taking with us is the first break he's had in two years, and even then he's combined the trip with a little work.'

'He seems very dedicated.'

'He is. When we first came across his NGO, Tim and I did quite a bit of research on him and his organization. He's got an excellent reputation in the aid world, both personally and in terms of the work his organization has been doing. Ultimately that's why we decided to throw our lot in with him. And the little we've gotten to know him so far, we haven't been disappointed. Plus he's absolutely gorgeous!'

'Bel!'

Bel put her hands up and laughed. 'What? I might be happily married to the love of my life but I'm not blind. And don't tell me you haven't noticed because I won't believe you.'

Danni looked across the pool where Rama was sitting in waist deep water talking to Tim. Even as a distance he was undeniably attractive. Actually she was a little disturbed by just how attractive she found him, but that was a conversation she wasn't going near. Instead she simply grinned and said, 'Alright, I'll concede. I'm not blind either.'

Once everyone had cooled off, Rama produced the food packs from his backpack and handed them each a brown paper package. Inside was a tightly bound banana leaf containing a meal of rice and vegetables topped with tiny dried fish which they ate straight off the banana leaf with their fingers. Despite being cold it was tasty and followed up with one of the small, fat local banana's, the meal more than satisfied the hunger they'd worked up with the mornings hike. After collecting everyone's rubbish and packing it away, Rama and Tim set off to climb to the top of the waterfall whilst the girls had another quick dip then lay on one of the big granite boulders to dry off and soak up the sun. Danni closed her eyes and was close to dozing off when a 'cooee', the quintessential Australian bush call, penetrated the air. Shielding her eyes from the sun she looked up and waved at the men standing at the top of the falls. They waved back then carefully started making their way back down, as Danni put her head back down on the pillow she'd fashioned from her bunched up shirt and closed her eyes again.

Whether or not she fell asleep she wasn't sure but the next thing she was aware of was Rama's voice in her ear. 'Wake up sleepy head.'

'I wasn't asleep,' she denied, forcing herself to sit up. 'Time to go?'

'Yep, we've got a bamboo raft to catch.'

Once everyone had donned their clothes and collected their belongings, Rama led the group off on another path Danni hadn't noticed before. They only had a short hike to reach the main river where two bamboo rafts were pulled up on the rocky shore ready for them. As they arrived, two young Dayak men stepped out of the shadow of the trees and came over to greet Rama with friendly handshakes. Rama introduced the men as their *joki's*, who would pilot them down the river and after smiles all round, they headed to the rafts and refloated them on the river. The rafts consisted of about twenty thick bamboo poles strapped tightly together to form a flat, six metre long deck. In the middle was a bench, made from more tightly strapped bamboo, its purpose as Danni soon realized was a seat that the passengers straddled, one in front of the other. Since Bel and Tim naturally wanted to ride together that left Danni sitting in front of Rama on the other raft.

The *joki's* showed them how to tuck their sandals under the strapping and where to hang on so that they wouldn't jam their fingers between the bamboo poles that would flex and move in rough water and once they were all settled, they pushed away from the shore into deeper water. Taking up their positions at the very front of the rafts, the *joki's* used a long bamboo pole to push and guide the rafts into the current and down the river, their skill and strength becoming evident very quickly as they hit their first lot of rapids.

'Hang on,' Rama warned as the raft speed up, lifting and flexing with the white water, lurching one way and then another. Their *joki* leaned heavily on his pole to keep them away from protruding rocks, others they just scraped over, the raft creaking and groaning in protest. As water rushed across the raft and splashed into her face, Danni held on to the strap on the front of the bench for all she was worth, both terrified and exhilarated, but when they emerged safely through the rapids she realized she was smiling broadly and laughed. The *joki* looked over his shoulder to check on his passengers and grinned at Danni who gave him the thumbs up sign, then turned around to watch Bel and Tim who were coming through the final stages of the rapids behind them. They too were grinning broadly and Bel whooped aloud to signal her approval. Their *joki* brought their raft alongside and Danni saw the two men grin at each other, obviously pleased to have appreciative passengers aboard.

'That was great fun,' said Bel, her face flushed and eyes shining. 'Is there much more of that Rama?'

Rama translated the question to the *joki's* who nodded and grinned some more and Danni got the decided impression that Bel had just sealed their fate. These guys were definitely going to give them a raft ride to remember. And it was a ride to remember indeed; for the beauty of the jungle, the crystal clear river, the adrenaline rushes as they shot more rapids and the tranquil sections where they simply drifted quietly and peacefully along with the gentle current.

It was during one of these quiet moments of the trip that Danni asked Rama how bamboo rafting had come about. 'It's a long tradition among the Meratus Dayaks, several hundred years at least,' he explained. 'Like most of Borneo the rivers were, and still are to a large degree, the easiest way to move about so the Dayaks used bamboo rafts to take their produce down to the lowlands to market. Bamboo is the obvious choice because it's plentiful, tends to grow close to the rivers, it's light and easy to handle and extremely buoyant. And because the mountain rivers are so shallow most of the time, a vessel with any draft is out of the question, so the flat bamboo rafts, or *lanting* as the locals call them, are perfect. There's also the added bonus of being able to easily dismantle them and sell the bamboo at their final destination because obviously they can't bring them back upriver against the current.'

'Is that what they'll do with our rafts at the end of the day?'

'No, more than likely they'll dismantle them and load the bamboo onto scooters to transport them back to Loksado for the next group of students or tourists that come along.'

'You're kidding!' The idea of transporting six metre long bamboo poles on a scooter seemed incongruous.

Rama grinned. 'No honest. Keep an eye on the rafts at the end of our trip and you'll see for yourself.'

Around one and half hours into the trip, the *joki's* guided the rafts to a rocky beach on the bend of a river where all six of them swam and had a competition to see who could skim rocks the farthest across the river, a competition soundly won by Danni and Rama's *joki* to much applause. After the break, their journey along the river continued for another couple of hours. Eventually they noticed a few farm plots on a distant hillside and shortly after that some thatched huts came into view along the river bank. As they passed under a hanging bridge, something Danni now recognized as ubiquitous to the region, their *joki's* guided the rafts to the riverbank signalling the end of the trip. As wonderful as it had been, everyone professed themselves ready for it to end as sitting on the hard bamboo benches for several hours, especially over the rapids, was hard on their backsides so there was plenty of good-natured moaning and groaning when they all stepped ashore. Their *joki's* had been good fun and despite the language barrier, they'd all enjoyed each other's company.

'Where are we?' Danni asked.

'Muara Tanuhi village,' Rama replied.

'Halo everyone!' Danni looked up to see Yusuf waving and walking towards them.

'Yusuf! Where have you been? You missed a great day out.'

'You certainly did,' agreed Bel. 'We've been hiking, swimming, visited a village and rafting of course.'

Yusuf smiled. 'I've been visiting with friends, but I knew Rama would show you a good time.'

'Well that he did. We've had such fun,' gushed Bel.

'Good, good. Now I've come to take you back to Loksado. My van is parked up there,' Yusuf explained gesturing towards his van.

After conferring with Rama, Bel, Tim and Danni pooled their funds for a generous tip for the *joki's* who were obviously pleased with the gesture and after warm farewells, they walked up the river bank to Yusuf's van to deposit their gear. No one was in any hurry to leave and Danni for one was more than happy to stretch her stiff muscles, so they lingered by a pergola in what appeared to be the village centre.

'Rama!' The call came from a young man holding a machete and walking towards them.

Rama acknowledged him with a wave and walked out to meet him. The two men exchanged warm handshakes and some conversation before Rama broke away and came back to the three friends. 'Would you like to come and have a look at one of my projects? It's fairly modest but you might find it interesting.'

They all agreed without hesitation and followed Rama across to where the young man was waiting. Rama introduced him as Kali and explained that he was one of the workers in the village owned project. They followed Kali to a work area further along the river bank where a group of young men and women were working together splitting bamboo poles into battens of varying sizes. The visitors watched with interest as one end of the long pole was propped into a forked frame stuck firmly into the ground. Using his machete the worker split the raised end of pole with a sharp whack, then pushed the blade down the full length of the pole to split it, then repeated the process several times until the desired batten size was achieved. The bamboo splitters worked with impressive speed, making the process look deceptively easy. The split battens were then cut to the desired length, bundled together with twine and stacked ready for market.

'The bamboo is harvested from the forest hereabouts then brought here for processing. The split bamboo then goes down to Kandangan, the closest big town to here, and from there it's traded further. This has been a really good project for this village because it has created a lot of jobs for the young folk, many of whom may otherwise have been forced to leave the village for work in the city.'

'So how was Helping Hands involved Rama?' Tim asked.

'As you can imagine, the villagers have been using bamboo extensively for centuries so they already know everything there is to know about harvesting and working with the stuff. However, there is a big difference between utilizing the naturally occurring bamboo forests for personal needs and harvesting commercial quantities. Compared to timber, bamboo grows very quickly, usually only three to five years to reach maturity but there are examples of over exploitation of bamboo forests all over Indonesia and other parts of Asia, sometimes to the point of completely wiping out them out. So the biggest part of my organizations involvement was ensuring that the same mistakes weren't repeated here. Apart from developing a plan for selectively harvesting the naturally occurring bamboo forests, we've helped the villagers re-establish bamboo forests in previously degraded areas. In other area's we've planted bamboo to help combat soil erosion. But propagating bamboo isn't easy because Indonesian bamboo doesn't generally flower or produce seeds; the locals establish new clumps from rhizome cuttings or by taking cuttings from the culm, the stem, itself. My organization not only helped negotiate the necessary government approvals, we also dug up some useful research and brought in some experts to help identify suitable locations to re-establish the bamboo forests and under the guidance of a principal researcher from the Indonesian Institute of Science, we're running ongoing trials into more efficient propagation techniques. There's also an NGO in Bali whose focus is the promotion of bamboo as a viable environmental alternative to timber. They've done a huge amount of work promoting bamboo internationally, preservation research, agro forestry projects, watershed reclamation, plantation development, policy development and providing education and training to local growers and other NGO's. We've sent several key people from the co-op down to their training centre in Bali and we receive on-going support from them which has been invaluable. On the business side of things we organized the village into a co-operative and establishing distribution channels for the product. Bamboo and rattan trading traditionally involves a lot of middle men between the supplier and the end-user so to ensure our co-op is getting the best price for their product, we've worked hard to weed out as many of those middle men as possible.'

'And who are the end users? What is the bamboo being used for?'

'Currently it's being used in building applications such as scaffolding or furniture. The battens are used to make trellises, bamboo fences and chicken cages. In the future there's potential for value adding and producing some of those products, or other products like chopsticks and toothpicks, right here in the local villages. Our people have even been learning how to make ply-bamboo at the Bali training centre.'

For Danni, Rama's commentary was both fascinating and an eye-opening. Unlike Bel and Tim, she didn't have the benefit of background research into Rama's organization so seeing and hearing about his work first hand was especially interesting and she was beginning to understand what had compelled her friends to commit twelve months of their lives to Rama's organization. The three friends and Yusuf accompanied Rama as he made the rounds of the work area where he inspected the raw material and market-ready products and spoke personally to nearly everyone there. By the time he said his goodbyes the sun had dropped below the tree line and was casting long shadows across the ground.

It was a pretty tired group that Yusuf delivered back to the Loksado. As Danni pointed out and everyone agreed, they had seen and done so much in just a single day. By popular choice they all elected to have an early dinner at the warung, followed by an early night so it was still dusk when they parted company outside their rooms after thanking Rama profusely for a wonderful day.

CHAPTER NINE

Taking Rama's advice to sleep in, when the village rooster woke Danni the following morning she stuck her head under the pillow, rolled over and tried to go back to sleep. Half an hour later she gave up and headed into the bathroom, bracing herself for another cold shower.

Morning ablutions finished, she let herself out of the room, quietly shutting the door behind her since there was no sound from the rooms beside her and she assumed her friends were still sleeping. Deciding to take a walk, she crossed the hanging bridge to the village and turned right; following the narrow track up passed the other bridge and a few village homes. There were a few villagers up and about but apart from one or two curious looks they just ignored Danni as she walked past. The track soon narrowed into a well-worn trail that followed the meandering river through the narrow valley. Apart from a few birds and the gurgling river, all was quiet and peaceful and just as the day before, Danni found the jungle comforting. When the trail turned away from the river and started tracking upwards, she hesitated for only a moment before deciding to continue. The higher she climbed, the steeper the track became until her legs started screaming in protest but determined to reach the top she pushed onwards. Her reward, on reaching the top of the ridge a short time later, was a stunning view across the adjacent peaks and the Amandit River curling through the valley floor below. From that height, Loksado looked like a miniature village with its smoking chimneys and tiny people moving about.

After resting for a few minutes she began the descent, taking extra care with her footing lest she strain an ankle on the way down. Back in the village, Danni crossed the bridge to the lodge but instead of going back to her room she walked down to the riverbank and bent down to splash some water on her face, washing away the light sheen of perspiration on her forehead. Kicking off her sandals, she perched on a rock and dangled her feet in the water, enjoying the feel of the bubbling water massaging her soles and sighing with contentment as she closed her eyes and raised her face to the sun. What a way to start the day she thought; beats battling it out in peak hour traffic.

At the sound of crunching gravel nearby, Danni snapped her eyes open and glanced around, seeing Rama approaching. 'I see you ignored my advice to have a sleep in,' Rama greeted her.

Danni grinned up at him. 'Couldn't. Apparently you didn't take your own advice either.'

'Couldn't,' he said, flinging her own answer back at her with a grin. 'How long have you been sitting here like a shag on a rock?'

'Not long. I've been for walk up there,' Danni said pointing to the adjacent ridge. 'Great view. Pity I didn't have my camera with me. And now I've been sitting here thinking about how much better it is to start the day like this rather than the commuter crush I normally deal with back home.'

Rama sat down on the river bank beside her, gazing at the ridge where Danni had pointed as he spoke. 'I don't think I could handle living like that. I've been working over here too long to go back to that sort of existence.'

'Have you ever worked in Australia?' Danni asked curiously.

Rama nodded. 'When I first graduated from uni as a junior intern with AusAid, the Australian Government Agency for International Development. I had to learn the ropes before they gave me my first international post.'

'Is that how you got into this line of work?'

Rama shrugged. 'That was the start of it but I think it was always destined by my background and events that happened.' Seeing the quizzical look on Danni's face he continued. 'Growing up with a white father and a Balinese mother always set me apart from my peers. Not in a bad way. I always had plenty of mates both in Australia and Bali, but I stood out. In Australia it was the way I looked but in Bali it was more that I had privileges most of my peers didn't. Dad wasn't a rich man, just a self-employed bricklayer who worked hard to support his family, but compared to the typical Balinese family, particularly thirty years ago, we were wealthy. I went to school in Australia, we owned a car, we had our own home and we travelled between Bali and Australia regularly. So yeah, compared to my Balinese friends and family I was the rich kid. We never flaunted our wealth, Mum was always very strict about that, but they did put it to good use to help my Balinese relatives.

It's surprising how little money and effort it takes to give someone a leg up. Dad spent a bit of time showing a couple of mum's brother-in-laws how to lay bricks and form concrete and some other trade skills and set them up with a bit of equipment and they ran with it. At first they just did small jobs but over time as their skills, confidence and business acumen improved they started winning bigger jobs. For the first time in their lives they were able to make a living outside the rice paddies and their village, they could send the kids to school and generally just lift their standard of living. And of course, the whole family and even the village benefited as more family members and neighbours were employed. Because they had access to good education, many of my cousins now have good jobs in other fields.

I saw all this happening as I grew up. Mum was always celebrating some new success or achievement within the family; a new cement mixer, a contract, a cousin starting school for the first time. It was a major celebration when the family managed to buy their first vehicle. It was a small truck, a bomby old thing that probably should have been retired years beforehand but I still remember Uncle Wayan giving all the villagers, kids and adults alike, rides up and down the village streets.' Rama smiled fondly at the memory.

'Anyway I went to uni and did a double degree in social science and economics. I got a job working for AusAid and was still in my internship when the first of the Bali bombings happened. The Australian Government moved quickly to provide emergency medical support but even after the initial crisis response they wanted to help the Indonesian Government improve health services in Bali as a lasting memorial to the Australian victims. Not surprisingly given my ethnicity and fluency in Indonesian and Balinese languages I was pulled into a team to help co-ordinate things on the ground in Bali. Then just as things were settling down the Indian Ocean tsunami hit. I was on the ground in Banda Aceh within days as part of the first AusAid contingency...' he trailed off, shuddering at the memory.

Danni reached across and squeezed his hand offering what little solace she could. 'That must have been awful,' she whispered.

Rama nodded and stared into the river, lost in thought. After a minute he gave himself a mental shake and squeezed Danni's hand appreciatively before breaking the contact and giving her a sad smile.

'Anyway, that's where I spent the next few years; disaster relief first then focusing on reconstruction and restoration.'

'Sounds like your time with AusAid was a real baptism of fire,' Danni observed.

Rama nodded ruefully. 'It was that. I saw more in those six years than I ever imagined I'd see in a lifetime. It was pretty stressful,' he added and they both knew that was a massive understatement.

'Is that why you left?'

'Yes and no. Despite the stress and the emotional trauma, my time with AusAid was a positive experience. We really were doing good work in the field and I learned a lot about international relations, program development and aid delivery but eventually I found the bureaucracy a bit stifling and decided I was better off working in a non-government organization.'

'But you've ended up running your own NGO now,' Danni commented.

'True. It wasn't something I set out to do. Like a lot of things in life it just happened. After AusAid I worked for a few different NGO's but I couldn't find one that fit my own ideologies in terms of their mandate or administration or both. You see, NGO's are filled to the brim with well-meaning, dedicated people but that doesn't always result in efficient or effective aid delivery. Others in my opinion are too patronizing, politicized or simply misguided in their efforts.'

Rama shrugged. 'In the end it just seemed logical to start my own NGO. I'd made a lot of good contacts during my time with AusAid and I managed to convince a few companies to put up some money or provide services at reduced or nil cost and the rest is history.'

'You make it sound easy but I'm sure it wasn't.'

'No it wasn't easy and I doubt it will ever be. No amount of funding or volunteers will ever be enough because there are so many people in need of help.'

'And what about yourself Rama? You've spent so much of your life helping other people, at what point do you start looking out for yourself?'

Rama looked at Danni askance. 'You know, no one has ever asked me that before.' He paused, considering his answer. 'Right now my needs are simple and the small wage I draw from Helping Hands is adequate. With no other demands on my time I can devote myself to Helping Hands and travel between projects as I need to but someday I would like to have a family of my own and things won't be so easy then. I suppose it is inevitable that eventually I'll have to employ more people to help me but I don't want to turn into one of those NGO's with top-heavy administration that sucks up funding that should be going to the people they're supposed to be helping.'

'Rama, you'll never let that happen,' said Danni with absolute conviction. 'Even in the short time I've known you I can see how dedicated you are and the connection you have with the people you help.'

He smiled up at her and reached across and gave her hand a quick squeeze. 'Thanks Danni, that means a lot to me.' And suddenly just like that, Rama was keenly aware of just how much Danni's opinion did matter to him. If only she wasn't already married…

***

Shortly after lunch, Yusuf collected the travellers for the next leg of the trip to Negara, a rural town located on a river of the same name in the lowlands to the west of the Meratus Mountain ranges. It was an uneventful drive, much of it backtracking on the same mountain road they had travelled two days previously. Once out of the mountains they turned westward, passing through rubber plantation country until the terrain flattened completely and rice fields took over. Several villages and several hours later they arrived at the reasonably large town of Kandangan where they would spend the night since there were no hotels at Negara. Yusuf navigated the streets with familiarity, locating the small guesthouse he knew. It was clean and tidy and as with the lodge, the travellers were allocated adjacent rooms.

The air was hot and still so when Rama told them they had a couple of hours to kill until their trip to the wetlands and Bel suggested going in search of ice creams, everyone agreed. Knowing the Indonesian's propensity for sweet things an ice cream shop wouldn't be far away. Since Yusuf had disappeared into the guesthouse they set of without him, sticking to the shady side of the street. Sure enough, within a few hundred metres they found a convenience store selling ice creams and cold drinks. Eating their ice creams as they went, they ambled slowly back to the guesthouse where they dragged the chairs from their little patios under a big banyan tree in the front yard and whiled away the rest of the afternoon chatting and lounging in the shade.

At four o'clock on the dot Yusuf re-appeared and after a flurry of activity returning their chairs and grabbing camera's and water bottles, everyone piled back into the van for the short drive to Negara. They drove out of town following a narrow road that traversed the levy banks above the flooded rice fields. Irrigation channels crisscrossed the country side and at every road crossing, locals dangled fishing lines from the bridges. The road passed through several villages where homes and shops were suspended on stilts above the rice fields hard up against the levy banks so the road served as the village common, footpath and playground.

On the outskirts of Negara, in front of a row of such houses, Yusuf pulled to a halt and bustled everyone out of the van. They scrambled down the steep levy bank behind him and onto a narrow, timber walkway between two village homes. One glance down between the gaps in the timber planks at the muddy brown water swirling below had Danni reaching for something to hold onto as she gingerly made her way to the waiting longboat. The water levels were obviously low at that time of the year as the roof of the longboat was level with the pier and it required a bit of scrambling and a helping hand from Yusuf to climb down into the passenger compartment. Only when she was safely on board did Danni realize the boat was of the same ilk as the crowded ferries she'd seen plying the river at Banjarmasin. What she hadn't realised then was that there was no seating aboard; passengers simply sat on the flat deck and with the roof barely a metre above their heads, standing was impossible. Thankfully on this occasion, they had the boat to themselves, Yusuf having arranged a special charter for them. Once everyone had scrambled in behind her, the driver pushed away from the pier, took his seat at the front of the boat and guided them out into the canal.

'This is different,' commented Bel, practically having to yell above the chugging engine.

'Glad we're not sharing with thirty other people,' Danni yelled back grinning. Turning her attention outside the boat, Danni peered through the open sides at the passing scenery. After the canal and river trips in Banjarmasin it all looked familiar although there were some subtle differences. For starters, Negara obviously experienced much bigger changes in water level as the simple wooden houses were perched on stilts high above the water, and unlike Banjarmasin where corrugated iron proliferated; most of the homes here were constructed of timber. Fishnets, suspended by the corners, hung from long bamboo poles poked out over the water so the owner simply had to reach out through an open window to lower the net. Frustrated with her low vantage point, Danni inched towards the back of the boat where the roof stopped just shy of the stern and she could stand.

'Climb up on the roof if you like,' said Rama behind her. 'Here, I'll give you hand.'

He helped Danni onto the low roof then climbed up behind her where they sat side by side with their legs dangling off the back. 'This is much better,' said Danni, appreciating the unobstructed view and the slight breeze at their backs as the boat chugged steadily through the canals. She waved to some children playing in the water on an old rubber inner tube and snapped off a photo as they waved back. Soon they left the canals and joined a larger river. They passed a dock where young men loading pineapples onto a small barge paused to watch them go by. Danni lifted an arm to wave and smiled back when they responded in kind. Long boats and canoes plied the waters; some brightly painted, others wearing the dull patina of untreated timber left to the elements. In the distance, the sun shone on a great golden dome of a mosque. Danni soaked it all in, imprinting every detail into her memory.

Beside her, Rama leaned back on his hands so he could watch her without it being obvious. He enjoyed her insatiable curiosity and the way her emotions played across her face; the wonder and the delight at all she was seeing and the genuine way she waved and smiled at the locals without a hint of self-consciousness. He itched to reach out and pull the loose tendrils of her hair away from her face, but he wouldn't do it, couldn't do it, for he knew Danni wasn't a free woman, not his for the taking. There was a husband at home waiting for her, although he wondered about their relationship. He knew about her husband's injury, Tim had given him a brief rundown when he rang to tell him Danni would be joining them in Borneo, but still he wondered. Why was Danni here alone, just as she was the day he met her in Sanur? If her husband's injury had been so bad he needed to go home, surely Danni would be with him? The warm, generous woman he was beginning to know wouldn't have left him to fend for himself of that he was certain. But he could speculate all he liked; it wasn't his place to ask. His place, it seemed, was to covet a woman that would never be his.

Danni leaned forward and poked her head below the roof line. 'Come up here guys,' she called to Bel and Tim. 'The view's much better.' When they appeared at the stern a few seconds later, Rama and Danni shuffled further along the roof to make space for them.

'You're right, it's much better up here,' said Bel, settling herself onto the roof. 'Oh look, we're entering the wetlands.' And she was right. The houses were thinning out set further back from the water's edge. Soon there was nothing but a vast, flat wetland thickly carpeted in swamp grass stretching as far as the eye could see. Water hyacinth grew in patches alongside the waterways and Danni watched fascinated as several locals harvested the crop from their narrow canoes. There were a few fishermen out and about, some casting nets from their canoes, others setting or retrieving fish traps. The puffy white clouds reflected on the water and the entire wetland glowed in the late afternoon sun.

'This is beautiful,' enthused Danni. 'Now I know why we came out so late in the day.'

Rama grinned, knowing he was about to drop a surprise on them. 'That and also because this is when the swimming buffalo of Negara come in.'

'What buffalo?' cried Danni and Bel in unison.

'The buffalo that live out here on the wetlands. See those structures over there?' Danni, Bel and Tim looked to where Rama was pointing off into the distance, noting the rough timber platforms perched above the water. Danni scanned the wetlands spotting more platforms. 'That's where the buffalo come home to each night. They spend their days grazing out in the swamp grass and each evening they swim back to these platforms to spend the night up out of the water. If we're lucky, we'll catch some of them as they return.'

'Oh I hope we get lucky,' said Danni, practically hugging herself with excitement. So do I, thought Rama, thinking he couldn't bear to disappoint her.

As the boat driver steered towards one of the platforms, Danni scanned the plain intently, hoping to spot the buffalo. Finally, just as the driver brought the boat to a halt near the platform, she spotted a small herd of buffalo slowly making their way towards them.

'Look, there they are,' she said springing to her feet.

'And look over there,' said Bel standing beside her pointing at a man standing in a canoe nearby. 'I wonder if he's the owner.' Danni had been so intent on the buffalo she hadn't even noticed him, but he seemed to be waiting and watching the buffalo so she supposed Bel was probably right. As she watched, he used a long pole to slowly push his way over to their boat where he, Yusuf and the boat driver smoked and chatted among themselves.

Slowly the buffalo came closer, alternatively walking through the long grass and swimming. As they neared the platform the man in the canoe poled away from their boat and positioned himself opposite the steep ramp onto the platform. Following the lead buffalo the herd plunged into the deep water and swam towards the platform, groaning and snorting, until their hoofed feet found purchase on the ramp and they heaved their great, lumbering bodies from the water. The herdsman moved in behind the herd, gently urging the stragglers on. When the last of them was safely on the platform, he climbed the ramp behind them and pulled a rail across to contain them, although none seemed inclined to leave. They were home for the night.

'That was worth coming to see,' commented Tim. 'Somewhat different to the cattle musters back home.'

'What an amazing place Borneo is. It just keeps throwing up surprise after surprise,' said Danni, shaking her head in wonder. Impulsively she leaned forward and caught Bel and Tim in a big hug. 'Thank you guys for bringing me here. If not for you I'd be sitting at home bored out of my brain right now. Instead I'm here having this wonderful adventure. I can't thank you enough. And you too Rama,' she added, smiling over her shoulder at him. But Negara hadn't quite finished with them yet; as they cruised back the setting sun turned the sky into a fiery orange blaze and Danni wore her smile all the way back to the pier.

That night Yusuf took them to a roadside warung consisting of nothing more than a rough wooden frame draped with tarpaulins and big canvas banner advertising the cuisine. They sat with the locals, on plastic stools at a long wooden bench where they ate heartily, enjoying the tasty, wholesome food. It was a family run affair; mum, dad and several kids all pitching in to serve the steady stream of customers. Looking around, Danni realised how much she enjoyed mixing it with the locals and the simple honesty in the way they lived.

The next morning after a breakfast of *nasi goreng* and fried egg, eaten straight off the waxy brown paper in which it was wrapped and delivered to their rooms, the travellers got away to a fairly early start. They made good time arriving at the Cempaka gem fields, the final sight-seeing stop of their trip, by mid-morning. On the way there, Rama explained a bit about the fields.

'South Kalimantan is well known as a diamond producer and there are several big mines in the province. Cempaka is probably the best known of the diamond fields, mainly on account of the *Tri Sakti,* meaning Thrice Sacred, diamond that was found there in the mid-sixties. It was massive in diamond, about the size of a grape, and a rare pink diamond to boot. There's been other big finds. One story has it that a local fisherman was looking for a stone to weigh down his net and picked up a 62 carat diamond worth US$100,000. They're the exceptions of course; most of the diamonds found at Cempaka are quite small but everyone lives in the hope of finding the big one. What's surprising about the Cempaka field is that it's still mined in the traditional way by hand, by locals so I think you'll find it an interesting experience.'

'Keep your eyes peeled to the ground girls,' Tim joked. 'You might find yourselves a nice diamond.'

'You might find something else too,' said Rama. 'As well as diamonds the field turns up gold, sapphires, amethysts, jasper and a lot of other semi-precious stones. The touts will be out so you'll have plenty of opportunity to buy yourselves a souvenir if you want.'

Bel and Danni looked at each other eagerly. 'Well I'm sure the diamonds will be out of my price range but I might be able to stretch to something a bit cheaper,' said Bel grinning.

'There goes the budget,' Tim grumbled good-naturedly.

As soon as Yusuf pulled up at the mine site the van was surrounded by eager touts, some offering their services as guides, others pushing fistfuls of semi-precious stones under their noses. They backed off as Yusuf and Rama both spoke sternly to them and only then did Danni get a chance to look around. The gem field covered a large area; a crater strewn, watery mess of mud and sand. Several crude timber sluices were perched on high ground above the pit but it was the miners down in the shallow pit that captivated her attention; digging at the muddy ground, chopping into the banks, others standing chest deep in muddy water swirling wash pans. It looked like a scene from some ancient excavation, the sort of thing you usually only saw in Hollywood movies.

'Jesus!' said Tim, mirroring all their thoughts.

'C'mon, let's have a closer look,' said Rama after giving them a few moments to make sense of the scene. 'Watch your footing,' he cautioned as they followed him across the uneven ground towards a group of men working nearby. In a deep shaft of sorts, several men were pounding crowbars into the ground, breaking the thick mud into chunks that others scraped into an assortment of rattan, tin, or plastic tubs that they hauled up the slippery slope to the sluices. Most of the miners took no notice of the group but a few looked up and acknowledged them with a nod. Rama spoke to a man who appeared to be in charge and then translated for the others.

'He said they've been digging this pit for several weeks now. It's turned up a few small diamonds and but nothing remarkable yet. But he says most diamonds are found at a depth of ten or fifteen metres so they'll keep digging until then. In another metre or two they'll hit water, so they'll pump it out of the shaft and up the hill to the sluices.'

'What happens if they don't find any diamonds at that depth?' Bel asked.

Rama spoke to the man again before he answered. 'They'll start tunnelling horizontally to see if they can pick up a deposit. If not, then they start another pit.'

Rama thanked the man then led the group up the slippery slope to the sluices where they watched the men dumping basketfuls of mud into the hopper. Using water from the pumps, the mud was gravity flushed down a long, narrow sluice box lined with timber battens to trap the heavy particles and rocks. What wasn't trapped flowed into a capture pit where more men were standing in the water swirling large wash pans of silt looking for smaller gems that may have escaped the sluice. After a while the sluice was stopped, the trap removed in sections and emptied of its contents which were carefully examined for a precious payload. Danni could almost sense the men holding their breaths in anticipation and she almost cried for them when their shoulders slumped with disappointment. 'Poor guys, it's a lot of hard work for not much.'

Rama nodded. 'Most of these guys just scrape by but they all live on the hope of striking it rich one day. But there are a lot of fingers in the pie. Half of whatever they find goes to the land owner and the village chief. And in the case of these guys here, they're working as part of a team so whatever is left has to be shared between them all.'

Tim was staring down the slope. 'What about those guys down there Rama? They look like there panning without a sluice.'

'They are. Let's go and have a look shall we.' They clambered down the slope to the muddy pool that had formed in the basin of the gem field. 'Believe it or not, those outfits back up there on the hill are the flash ones. These guys generally work alone or in pairs, panning mud they've scraped or gouged from around the pit or the muddy sediment that collects in here after heavy rain. It's not unusual for them to spend all day standing in the water swirling their pans over and over again.'

The travellers milled around, moving from one group of panners to the next until a shout of excitement went up and other workers nearby rushed to see the cause. Danni and the others hurried over, craning their necks to see over the small group that had gathered around a shirtless man who was climbing from the water. Carefully, he laid his pan on the ground and picked out a small stone, holding it up to the sunlight, rolling it between his thumb and forefinger as he examined it for faults. Satisfied, he grinned at the crowd around him and carefully handed it over to a woman Danni assumed was his wife. She wrapped it in a piece of paper then tucked it into a pouch and hurried away and slowly the crowd melted away with an extra spring in their step. Next time, they might be the lucky one.

'Seen enough folks?' Rama asked. When everyone nodded and they made their way back to the van where the hawkers were waiting for them. This time Bel, Tim and Danni were keen to have a look at their offerings and carefully examined the polished stones that were presented. Danni quickly looked past the sapphires and amethysts, preferring instead a large piece of black onyx which she decided would make a nice pendant and on a whim, tossed in some small polished stones in bright blue, red and orange, thinking maybe she could get them set into a silver bracelet. At US$5 for the lot, she was very happy with her souvenirs. Bel bought herself a lovely brown stone flecked through with tiny particles of gold that glittered and sparkled in the sunlight which like Danni she intended to have made into a pendant. They might not have come away with diamonds but both women were very happy with their purchases.

CHAPTER TEN

They arrived back in Banjarmasin around midday, all feeling slightly travel weary. After assuring Yusuf that they planned to spend the afternoon doing not much, he left them at the hotel and headed home to see his family. Bel, Tim and Danni were pleased when Rama elected to join them for lunch; over the past few days they'd all become firm friends and slipped into a comfortable foursome. From Danni's point of view, having Rama along made her feel less like a 'third wheel', aside from the fact she enjoyed his company immensely. But unlike the rest of them, Rama didn't have the luxury of being on holidays, he was here to work, a fact Danni was reminded of when he settled down in foyer to make some calls whilst the three of them checked back into the hotel and retrieved their luggage from storage.

After regrouping they decided to walk up passed the main market into the old riverside quarter, an area they hadn't so far explored. Keeping as close to the riverbank as possible, they skirted around the main market and warehouses until they reached the old bridge their boat rides had taken them under. Here they found themselves among porcelain sellers, their tiny stores crammed so full Danni wondered how anyone could possibly go in an out without sending the whole lot crashing to the ground. Passed the porcelain sellers they delved into a wooden and corrugated iron cloaked labyrinth of covered boardwalks, homes and tearooms. The air was hot and thick among the cramped confines but the locals seemed not to notice as they scurried along the narrow boardwalks whilst others lounged in doorways, smoking and gazing about with apparent indifference. To Danni, it was a strange and bewildering place that set her head spinning and her senses reeling. When they finally emerged on the other side she stood blinking in the bright sunshine, momentarily disoriented. Rama led them to a warung on the very edge of the old quarter, a rickety construction jutting out over the river that was clearly visible between the gaps in the planks at their feet. They sat at a vinyl covered table flanked by simple wooden benches, right beside a single rail that separated them from the fast flowing river, grateful for the slight breeze blowing across the porch.

'It's a bit rough looking I know but I assure you the food is good,' promised Rama, 'and I figured you'd rather look at the river than the street.'

'This is fine,' Tim reassured him and it was. They were becoming accustomed to the simple local food; the lack of pretence. Even the dilapidated surroundings had a sense of comfortable familiarity about them now.

Over lunch Bel, Tim and Danni discussed their options for the next week, appreciating the input Rama was able to provide. There was still more to see around Banjarmasin; a visit to the nearby islands; Palau Kembang where a troop of long-tailed macaques inhabited an abandoned Chinese temple or Palau Kaget for a chance of spotting some shy proboscis monkey's. Or they could head north into East Kalimantan province to the coastal cities of Balikpapan or Samarinda and take a three or four day boat journey up the mighty Mahakam River, one of the last remaining strongholds of traditional Dayak longhouse communities. From Samarinda, drift further north to stand on the equator near Botong, also the gateway to the Kutai National Park, home to wild orangutans, sun bear, deer, slow loris, proboscis monkey and other exotic species. Since Bel and Tim's mobilisation point for their volunteer work was Samarinda, heading north seemed logical; the only issue was transport and choosing between a long ten hour bus ride or a short domestic flight. For help with that they would need to find a booking agent but with plenty of time up their sleeves, they decided to finish their riverside walk and loop back to the hotel through the city centre.

'What's that over there?' asked Bel pointing towards a large gathering across the street. 'It looks like a market of some sort. Shall we have a look?'

The group nodded in general agreement and crossed the street to the market, realizing straight away that this was no ordinary market. Hundreds of bamboo and rattan bird cages containing thousands of birds were stacked three or four high on the ground or hanging from overhead beams. The air was thick with the musty scent of the avian captives and filled with non-stop squawking and chirping.

'Oh it's a bird market!' exclaimed Bel.

Tim let out a long, low whistle. 'I've heard about Indonesia's bird markets. Never seen one before though.'

Rama looked grim. 'Unfortunately Indonesia has many bird markets and I've seen more than I care too.'

'I once overheard some tourists in Bali talking about a bird market they'd visited but I've never been there myself.'

Rama nodded. 'There are a couple of big bird markets in Denpasar, although they were probably referring to Pasar Burung Sanglah bird market. It shares the same location as one of Denpasar's main traditional markets so tourists sometimes inadvertently find themselves at the bird market. Unfortunately over the years it's become a bit of a tourist attraction in its own right, many drawn to the exotic nature of the place.'

'I have to admit I'm curious to have a look myself if no one has any objections,' said Tim.

Although Danni wasn't a fan of bird-keeping, in her view birds should be flying around free, she had to confess a morbid curiosity herself and trailed into the undercover market with the rest of the group where they soon found themselves swallowed up in a labyrinth created by thousands of bird cages of all sizes hanging and stacked so closely together that in some places the group was forced to squeeze through in single file. It was hot inside under the tin roof and the scent of birds, faeces and dust was almost overpowering.

It was obvious that the standard of care for the birds varied widely from vendor to vendor. Many appeared well cared for in clean cages that they occupied solely or with only one or two mates. But other cages contained twenty or thirty or more mangy looking birds crammed into too small cages with faeces piled up inches high, dirty water and food dishes. With no perch to use the birds had little choice but to cling awkwardly to the bars on the side of the cage or sit among the dried faeces. All four friends were horrified.

'Rama, what are all the birds for?' Danni asked.

'It depends. Some are bought as pets or for breeding, others may be eaten. The lucky ones are bought then set free as a way of earning good luck as the Indonesian's can be a superstitious lot. Unfortunately a lot, particularly the rarer species, end up illegally traded overseas as pets. It really depends on the buyer.'

'But where do they all come from?' asked Bel looking around. 'There must be thousands of birds here.'

'Some are domestically bred stock but the majority are probably wild birds that have been trapped or stolen from nests as chicks. Do you remember we saw those people setting bird nets on our way up to Loksado? Well there's every chance whatever they caught has ended up here.'

'It's awful.'

'Yes it is but bird keeping is very popular throughout in Indonesia. Has been for hundreds, if not thousands of years. It's also somewhat of a status symbol too. The richer you are, the more exotic or rare the type of bird you're likely to own.'

Rama pointed to a cage of small, yellow breasted birds. 'These little finches are pretty but they're not particularly uncommon so they're cheap. In terms of status, they're very much entry level. Parrots are definitely a step up but they cost a bit more. Songbirds like the starling, the perkutut and other sunbirds are very popular, price depending on their age and rarity. Then you've got cockatoos, kingfishers, owls and even eagles. At the very top of the list is the highly endangered hornbill. In all the years I've been kicking around Borneo I've never seen one in the wild, yet I once saw two openly being offered for sale at the Pramuka bird market in Jakarta.'

'How do they get away with selling rare and endangered species so openly?' Danni asked and then held her hand up to stop anyone answering. 'No don't answer. I get it – corruption!' she stated flatly.

Rama gave her a sympathetic look. He hated seeing the disillusionment on Danni face even though she was right.

'Unfortunately yes. There's a lot of money involved and the illegal traders run very sophisticated operations. With the help of wildlife crusaders and the media there have been attempts by some officials to crack down on the illegal wildlife trade but it varies widely across the 1500 islands that make up the Indonesian archipelago. In some places illegal traders operate quite openly with relative impunity, in other places you won't find protected species on display in the markets but that's not to say you can't make a purchase if you're so inclined. The animals are simply kept out of sight in warehouses or at the trader's home. And don't think the problem is worse in the outlying regions. Jakarta's Pramuka bird market that I referred to earlier is widely regarded as the world's biggest illegal animal market and it's only a stone's throw from the nation's parliament.'

'It's not just birds either,' said Tim pointing to the adjacent stall. 'Look here. There are squirrels in these cages and a python over there.'

The four of them stared at the caged animals sadly. Bel shuddered. 'I'm with you Danni, this is awful. Let's get out of here.'

'Yeah I've seen enough too,' agreed Tim.

They turned and headed back in the general direction from which they'd come although it was impossible to be sure given the closeted environment. As they made their exit Danni tried not to look at the poor animals but her eyes were constantly drawn back to the cages.

'Oh my God!' she exclaimed suddenly, pointing towards a dark recess of the market. 'Is that an orangutan?'

'Where?' Bel squeezed up against her, peering in the direction of Danni's outstretched hand. 'Oh I think you're right.'

Tim and Rama quickly spotted the hapless animal also.

'Damn it,' Rama cursed and there was no mistaking the angry set of his face. It was the first time Danni had seen Rama's calm, even temperament desert him.

Turning her gaze back to the orangutan Danni realized with a start that Bel was already stomping off towards the orangutan with Tim hot on her heals. Rama set off after them with Danni trailing behind.

'Oh it's just a baby, poor little love,' she heard Bel say when she caught up. Sure enough, sitting in the bottom of a wire cage about the size of a small dog kennel, a small orangutan stared at them with huge brown eyes. Too young to have attained a full coat, the baby's dark skin and skinny limbs were clearly visible beneath the thin tufts of orange hair. There was a thin blanket in the bottom of the cage, meagre comfort for the poor creature and someone had placed some pieces of durian fruit in the cage but they were untouched. As they watched, the baby rolled onto her side and lay on the thin blanket. Apart from the rise and fall of her chest, she lay unmoving.

Danni felt sickened and she put her hand to her mouth to stifle a cry of alarm. 'Oh god that's awful. Absolutely awful. We have to do something.'

Bel nodded vigorously, 'Yes, we can't just leave her here.'

'Rama…' Danni appealed.

The stall holder, a middle aged man, had materialized by now and was watching their reaction curiously and without any apparent embarrassment or compunction about offering an endangered animal for sale. A woman, whom Danni guessed was his wife, sat on a low stool towards the back of the stall and watched on silently.

'You buy? Good pet. Very special,' said the man in heavily accented English.

'Rama, we need to do something.'

Rama stepped forward and spoke to the trader in rapid Indonesian for several minutes. Danni listened intently even though she couldn't understand a word they were saying. Feeling helpless, her frustration was growing by the minute. She noticed Tim giving Bel's hand a squeeze and realized they were feeling just the same. Finally Rama turned back to the small huddle Danni, Bel and Tim had formed.

'What did he have to say?' Bel asked.

Rama kept his voice low so they couldn't be overheard. 'Apparently the infant's mother was killed several weeks ago after she raided a palm oil plantation. One of the workers, this man's brother, rescued the infant and then passed her to him to sell. He's asking US$150 for her.'

'So let's buy her. I'll happily pay that to see her set free,' said Danni without hesitation.

Rama shook his head. 'It's more complicated than that Danni. For one thing, purchasing any animal from illegal traders just perpetuates the problem, no matter how good your intentions. The next issue is what to do with her if you did get your hands on her. She's too young to fend for herself and I'm no expert but she looks pretty sick to me.'

'But we can't just leave her here.'

'I'm not for one moment suggesting we do, but I think we need some help here. I've got a friend who works for the World Wildlife Fund. Among other things, animal rescues are a big part of what he does. Let's get out of here so I can give him a call.'

Rama spoke briefly to the trader then indicated they should leave. Danni and Bel gave the baby orangutan long sorrowful looks and followed the guys out with watery eyes. Back on the street, Rama pointed them to a nearby warung.

'Why don't you guys order up some coffee whilst I ring my friend?'

Rama looked grim when he joined them twenty minutes later. 'It's not good news I'm afraid. Jon is away up north with the rest of his team trying to intercept a shipment of gibbons and macaques they got a tip-off about. He's not sure when he'll be back but expects it won't be for several more days. Unfortunately, I don't think that poor baby has that much time left.'

'So we're on our own?' asked Tim.

'Not entirely. Jon's wife Maya has been working alongside him in this business for years so she knows her way around the illegal animal trade almost as well as he does. Fortunately she stayed home in Banjarmasin with the kids this time around. Yusuf is on his way to collect her now. There are no guarantees with this sort of thing but we stand a far better chance of success with Maya's help than we do on our own. But if, and it's a big if, we manage to convince the trader to hand the orangutan over to us we're going to have to get it to safety ourselves. Like most organizations that depend on donations for funding, WWF runs on a very tight budget. Jon and his team have limited resources and currently their vehicles and the volunteer vet are up north with him.'

It was over an hour before Yusuf arrived with a small Indonesian woman in tow. Rama stood to greet her and the two exchanged a quick hug.

'Maya, it's good to see. I just wish it was under better circumstances.'

Maya gave his cheek an affectionate pat and shrugged philosophically. 'Rama, you know as well as I do that there are no holidays in this business. Every day and every night Jon and I are on call. Now,' she continued, 'introduce me to your friends and tell me what you know and then we will work out our strategy.'

Rama made the introductions as Maya and Yusuf joined them at the table. Over more coffee Rama filled them in on the details. Maya listened carefully and asked a few questions of her own about the trader, his other stock and the condition of the baby. Despite her small stature, she oozed confidence and strength and Danni was very pleased to have her on their team.

'Okay Rama, from what you have told me I don't think we are dealing with an experienced illegal trader. For one thing, if he had contacts in the industry I think the baby would have been moved on already. Secondly they clearly have no idea how to look after the baby. Whilst illegal traders can be cruel and callous an orangutan is a valuable animal. It is worth far more to them alive than dead.'

'Yes, I think you're right,' agreed Rama.

'So in terms of trying to secure the poor animal's release this is a good thing.'

Maya turned and spoke briefly in Indonesian to Yusuf and then the two of them stood. 'Yusuf and I will go and find this baby and confirm what you have told us. For now it's better that we go alone. A Banjarese man and woman strolling through the market together won't raise any suspicions.'

Once again Danni and her friends had an anxious wait. Tim had his arm around Bel for moral support and Danni felt a twinge of envy, wishing Rob was with her offering his support. With a start, she realized it was the first time in days that she'd actually thought of Rob at all. Guilt washed over her but she pushed in aside. Right now there was enough to worry about.

Maya and Yusuf were back relatively quickly. 'You were right Rama. The baby is a very sick little one. We must move quickly although it may already be too late to save the poor thing.'

Rama, Maya and Yusuf conversed some more in Indonesian, obviously working through their plan of attack. Finally Rama stood and nodded to Danni, Bel and Tim.

'It's time now. Let's go see what we can do. Maya and I will do the talking. Please just stay in the background. I know it will be hard for you all, especially if things don't look like they are going our way but please don't get angry, don't interject or raise your voices. We don't want to inflame the situation or create a scene.'

All three of them nodded and once again they crossed the street and entered the market. This time Danni was so focused on rescuing the orangutan she didn't notice the smell or the stifling environment. Despite the labyrinth of bird cages, Maya led the group directly back to the traders stall without hesitation. The trader's wife was the first to notice the group descending on them. She motioned to her husband who turned and eyed the group nervously.

Although speaking Indonesian once again, Danni could tell from Rama and Maya's body language that introductions were being made and the two of them were trying to put the trader at ease. Danni was surprised to see Rama, who didn't smoke, pull a packet of cigarettes from his pocket and offer one to the trader who took it with a grin. Unable to follow the conversation any further, Danni turned her attention to the baby orangutan who was still lying in the bottom of the cage, staring at nothing in particular. She was no vet but to Danni, the baby's breathing seemed shallower and more laboured that it had been only a few hours before. When Danni stepped forward for a closer look the baby's gaze barely flickered. That's when Danni realized how close to death the poor thing was. She pressed her fist to her mouth to stifle a sob but there was nothing she could do to stop the tears that filled her eyes. She fumbled in her pocket for a tissue and hurriedly wiped the tears away but they kept coming and pretty soon the tissue was saturated and useless so she used her hand to brush the tears away instead.

Suddenly Danni realized the trader's wife was at her side. Wordlessly she took a key from her pocket and unlocked the padlock on the orangutan's cage then reached in, carefully lifted the baby out and placed her in Danni's arms. Stunned, Danni simply stared at the orangutan, then the trader's wife and back to the orangutan.

Ten feet away Rama, Maya and the trader were still deep in conversation, completely unaware of what had just taken place.

'Ah guys...Rama, Maya,' called Tim to get their attention.

In unison all three turned to stare at Danni cradling the baby orangutan. Rama and Maya looked delighted but the trader spoke angrily to his wife who was just as heated in her reply. Finally the trader nodded and turned back to the group, waving them away with the orangutan. Before she was herded out with the rest of the group, Danni caught the trader's wife's eye.

'Thank you,' she said simply.

The woman nodded in understanding and gave her a sad smile then busied herself about the stall, effectively dismissing Danni and the rest of the group.

Cradling the precious bundle in her arms, Danni was still in a state of shock and only dimly aware of climbing into Yusuf's van and the excited conversation going on around her.

'Oh my God, I can't believe that just happened,' said Bel.

'What exactly did happen?' asked Tim.

'Well it seems that whilst the trader was still trying to convince us to pay for the orangutan, his wife agreed with us that the baby was too sick to sell and would surely die without specialist care. So she took matters into her own hands.'

'Is that likely to cause trouble for her?'

Maya shook her head. 'No, the matter is already settled.' As she spoke Maya moved into the vacant seat beside Danni in order to give the baby a closer look.

'This little one is not out of the woods by a long way. The most important thing now is to get this baby back to my home where we have some things to help her.' Danni hugged the baby closer to her and prayed silently to God to save her.

On the outskirts of town Yusuf pulled off the main road onto a narrow gravel track running between some rice paddies. A few hundred metres along they reached a small group of modest village homes where some children playing on the roadside waved as Yusuf pulled up outside a double story concrete home.

'Okay here we are.' Maya slid the van door open and held a steadying hand out to Danni as she stepped down with the baby orangutan in her arms.

'Come, come, this way,' she said without waiting for the others. Knowing it was considered bad manners to wear her shoes inside, Danni hesitated at the door unable to undo her sandals without relinquishing her hold on the baby.

'It's okay, don't worry,' said Maya waving her inside, so Danni followed her through to a room at the back of the house. It was immediately apparent that this was a holding room of sorts for rescued animals with several cages spaced along the walls, a couple of cots that would normally be used from human babies and a big comfortable armchair in one corner. A small adjoining room contained a stainless steel table, a wide bench, shelves and cupboards that appeared to be stocked with first aid supplies; a basic but adequate veterinary treatment room. Both rooms were spotlessly clean and tidy and well lit from large windows.

It was the latter room that Maya waved Danni into, grabbing a soft blanket from a shelf and tossing it onto the bench. 'Come, put her down here.'

Carefully Danni laid the little orangutan on the blanket leaving a comforting hand on her shoulder. There was no hint of protest or struggle from the infant; she was too ill. Maya busied herself in cupboards then left the room briefly before returning with a large baby's bottle.

'Special formula,' she explained as she tested the temperature of the formula on the inside of her wrist, just as one would for a human baby. Satisfied, she brought the nipple to orangutan's mouth, slipping it between the baby's lips. There was no response. Maya clicked her tongue then withdrew the nipple so she could dribble some onto the baby's lips in an effort to entice her to taste the formula. Still no response. After several minutes of perseverance, the baby had still shown no interest in the bottle.

'This is not good. This little one is very badly dehydrated and almost starved. We must get fluids into her. If Alison, our vet was here she would have her on a drip by now.'

Maya shoved the bottle into Danni's hands. 'Here, you keep trying. I will try to raise Alison on the phone to see if she has any ideas.'

Lifting the bottle to the orangutan's lips, Danni tried again to get her to suckle to no avail so she gathered her up in the blanket and moved over to the armchair where she sat with the baby cradled against her chest. She dribbled some of the formula into the baby's mouth and detected an almost imperceptible movement from her. Bringing the bottle back to the baby's lips, she dribbled in some more formula. This time the infants response was unmistakable so Danni gently pushed the nipple between her lips and felt her heart skip a beat when the baby began to suckle.

'Yes!' Bel punched the air. 'Way to go Danni, way to go baby.'

Danni looked up in surprise; she'd been so focused on the baby since they arrived she hadn't even noticed they had an audience. Bel, Tim, Rama and Yusuf were grinning at each other, their relief as palpable as Danni's. Maya bustled back into the room, pulling up short at the sight of Danni nursing the infant. She came and stood by the chair, clicking her tongue with satisfaction as the baby suckled strongly. When Danni smiled up at her she gave her shoulder a squeeze.

'Good girl,' she said then turned to the rest of the group. 'Okay everyone, out now please. This little one still has a very long way to go. For her, no excitement, no stress. Rama you know the way to the kitchen. Take your friends and make yourselves some tea or coffee. I will join you shortly.'

Once the group had obediently left the room Maya returned to Danni's side. 'Once the baby has finished the bottle we need to examine her, give her a clean and I will administer some antibiotics.'

As the last of the formula drained from the bottle the baby closed her eyes and fell into a deep sleep, just as Danni had seen her nieces do after nursing. She stared down at the little brown face, the pale rings around her closed eyes, the tiny ears and the shock of orange hair and felt a rush of love for the hapless creature. Lifting her face Danni closed her eyes and made a silent promise to the baby's slain mother that she would do whatever it took to protect her little one.

Danni rose and took the tiny bundle back over to the bench that Maya had prepped, conscious that the other woman was watching her closely as she lay the still sleeping orangutan down. Maya reached out and clasped Danni's arm. 'Danni, I can see how much you care for this little one. But I must caution you that her chances of survival are slim.'

'We can't let her die Maya.'

'We will fight for her Danni, but ultimately her fate is up to God. Sometimes, despite our best efforts…' Maya left the rest of the sentence hanging but her meaning was clear.

'Is this how it always is?' Danni asked. 'I mean with the other animals you and your husband rescue? How do you keep doing it?'

'The question is how can we not keep doing it? For every animal that we rescue there are countless others that slip through the net.'

'But it must break your heart.'

Maya nodded. 'Yes it can and does regularly. But there are also joyous moments when an animal that we have saved is released back into the wild or at least placed into a protective environment where they will be nurtured and cared for over their lifetime. So when things get tough, we cling to those memories and hope we can create more like them in the future.'

The admiration Danni felt for this small, determined woman was immeasurable and she mentally shook her head in amazement. Over the next hour Danni assisted Maya whilst she gently examined, bathed and treated the baby. Apart from a few chafe injuries which Maya cleansed and applied antiseptic lotion to, there were no other visible injuries. The infant's biggest problem was malnourishment. After weighing the baby, Maya made a quick call to the WWF vet and then carefully measured the prescribed dosage of antibiotics and injected the infant after explaining to Danni that orangutans were very susceptible to human diseases such as influenza. After fitting her with a disposable nappy Maya stepped back declaring she was done. Amazingly the baby had remained asleep throughout the entire examination and was still sleeping when Danni, under Maya's instruction, transferred her to one of the cots and covered her with a furry blanket. When Maya secured a top over the cradle to confine the baby, Danni gave her a quizzical look.

'For her own safety,' Maya explained. 'Even with a full tummy she will be too weak to climb out but I've been surprised before.'

Finally Maya closed the curtains to darken the room and the two women quietly slipped out.

'Come. I'll show you where to freshen up before we join the others.'

Danni was surprised how much better she felt after the wash. Somehow the unpleasantness of the bird market and the stress of the past few hours washed away with the soap and water. Following their voices, Danni found the others on the front patio of the house. As she sat down beside Tim he threw a friendly arm across her shoulders and gave her a brotherly hug.

'Hey girl, how're you doing?'

Danni let out a long pent-up sigh. 'To be honest I'm feeling kind of wrung out.'

'That's not surprising,' said Bel. 'But you we're amazing in there. I'm really proud of you.'

Danni shook her head. 'No, Maya is the amazing one. I feel completely humbled by her.'

Just then two small children ran onto the patio and launched themselves at Rama who was perched on the patio railing. '*Parman, parman*!' they sang out excitedly. Uncle, uncle.

Rama bent down and hugged both children to him, lifting them off their feet. 'Bejo, Dian. It's good to see you. But boy you two are heavy now. Have you grown?' With exaggerated effort, Rama set the little boy and girl back on their feet.

Both children giggled and squirmed out of Rama's embrace to stand tall and proud in front of him.

'Hmm yes you have both grown. You must be eating all your vegetables.'

Maya joined them on the patio. 'Ah there you two are. I went to the neighbour's house to collect them and they came running back as soon as I mentioned you were here Rama,' she said with a fond smile at the children, then turning to the rest of them, 'These are my children. This is my firstborn Dian,' she said indicating to the pretty girl, 'and this is my baby Bejo.' Suddenly shy in front of the strangers the little boy clung to his sister's arm and nestled against her side.

'Nice to me you both,' said Bel with a big smile as she knelt down in front of them. 'Rama is right, you are both big children. Let me guess your ages. Hmm…Dian I think you must be six and Bejo, you must be at least four.' Danni could see Bel's experience as a school teacher coming to the fore as the children responded with wide-eyed amazement.

'Yes! How did you know?' Dian was clearly impressed.

'Well I'm a school teacher so I get to hang out with kids your age every day.'

Overcoming his shyness, Bejo stepped forward. 'I started going to school this year.'

'Did you now? What's your teacher's name? My students call me Ms Masters but,' she said with a conspiratorial wink, 'since we're not at school you can call me Belinda, and this is my husband Tim and my friends Danni and Yusuf.'

Bel continued chatting to the children who now the ice was broken, were bombarding her with questions about her school and her students and hanging off every word.

'Bel's very good with children,' Danni commented.

'Yes she definitely seems to have a natural rapport with them,' agreed Rama. 'She'll do very well with the local kids. With Tim's background as a builder and their overall experience, I'm certainly glad to have their services. Its people like that who make it possible for NGO's like mine to continue the work they do.'

Maya agreed. 'Yes it's the same with WWF and the support team that Jon and I have. Without them we wouldn't have a hope.'

'How hard is it to get volunteers?' Danni queried.

'A lot depends on the NGO and their mandate. Correct me if I'm wrong Maya but I suspect WWF has no shortage of volunteers because the kind of work they do, campaigning for and saving endangered animals, has a lot of public support and the organization has a fairly high profile. As volunteer work goes it is perceived as rather glamorous although the reality is actually far from it.'

Maya agreed. 'That is true to an extent. There is never a shortage of would-be volunteers but despite the best of intentions not everyone who applies has the necessary skill set. It's not about quantity of volunteers, more so the quality of volunteers. You see unless they have a specific skill set that we need, a well-meaning westerner who doesn't speak the local language, doesn't understand local customs or culture and in a lot of cases can only make a short-term commitment, is much less effective than a local person. Keeping in mind of course that labour in third world countries is very cheap, so NGO's can usually afford to pay a small wage to a local person and in doing so they get more bang for their buck, they provide much needed jobs and training to the locals and effectively empower them to one day take ownership of the issues themselves.'

'Plus there is some risk involved in foreign volunteers,' Rama added. 'Not everyone who offers their services has altruistic motives. There have been some horrifying scandals involving NGO's and volunteer behaviour. Paedophiles volunteering at orphanages to gain access to children, men taking advantage of the under-privileged women they're supposed to be helping, theft, criminals using NGO's as a front to hide or facilitate illegal activities. Fortunately these kinds of issues are few and far between but no good NGO will take on a volunteer without putting them through a rigorous application process and running background checks. All that takes a lot of time, effort and money. Then after all that, you'd be surprised how many volunteers arrive in country only to find they just can't cope with the conditions, the culture or being away from home, family and friends. Nearly every NGO has stories of volunteers who turned tail and head for home within a week or two of arrival. That's why a lot of NGO's like mine require volunteers to cover their own airfares and travel costs.'

'Yes, I get that,' said Danni. 'I have to confess that I've never given any thought to volunteering until I met Bel and Tim and yourselves and now I realize I don't really have anything to offer anyway. I feel rather useless to be honest.'

'You're being too hard on yourself Danni. Do you know the biggest hurdle most NGO's face is funding, or rather lack of funding. Most rely on donations or grants and expend an inordinate amount of time and effort looking for and trying to convince potential donors to support their cause. Plus there's only so much money to go around so it is very competitive among NGO's. With your marketing background you'd be a great asset and I for one would love to have you on my team.' Rama grinned and gave her a gently nudge, 'I just have to figure out how to convince you to join us.'

Danni grinned back without commenting. She could see the truth in Rama's words and her mind raced with possibilities but at this point she wasn't ready to make any sort of commitment. It was one thing to be all inspired when she was right amongst things in Borneo, quite another keep the torch burning when she returned to her normal life in little more than a week's times. And right now, her primary concern was for the little orangutan fighting for her life in the back room.

'Maya, what happens now with Sweetie-pie?'

'Sweetie-pie?' Rama grinned and raised an eyebrow.

Danni grinned, 'Well we've got to call her something.' Which Rama acknowledged with a shrug but his eyes twinkled with amusement.

'The next few days are critical for her,' answered Maya. 'It's good, very good, that she has taken a bottle but we won't know for a while how her body will respond. She's so badly malnourished that her body may have suffered permanent damage.'

'I just can't understand how anyone could cage and starve an innocent creature like that,' said Danni with disgust.

'Most of the time it's ignorance. I don't think the trader or his wife or whoever had her before that willfully starved poor Sweetie, in fact they gave her to us once they accepted that she was dying but they simply didn't understand her needs. Did you notice the pieces of durian fruit in her cage? Sweetie had no hope of eating that. Orangutans don't start weaning from their mothers until around three years of age. Yes they will start trying to eat certain soft types of fruit from about three or four months of age when their first little milk teeth come in, but the fruit must be chewed and ground up by their mothers first and it's really only a taste. Most of their nutritional needs are derived from their mother's milk.

Orangutan babies are very similar to human babies in a lot of ways. At her age Sweetie would normally feed at least five times a day but given her current state Alyson our vet, has recommended smaller, more frequent feeds. She's concerned about overloading her system.'

'Maya you can't manage that on your own, particularly not with the kids to look after too. Please let me stay and help,' Danni offered without hesitation.

Maya looked relieved. 'I was hoping you would.'

Tim, who had been listening to Bel and the children's conversation on one side and the adult conversation on the other, piped up. 'We're all keen to help Maya. Danni since you've already made a start with Sweetie, why don't you take the night shift then Bel and I will be here bright and early in the morning to relieve you.'

'Maya, if it's okay with you I'll stay and give Danni a hand overnight,' Rama offered.

'Thank you all. Between us Sweetie-pie will be in good hands.'

With that settled the assembled group made moves to head off in their various directions. Bel and Tim left with Yusuf, Maya shooed the children inside to wash up and then took Danni and Rama back to Sweeties room and after giving them strict instructions to first clean their hands with sterilizing solution, showed them how to make up the special formula before leaving them to it.

Sweetie didn't appear to have moved at all but was awake and Danni felt she was taking a little bit of interest in her surroundings although it may have been wishful thinking on her part. Rama opened the top of the crib and held the bottle whilst Danni gently scooped up Sweetie and moved over to the big armchair. After making herself and Sweetie comfortable, she took the bottle from Rama and held her breath as she offered it to Sweetie. To her relief, Sweetie didn't need any coaxing this time and suckled on the teat without hesitation. Danni and Rama grinned delightedly at each other.

Rama perched on the arm of the big chair watching Sweetie feeding. It was a casual intimacy, in no way sexual, but Danni's senses zinged with awareness. She could feel the heat of his body and stir of his breath on her neck and when her body tightened in response she felt a creeping sense of guilt that set off an internal dialogue. Don't be stupid she admonished herself. You haven't done anything inappropriate and nor has Rama. Okay so you find him attractive. So what? You're married, not blind. Doesn't mean you're going to act on it. But even as she debated with herself, Danni couldn't quite shake a nagging sense of disquiet.

A sound of sucking air pulled Danni's attention back to Sweetie whom she was satisfied to see had finished the bottle and was staring up at Danni with big, fathomless brown eyes. Danni murmured softly to her and gently stroked her cheek with the back of her finger. 'Hello little one. You're going to be okay now. We're going to take care of you,' she murmured. Sweeties eyes flicked across Danni's face, almost as if she was trying to decide whether or not to trust her. Gently Danni drew her closer and when Sweetie turned her head slightly, Danni was sure the infant was listening to her heartbeat. The surge of love and protectiveness that swept through her was so strong she caught her breath.

When Rama stood and went to the bench to spread a towel and then straightened the blankets in the crib, Danni took it as her cue to get Sweetie ready for bed. Just as Maya had shown her earlier, Danni changed Sweeties nappy then tucked her into the crib, giving her face one more gently stroke before closing the top. Sweetie watched her through the bars for another minute or so before her eyes drifted closed. Only then did Danni leave her side.

'You have a way with her,' Rama said softly.

'Not really. She's had such a trauma that right now I think Sweetie would respond to anyone who shows her a bit of love and kindness.' Danni shuddered, 'I hate to think about what's she's been through.'

Rama agreed. 'That's behind her now. Let's just concentrate on getting her well again.'

'But what's to become of her after that? Where will she go?'

'Once she's passed this critical point, she'll be transferred to one of several specialist Orangutan rehabilitation centres that we have here in Kalimantan. She'll get the best of care there and they'll do everything they can to equip her with the skills she'll need to survive in the wild. There's no guarantee that she can be released, that all depends on how well she does, but ultimately that's the aim for every orangutan that enters the system. Some make it, some don't. The worst case scenario is that she remains in a protected environment with dedicated carers and surrounded by other orangutans. It's not ideal, but even if that comes to pass Sweetie will still be one of the lucky ones, one of the few that actually got rescued.'

Danni didn't know whether to feel relieved or cry and it must have been written all over her face because Rama placed his hand in the small of her back and nudged her towards the door.

'Come on, I think you need to take a break whilst you can, get a bit of fresh air. With two to three hourly feeds scheduled we've got a long night in front of us.'

They found Maya talking on her mobile phone. She waved and mouthed 'Jon' to them so Danni gave her the thumbs to indicate all was well with Sweetie-pie before they left Maya to her call and wandered back out onto the patio. The children, cleaned and dressed in their pajama's and slippers were playing with a skipping rope and paused to wave at the two adults as they sat down to watch.

'Their English is very good,' Danni commented indicating to the children.

'As you've no doubt gathered their father Jon, is an *orang putih*, a white man. He's English. Been knocking around Indonesia for the WWF for at least ten years. He met Maya way back in the early days, married her and never left. The kids have never known anything other than a bilingual household so they just slip in and out of Indonesian or English without a thought.'

'Actually I've been surprised how many of the kids and young adults we've met do have a basic grasp of English.'

'That's because English is part of the school curriculum in Indonesia. Plus there's a constant stream of English language television content, subtitled in Indonesian of course but inevitably most youngsters pick up a least a few English phrases.'

'Well I'm impressed anyway. Despite our multicultural reputation, very few Australians have a second language.'

Maya came onto the patio with her usual determined stride. 'I take it all is well with Sweetie-pie?'

Danni grinned. 'Yep, she took the bottle straight away and drank the lot. I think she even looked at me.'

Maya clapped her hands together happily. 'Excellent. Maybe, we got to her in time after all. Jon was thrilled to hear she is hanging in there.'

'Any word on when he'll be home?' Rama asked.

'Not for a few more days yet, it's not going so well,' Maya said grimly. 'Now it's time I fed everyone I think.'

'Can I do something to help?' Danni offered but Maya waved the offer aside on the basis that Danni had a long night ahead of her.

Later Danni and Rama joined Maya and the children for dinner in the family living room. The meal of spicy noodles, chicken and vegetables followed by fresh fruit and sweet tea was simple but delicious. Afterwards, Rama played with the children whilst Danni helped Maya clean up and later when Sweetie-pie's next scheduled feed coincided with the children's bedtime, Maya once again left that task to Rama and Danni. As before, Sweetie took to the bottle well and suckled strongly causing the little flicker of hope in Danni's heart flare just a little bit brighter.

Maya came in as Sweetie was finishing the bottle and like Danni, felt that Sweetie-pie seemed just a little bit brighter and showing some interest in her surroundings which was a good sign. Danni smiled happily at the precious bundle in her arms, feeling the tension and adrenaline that had been coursing through her body since she first spotted Sweetie at the market ease out of her, only to be replaced by deep weariness. When Maya saw her stifle a yawn, she offered Danni the use of a spare bedroom and Rama offered to take the next feed but Danni was adamant about staying with Sweetie. So in the end, Maya brought in a thin foam mattress and a couple of blankets for them and after checking the supplies to ensure Rama and Danni had everything they needed to get Sweetie through the night, she bid them goodnight and left them to it.

It wasn't until after Danni and Rama had re-settled Sweetie into her cot that it occurred to Danni that she would actually be spending the night alone with Rama, a realisation which left her feeling a little awkward. Although the circumstances were perfectly innocent, Danni had never slept alone in a room with any man other than Rob.

'Do you want the mattress or the armchair?' Rama asked.

'I'll take the armchair if you don't mind.' Lying on a thin mattress on a hard tiled floor didn't look too comfortable.

'I don't mind.'

Danni stifled another yawn and stretch her arms up over her head.

'Danni why don't you grab a nap before Sweetie-pie's next feed? I'll wake you when it's time.'

'Thanks, I think I will.' Danni gave him a tired smile, then curled up in the armchair under one of the blankets Maya had supplied and promptly fell asleep.

***

'Danni, wake up.' The soft masculine voice and a gently hand on her shoulder penetrated her sleepy cocoon. 'Danni.' There it was again. Reluctantly she dragged her eyelids open to find Rama leaning over her. It took a full second to remember where she was but once the fog cleared she sat up with a start.

'Sweetie!'

'She's fine,' Rama assured her, 'but it's time for her next feed. I'm happy to do it if you want to go back to sleep.'

Danni shook her head and let her feet drop to the floor. 'I'm okay. I'd like to do it.'

'I thought you might,' said Rama tenderly, 'but stay there, I'll bring Sweetie to you.'

Gently, Rama lifted Sweetie from her cot and placed her in Danni's arms, then passed her the bottle he had already prepared. Sweetie suckled eagerly as soon as Danni placed the nipple between her lips.

'Thanks Rama, but you should have woken me sooner so I could help.'

'No need. Preparing the bottle is no trouble. Besides, you looked so out to it I didn't have the heart to wake you any sooner.'

'Did you sleep?'

Rama shook his head. 'No, I just rested in between checking on Sweetie.'

There was much excitement when they changed Sweeties nappy.

'Oh Rama, I think she's done a little wee!' exclaimed Danni.

'I think you're right. That has to be a good sign.' They grinned delightedly at each other until Danni burst out laughing.

'Look at us celebrating a wet nappy. Anyone would think we'd won the lottery.'

'Nah, this is better than a lottery win.' Rama reached out and tenderly stroked Sweetie's arm and not for the first time, Danni marvelled at what an unusual man he was; in fact quite unlike anyone she'd ever known.

By the time dawn rolled around Danni was exhausted. Some people managed quite well with short power naps but she wasn't one of them. Having to drag herself out of a deep sleep every couple of hours was exhausting in itself so in the early hours of the morning she gave up trying to sleep at all. Rama didn't seem inclined to sleep either so the two of them passed the hours talking softly about anything and everything. Sweetie-pie continued to improve steadily with each feed and although she was still too weak to move around, sometime in the wee small hours Danni looked across at the cot and found that Sweetie-pie had turned her head towards herself and Rama and was watching them.

Bel, Tim and Yusuf arrived just after six o'clock in the morning, Tim announcing that the 'Cavalry have arrived.'

After quietly checking on Sweetie-pie they were thrilled to see the change less than twenty-four hours had made. Bel hugged Danni enthusiastically. 'Oh Danni, she looks so much better. Has Maya seen her this morning? What does she think? Is she going to make it?'

Danni laughed tiredly and held her hands up to stave off any more questions. 'Whoa, slow down Bel. Yes Maya came in earlier this morning to check on her and like Rama and me, she's feeling optimistic. Maya was quick to remind us that she's not a vet, but for my money she does have a lot of experience nursing sick animals so her opinion means a lot to me. But Sweetie is still so weak she's very vulnerable to infection and other problems. It's going to be a long road back to health and she needs a lot of TLC.'

'Well we're all here to help her,' said Bel, 'and I just feel it in my bones that she's going to be okay. Now Danni you look exhausted and Rama, you don't look much better. We knew you wouldn't get much sleep last night, that's why we came early to relieve you. So show us what we need to do so we can take over and let you guys get some sleep.'

Rama and Danni ran through the bottle making process and hung around until Bel had Sweetie-pie feeding strongly, then said a quick goodbye to Maya on their way passed the kitchen as they headed to Yusuf's van. Feeling bone weary, Danni put her head back against the seat and closed her eyes, oblivious to the city stirring with a new day. It was only when the van slowed and bumped its way over hotel's rough driveway that she opened her eyes.

Rama jumped down from the front passenger seat, slid the rear down open for her and helped her out. 'You look done in Danni,' he said sympathetically.

Danni answered by way of heavy sigh and a tired grin, but when she noticed the concerned look Yusuf was giving her over his shoulder from the driver seat, she made a better effort. 'Nothing a few hours' sleep won't fix. Thanks for coming to get us Yusuf and for your help yesterday.'

'No problem Danni. It was a very bad business so it was my pleasure to assist.'

Danni smiled and nodded in acknowledgement, then turned back towards the hotel.

'Get plenty of sleep,' Rama told her. 'We don't have to be back to relieve Bel and Tim until this evening. I'll give you a ring later today to give you an update on Sweetie-pie.'

'Thanks Rama. Until later…' Danni stepped through the wide door the hotel concierge was holding open for her and took the elevator straight up to her room. She was too tired to worry about breakfast so after a nice hot shower she closed the curtains to darken the room, hung the Do Not Disturb sign on her doorknob then collapsed into bed and was instantly asleep.

***

Sometime later, Danni became aware of a shrill ringing somewhere close to her head. It took a few moments to realize it was the telephone and in her half dazed haste to answer the call she fumbled and dropped the handset down beside the bed. By the time she retrieved it she was wide awake.

'Hello.'

There was a low, masculine laugh on the other end of the line. 'Dropped the phone did you? Guess you were still sleeping.'

Rama! 'I was,' said Danni without any rancour. 'What time is it?'

'Two o'clock in the afternoon.'

Danni sprang up into a sitting position on the edge of the bed. 'You're kidding.'

'Nope, afraid not. Sorry I woke you though, I thought you would be up by now.'

'No I'm glad you rang. I need to get a few things done before we head back over to Maya's. By the way, any news?'

'Yes, I just got off the phone to her. Sweetie-pie is doing well, starting to show more interest in her surroundings and even moving around a little. Maya has been in touch with the vet again who recommended increasing the volume of Sweetie-pie's bottles but reducing the number of feeds so the good news is we should get a little more sleep tonight. '

'Oh that's fabulous,' said Danni enthusiastically, then clarified herself. 'I mean for Sweetie-pie, I'm not worried about the lack of sleep.'

Rama laughed. 'It's okay, I know what you meant. Anyway, before we head back over there, how about we grab an early dinner somewhere? That way Maya doesn't have to worry about feeding us, although I'm sure she wouldn't mind.'

At the thought of food, Danni's stomach grumbled loudly, reminding her that she hadn't eaten since dinner time the previous evening. 'Sounds like a plan.'

'Okay, I'll swing by the hotel for you at five. See you then.'

Needing something to hold her over until dinner time, Danni made herself a cup of sweet tea, selected some of the bright red, spiky skinned rambutan from the complementary fruit basket in her room and dragged a chair out onto the small balcony so she could watch the comings and goings along the river whilst enjoying her picnic. A gentle breeze swept across the water and over Danni, cooling her skin and bringing the rhythmic chug-chug of the longboat engines to her ears and lulling her into a deeply relaxed state. It was only a nagging sense of responsibility that forced her to leave her balcony view and pick up the telephone.

Danni dialed Rob's mobile phone and waited through a series of clicks and buzzes and several rings before her call connected.

'Rob Pollard,' her husband answered in his usual brusque manner.

'Rob, it's me.'

'Danni! Where the hell have you been? I've been worried about you.'

'Sorry Rob, I didn't mean to worry you. I did warn you I may be out of touch for a few days.'

Rob grunted, then softened. 'Yeah well I was just worried when I hadn't heard from you.'

'Well like I said, I am sorry. But I've got so much to tell you,' Danni said excitedly, going on to tell him all about Sweetie-pie's rescue. Unfortunately Rob didn't quite share her enthusiasm.

'Jesus Danni, are you mad? I can't believe you would let yourself get mixed up in something like that!'

Rob's angry reaction left Danni momentarily stunned into silence. Finally she asked, 'What on earth do you mean by that?'

'I mean I can't believe you would get yourself mixed up with the illegal animal trade. You could have put yourself in danger and frankly I have to say, this is exactly the sort of thing I was worried about when you took off with Tim and Belinda.'

Danni's surprise at Rob's anger was swiftly replaced by her own anger. 'That's completely out of line Rob. For starters, this wasn't a sophisticated illegal trading network, just a couple of locals trying to take advantage of a situation they found themselves in. Secondly, Rama and Maya, the lady from the WWF, assessed and handled the situation and as for Bel and Tim, whatever you're implying is unjustified. I've never met a less selfish couple in my life. For that matter, the same goes for Rama and Maya. But you know what, none of that matters because there's no way I could have walked away and left Sweetie-pie to die in some cage in the market and lived with myself.'

'Come off it Danni. Since when did you give a hoot about animal welfare and helping out the less fortunate?'

'That's unfair Rob. I may not have spent my weekends volunteering at animal shelters or soup kitchens but I've always cared. You make it sound like I'm a heartless bitch. Do you really think so little of me?'

'Well you weren't exactly acting like a concerned wife when you took off to Borneo and left me to fend for my crook leg myself.'

'Oh there it is,' said Danni sarcastically. 'That's the crux of it isn't it? Good little wifey didn't go running home with you when your leg got infected after you ignored her pleas to see a doctor in Bali and stay out of the water. You and I both know you could have stayed in Bali and gotten your leg treated there but once surfing with your mates was off the agenda, you decided to cut your losses and go home. Apparently spending your days hanging out with me instead wasn't particularly appealing. The truth of it is had you not been injured, you'd still be spending your days surfing with your mates and leaving me to my own devices. Either way I was still going to be on my own.'

'It's never bothered you before. I thought you liked hanging out with the girls.'

'You know what Rob, the fact that you'd rather spend time with your mates instead of me has been bothering me for a long time. But I've been so busy making excuses for you that wasn't ready to admit before now.'

'Nicely done Danni. Congratulations on turning the tables and making me out to be the bad guy.'

Suddenly Danni felt the fight go out of her. They had both said things that they would probably regret, but on the other hand maybe they needed to be said. But right now, on an international call, thousands of miles apart, was not the time. 'Look Rob, this conversation isn't going anywhere. I didn't ring to have an argument. I actually thought you'd be interested and share some of my excitement.'

Sensing Danni backing off, Rob adopted a more conciliatory tone. 'Yeah well, like I said I was worried about you. I'd appreciate it if you checked in a little more regularly in future.'

Danni bit back a retort, saying instead, 'I'll be here in Banjarmasin for at least another few days I expect. I'll call you in a couple days and in the meantime you've got my number here at the hotel if you need to get in touch with me.'

'Righto.'

They lapsed into an awkward silence, both struggling to find their way back to neutral territory. 'Listen I'd better go Danni, I'm still at work and I have a few things to do before knock-off time.'

'Okay Rob, I'd better go too. I need to give mum and dad a call. Talk soon.'

'Yep, talk soon. Bye.'

The call to Rob left Danni shaken and upset. His attitude towards Sweetie-pie's rescue surprised her. No one would ever accuse Rob of being a bleeding heart but neither was he mean spirited or unfeeling. Mistreatment and abuse of animals or people upset him as much as it did Danni and in her heart of hearts she honestly believed that Rob would no more have walked away from Sweetie than she could. So that left Danni with the uncomfortable conclusion that what was really bothering Rob was that Danni was having this adventure without him. Apparently it was okay for him to have trips away with his mates but when the shoe was on the other foot there was a definite double-standard at play. Well buggar him, she thought, he'll just have to get over it. But despite her bravado, deep down Danni knew it really wasn't that simple. Like most couples, they had their occasional blow-up but for the most part their relationship was steady, caring and respectful and Danni certainly didn't want to jeopardize that. There was no denying though, that this Borneo trip would mark a change in their relationship, one that would require some adjustment by both of them. But they weren't insurmountable issues and once she returned home to Perth, Danni was confident they could sort them out.

Feeling a little better, Danni put in a call to her parents.

'Hello.'

'Hi Dad, it's Danni.'

'Sweetheart! It's good to hear your voice. Hang on a sec, I'll get your mum and put you speaker phone.' There was some muffled noise at the other end of the phone whilst her parents got themselves sorted.

'Hi honey. Where are you calling from?' The sound of her mother's voice instantly lifted her spirits and her earlier enthusiasm to share her adventures came rushing back.

'I'm still in Borneo. Banjarmasin to be exact. I assume Rob told you where I was. He promised he would.'

'Yes he called around a few days ago and filled us in on your plans. I must say we had no idea where Banjarmasin was; your father had to look it up in the atlas. You're a bit off the beaten track.'

'I guess I am. Actually I've just gotten back from a trip into the hinterland region which was fabulous.' Danni proceeded to fill her parents in on all that she'd seen and done since arriving in Borneo; the canal trip, the floating market, the Dayak villages, the swimming buffalo and the diamond mining at Cempaka.

'Sounds like you've been having a real adventure.'

Danni laughed. 'I sure have. This really is an amazing place and I'm so glad I came. But I haven't told you the best bit yet.' After Rob's reaction Danni was a bit nervous as she relayed the details of finding and rescuing Sweetie-pie, but she needn't have worried. Her parent's unconditional approval nearly brought a tear to her eye.

'That's fabulous Danni. I'm really proud of you. I'd say the little orangutan was very lucky you and your friends found her when you did.'

'Yes Maya thinks we got to her just in the nick of time. I can't wait to see how she's improved during today.'

'So you're going back?'

'Definitely. Sweetie-pie needs twenty-four hour care for at least a few more days. Maya can't do that on her own since she's got two small kids to care for as well as manning the WWF office so Bel, Tim, Rama and I have all volunteered to look after her. We've got a roster worked out; Bel and Tim on days, Rama and myself on nights.'

'What happens to her after that?' her father asked.

'Rama seems to think she'll go to an orangutan rehabilitation centre. Unfortunately, her situation isn't uncommon so there are several of these centres operating in Kalimantan. The aim is to return the orangutans to the wild but it's not always possible. Either way, Sweetie will be well cared for.'

'Well love, you've certainly got a story to tell when you get home. Speaking of which, when are you coming home?' her mum asked.

'I've still got a bit over a week of holidays left and I'm keen to see more of Borneo so I'll be using up every one of those days. Apart from that I don't have any fixed plans. I've left it to Rama, Bel and Tim to set the itinerary since they know so much more about the region than I do. I think Rama needs to get back to work but Bel, Tim and I may go further north to a place called Balikpapan and spend a few days travelling up the river on a *klotok*. That's what they call the larger riverboats here. Further north again there's a national park we might visit but we'll have to rough it. Over here on the Indonesian side of Borneo there aren't any flash resorts so it's all pretty basic, but that's part of the appeal I think. Borneo conjures up all sorts of images of explorers gamely hacking their way through the jungle, or paddling dugout canoes along some unknown river with a posse of natives and frankly even today it's not so hard to get a sense of that. Personally I would have been disappointed if I'd found the place too well developed.'

'My daughter the adventurer,' Bill teased.

'You should see me in my pith hat and safari suit,' Danni quipped.

'Well love, I'm pleased you're having a good time and I know your brother will love hearing about what you've been up to. We'd never admit it to Rob, but your dad and I and Chris and were all pleased you decided to continue your holiday without him. Doesn't hurt to remind him not to take you for granted.'

'Probably not. He's not too thrilled about it,' Danni admitted.

'Giving you grief is he?' Trust her father to read between the lines.

'A little, but not so much that I'm going to rush home. He'll get over it.'

'That a girl, stick to your guns. Rob's not a bad bloke, he just needs a bit of shake up to help him realize what's important.'

'You're right dad. I've been slowly coming to that conclusion myself. But I don't blame Rob; he's never stopped me doing anything because until now I've never wanted to step outside the square. And in all fairness I can't expect him to adjust his thinking overnight though I'm sure he'll will in time. He has to really, as I just can't see myself being happy to spend future holidays lying around on the beach in Bali. On the flip side though, Rob loves his surfing and all that boy stuff and I can't expect him to give that up. We just need to compromise a bit.'

'That's true of any relationship love, just be sure it's not all one sided,' said her mother firmly. 'Now listen, it's been lovely chatting with you honey but we've been on the phone for ages. I hate to think what this call must be costing you.'

'Hmm you're right. I just had so much to tell you though. Say gidday to Chris and Jenny for me and tell them I've got lots of photos to bore them with when I get home.'

'Will do and we'd love to see your photos too.'

'I'll organize a slide show at my house for everyone once I'm settled back in,' Danni promised.

'Alright love. Take care and give that orangutan of yours a pat for me.'

'Thanks dad. Love you both.' Danni hung up with a broad smile on her face. The long chat with her folks was just what she'd needed to cheer herself up. Good old reliable mum and dad!

CHAPTER ELEVEN

Danni showered and dressed and organized a bag of washing for the hotel laundry service to collect then sat back out on the balcony to write a postcard to Emily who would be home from Bali by now. She struggled to fit all her news on the back of the postcard so the result was a fairly succinct narrative that would no doubt leave Emily with more questions than answers, but at least she had made an effort which Em would appreciate. Whilst she was in the postcard writing mood, Danni penned one to her four year old niece knowing Nicola would be thrilled to receive her very own mail. Danni was down in the lobby arranging postage with the receptionist when Rama arrived for their dinner date.

'Hey, you look well rested,' Rama said by way of greeting. And she did. Wearing a form fitting singlet, loose Bombay style cotton pants, strappy sandals and a silk scarf around her ponytail Danni looked young and fresh and alluring and not for the first time Rama thought what a beautiful woman she was.

'I could say the same for you. I think we both had our eyes hanging out of our heads this morning. I don't know about you but it's been a long time since this old married woman has pulled an all-nighter,' Danni laughed.

'Can't say I've ever been an old married woman,' Rama joked. 'But I know what you mean. My nights of partying until dawn are a distant memory too. Apart from an occasional crisis at work I prefer to be tucked up in bed well before midnight.'

'So are you ready to go? There's a good little restaurant about ten minute's walk from here and I've organized for Yusuf to pick us up from there in an hour.'

'As long as the food is good and there's lots of it I'm happy,' said Danni, falling into step with Rama. 'I'm absolutely famished. Apart from a few rambutan I haven't eaten since dinner time last night.'

Rama grinned down at her. 'I'm sure Ahmed, the owner will be able to do something about that.'

They walked on in companionable silence, Danni's attention drawn to the street scenes around her, now and again slowing or pausing to peer into a shop, stall or the food on a peddler's cart. Rama adjusted his stride to match Danni's, happy to indulge her fascination with the everyday life in Banjarmasin. Danni stopped to examine some seafood smoking over a charcoal grill on the sidewalk, watching as the cook brushed everything over with a thick, brown marinade before quickly and efficiently turning everything over and repeating the exercise. The aroma of the smoky marinade and the sizzling seafood was heavenly.

'Smells delicious.'

'It tastes as good as it looks too as you'll discover,' said Rama. 'This is our dinner spot.'

Before Danni could respond a large Banjarese man emerged from the restaurant and descended on Rama with such boisterous enthusiasm that Danni took a step back to make some room.

'Rama my friend. It is wonderful to see you again,' he said grasping Rama's hand between his own and pumping it up and down.

'And you to my friend,' Rama responded warmly. 'How is your family?'

'Very good. Life is good. My oldest child is about to graduate from high school, praise Allah, but I also think praise Rama.'

'I'm glad everything is working out for you.' Rama chuckled then gestured to Danni. 'Now let me introduce you to my friend Danni. She's visiting from Western Australia. Danni, this is Ahmed, owner of this establishment.'

'Ah yes I saw that you brought a beautiful woman with you,' said Ahmed as he turned to Danni and repeated his enthusiastic hand-pumping exercise with her. Danni bit down on her bottom lip to stop herself from giggling. 'You are a very lucky woman to have such a good man as Rama.'

'Oh we're not—'Danni's protest died on her lips as Ahmed continued.

'Welcome to Banjarmasin Miss Danni and welcome to my restaurant,' said Ahmed gesturing around him. 'You will be my very special guest. Tonight you will enjoy the best food that Banjarmasin has to offer.'

The radiant smile Danni wore was half in response to Ahmed's expansive personality and half in response to the wink Rama shot her. 'Thank you Ahmed. I'm looking forward to trying your food. It certainly smells nice.'

Still clasping Danni's hand, Ahmed led them into the dimly lit restaurant which was decorated in a jungle theme consisting of rough-hewn tables and chairs, mud rendered walls decorated with traditional hand-woven mats and Dayak artefacts. A large bamboo frame was suspended from the ceiling and draped with creeper vines. Tall bamboo in pots and traditional fish traps were strategically placed around the room to partition the large space and provide some privacy to the individual tables. Noticeably absent from the tables were the gaudy plastic serviette dispensers and condiment bottles that seemed to grace every other table in Kalimantan, at least in Danni's experience.

'Oh Ahmed, it's just lovely,' Danni's praise was genuine.

Ahmed beamed with pride. 'Okay, now you sit here please and then tell me what you wish to drink.'

Rama and Danni sat opposite each other at a small table at the front of the restaurant from where they had a good view of the street and the grills at the front of the restaurant. Deciding against an alcoholic drink with a long night caring for Sweetie-pie in front of her, Danni ordered a fresh lemon and lime juice whilst Rama opted for a beer. After personally taking their drinks order Ahmed relayed it to the young waitress hovering nearby and passed them each a menu. Realising it was written in Bahasa Indonesian, Danni handed the menu straight back to Ahmed.

'Ahmed, I think I can trust you to bring me your very best chefs special.'

Ahmed beamed with delight. 'For you Miss Danni, only the very best, and Rama what do you fancy?'

Rama looked at Danni and Ahmed then closed his menu. 'Ahmed, like Danni I will leave it you to choose.'

Ahmed clapped his hands together happily. 'It will be very good, you will see.' And with that he bustled off to the kitchen.

'He's a bit of a character,' Danni commented with a grin.

'He sure is. I think he gets more effusive every time I see him,' laughed Rama.

'How long have you known him?'

Rama thought for a minute before responding. 'About five years now. Ahmed was one of the first people my organization helped and has since become one of our best success stories.'

Danni was intrigued. 'Tell me about it.'

'When I met Ahmed he was selling seafood from a mobile cart or what the locals call a *kaki lima,* meaning five legs in reference to the wheel and two stands on the cart plus the vendors legs. He had a little charcoal brazier on which he grilled fish, octopus, prawns and sometimes lobster but what made it really delicious were the marinades he used. Anyway, Ahmed's daily route took him past the guesthouse where I keep a room when I'm in Banjarmasin and I became somewhat of a regular customer. We started to chat and eventually I got to know his situation, which was pretty difficult to say the least and I realized I was in a position to help him out through Helping Hands.'

They were interrupted momentarily as the waitress shyly set their drinks on the table in front of them. *'Terima kasih,'* Danni said giving her a smile. Thank you. She took a long sip of the cool, sweet, tangy drink then sat back in her chair.

'Wow. It's a heck of leap from cart vendor to restaurateur.'

'Yes it is. Running a mobile cart is an awfully hard way to make a living. Believe it or not, you don't just buy a cart and set up shop. Most vendors serve an apprenticeship of sorts learning how to make *bakso* or noodles or spring rolls or whatever. Then when they're ready to go out on their own they rarely have the funds to buy a cart so they have to lease one instead. By the time they've paid the lease, bought supplies like gas or charcoal and purchased ingredients most are lucky to net fifteen or twenty percent of their daily takings, which can vary tremendously from day to day. Some days they do okay, other days they're lucky to cover costs. Little wonder most cart vendors barely scrape together a decent living.

It's hard work too. A cart vendor's day can start at 5am to visit the market for fresh supplies followed by a couple of hours of food preparation. Then he'll have breakfast and rest for a couple of hours before heading out on his route. Typically the route is short-haul covering a few blocks but he'll likely go around four or five times in the course of a day, covering up to four or five kilometres in all, pushing or pulling a heavy cart the whole way. In Ahmed's case he would have to swing home to restock between routes because without refrigeration he had to keep his seafood stock alive in a rudimentary wet tank set-up he kept at home. Most days Ahmed worked his route until 6pm or evening prayer time. And because vendors mostly just scratch out a living they can rarely afford to take a day off. They're out there working their route day in, day out, rain or shine.

Anyway, when I got to know Ahmed I realized how tough he was doing it. He had a wife and three children as well as his elderly mother to support. But he also had dreams of one day owning his own restaurant as unlikely as it seemed, but sometimes dreams are all people like Ahmed have to cling to.'

Danni shook her head sadly. 'That's a tough way to make a living. I really had no idea how hard the *kaki lima* have worked for the few rupiah that I've spent with them over the years. In Bali, I suspect most tourists buy *bakso* or grilled corn cobs from a cart vendor just for the novelty value, never realising how much effort the vendors have put in for so little reward.'

'Unfortunately that's true of so much work and enterprise in Indonesia and other third world countries. So much effort, just to eke out a living. That's the poverty cycle and that's what NGO's like mine are trying to break, one person, one family, one village at a time.'

'So what's your strategy Rama? How do you lift someone like Ahmed up from cart vendor to restaurateur?'

Unfortunately the question went unanswered because Ahmed was trooping towards them with two waitresses in tow and carrying a long platter which he ceremoniously placed on the table between Danni and Rama. A large whole fish was propped upright in a wooden stand, providing easy access to both sides of the succulent grilled flesh. Around the fish a bevy of prawns, baby octopus and a sand crab, conveniently halved, the whole lot garnished with chopped red chilli, shaved carrot and coriander leaves.

'Oh Ahmed, it looks and smells divine,' enthused Danni.

Two young waitresses stood behind Ahmed both holding trays loaded with dishes. Ahmed turned and retrieved two small bowls from one of them. 'Two of my special marinades to have with your seafood.' He reached for more bowls, 'Saffron rice and a fresh salad of mango, cucumber, coriander, lime juice, chilli and a little palm sugar to sweeten.'

He stood back beaming expectantly at Danni and Rama. 'Well Ahmed, I think you have outdone yourself,' said Rama.

'I'll say,' seconded Danni, 'although I don't know how we'll possibly get through it all.'

'You will not be able to resist, you will see,' predicted Ahmed confidently. 'Now we will leave you to enjoy your meal in peace.' He turned and bustled away, shooing the two waitresses ahead of him.

Once Ahmed was out of hearing, Danni whispered quietly to Rama. 'Seriously, how on earth are we going to get through all this?'

Rama grinned. 'Let's at least make a decent dent in it or Ahmed with be devastated. Besides, I thought you were famished.'

Danni was already filling her plate. 'I am but a girl's got her limits.' She bit into one of the large prawns and groaned. 'Hmmm yum. I think my limit just shifted. I don't know what Ahmed puts into his marinades but that is delicious.'

'Told you so,' said Rama smugly as he turned his attention to the food on his plate.

With the arrival of their meal, their previous conversation was forgotten. They ate in companionable silence apart from commenting on the various elements of the meal, every bit of which was perfectly cooked and very tasty. The mango salad was crisp and light, a perfect foil for the smoky, grilled seafood and the complex spices in the marinades. Despite Danni's concerns, she and Rama devoured almost everything on the table. The young waitresses were attentive throughout, refreshing their drinks, removing the seafood scraps and finally bringing them wet towels and a bowl of lemon scented water in which to wash their fingers after the messy task of de-shelling the seafood.

'Rama that meal was delicious. How do I say that in Bahasa Indonesian? I'd like to thank Ahmed properly.' Rama told her the words which Danni repeated a couple of times so when Ahmed came to the table she turned to him and said, '*Terima kasih* Ahmed, *makanan lezat.*' Thank you Ahmed, the food was delicious. Danni's tongue stumbled over the unfamiliar words so she finished with a self-conscious laugh but Ahmed obviously understood her because he clapped his hands together delightedly and beamed.

'Well done Miss Danni. I am happy you enjoyed your meal and that you learn a little of our language. Rama, you must teach her more.'

Rama inclined his head. 'I will,' he promised.

'Now, would you like dessert? Rama I have your favourite *Bingka Barandam.*'

Rama laughed. 'You know me well Ahmed but,' he said patting his stomach, 'I couldn't possibly eat another thing. What about you Danni?'

She shook her head. 'No I'm full but I'm intrigued to try some of this *Bingka Barandam.* This is the second time I've heard it's your favourite Rama so it must be good. But not today; I'll come back and try it before I go home Ahmed. Besides, we have some friends to meet very soon.'

'You have more friends here Rama? You must bring them to my restaurant!'

'I would Ahmed but it's a little bit complicated at the moment. We are all sharing the care of an orphaned orangutan for the next few days at least.' Rama quickly explained the situation to Ahmed who shook his head gravely. 'The people of Borneo must stop this terrible business. Rama, you must tell me if you need some help. I can send my daughters to help you care for this baby.'

'Thanks Ahmed, I'll keep in mind.'

'Okay but now, you must tell your friends where to find my restaurant. I will look after them very well.'

'Ever the businessman Ahmed,' Rama laughed. 'But yes I will tell them to come. However right now I see Yusuf is waiting for us across the street so we must get going.'

Ahmed signalled for their bill which one of the waitresses quickly brought to the table. Danni reached for it as did Rama, their hands meeting on the billfold. 'Rama please let me get this.'

'No Danni, this is my treat.' Rama opened the billfold and scanned the bill. 'Ahmed, I hope you haven't given us a discount? You know how I feel about that.'

Ahmed sighed sadly and spread his hands wide. 'Rama my friend, it is always my pleasure to feed you and I would gladly do so without charge, but alas I have come to accept that you will not allow it to be so.'

'My reward is seeing you doing so well Ahmed and that you continue to work with my organization.'

Danni was rather intrigued by the exchange and made a mental note to quiz Rama about it later on. Leaving him to sort out the bill she went to use the bathroom, pleased to find spotlessly clean, western style facilities complete with scented hand soap and a stack of tightly rolled cotton hand towels. Over the previous week, out of necessity she'd gotten used to using the Asian style squatter toilets but they were one thing about Borneo that she wouldn't miss.

Danni rejoined the men who were chatting by the restaurant entrance as they waited for her. Making their goodbyes, Rama shook Ahmed's hand. 'Until next time Ahmed.'

'It was lovely to meet you Ahmed and I promise to come back before I go home to Australia,' said Danni genuinely.

Ahmed captured her hand between his. 'You are most welcome anytime Miss Danni and perhaps Rama can persuade you to stay in our country.' He gazed expectantly at Danni and she just didn't have the heart to tell him she and Rama weren't romantically involved.

'We'll see,' she said noncommittally.

They were saved from a more drawn out farewell when another couple stepped into the restaurant and with a final 'Farewell my friends,' Ahmed turned his attention to the new arrivals. Danni and Rama exchanged grins as the other couple were swallowed up in Ahmed's natural effusiveness then headed across the road towards Yusuf who was leaning against the van smoking a cigarette whilst he waited for them. Seeing them approach he straightened, snuffed out his cigarette and lifted an arm in greeting.

'Good evening Rama, Danni.'

'Hello Yusuf, I hope we haven't kept you waiting too long.'

'No problem,' he said sliding the van door open for Danni. To her surprise, Rama climbed in behind her and sat beside her rather than riding up front with Yusuf.

'How was your meal?' Yusuf asked as he eased the minivan into the traffic.

'Lovely. That was probably best seafood meal I've ever had. I'd love to know what Ahmed puts into his marinades.'

'Yes I hear that comment often from other people I have brought here,' said Yusuf.

'Tourists you mean?' Danni asked curiously.

'Yes tourists. Often they ask me for recommendations and of course I take them to Ahmed's.'

'Of course.'

They reached Maya's house just a little after six and found Maya, Bel, Tim and the children relaxing on the front patio. The children immediately descended on Rama, literally hanging off him as he made the short walk from the van to the patio but he didn't seem to mind in the least. After the adults exchanged greetings Danni was straight down to business.

'How's Sweetie-pie doing?'

'Wonderful! You wouldn't believe she's the same sick little orangutan we rescued yesterday. With good nutrition, the antibiotics and a stress free environment she's coming on in leaps and bounds,' Bel gushed. 'She's not long had a feed so you're off the hook for another couple of hours but why don't you go and look in on her anyway.'

Danni smiled. 'I think I will.'

'Me too,' said Rama extricating himself from the children.

They slipped through the house and quietly let themselves into the back room, treading softly to the cot where Sweetie-pie was sleeping under a light rug. The curtains were drawn to block out the late afternoon sun but even in the dimness, the improvement in Sweetie-pie's condition was obvious. Instead of lying prone on her back, limbs flung out as she had done, Sweetie was curled onto her side, one tiny fist drawn up to her face. Her breathing, previously shallow and erratic was now deep and regular. For all the world, she looked like a contented baby.

To her embarrassment Danni's eyes filled with tears and she tried to blink them away. Rama glanced at her and moved to the treatment area, returning with a tissue that he held out to her without a word. Danni took it from him and wiped her eyes. 'Sorry, I'm not normally a cry-baby.'

'No need to apologize. You have a soft heart Danni, compassionate, that's nothing to be embarrassed about.' The irony of Rama's comment was not lost on Danni. She was still smarting over Rob's insinuation that she was uncaring, heartless even, and although she knew the comments had been flung in anger but they still stung.

'Maybe, though I'm not sure everyone would agree,' she murmured then instantly regretted it when the comment drew a sharp glance from Rama. Danni wasn't about to air her marriage woes with Rama or anyone else for that matter but thankfully he chose to let the comment slide. Instead he said, 'Come on, let's leave Sweetie sleeping and go join the others.'

'What do you think?' Bel asked as they stepped back onto the patio.

'I'm thinking what a difference a day makes. She looks so much better,' Danni answered with a smile. 'By the way, I'm sorry we didn't get here a bit earlier. You guys have had a long day.'

'Actually we've had a lovely day,' said Bel. 'In between feeding Sweetie, Tim put his building skills to work and did some repairs on Maya and Jon's shed and these little munchkins have been keeping me entertained.' Bel reached out to tickle the two children who squealed and giggled with delight. 'What about you two? I suppose you slept most of the day?'

'I sure did. I was still sleeping when Rama rang about two to give me an update on Sweetie-pie. I rang home and took care of a few other chores then Rama took me for an early dinner to his friend Ahmed's restaurant, which by the way we are under strict instructions from Ahmed to send to you to. The food is absolutely divine and Ahmed is such a character.'

Tim looked impressed. 'Sounds good to me. I'd be happy to go there for dinner tonight. What say you Bel?'

Bel nodded. 'Definitely, but a shower and change first I think,' she said wrinkling her nose.

Tim rose to his feet and held a hand out to his wife. 'Come on then, let's not keep Yusuf waiting.'

As they all walked together out to the van with the children milling around them, Bel gave Danni some handover instructions for Sweetie-pie's care whilst Rama gave Tim directions to Ahmed's.

'Enjoy your dinner and don't forget to tell Ahmed you're Rama's friends,' called Danni as they pulled away.

'We will!'

Danni linked arms with Maya as they walked back to the house. 'Looks like you're stuck with us again Maya.'

'No problem, I'm enjoying everyone's company,' Maya answered graciously. 'Danni you and your friends are welcome in my home anytime. Now, I gather you have already eaten?'

'Yes, we didn't want to burden you with having to feed us.'

Maya clicked her tongue. 'It's no problem, but my food cannot compare to Ahmed's.'

Danni grinned, 'I don't think too many can.'

'Okay Danni,' said Maya patting Danni's hand before unlinking their arms. 'Time for me to feed my brood now.'

'Can I help?'

'No it's okay. Stay and keep Rama company,' she said over her shoulder as she headed off to the kitchen.

Danni went to check on Sweetie-pie again then sat on the patio watching Rama play with the children until they were called to wash and have dinner.

'You're good with kids,' Danni observed when Rama came to sit with her.

Rama shrugged. 'Probably because I've always had a lot of kids around me.'

'How so?'

'Lots of Bali cousins of all ages and now many of them have their own kids. You know how it is there, everyone together in family compound. That's changing a bit as many young ones are moving away for work and families are becoming more urbanized, but the family compound still remains at the heart of Balinese life. Those that live away always return for important events and celebrations. Just like my mum and me I guess. What about you Danni? What's your family like?'

'Small compared to yours. Just mum and dad and my brother Chris who's only thirteen months younger than me so we're pretty close; at least these days we are, during our teenage years we were arguing one minute, best of friends the next. He's married now and has two little girls and Jenny his wife is lovely. But both mum and dad were only children so there's no other family, no cousins.'

'Tell me about them,' Rama prompted. He liked listening to Danni talk; her voice was low and even and washed over him like a soothing ballad.

Danni glanced at him, unsure if he was really interested or just being polite, but he was looking at her expectantly. 'Well let's see…mum and dad have been married forever, at least it seems that way. They were childhood sweethearts who married straight out of school. Apparently neither set of parents was too happy about it; they thought they were too young and it would end in disaster but mum and dad proved them wrong. They worked hard and scrimped and scraped to buy their first home and later a small business which dad built up over the years into a thriving concern. Along the way of course they had me and Chris. Dad retired early about a year ago and handed the reins of the business over to Chris then took mum on the round-the-world trip he'd always promised her.'

'Sounds nice. No place for you in the family business?'

'There could be if I wanted it but I spent lots of school holidays helping out and it was enough to convince me that it wasn't for me. I was more interested in marketing. Chris on the other hand thrives on it and he's worked hard for years alongside dad. I think it got to the point that dad really felt Chris had earned the top job which was part of the reason he took early retirement. But now he's done the big trip with mum he's struggling to fill his days. He and mum spend a lot of time together and they've got lots of friends and dad plays golf a few times a week but it's not really enough. Mum's happy to spend her days looking after her granddaughters and painting, which she's quite good at, so it's not really a problem for her.'

'Can your dad go back to work in the family business?'

'Yes he could but he's really concerned about stepping on Chris's toes. That's not the way Chris see's it at all, in fact I know he quite likes having dad to help out, but dad doesn't want to be seen as interfering.'

'There's always volunteer work,' Rama suggested, causing Danni to throw her head back in laughter.

'Oh Rama, trust you to suggest that.'

'I'm serious Danni. A man with his experience running what sounds like a successful business would have a lot to offer. He could offer his services as an advisor or business mentor or do some paid consultancy work if he doesn't like idea of working for nothing; some people don't. There are a lot of possibilities.'

'Hmm, I hadn't thought of that. I'm sure he'd like to be doing something useful. I'll definitely suggest it to him when I get home.'

Rama checked his watch. 'Just about time to feed Sweetie-pie,' he said standing up and holding a hand out to Danni. It seemed entirely natural to accept it until their hands met and the contact suddenly seemed too familiar, too intimate. Springing to her feet she hurriedly pulled her hand away and stepped back to put some space between them. If Rama noticed her sudden awkwardness he gave no indication, casually gesturing ahead of him. 'Lead the way McDuff.'

The treatment room was in darkness now the sun had dipped below the horizon and mindful not to startle Sweetie-pie, Danni waited by the door until Rama located and flicked on the small lamp at the far end of the room, revealing a wide awake Sweetie-pie. She turned her head slightly so she could watch Danni as she approached the cot.

'Hello Sweetie, how's my precious one?' Danni crooned softly. 'Do you remember me? I'm very happy to see you looking so much better.' Although she remained calm, there was wariness in the infant's eyes, almost as if she couldn't quite decide what to make of these new people in her life.

Falling back into the routine they had established the night before Rama made up the bottle of formula, a larger one this time as per the vets orders, whilst Danni settled into the big armchair with Sweetie-pie still lightly wrapped in her sleeping rug, snuggled in Danni's lap. Sweetie-pie watched Rama approach with the bottle and greedily reached for it as Danni brought it to her mouth. 'Ooh you know what this is now don't you little one. Well drink up. This is the stuff that's going to make you big and strong so you can go back to the jungle.' Sweetie-pie gave every indication that she was listening to Danni, even as her eyes darted back and forth between Danni and Rama who was putting clean bedding in the Sweeties cot and then came and perched on the arm of the chair to watch Sweetie suckling.

'She's really getting her strength back,' he commented.

'I can't believe how quickly she's improving,' agreed Danni. 'I'd love to see her well on the road to recovery before I have to leave.'

'I think you will; she's well down that road already.'

Once Sweetie-pie finished the bottle, Danni cleaned her and changed her nappy. Although Sweetie remained awake throughout, she was fading by the end of the small amount of activity and was asleep almost as soon as Danni settled her back into the cot; a sobering reminder that despite the visible improvement in her condition, Sweetie was still a sick little baby.

Leaving her to sleep, Danni and Rama joined Maya and the children in the family room where they all played a spirited game of Uno until the children were sent off the bed. Maya rejoined Danni and Rama long enough to share a pot of tea before taking herself off to bed.

'That's the way it is over here,' observed Rama. 'Early to bed and up with the sun. Even in the cities it's a pattern that persists. Why don't we adjourn to the back patio so we don't disturb anyone?'

Danni followed Rama through the house, grabbing a sarong from her bag along the way to ward off the slight evening chill and the odd mosquito. 'Do you mind?' Danni asked Rama, gesturing to a hammock that was strung between two pillars.

'No, it's all yours.'

Danni carefully lowered herself into the simple string hammock. It wobbled precariously beneath her, threatening to dump her on her backside onto the ground until she finally found the centre of gravity and was safely wrapped deep inside the woven net. 'Well that was graceful!' said Danni with a self-mocking giggle, which had the effect of drawing a full throated laugh from Rama who was already struggling to maintain a straight face. Danni threw him what she hoped was an indignant look but failed miserably as she cracked up laughing also.

'It's alright for you,' she accused. 'You've probably been climbing in and out of these things since before you could walk.'

'True,' he conceded still looking highly amused. 'There's a technique for getting in and out of those string hammocks. If I'm feeling generous sometime I might show you.'

'Ha ha.'

Rama dragged a chair over closer to the hammock and propped his bare feet up on one of the pillars. 'I've had a nice evening Danni. You're good company.'

'I could say the same. You're incredibly easy to talk to Rama. Speaking of which, we never got a chance to finish our conversation back at the restaurant. By the way, you realize Ahmed thinks you and I are an item?'

Rama nodded, 'I picked up on that. A natural assumption I suppose when a man takes a beautiful woman to dinner. I figured it was easier to let him think we were together than explain how I came to be having dinner with a married woman.'

Danni laughed, 'Oh my, I didn't even think of that aspect. I think that little tit-bit would have scandalized the poor man.'

'Not to mention my reputation,' quipped Rama.

'Your reputation! What about mine? I'd be the scarlet women after all.'

'Nah,' said Rama deadpan, 'your reputation's as good as shot anyway once I tell Ahmed you dumped me. In case you didn't notice, I'm the golden haired boy in his eyes.'

Danni was mortified. 'Rama, you wouldn't!'

Once again Rama burst out laughing at Danni's expense. Well he's certainly in a good mood tonight she thought, shaking her head in mock disgust. 'Okay, now you've had your fun tell me about Ahmed. I'm really keen to know how you helped him go from cart vendor to restaurateur.'

Rama grinned at her a moment longer then switched into his serious mode.

'Helping Hands' mandate is to sponsor, both financially and practically, individual or community based projects that have the potential to benefit the wider community. Now this isn't a new idea by any means but where my approach differs is that I require a co-operative approach to trading within the network of projects and enterprises that we've assisted. It's a mutually beneficial approach that helps the projects reach commercial viability sooner as well as providing ongoing training opportunities for those involved. Also, most everyone I deal with is naturally hard working but they have little, if any education and rarely any previous exposure to business management, so by keeping the trading 'within the family' where possible, it provides a sort of nursery business training ground. And of course, Helping Hands provides additional training, education and support through the skilled volunteers that come and work with us.

So in Ahmed's case, I was convinced his marinated seafood was a product that could be taken further, albeit with a bit of refinement. I also realized that a restaurant within our network would provide a great opportunity for our other projects that could supply produce such as seafood, vegetables, herbs and spices. The initial establishment was also mostly handled within the network. The tables and chairs were made to order by a carpentry workshop we helped establish, the bamboo, fish traps, woven mats and artefacts were all supplied from other projects within the network. As well as coordinating everything, with Ahmed's involvement of course, Helping Hands brought in an experienced chef and restaurant manager, volunteers of course, to work alongside him during the initial start-up period.

In return, the restaurant provides on-the-job training opportunities for many of the young ones in our network interested in hospitality. Some kids that started out working at Ahmed's have gone on to work in some of the bigger hotels here in town, others have used the cashier and service experience as a stepping stone into the retail sector, We've also had a several apprentice chefs that have graduated and been picked up by high end resorts in Yogyakarta and Bali. I know aspiring to be a waitress or bar tender or cashier may not sound like much when you compare it to Australia where most parents want a university education for their kids, but here it's a big deal, especially when you consider where most of these kids have come from. Any job that pays a steady wage, in a clean, safe environment where there is real opportunity for advancement is highly regarded.'

'It sounds like a great idea but how far does the keep it in the family stipulation go? I mean, doesn't that have the potential to stifle enterprise and competition if they're limited to where they can buy and sell goods and services?' Danni asked.

'Good question and if we restricted trade to only within the network, you're right, it would be restrictive and ultimately unviable. The stipulation applies only where practical. Due to logistics and the relatively small size of our network - we're growing everyday but it takes time – it's simply not possible to always buy and sell internally. What we do is make introductions within the network so that our members know what goods and services are available within our group and we ask them to always give other members the opportunity to tender. It doesn't stop them from looking outside the network but we do require an open tender system so if a more competitive deal is obtained from outside the network, the buyer or seller must go back to the network member and give them the opportunity to match it. Sometimes our network member still can't match a price, but if nothing else it gives them feedback on the market pricing and helps them understand how other businesses are building up their bids, so it's a good learning experience.'

'That sounds reasonable. Now tell me, who actually owns the projects and enterprises you sponsor? Obviously your organization puts up the start-up money.'

Rama nodded. 'Yes we do, as well as providing a certain amount of initial working capital. The enterprises are owned by the stakeholders in whatever form is most appropriate. Ahmed is a sole-trader but within our network we have partnerships, family businesses and village co-operatives.'

'So Helping Hands doesn't retain an ownership stake?'

'No we don't. I felt it was important that the people we helped had full ownership so they didn't feel like we'd be looking over their shoulders forever. But equally I didn't feel it was appropriate to just gift the money to them. We're generally not talking big dollars because here in Indonesia things are a lot cheaper than in Australia, but it's important that we keep cycling the money through the organization so we can continue to fund new projects. Basically we provide interest free loans on a payment plan that the owners can see the end of and isn't unduly burdensome. Usually that means an amnesty period whilst the enterprise is in the start-up phase so repayments don't kick in until they reach a certain return on investment.'

'On the surface it sounds great, but given the corruption I've seen in this country, I can't help but be a little bit cynical,' said Danni. 'How do know when that magical return on investment figure has been reached?'

Rama gave her a rueful smile. 'That's a valid point Danni. I can see you're starting to understand the way this country works. Something we absolutely insist on is transparency; that means full access to the books, banking records, payroll, premises and so forth and we conduct regular audits and inspections. But of course, things are relatively unsophisticated here; handshake deals, cash transactions and the barter system still prevail much of the time so to a large extent we just have to have faith that the people we help are doing the right thing. And to be perfectly honest, our beneficiaries are just so grateful for the opportunity we've given them that loan repayments have never been an issue. In fact, a lot of our recipients have repaid their loan ahead of plan. You have to remember that the people of Indonesia have their pride just like anywhere else. Ultimately they don't want charity, they just want a hand up.

The bigger concern for us is corrupt business practices. It's a way of life here, endemic at all levels of society. There's no getting away from that. Other than those on the top of the heap, most Indonesians hate it and resent it but there is a certain tendency, borne out of generations of behaviour, to go with the flow. I'm not so idealistic that I'm blind to the risk that given the opportunity some of our beneficiaries would participate in corrupt behaviour, particularly as their circumstances and standing improves and they find themselves in a position to exert a little pressure themselves. I know everyone of them personally and I'd hate to think any of them would behave that way but they're human. That's my biggest concern and that's why it's imperative we have full transparency as far as possible. Also, we need to ensure that members are abiding by the keep it in the family mandate. Like the loan repayment, that's never been an issue but we have to be able to assure our donors that everything is above board.'

'And what about the keep it in the family stipulation? How long does that apply?'

'Like I said earlier, that requirement is really about providing a new project or enterprise with some early trade opportunities, helping them establish supply chains and creating a business training ground. Once the start-up funding is repaid, all of the obligations that were incumbent on them become null and void. They're free to operate as they wish. Think of what we provide as a kind of cocoon. We provide the funds and a protected environment in which learn and grow the business. By the very fact they've been able to repay the loan we know they've been successful and it's time for them to emerge from the cocoon into the big wide world. Honestly though, all of our former members have chosen to stay in the program in some capacity or other because they've developed good business relationships with each other and they also like to give back to the organization that has been so pivotal in changing their lives.'

'Rama, I have to say I'm very impressed. You obviously gave this a lot of thought and the logistics of just trying to pull it all together is mind boggling. It's like trying to run a whole lot of small business as well as your own organization.'

Rama shrugged modestly. 'It is challenging but it's always stimulating and the successes keep my motivation level up. But there's no way I could do it all on my own. I have a small but dedicated team of assistants and of course the volunteers without whom it would be nigh on impossible to deliver the expertise and training that are so important to our program.'

'Okay, one last question Rama if I may?'

'Ask away Danni. I'm more than happy to talk about Helping Hands. I'm still hoping to convince you to come on board and help us out with your marketing skills.'

'Rama! Is that why you took me to dinner so you could show me Ahmed's restaurant? How very under-handed of you.' Danni teased.

Rama clutched his chest in mock pain and did his best to look indignant. 'Danni, you wound me. How could you think such a thing?'

Danni laughed. 'If the shoe fits…'

'Okay I'll admit that I was happy to have an excuse to take you to Ahmed's but my main motivation was definitely to treat you to some of the best food Banjarmasin has to offer.'

Danni sighed and patted her stomach with satisfaction. 'Well you certainly did that. That meal was absolutely delicious. Ahmed's food would stack up anywhere.'

'So what's your question?'

'How do you find the projects you sponsor?'

'Another very good question but not one that has a straightforward answer. The first few projects we sponsored were community based projects. I'd done some work with another NGO delivering some basic education and medical assistance to some Dayak villages to the north of Banjarmasin. The NGO went in there quite a few years before I was involved and built a school and a very basic medical clinic and were doing a good job of improving the level of education, which was virtually nil before they got there, and health services. The problem was years later they were still there doing the same thing but for the next generation. Living standards remained very low and the villagers still only eked out a subsistence standard of living. There was no industry of any sort and no paid job opportunities so the kids that did get a bit of education from the NGO either did nothing with it or had to leave the village and move to the city for paid work. Some of their earnings were filtering back to the village but essentially for those that stayed, nothing really changed. I'm not knocking that NGO; their mandate was to bring education and health care to poor communities and they did that very well. Trouble is they'll still be there in ten, twenty, fifty year's time doing exactly the same thing for generation after generation unless the economy of those communities improves to the point where they can provide those things for themselves, or at least warrant enough attention from the government to do so.

So after spending a bit of time in the village and talking to both the elders and younger people, I realized that between them all they had lots of skills and ideas with commercial potential but what they lacked was the knowledge and capital to turn them into viable businesses.'

Rama paused for a second. 'I'm not boring you am I? I do tend to get pretty wrapped up in this stuff at times.'

'No not at all. I'm finding it fascinating. There's a lot more to what you and your organization does than meets the eye; please go on.'

'Well in the end I put it to the village elders; asked them what they could do best if they had access to capital and help to find suppliers and buyers. They came up with quite a lot of ideas like selling carvings to occasional tourists, making and selling woven mats at the local market to name a few. Great for making an odd dollar here and there but that was about it. It took a while to get them to start thinking bigger, but eventually they came up two ideas that we ended up running with.

The first related to some logging and mining camps upriver from them. As with a lot of Borneo, the river was the main means of transport so the workers for these camps were passing by the village every day and in quite high numbers. As well as targeting the workers, there was also potential to win some work from the companies themselves. So we started by establishing a large trading post right on the river bank, complete with a jetty to tie the bigger boats up to, in order to encourage the workers to stop in and spend some money. We knew what times they were passing so the women of the village started preparing meals that the guys could take away with them to eat on the boat ride. Traditional fare of course; rice, vegetable noodles, egg, fish wrapped in waxy brown paper and banana leaves. Once the word got out they had a steady stream of workers stopping in.

The next step was to set up a small river barge with a mobile shop to take it up river to the worksites or as close as we could get. Many of these guys are away from home for weeks at a time with little entertainment and they live pretty rough. We stocked our barge with the usual day to day essentials but also a few little luxuries these guys wouldn't normally see. The barge just cruised up and down the river servicing the various sites. After a few months we found that when the barge tied up overnight anywhere near the work camps they usually got a few visitors, mostly because the workers get bored and the barge provides a bit of a diversion. One of the young villagers who worked the barge then came up with the bright idea of setting up karaoke on the barge. The Indonesians love their karaoke so that has been a big hit.'

Danni shook her head in amazement. 'A mobile karaoke bar, who would have thought,' she laughed.

Rama grinned. 'Not so funny when you're expecting a quiet trip up the river and you encounter a blaring karaoke bar.'

'No probably not,' agreed Danni.

'Anyway, both enterprises were a good success and have made a big difference to the average income level in the village because they're run as a co-operative and everyone is involved in some capacity. Since then we've helped a neighbouring village established a floating fish farm that they move along the river to ensure freshness and reduce the impact on the environment. The co-op is now selling fish to many of those same logging and mining camps up the river as well as sending fish to the local markets. Currently they're in the process of expanding into manufacturing *pertisikan*, a dark salty fish paste that's a very popular condiment throughout Indonesia. I have a couple of volunteers working with them now to establish a small manufacturing plant that will meet commercial hygiene standards, which is essential if they want to distribute their product into city outlets. So far it's looking promising.

Based on what we learned with that first operation, we've established similar fish farms in other villages because the demand for fish is massive. Some of the produce is being sent down to Java and looking ahead, the possibility of exporting fish to other countries is not out of the question.

To give you an idea of how we choose other projects, because farm fish are fed with pellets we identified an opportunity to make and sell the pellets. Again using expert volunteer help that's another project my organization has been able to get off the ground.'

'So sometimes the ideas for new projects come from existing projects within your organization?' Danni asked.

'More or less. Now that Helping Hands has been around for a while and we're having a visible impact on so many lives, we get approached all the time for help. The Dayaks are a proud people and it's a big thing for them to reach out for help, so it's rare that a village will approach us without having an idea in mind already. We assess every proposal or idea very carefully. Working out who and how we can help is one of the hardest aspects of my job.

Often the proposals that come our way are just not viable for a number of reasons and sometimes we have to reject a proposal that does have merit because it doesn't meet our requirements. You see, the reality is that we have limited funds so we have to ensure we get maximum bang for our buck. Sometimes it's a matter of choosing one project over another simply because it has the potential to benefit more people. Other proposals may be rejected because they just don't fit anywhere in our network so there's limited opportunity to feed into an existing supply or distribution chain, which in turn compromises the level of support we can provide. That's not to say we'll reject a project entirely on that basis but it does increase the risk factor. There are also two criteria that we don't compromise on; the project must have long-term viability and must be ecologically sustainable with no adverse impact on the environment.

Sadly, I've had some really good ideas that tick all the right boxes come across my desk, but we haven't been able to get them off the ground because we lack the technical expertise we need. I advertise for volunteers with the skills we need at any given time but we're not always successful in securing a suitable applicant. Still, we never discard those ideas. When the opportunity presents, we'll run with it.'

'What about the one's you reject? Is there anything you can do to help those people?'

'Often there is. If an idea has been brought to us just doesn't fly we'll continue to work with those people to try and identify other possibilities, get them thinking outside the square. The fish food pellet project is an example of that. The village where that project is based came to us with an idea for something totally unrelated which we felt was unviable. But I was able to go back to them several months later with the pellet making plan and they grabbed it. Currently we have an idea to establish a fish hatchery because with all the fish farms in our network there's obviously a market for the fingerlings. But fish hatching is quite a specialized process. I'm meeting an aquaculture specialist in Sydney later this year to see what's involved. We have another village we'd like to help out with that project so we're working hard to get that one up.'

'Rama, I'm in awe of everything you and your organization is doing. Just meeting Ahmed and visiting Muara Tanuh village, I've seen firsthand how much difference you're making to people's lives. Honestly, I'd like to be able offer my marketing services but I need to give it some more thought before I do so. The last think I want to do is make promises I can't keep down the track.' There was a part of Danni that wanted to pledge whatever help she could give him right then and there, but a cautionary voice inside her head held her back. Here in Borneo, it was easy to feel drawn in to the local issues and motivated to help but once back home there were other demands on her time she had to think about. Not the least of which was mending some of the cracks in her marriage.

Rama reached across and squeezed her hand. 'Danni, I understand you've got commitments back home in Australia. Whilst I've made no secret of the fact I could do with someone with your skills on board, it's not my intention to pressure you into anything you don't want to do or haven't the time for,' he said sincerely, immediately putting Danni at ease as he was so easily to be able to do. She gave him a grateful smile and snuggled deeper into the hammock beneath her sarong with a deep sigh.

***

Bel and Tim arrived early the next morning with a box of goodies. 'Special delivery from Ahmed,' explained Tim. 'He sent two of his daughters over to the hotel with it this morning. The two children manoeuvred themselves between Tim and the table as he set the box down, standing on tip toes to peer inside. 'Whoa there kids, there's plenty for everyone,' he laughed, as he and Bel placed the contents on the table and unwrapped the parcels, revealing omelettes, fried garlic potatoes with *kangkung*, crispy fish morsels, fresh bread rolls and banana pancakes. There was even fresh fruit juice.

'Oh my, Ahmed has outdone himself,' said Danni, eyeing the banquet with relish. Maya was already handing out plates and within a few minutes everyone was tucking in with gusto.

'I don't know what exactly Ahmed does to his food,' said Tim between mouthfuls. 'But whatever it is, it works.'

'How was Sweetie-pie's night?' Bel asked.

Danni beamed across the table. 'Really, really good. She reached out her hand and grasped my shirt this morning when I was feeding her.'

'That's fantastic!' exclaimed Bel excitedly. 'Maya, that has to mean she's getting better surely?'

Maya smiled. 'It's a very good sign. She's getting stronger, more alert. Maybe in another day or two, when she's a little stronger, we can think about moving her to a rehabilitation centre.'

'That soon?' Tim asked, surprised.

Maya nodded. 'Yes, a specialist rehabilitation centre is the best place for her and the sooner the better. She is still very susceptible to infection, from us and other animals. Our facilities here are basic as you have seen, adequate only for short term transitioning until we can find a more suitable solution for the animals. We don't have the room to keep a too many animals separated, which puts the sick and vulnerable ones like Sweetie at extra risk. We've been fortunate so far that she has been alone but that can change very quickly, especially if Jon and his team have some success up north. Many of the animals we bring here are sick or dying and the stronger ones can make quite a ruckus in their cages, particularly the wild ones who have had no previous human contact. It can be a very stressful environment, one best avoided for Sweetie if we can. The rehab centre has specialist vets who can treat her, she'll be monitored around the clock and even in quarantine, she'll have a much nicer environment and be able to see other orangutans.'

'It does sound more suitable,' Tim agreed.

Maya smiled reassuringly at the group. 'Now it looks like she's going to make it, I'll start making some calls and see where I can secure a spot for her. There are several options but many are close to capacity. In the meantime, your job is to get her well enough to travel.'

Having spent so much time with Bel, Tim and Danni over the past several days, Rama ruefully conceded that he had a lot of work to catch up on. He felt bad about leaving Danni to her own devices for the day but there didn't seem to be any other option and although Danni laughed off his concerns and assured him that she was perfectly fine looking after herself, he was reluctant nonetheless. As he and Yusuf pulled away from the hotel, he admitted to himself that the root of his reluctance was that he was just plain going to miss her. Being around Danni, spending time with her was becoming bitter sweet torture.

Totally unaware of Rama's inner turmoil, Danni waved the van off and headed for her room. Halfway to the elevator, the receptionist caught her attention. 'Madame, you have a message.'

Danni changed directions and retrieved the note. 'I'm sorry' was all it said. There was no name, but there didn't need to be; Danni knew who it was from. She smiled her thanks to the receptionist and went upstairs to her room and straight to the telephone.

Rob answered on the second ring. 'I'm sorry too,' she said, not bothering with a greeting.

'Danni!' Rob sounded relieved. 'I wasn't sure if you'd call. I said some pretty nasty things yesterday; thought maybe you wouldn't want to talk to me.'

'Oh Rob, of course I want to talk to you. I just don't want to fight and you're not the only one who said some nasty things yesterday. I didn't even ask how your leg was.'

'The leg's coming along okay. I don't need to have it re-dressed at the clinic anymore; I can do it myself.' Rob paused for moment. 'But listen babe, getting back to the other stuff, I think I was just feeling a bit lonely and sorry for myself. Do you think you can forgive me and we can put it behind us?'

'Of course I forgive you Rob.' What Danni didn't say was yes, they could put it all behind them. They couldn't, or at least she couldn't. They needed to do some serious talking about the status quo in their marriage. She wasn't happy with it and hadn't been for a long time but it was only now with the benefit of time and distance that she could finally admit it to herself. But that wasn't a conversation she wanted to have over the phone; it could wait until she was home.

There was a momentary silence, as if Rob expected her to say more. When she didn't he changed the subject. 'So how's the orangutan coming along?'

'Good, really good,' said Danni cautiously, but her passion got the better of her. 'Oh Rob, you should see her. She's just the sweetest little thing, just like a human baby except she's covered in orange fur and she's got these huge fathomless brown eyes with cute white rings around them. And this morning, she even reached out grabbed my shirt.'

Rob chuckled. 'She does sound kinda cute. You'll have to take a photo to show me.'

'Good idea. I've been so busy caring for her I haven't thought to do it.'

They chatted on for a while longer, Danni filling Rob in on their trip into the hinterlands, since she hadn't had a chance the previous day, until she got the feeling Rob's attention had wandered. But even so, after the call she felt much happier knowing they had mended some bridges.

Feeling buoyed after the reconciliation with Rob and less tired than the previous day, thanks to Sweetie-pies friendlier feeding schedule, Danni felt a little too stimulated to sleep. She thought about Rama heading off to work despite the long night and everything she'd learned about him and his organization and the people he helped. That's when it struck her that she had to help him; she wanted to help him. She felt the beginnings of the familiar surge of excitement that struck her whenever a new marketing account landed on her desk; ideas and strategies starting to fill her head. Grabbing a notebook and pen from her bag, Danni propped herself up on the bed and started scribbling them down.

Nearly three hours passed before her energy finally waned and she gave in to drooping eyelids and lay down to sleep. She'd made a good start on formulating Rama's campaign. There was more research to be done and a long way to go before she could give him something useful but it was a start.

She woke a little after midday feeling refreshed and hungry so after showering she headed down to the hotel restaurant but on finding it empty, impulsively decided to walk up to Ahmed's instead.

'Miss Danni, you've come back!' Danni had barely stepped inside the restaurant when Ahmed spotted her and grasped her hands in his, beaming with his customary enthusiasm.

Danni smiled. 'I promised I would. Plus I had to come by to thank you for the wonderful breakfast this morning.'

Ahmed waved her thanks aside. 'It's no problem. Now tell me, how is the little orangutan?'

'She's great,' said Danni, eyes shining brightly. 'Maya thinks she might be well enough to move to a rehabilitation centre in a couple of days.'

Ahmed clapped his hands together. 'Wonderful, wonderful. Now, have you come for lunch? Ahmed will feed you yes?' Danni didn't need to answer; he was already leading her to a table and had a menu open in front of her as soon as she sat.

'I don't understand Bahasa Indonesian Ahmed,' she reminded him. 'Would you just bring me something light please? A salad?'

'I have just the thing,' he said, setting off for the kitchen like a man on a mission, sending the same young waitress that had served her and Rama the previous evening to the table to take her drink order.

Lunch was delicious, just as Danni expected; a green mango salad topped with marinated squid that was so tender it practically melted in her mouth. Thinking she'd like to try and replicate it at home, Danni carefully scrutinized the food on her plate and chewed slowly, letting the flavours roll over her tongue as she tried to identify the ingredients. Ahmed materialized beside the table looking deeply troubled. 'Is something wrong Miss Danni?'

'No, the food is delicious Ahmed,' Danni reassured him. 'Actually I was trying to figure out what ingredients you've used so I can try to copy it back home,' she confessed smiling.

Ahmed troubled expression cleared and he smiled. 'Ah I see. Since you are a friend, I will show you. When you finish eating, I will bring you into the kitchen, yes? But first you eat, then we cook.'

'Oh Ahmed, that would be great!'

And so, Danni spent the rest of the afternoon in Ahmed's kitchen receiving a personal cooking lesson from a man she now considered a culinary genius. He had the kind of instinctive understanding of flavours and texture that couldn't be taught and a style unrestrained by formal training, but most of all, it was Ahmed's love of food that shone through. Danni felt both humbled and privileged by his generosity. He showed her his salad recipe as promised but it was more than a just simple lesson; he taught her about the different Asian fruit and vegetables, many of which were strange and new to her, he showed her how to chop, slice and dice to extract just the right amount of flavour and texture, he taught her about spices and herbs and made her think about the subtleties of taste and the way different flavours interacted. When the time came to leave, Ahmed insisted on packaging up the food she had prepared to take with her and flatly refused to accept any payment from her, other than for her lunch. Danni felt a bit awkward about it but not wanting to offend, she graciously conceded the point.

'Come back tomorrow Miss Danni. If you wish, we shall have another lesson,' he offered and Danni was keen to take him up on it. She'd enjoyed herself immensely and not just because of the knowledge he'd imparted; Ahmed was fun to be around. Balancing her box of goodies under one arm, she reached out with the other and gave him a friendly hug. 'Thanks Ahmed. I'll see you tomorrow.'

Rama was leaning against a pillar outside the hotel foyer when she got back. 'Am I late?' she asked, smiling as she walked towards him.

Rama grinned and shook his head. 'No I'm early. I thought you might have been at a bit of a loose end and could use some company.' He inclined his chin towards the box she was carrying. 'What have you got there?'

'Food. I've been having a cooking lesson with Ahmed,' said Danni grinning.

Rama looked impressed. 'Have you now? I must say you're full of surprises Danni.'

Danni shrugged and laughed. 'It just kind of happened. Fancy helping me eat this lot? By the way, where's Yusuf?' she asked, scanning the car park for his van.

'I borrowed a scooter from my landlord and gave him the evening off so he could spend it with his family. Tim's happy to ride the scooter.' He reached out and took the box from Danni. 'This smells good. Your cooking or Ahmed's?'

'Mine. Well sort of mine, under Ahmed's tutelage.'

'Where shall we eat?' Rama asked.

'My room I guess. We can sit out on my little balcony overlooking the river. I'll just drop into the restaurant on the way through and borrow some plates and cutlery.'

Plates in hand, Rama followed Danni up to her room. Inside he set the box down on the bench, noticing the message Danni had discarded there earlier. 'I'm sorry'. What did it mean? Who was it from? It was none of his business he reminded himself, refocussing on the room instead. The unmade bed, the note pad and loose pages scattered across it. He looked away, trying to ignore the intimacy of being in Danni's private space.

But Danni had seen him look at the bed and look away, although she misinterpreted his discomfort completely. 'Sorry, I wasn't expecting company, but I've been doing some work on a marketing campaign for you Rama,' she confessed.

He looked surprised but pleased. 'Danni, I really appreciate it but I already told you I don't want you to feel pressured into anything.'

She laid a hand on his arm and smiled up at him. 'I don't. I really want to do this for you Rama and I have some great ideas. Let's get dinner served and we can talk about it whilst we eat.'

Rama set the food out on the little table on the balcony whilst Danni boiled the kettle and made them a cup of tea and over dinner she filled him in on her idea's, seeking his input and drawing out further information she needed. Rama was thrilled with the strategy that she mapped out for him and although there were still a lot of holes and a lot of work to be done, Danni's knowledge and professionalism shone through and he had no doubt she would deliver. And best of all, he was really pleased to have an excuse to stay in touch with her once she returned home to Australia. Even though he knew a relationship was out of the question, the thought of never seeing or hearing from her again was almost unbearable.

That night passed much the same as the previous. Sweetie-pie continued to make good progress and was even starting to move about in her cot. When Danni gave her the early morning feed, Rama opened the curtains and repositioned the big arm chair so that Sweetie could look out at the trees and the garden behind the house, which captured and held the little orangutan's attention for the entire feed. Ahmed seemed intent on keeping them all fed, sending breakfast once again and just like the previous day Rama dropped Danni at the hotel and headed off to work, promising to collect her from Ahmed's later that afternoon after her cooking lesson. Danni spent her morning catching up on sleep and doing some more work on Rama's campaign, this time using the public computer in the foyer to do some research on the internet.

At Ahmed's she passed up a formal lunch in favour of propping herself up in the kitchen, watching and chatting to Ahmed and his staff whilst they worked and munching on the little morsels that he passed her to try, each time testing her to see what ingredients she could identify. The kitchen staff seemed to enjoy the game, looking on expectantly, smiling when she got one right and groaning good-naturedly when she got one wrong. When the lunchtime crowd swelled she rolled up her sleeves and pitched in washing dishes and chopping vegetables and the staff, now over their initial shyness included her in their camaraderie making Danni really feel like one of the gang.

Once things in the restaurant died down Ahmed turned his attention back to Danni, announcing he was going to teach her to make *Bingka Barandam*, the sweet cake that Rama had previously declared was his favourite. Danni had a sneaking suspicion that Ahmed had chosen the recipe deliberately in an attempt to play match-maker but she kept her thoughts to herself and set herself to the task, beating eggs with vanilla bean seeds and adding sifted flour to make a light dough which she poured into individual moulds. Whilst the cakes were in the oven cooking, Ahmed guided her through the steps to make the sweet syrup in which the cakes would be soaked before serving. Into a pot of water went sugar, fresh cinnamon sticks and pandan leaves, the long thin leaves of the pandanus palm, tied into a knot and which when simmered gently added a heavenly, aromatic flavour and delicate yellow tint to the sweet sauce. The sauce and cakes, now cooked soft and golden, were set aside to cool.

Ahmed inspected the sweet treat and grunted with satisfaction. 'When Rama comes, you give him some and he will see how good you can cook,' he said matter-of-factly.

An hour or so later, Danni looked up from the spices she was grinding in the mortar and pestle and got a surprise to see Rama propped against the kitchen doorway watching her. 'Hey, having fun?'

Danni smiled, doing her best to ignore the giggles and nudges passing between the staff. 'I am actually. Ahmed's determined to turn me into a decent cook.'

'I saw him out front. He made a point of telling me you're a very good cook,' said Rama, trying not to burst out laughing. 'For some reason he seemed to think I should know.'

Danni cringed and bit her bottom lip to keep herself from laughing. 'Poor guy is going to be heartbroken you know.' He's not the only one, thought Rama.

Ahmed bustled into the kitchen and sent Rama packing to a table, then supervised Danni as she plated up the *Bingka Barandam*, carefully dropping the little cakes into the sweet syrup. With a flourish, Ahmed garnished the bowls with a tiny knotted piece of pandan leaf and stepped back to admire the finished product, then he picked up the bowls and handed one to Danni and marched out of the kitchen with Danni bringing up the rear. At Rama's table he stood back so Danni could set her bowl in front of Rama, then waited until she sat down opposite to set down the other bowl in front of her.

'Rama,' he announced. 'Miss Danni has made your favourite treat for you. You will see it is very good.'

Danni and Rama waited until Ahmed was safely back in the kitchen then looked at each other and burst into laughter. 'Not very subtle is he?' said Rama drily, eliciting more giggles from Danni. Rama grinning at her like an idiot didn't help. 'Stop it!' she growled, giggling again. Finally she took a deep breath and slowly released it, calming herself enough to take a bite of the sweet treat. Following her lead, Rama tucked in as well, demolishing the entire contents of the bowl in seconds.

'Hat's off to you Danni. That was really good,' he said leaning back in his chair and patting his stomach appreciatively.

'It is nice,' Danni confirmed between mouthfuls. 'I can see why you like it. And such a simple recipe too. I'm sure I can make it again at home, although I'm not sure where I could possibly buy pandan leaves.'

'Maybe you could substitute them with something else.'

'Maybe…I'll have to ask Ahmed.' Danni finished the last of her dessert and sat back satiated. 'I'm not sure eating that so close to dinner time was such a good idea.'

'Don't worry about it. We can skip dinner and if we get hungry later on I'm sure Maya will find something for us.'

Ahmed came to the table on the pretext of collecting their empty bowls and Rama nearly set Danni off on another fit of giggles when he winked at her. 'What did you think Rama? It was good yes?'

Rama made a show of licking his lips and giving the question serious consideration. 'Yes very good. I think Danni has some talent,' he said seriously, earning him a kick him under the table from Danni.

Ahmed beamed delightedly. 'With Ahmed's help she will be cooking Indonesian food very soon.' He turned to Danni, 'Tomorrow you come back again and I will teach you some more.'

Danni opened her mouth to reply, but Rama cut her off. 'Actually, before you decide Danni I should tell you there have been some developments with Sweetie—' He held up a hand when Danni started, '— it's alright, every things okay. You see, Maya's husband Jon and Alyson, the vet arrived back a few hours ago and Alyson thinks Sweetie is well enough to travel so there's talk of transferring her to a rehabilitation centre tomorrow.'

'Oh Rama,' was all Danni could say before tears welled in her eyes. Embarrassed, she reached into her pocket for a tissue. 'Sorry, just ignore me,' she said to the two men who were both looking at her askance. 'I'm just being silly. I'm really happy for Sweetie, of course the rehab centre is the best thing for her,' Danni blew her nose before continuing, 'but I'm going to miss her.'

Rama stood up and came around the table. Dropping down on his haunches beside her, he reached for her hand. 'Don't apologise Danni. It's only natural that you'll miss her. How about I have a talk to Jon and see if you can go with him to the rehab centre? I'm sure once you've met the carers and seen the facilities there you'll feel much happier. In fact, we should all go since we've all had a hand in caring for her.'

'Thanks Rama, I'd really appreciate that,' she whispered, looking at him through teary eyes.

Rama caught and held her gaze. The urge to lean in and kiss her tears away was so strong he was sure he'd already started moving towards her before he caught himself. Abruptly he dropped her hand and stood up, trying to put some distance between them. Danni was looking at him strangely, but he kept his eyes averted and pretended not to notice. 'We should get going,' he said, sounding a whole lot calmer than he felt. 'Ahmed, what do we owe you?'

Ahmed hadn't noticed anything odd about their exchange, in fact he was beaming at the two of them as if Rama comforting Danni was confirmation that they were a couple in love. 'No payment,' he said holding his hand up. 'Miss Danni worked very hard today. Good worker in the kitchen. So tomorrow maybe I see you, maybe I don't. You come back anytime you want.'

Danni smiled her thanks, then excused herself to use the bathroom which was really just a ruse for some privacy and a bit of time to gather her thoughts. Rama was attracted to her! She'd seen it in his eyes in that split second before he caught himself and looked away. For a moment, she thought he might have kissed her and she actually wanted him to! There was no denying the sharp stab of disappointment in her chest when he didn't. Leaning over the basin, she splashed some cold water on her face and stared at herself in the mirror. Never in her wildest imagination had she ever thought of herself as the sort of woman who would cheat on her husband and yet in that moment she'd yearned for Rama's touch. How could she? Because you love him. You love Rama.

It was a shocking revelation but there was no denying it. Somehow over the last week, perhaps even since their first meeting in Sanur after she'd watched him meditating on the beach, she'd fallen for him. Danni splashed some more water on her face and leaned on the basin gulping for air, trying to will away the adrenaline surging through her body. Looking back there'd been signs; the physical attraction, the easy camaraderie, her growing respect and admiration but she'd been too naive to recognize the danger signs. Idiot!

She thought of Rob, her first love, the man she had fallen for at the tender age of twenty and spent her entire adult life with. Yes he could be stubborn and exasperating but also sweet and gentle and Danni loved him, faults and all. And never had she doubted his feelings for her. So there it was, the simple truth; she was in love with two men.

So what now Danni asked herself? Could she simply ignore her feelings for Rama, tuck her love for him away in a secret compartment in her heart and go home to Rob as if nothing had changed? She had to. When she married Rob she'd stood in front of the celebrant and sworn her love to him, promised faithfulness and pledged to share her life with him. She took her vows as seriously then as she did now and had no intention of breaking them.

The smart thing to do would be to take the very next flight home and put as much distance between herself and Rama as possible. But for tonight at least, she was stuck. Sweetie-pie still needed around the clock care and Danni wasn't about to renege on her. Sure she could beg off sick and between them Bel, Tim and Rama would cover for her but that would be entirely selfish on her part. Besides Danni reasoned, what had really changed between yesterday and today other than she now recognized her feelings for Rama? After all she hadn't fallen in love with him overnight, although she reminded herself ruefully, a week wasn't much better. But the fact remained things had been good between herself and Rama until now and logically there was no reason for that to change. He didn't know how she felt and she wasn't about to tell him. Was it wrong to want to spend a few more hours in his company? Once she left Borneo there would be no reason to see him again. There'd be some emails back and forth while she finalized the marketing campaign for Helping Hands but after that it would be best for all concerned if she ended their contact, however painful that might be. Surely she was mature enough to be able to maintain the friendly camaraderie between them until then?

That settled, Danni washed her face again, fluffed her hair and plastered what she hoped was a normal expression on her face and stepped from the bathroom, waving to Ahmed as she crossed the floor towards Rama who was waiting by the door. 'I was starting to think you'd got lost in there,' he commented lightly as they walked to his borrowed scooter.

'I needed a bit of a wash-up after working in the kitchen all afternoon,' Danni lied, doing her best to act nonchalant.

'Fair enough.' Rama handed her a helmet and swung a long leg over the bike. Once Danni was settled behind him, he pulled out into the traffic doing his best to ignore the feel of her hands around his waist and his heart thumping in his chest. Unknown to him, Danni was struggling with exactly the same problem.

Jon Macklin turned out to be an entirely personable guy. Despite his years in Indonesia, he still had a broad Cockney accent and a lively British sense of humour, a valuable asset Danni decided, given the serious nature of his work. He retained another English trait too, a love of beer, which out of courtesy to the Muslim populace in his adopted home he enjoyed in the privacy of his own home but was more than happy to share his precious stockpile with his non-Muslim visitors. Alyson, the WWF vet was somewhere in her early fifties having flown the coup once the youngest of her brood of kids had left the nest. She was forthright and efficient but beneath the gruff exterior was a heart of gold. With Jon's beer flowing and chicken grilling on Maya's charcoal brazier on the front patio, the evening turned into a long, happy affair. In the expanded company, Danni's concerns about being alone with Rama melted away and despite her troubled thoughts she relaxed and enjoyed herself.

Sweetie-pie was active and alert when Danni and Rama went in to feed her, eagerly reaching for the bottle and moving her head slightly as she suckled to watch Rama as he put the formula makings away and straightened her cot. Towards the end of the feed Alyson came in to check on her and after a careful examination confirmed that Sweetie-pie was definitely well enough to transfer to the rehabilitation centre the following day, news that she relayed to the rest of the group when they rejoined them on the patio.

'I'm okay,' said Danni when Rama threw her a concerned look, then for everyone else's benefit she elaborated. 'I had a bit of moment this afternoon when Rama told me Sweetie-pie was going to be transferred. Entirely selfish on my part but I am going to miss her.'

'Don't worry, you weren't the only one,' said Tim, looking pointedly at Bel.

'Jon, any chance our carers here can come along for the transfer tomorrow?' Rama asked. 'I think it would benefit everyone to see Sweetie's new home.'

'I don't see why not. You've all been instrumental in getting Sweetie this far, so I think it's only fair. It's a long drive up to Palangka Raya where the rehab centre is though so it will be a long day and we'll need to get an early start.'

With that in mind, after working out the logistics of transporting Sweetie and everyone else, the gathering broke up; Bel, Tim and Alyson heading off in their respective directions, Jon and Maya to bed and Rama and Danni to the back patio where they wouldn't disturb the household. Enveloped by the warm tropical night, Danni lying in the hammock and Rama lounging in a chair, feet propped up the pillar just like the previous evening, they talked softly between themselves until Sweetie's next feed and then retired inside to snatch whatever sleep they could before the long day ahead.

CHAPTER TWELVE

The sky still wore the purple hue of pre-dawn when the household stirred. Now familiar with Maya's kitchen, Danni had a pot of tea made when Alyson arrived, followed shortly afterwards by Bel and Tim. Despite the early start, Ahmed had once again insisted on supplying breakfast even though Bel and Tim had called in on their way home the previous evening to tell him not to bother. After everyone had eaten, the men helped Jon load a cage for Sweetie into the back of the WWF four wheel drive wagon, whilst Bel and Danni gave Sweetie another bottle. Alyson had already explained that to reduce stress, Sweetie would be tranquilised for the journey so they were prepared when the vet administered the drug that put Sweetie into a deep sleep, then very carefully carried her out to the vehicle where she was settled on a soft bed in the cage. The travellers followed her into the vehicle, Alyson insisting on taking the dickie seat in the back with Sweetie so she could monitor her. So with Maya and the children waving to them they set off.

It took four hours to travel to Palangka Raya, the capital of Central Kalimantan province. The mood in the vehicle was rather pensive and no one seemed inclined to chat much so Danni spent most of the journey looking out the window or dozing, although the constant change of pace that was synonymous with road travel in Borneo made sleep near on impossible. Danni was still deeply troubled by her feelings for Rama but determinedly refused the think about it and if anyone else noticed her pensive mood, they naturally assumed it was entirely due to Sweetie's transfer. As they neared Palangka Raya, Jon gave them a brief rundown on the rehabilitation centre.

'The centre is located just outside the city in a forest reserve called Nyaru Menteng. It's operated by BOS, the Borneo Orangutan Survival Foundation and is the largest orangutan conservation facility in the world with the largest rehab program to match. BOS is absolutely dedicated to returning orangutans to the wild wherever possible so their program is focused on preparing orangutans for release. I can assure you Sweetie-pie will be in the very best of hands.'

Shortly afterwards they turned off the bitumen onto a gravel road and after a few more kilometres arrived at the centre, a modest complex at the edge of a lush, green forest. Jon ignored the sign pointing to the visitor information centre and drove up to a gate which was soon opened for them by a centre employee once he'd established the purpose of their visit. Jon knew his way around from countless previous visits and headed across the grounds to another building where he parked and asked them to wait whilst he checked in. Five minutes later he was back with several people in tow, one of whom he introduced as Pieter, the centre manager. He was a tall man, with a rugged complexion, greying hair and a confident, friendly demeanour.

'Jon tells me you've all done a remarkable job rescuing and looking after the young orangutan you've brought us. Let's have a look at her shall we?' he said, peering into the open back of the vehicle. Sweetie-pie was still lying in the bottom of her cage and although still drowsy, she regarded the new people warily. Pieter looked her over quickly then stepped back so as not to unnecessarily frighten her. 'She's a young'n, malnourished but otherwise doesn't seem too bad. What say you Alyson?' he asked, obviously well acquainted with the WWF vet.

'I agree. The guys here have been feeding and caring for her around the clock and she's responded well, become more alert and active every day. I haven't seen any signs of disease but we've had her on a precautionary course of antibiotics just in case. That's not to say you guys won't turn up something when your vets run their labs.'

'All right folks,' said Pieter turning back to the assembled group, 'I presume you've given this little one a name?'

'Yes, it's Sweetie-pie,' Danni confirmed smiling.

'All right, I'm afraid it's time for you all to say your goodbyes to Sweetie-pie. We'll pass her into the care of our veterinarians now and then she'll go into quarantine.' He held up his hands, 'Now I know you've probably got lots of questions so I'll make you a deal. Let's get Sweetie organized and then I'll give you a tour of the complex. Visitors aren't normally given access beyond the information centre but in view of the efforts you've all put in to save Sweetie, I think we can make an exception for you folks,' he said smiling at the group.

One by one, Bel, Tim, Danni and Rama went to the back of the car and said their goodbyes to Sweetie-pie. Danni wished more than anything that she could hold her one more time but it was clearly out of the question. Instead she reached out and threaded her fingers through the mesh, her heart clenching when Sweetie grasped her finger in her hand and looked at her with her big, fathomless brown eyes, almost as if she sensed this was goodbye. Tears rolled down her cheek but Danni made no attempt to wipe them away until Pieter and a couple of helpers shuffled forward to lift Sweetie's cage from the vehicle. Reluctantly Danni stepped back and it seemed like the most natural thing in the world when Rama put a comforting arm around her shoulders whilst they stood and watched Sweetie disappear into the clinic. Jon and Alyson followed Sweetie into the clinic, leaving an equally upset Bel sniffling into Tim's shoulder and Danni trying to compose herself in the comfort of Rama's embrace. They were still drying their eyes when Pieter and Jon emerged from the clinic several minutes later.

Pieter threw his arms wide. 'Ladies, there's no need for tears. This is a good place for Sweetie, she'll be happy here and maybe one day God willing, we can send her home to the forest.'

Danni stepped out of Rama's embrace and forced a watery smile. 'I know Pieter. I really am happy for her, we all are, it's just saying goodbye that was hard.'

'It's always hard to say goodbye,' agreed Pieter. 'Everyone here gets very attached to our orangutans, especially our carers in the nursery who can spend five or more years looking after their infant.'

'So do the carers get assigned to a particular infant?' Bel asked.

Pieter nodded, 'Yes indeed. Baby orangutans need twenty four hour care, so we assign two carers to each infant. They become substitute mothers so as you can imagine a very strong bond develops between the infant and their carers. In fact, a baby orangutan can become very upset and cry and scream if left alone by their carer.'

'I had no idea they were so needy for so long,' commented Tim.

'Oh yes. The long nurturing period is just about the longest of any animal in the world and its one of the reasons orangutans are so vulnerable to extinction. In the wild, a baby orangutan stays with its mother until about seven years of age. For the first few at least they remain constantly with her clinging to her fur then gradually they start to move away; at first sticking to her side, then little forays a further afield as they develop their climbing skills and independence. They also suckle until about five years of age. It takes that long for their digestive systems to be able to handle a diet exclusively of fruit, leaves, bark and a little protein from termites and grubs.'

'And I suppose a nursing mother won't breed until her little one is fully weaned?'

'That's right Tim. Now do the sums; seven years of nurturing, time for reproduction, add another year for gestation and you have a breeding cycle of one baby every eight or so years. That means the average healthy female orangutan will only reproduce two or three times in her lifetime.'

'So throw man-made threats like logging, forest fires, palm oil plantations and poaching into the mix...' said Tim looking alarmed. 'Jesus, they're up against it. I had no idea!'

'I can see you're starting to comprehend the magnitude of the problems the orangutans are facing. Extinction of orangutans in the wild is a very real possibility within the next ten years or so,' said Pieter sadly. 'Rehabilitation centres like this one are doing what they can but really we're just a drop in the ocean. Believe it or not your Sweetie-pie is one of the lucky ones. Only one in six orphaned orangutans are rescued and taken to rehab centres. The rest face almost certain death. Realistically the only way to save the species in the wild is to protect their habitat and safeguard them from poachers and that's a very big, ongoing battle that's a long way from being won,' Pieter said grimly. 'All right folks, let's begin the tour shall we?'

He shepherded the group away from the clinic to a neat, white washed building nearby and skirted around the back where there were several rows of cages nestled among a leafy, forested garden. The cages where of varying sizes and blended quite well with the surroundings. 'This is our quarantine centre,' said Pieter. 'We won't go any closer as access is limited to essential staff. All new comers to the centre spend at least their first few weeks here. You see many of the orangutans that come to us are diseased, often with diseases that have been transmitted by their human captors and until they're declared disease free by our veterinary staff, we can't risk introducing them into the rest of our population. Once the vets have finished with Sweetie she'll be brought up here. We've put a lot of care into the design of our cages to ensure our charges are comfortable and able to move around, but most importantly, they're able to spend time out here in the garden and although they can't physically interact, they can see other orangutans which helps keep their spirits up and gives them something to look forward too.'

'Are orangutans able to pick up human diseases then?' asked Bel.

'Absolutely,' said Pieter emphatically. 'They share ninety-seven percent of our DNA but they don't have the immunity that we humans have built up so they're very susceptible.'

From the quarantine centre Pieter took them over to the nursery. 'Oh my,' said Danni as they entered the nursery. She counted eight infant orangutans, each one with a carer just as Pieter had told them.

'All orangutans two years or under live here in the nursery, where our carers try to replicate the sort of nurturing they would normally get from their natural mothers; diet, physical contact, climbing training, everything. So for example, the little ones are bottle fed entirely until they're milk teeth come in and then we gradually introduce various fruits, mashed up soft fruits to begin with. Come outside and have a look,' he said leading them through the back of the building out into a large thickly treed yard with various climbing frames and obstacles.

'It looks like a playground for orangutans!' commented Bel.

Pieter laughed. 'That's exactly what it is, except this one is designed specifically to get the little ones climbing and gripping because although orangutans are born for life in the trees, climbing is a skill they still need to learn as well as developing their muscles so they have the strength for it. As you can see,' he said indicating to several carers in the yard with their young charges, 'our carers spend a lot of time out here encouraging the little ones to use their hands and feet to grip.'

The group lingered around the nursery for a while, intrigued by the interplay between the carers and the babies. The bond that Pieter had spoken of was obvious and touching and one that they could all relate to after only a few days caring for Sweetie. As they watched one carer playing with her charge, Rama grinned at Danni, 'I think Sweetie is going to be very happy here.'

Danni's eyes were glistening but this time they were happy tears. She beamed at Rama. 'I think she's going to be very happy too. What a wonderful place!' On hearing her comment, Bel wandered over and threw and arm around Danni's waist. 'She's going to love it! I wish I could come back and see her here in the months to come.'

Overhearing the comment, Pieter smiled at the girls. 'You're welcome to come back anytime you're in the area. Just come to the main office and ask for me.'

'Before we leave Borneo, Tim and I might just take you up on that Pieter.'

'Okay, time to move on folks. Let's head over to the forest school which is where we move the little ones to after they leave the nursery.'

They followed Pieter deeper into the forest until they reached a small building perched on the edge of large grassed clearing. Like the nursery school, there were several climbing apparatus spaced around the clearing, but these were bigger and higher and incorporated platforms suspended high above the ground.

'Where are all the orangutans?' Bel asked.

'In there,' said Pieter indicating towards the adjoining forest. 'At forest school the orangutans spend most of the day in the jungle in groups of eight or more. This is where they really hone the skills they'll need to survive in the wild. They spend their days climbing and swinging in the trees, learning to build nests, learning more about what they can and can't eat and also about the natural dangers they'll encounter such as snakes. All under the watchful eye of our carers. Late in the afternoon they come back here to the main lawn for a snack and some milk and to get some rest.'

'Sounds like a good life,' commented Rama.

Pieter nodded, 'It is and it's here that our young charges really grow up. Why don't we walk into the forest a little way and see if we can find a group of orangutans?'

His suggestion was met with enthusiasm so Pieter led them off along a well-worn trail into the forest. After a few minutes, he stopped and cocked his head, listening carefully. 'Hear that?' he asked. They all nodded. The sound of rustling trees and snapping branches was clearly discernable. 'I think we've found a group. Watch your step,' he warned as he set off through the forest towards the noise. After scrambling for a few minutes through the thick leaf litter, over logs and around sprawling buttress roots, Pieter stopped again and pointed up into the trees. 'There you go.'

The dark orange fur of a young orangutan was easy to spot high up in the tree. Casting their gazes wider they soon picked out five or six more as well as a couple lumbering across the forest floor. 'Oh look at them!' exclaimed Danni excitedly. There were collective oohs and ahh's from the group as they watched the orangutans moving through the trees. The older ones moved quite effortlessly, swinging casually from branch to branch, but Pieter pointed to one of the younger ones who was hanging from a thick vine by a hand and foot. She was absolutely adorable; short with a cute round belly and bright orange fur that would darken as she matured. 'See how she's reaching out for that branch? She can't quite reach it so she needs to learn to swing over to it. Watch her now.' Unaware of her audience the little orangutan stretched away from the vine she was holding then swung her body forward trying to generate the momentum she need to close the gap to the other branch. Just missing it she tried again but this time as she swung forward she let go with her foot and used her lower body as a pendulum and easily reached the other branch. The onlookers let out a collective sigh. 'Well done little one,' said Danni smiling broadly.

Even Pieter was grinning. 'She's learning. As she gets stronger and improves her co-ordination, manoeuvring between the trees will become effortless.' Spotting the carer nearby, Pieter left them happily watching the orangutans whilst he went over to chat with him. 'That little one is Kesi,' he told them when he returned. 'She only came to the forest school about two months ago but she's doing very well.'

'Pieter, when do the orangutans get released back into the wild?' Tim asked.

'Once we're confident an orangutan can build nests and find their own food we move them to a special protected area known as the 'Orangutan Islands', a group of five uninhabited islands located in the middle of the river just behind the veterinary clinic. We keep the islands as natural as possible with minimal human contact. Before they're released into the wild, the inhabitants spend at least two dry seasons and one wet season there to prove they can cope with the changes in food supply and living in the tree tops during the wet season when the islands become flooded.'

'So they're entirely self-sufficient then?' Danni asked.

'As much as is practical. Obviously being on an island restricts their ability to forage as widely as they would otherwise so we do give them two small supplemental meals a day. Importantly though, during the dry season when food is naturally in shorter supply, we don't increase the supplemental feeds. This is to ensure they learn to cope with naturally occurring fluctuations in supply. Also the orangutans remain under our observation. We have a strict policy of sighting each individual orangutan daily. If one goes missing we'll send out a search party until they're found. That way we can intervene in the case of illness or injury,' Pieter explained.

'I must say I'm impressed with everything I've seen here Pieter,' said Rama. 'Very impressed. Can I ask how many orangutans have been successfully released back into the wild?'

'Just over a hundred and fifty. We've got quite few on the Islands ready for release now but it's always a challenge to find a suitable location for them; somewhere that's relatively untouched environment and has adequate food sources and is safe from humans. To complicate matters, orangutans have to be released into the area they originated from to prevent genetic mix-up with other populations. For instance, an orangutan from east or central Kalimantan can't be mixed with one from west Kalimantan. Then once we've identified a suitable location, the logistics of getting the orangutan there come into play. The season has to be favourable and as you can imagine, the release sites are pretty remote so we often have to use helicopters or light planes that can land on rivers. It's always an expensive operation so sometimes its lack of funding that holds us back.'

'And I suppose you need to get them off the islands to make room for others coming through?' surmised Tim.

Pieter nodded, 'Precisely and we're not talking one or two individuals. We try to release new orangutans onto the island in small groups that they're already familiar with. It helps the transition process. Some will eventually leave the group and go off on their own but others prefer to stay together. It's the same story when we release them into the wild.'

'How successful have the releases been Pieter? I presume there's some sort of ongoing monitoring?' Rama asked.

'Absolutely. Not only do we want to know how our orangutans are doing, the feedback is vital to ensure our rehabilitation program is working so periodically we send field teams out to run check-ups if we can entice them out of the trees. So far, most of the orangutans we've released are doing well.'

'Pieter, I can't thank you enough for showing us around,' said Danni, voicing a sentiment that was backed up by everyone else. Taking that as a signal to head back to the main complex, Pieter led the group back through the forest to the veterinary clinic where they collected Alyson who had been tending Sweetie with her BOS counterparts.

'How is she Alyson?' Bel asked.

'She's doing okay. The vets here are pretty happy with her overall and she's been moved to one of the quarantine cages now. Her new carer is already with her and they're getting acquainted. She's in good hands folks,' said Alyson confidently.

'Now I've seen the facilities I've got no doubts about that,' said Danni smiling.

'Looks like our work here is done then,' said Jon. 'But we've still got a long drive back. How about we grab some lunch then hit the road? Pieter, is the warung over at the worker's village open? Will you join us for lunch?' he asked when Pieter nodded. Agreeing, Pieter walked them back up to a small village adjacent to the main entrance where they sat at one big table in the village warung.

'I assumed all your workers would be local,' said Tim as they waited for their meals.

'Most are but some come from further afield and we also have international volunteers, researchers, specialist technicians and veterinary staff who come and work for us. So we've built this village and common-housing to accommodate everyone,' Pieter explained.

'It's a pretty big operation, much bigger than I imagined.'

'Yes it is,' agreed Pieter, 'and it takes a lot of effort and funding to keep it going. At the moment we've got about two hundred workers and just over six hundred orangutans in our care. We've had to expand considerably over the years to keep up with the growing numbers of orangutans coming to us.'

'How many orangutans are left in the wild?' Danni asked curiously.

'Current estimates put the number at around 40,000 in Borneo and Sumatra. It may sound a lot but that number represents a fifty percent decline in the past decade alone.'

'We're thinking of heading up to Kutai National Park to try and see some orangutans in the wild,' Bel said.

Pieter looked doubtful. 'Well there are wild orangutans in the park for sure, but to be honest your chances of seeing them are very slim. The only place I can guarantee you'll see orangutans in the wild is Tanjung Puting National Park about four hundred kilometres west of here.'

'Fabulous place,' Jon enthused. 'Maya and I visited the park several years ago and had an amazing time.'

'I've never heard of it,' said Tim looking interested. 'Bel and I didn't really consider travelling that far west.'

'Tanjung Puting, or Camp Leakey to be specific, was where orangutan conservation really started when a Canadian researcher by the name of Biruté Galdikas set up a research station there in the early seventies. Galdikas was one the so-called Trimates, three women that renowned paleo archaeologist Louis Leakey sent to study primates in their natural environment. You may not recognize her name but you'll probably have heard of the other two; Dian Fossey—'

'—yes, of 'Gorillas in the Mist' fame,' Bel interjected.

Pieter nodded, 'That's the one; that movie made her a household name. She went to Rwanda to study the mountain gorillas. The other lady was Jane Goodall who studied chimpanzees in Tanzania. Anyway, as well as her studies of wild orangutans, Galdikas established rehabilitation and release programs for captive, injured and orphaned orangutans, education programs and campaigned relentlessly for their protection. After years of pressure from Galdikas, Tanjung Puting was eventually declared a national park. Over the years, Galdikas rehabilitation program successfully returned nearly two hundred of the orangutans to the wild and Tanjung Puting now boasts the largest wild orangutan population in the world. It's one of the few places where tourists can see them in their natural environment.'

'It certainly sounds intriguing,' said Tim. 'What's involved in visiting the park?'

Jon and Pieter grinned at each other. 'Well now, that's the fun part,' said Jon. 'The park can only be accessed by boat so you fly into Pangkalanbun, then catch a *klotok* from the nearby port town of Kumai and spend the next few days eating and sleeping on the boat whilst you cruise up the Sekonyer River dropping into the various camps to visit the orangutans at their feeding stations. Picture yourselves lounging up on the deck with proboscis monkeys watching you from the riverbank and macaques leaping from tree to tree. If you get lucky, you might see a crocodile or two, maybe even a gibbon; if you don't see them you'll certainly hear them whoop whooping to each other.'

'Oh my, that does sound like an experience not to be missed,' ventured Danni, looking at Bel and Tim who were nodding in agreement.

'I think we've just had a change of plans,' Bel grinned.

On the long drive back to Banjarmasin there was a lot of excited chatter about the Tanjung Puting expedition as they dragged every detail of Jon's previous visit out of him. Jon even phoned ahead to Maya and asked her to dig out their guide's name and make contact with him to check his availability. By the time they arrived back in Banjarmasin, Maya greeted them with the news that the guide was on standby to take them to Tanjung Puting. All they had to do was book their flights and when Bel and Tim suggested Rama join them, it hadn't taken much persuasion to convince him to do so. For her part Danni had mixed feelings about that; on the one hand she thrilled to be able to spend a few more days with him and share what promised to be a real adventure, but on the other hand she knew prolonging her time with him would probably only make matters worse. But it was a done deal; Rama was coming with them and Danni could hardly protest without a valid reason and she certainly wasn't about to confess her feelings for him to anyone else.

After such a long day everyone was keen to have an early night but as they waited for Yusuf to come and collect them, Danni made the bittersweet realization that her time in Banjarmasin with all the wonderful people she had met was coming to an end since the Tanjung Puting adventure would mark the final stage of her holiday and she would begin her homeward journey from there.

Their last day in Banjarmasin was fairly leisurely, starting with a much needed sleep-in. Rama met them at the hotel and they walked back along the main street to a travel agent who was able to arrange flights to Pangkalanbun the following morning and in Danni's case her onward flights from there to Bali to connect with her return flight to Australia.

Whilst they ate lunch at the markets, Rama put in a call to the Tanjung Puting guide to confirm their arrival time and just like that everything was arranged. Danni's excitement however, was tinged with a little sadness knowing that over the next few hours she had to say goodbye to some people that she'd grown very fond of and in all reality, would probably never see again. So with Bel, Tim and Rama along for moral support, they all walked up to Ahmed's.

Ahmed's greeting was expansive as always. 'Hello everyone.' But his smile quickly faded in response the friend's forlorn faces. 'What is wrong? Did it not go well with your little orangutan?'

Danni gave him a weak smile. 'She's fine Ahmed and the rehab centre is wonderful. She'll be well cared for.' She paused, 'Actually, I've come to say goodbye Ahmed. We're all flying over to Pangkalanbun in the morning and I'll be going home to Australia from there, so this is it for me.'

Ahmed looked aghast. 'Oh no, no, no, Miss Danni. Surely you will be back again sometime? Rama, you must convince her to stay.' To which Rama merely shrugged as if to say it was out of his hands, but Danni found Ahmed's unwavering efforts to push her and Rama together amusing enough to bring a grin to her face.

'I'm afraid that's not possible Ahmed. I have a home and a life to go back to in Australia,' she told him as she threaded her arm through his. 'But you've become very dear to me Ahmed so I fully intend to keep in touch and I'll be thinking of you every time I make one of your recipes.'

Ahmed sighed heavily and patted her arm. 'This is a very sad occasion Miss Danni. Tonight, you must all come back here to Ahmed's for your last dinner in Banjarmasin.'

Danni looked around the others who all nodded in agreement. 'Thank you Ahmed, I'd like that immensely.' Then as she extricated her arm from Ahmed's, 'Well I still have a few more friends to say goodbye to so I better get on with it.'

Ahmed's face suddenly brightened as an idea struck him. 'Bring them all here Miss Danni, all your friends. Tonight, we will have a party at Ahmed's.'

'Ahmed that's a great idea! My treat, my way of thanking everyone who has made my time here so special.' said Danni smiling happily. 'What do you think guys?'

Once again, everyone nodded. 'Good thinking Ahmed,' complemented Bel.

The prospect of a party lifted everyone's spirits no end. Rama jumped on the phone to call Jon and Yusuf to invite them along and then took his leave citing work to do ahead of the upcoming trip, arranging to meet up again at Ahmed's later that evening. Realising they could be in for a late night, the rest of them decided to have a lazy afternoon back at the hotel and get their packing done, although Danni used the time to do some more work on her marketing campaign for Rama and call Rob.

'Hey Rob, it's me,' she said when the crackling phone line connected.

'Hi babe. How's it going over there?'

'Great. We transferred Sweetie-pie to a rehab centre yesterday and got a tour in the process. It's an amazing facility but awful to learn about the plight of the orangutans.' She went on to fill Rob in on the details and was pleased that he seemed genuinely interested. 'Anyway, tomorrow we're flying over to a place called Pangkalanbun where we're going to catch a *klotok*, that's a local houseboat, into Tanjung Puting National Park. We've been told it's the best place to see orangutans in the wild.'

'You're really into the orangutans aren't you?' Rob observed.

'I guess I am. It's funny, until Sweetie, I never really given them any thought but now I just love them. There such amazing creatures and so vulnerable. It breaks my heart to think that our kids or grandkids may never have the chance to see an orangutan in the wild.'

'I guess the same can be said for a lot of other threatened species,' said Rob.

'It's a sobering thought isn't it? This whole trip, including some of the things I learned in Bali, has really opened my eyes to the pressure that we humans are putting on our planet and everything on it. Thank God there are people like Jon and Maya and Pieter at the rehab centre who are trying to raise awareness and clean up some of the mess we humans are making.'

'It might not be enough babe.'

'Then this planet is in serious trouble Rob.' There was a brief silence as they both digested the implications then Rob said, 'Hey, I better get back to work. Give me your flight details so I can meet you at the airport.'

Danni gave him the details and promised to call along the way to let him know how she was travelling, then disconnected the call with Rob's parting comment that he was looking forward to having her home ringing in her ears. Whilst she was looking forward to seeing Rob, she honestly didn't feel a lot of enthusiasm about going home. Borneo had definitely gotten under her skin and made her question her life back home and how she was living it. Then there was the whole Rama issue; the thought of never seeing him again was unbearable but at the same time she knew for the sake of her marriage it was the only way forward. She'd promised Rama a marketing campaign and she intended to see it through, not just for him, but also the hundreds, perhaps thousands of people that he could help through Helping Hands, but once the launch was over she would bow out.

***

The party at Ahmed's was a happy, raucous affair. Jon, Maya and the children were there, as was Alyson. Yusuf brought along his wife and son who after some initial shyness seemed to enjoy themselves. Ahmed's family also joined them; his wife and three daughters. Bel and Tim had already met the eldest two when they'd made the breakfast deliveries but it was the first time Danni had met any of his family and she immediately warmed to them all, making a point of spending time getting to know them. Ahmed had set up a long table for the big group and arranged trays of food to be brought out at regular intervals and in between attending to the other restaurant patrons and supervising the cooking, he still found time to enjoy the party. Later on when the restaurant was empty but for their large group, Danni was thrilled when the staff, who's friendly banter she'd enjoyed during the cooking lessons, drifted over and joined in.

As predicted, it was late when the party finally started to break up. First to leave, Jon and Maya with the children who had long since fallen asleep on a rug Maya had spread out in the corner. Danni hugged them both warmly and promised to keep in touch via email. Yusuf and his family followed them out the door then Alyson and Ahmed's staff drifted off one by one. When Ahmed's wife and daughters headed upstairs to their apartment above the restaurant the time had come to bid her final farewell to Ahmed. He looked inordinately pleased and a hint watery eyed when Danni gave him a big hug. 'Thank you for a lovely party Ahmed.'

'Ah it was my pleasure. You keep practicing your Indonesian cooking Miss Danni and when you come back one day, I will show you some more.'

Danni didn't see any point in telling him she may never get back to Banjarmasin but then who knew, maybe one day she could convince Rob to come to Borneo together. 'I fully intend to show off my new cooking skills to my family and friends Ahmed and of course you'll get full credit. I can't thank you enough for your hospitality,' she told him as she stood on tip toe and gave him a peck on the cheek, then with one final wave she turned and left the restaurant.

'You all right?' Bel asked, walking alongside her.

'Yeah, I am. It was a really enjoyable evening but it just seems like the last couple of days have been all about goodbyes. I feel very fortunate to have met such wonderful people. The funny thing is the friendships I've developed over the last couple of weeks, yourself and Tim included, are stronger than many of those I have with people I've known and considered friends for years. Things just seem more real over here.'

'Tim and I've made the same observation over the years we've been volunteering. I think in poor countries where people are working hard just to survive, there's no time or energy for the sort of conditions we westerners tend to put on friendships; do they have the right job, drive the right car, live in the right suburb and so on. None of that comes into it in places like this; you're just accepted for who you are, even among the expats.' Danni could see an element of truth in Bel's comments, even recognizing some of that in her own relationships with people over the years and she vowed then and there to be a better person.

CHAPTER THIRTEEN

As the twin prop airplane descended through the light cloud on approach to Iskandar airport, Pangkalanbun, Danni leaned forward eagerly peering out the window. Conveniently, the plane banked right giving her a birds-eye view of the countryside as they turned inland to follow the course of a wide inlet away from the Java Sea. The countryside all around looked relatively flat, a vast green mosaic of cultivated fields and swathe of jungle dissected by a wide, brown river meandering lazily away from the head of the inlet into the interior as far at the eye could see. As they flew lower, Danni made out several large ships and a small port surrounded by a smattering of rural homes. Aware that Rama was peering over her shoulder, she sat back to give him a better view. 'That must be Kumai,' he said pointing to the port. 'I believe that's the home port for the *klotok* fleet.'

Danni grinned, feeling a rush of excitement. 'So our *klotok* is down there somewhere waiting for us. I'm so looking forward to this trip.'

Rama sat back in his seat and returned her grin. 'Me too,' he answered just as they touched down.

They disembarked and walked across the tarmac to the neat, terminal building with the big *Selamat Datang Pangkalanbun* sign, *Welcome to Pangkalanbun. Inside,* posters of Tanjung Puting and orangutans were adorned every wall leaving no doubts about the region's main attraction.

'Rama?' The tentatively spoken inquiring came when they had barely stepped inside the terminal building.

'That's me,' Rama confirmed offering his hand. 'You must be Isy?' When he nodded, Rama quickly introduced the rest of them.

'I am pleased to meet you. Did you have a good flight?' he asked politely. Compared to most of his countrymen, Isy was fairly short and stocky but looked as strong as an ox. He seemed a little shy which struck Danni as rather unusual for someone who made their living as a guide, but his English was good and Jon and Maya had both been full of praise for him so he obviously knew his stuff.

Isy stood back whilst they collected their luggage but quickly stepped forward to take Danni's bag as she pulled it off the carousel. 'Thanks Isy,' she said smiling. Once they had everything he led them out of the terminal to a small mini-van they piled into. Isy climbed into the driver's seat, explaining before they drove off that they had a fifteen minute drive to Kumai where their *klotok* was berthed. If the scenery on the short drive was relatively benign the little port town was anything but. Isy slowed the van to walking pace as he inched his way along the main street, pushing his way through the tightly packed market stalls, shop houses and pedestrians. It was bustling and colourful and exotic. Danni followed Tim's lead and slid open her window for a better look, only to be assaulted by a screeching din.

'Holy crap, what's that noise?' exclaimed Tim.

'Swiftlets,' answered Rama. 'See those concrete buildings?' He pointed to several tall concrete buildings looming over the town. As high as twenty metres, the slab sided buildings were pockmarked with small openings about the size of an A4 page and were incredibly ugly. 'They're bird houses, built to provide artificial nesting sites for thousands of Swiftlets. They make the nests from their solidified saliva and as awful as it sounds, the nests are edible. They're the prime ingredient in bird's nest soup which you've no doubt heard of and are said to be an aphrodisiac—'

'I think I'll stick with Viagra thank you very much,' Tim joked, drawing chuckles from everyone.

'Well anyway,' Rama continued, 'the nests fetch pretty high prices. In the old days they were harvested from caves and rocky crevices in the jungle but then some bright spark came up with the idea of building these birdhouses. They're springing up all over Borneo now, even in places like this which on account of the flat terrain, are well outside the Swiftlets natural nesting habitat.'

'They're damn noisy,' said Danni, closing her window.

'They are,' agreed Rama. 'But most of the noise you're hearing now is actually Swiflet recordings played out over a loud speaker. It's supposed to attract the birds into the bird houses.'

'So they just keep playing the recordings incessantly over and over again?' asked Danni, thinking it seemed too incredulous to be true.

'From early morning to late at night they play it,' said Isy over his shoulder. 'The Chinese come here and build them. They pay the right people to be allowed to build them and then grow rich whilst the locals are driven mad with the noise and the bird poo.'

'That's outrageous!' exclaimed Bel. 'Is there nothing that can be done to stop them?'

Isy shook his head. 'Not really. The locals complain and maybe they get a little compensation money to keep them quiet but the noise doesn't go away.'

A few hundred metres past the crowded market place they reached the river's edge. Isy parked adjacent to a large, rather tawdry orangutan sculpture which they gave only a cursory glance, everyone being more interested in the small *klotok* fleet moored alongside the dock. Eagerly, they grabbed their luggage and followed Isy to one of the *klotoks*, handing their gear up to a waiting crew member and following it aboard. They barely had time to get their bearings before Isy introduced them to the captain, his wife who was also their cook and the younger crewman, none of whom spoke any English. Introductions complete, the captain had them underway within minutes whilst the four friends stared curiously around them.

The *klotok* was about sixteen metres long with a narrow beam, shallow draft and solid timber construction. It had an enclosed lower deck but for the bow and stern and a covered upper deck where the four friends now found themselves. It was open-sided with a low rail and simply furnished with a rattan floor mat, thin mattresses and big lounging pillows and a hammock suspended from the roof beams. On the foredeck were two canvas sun lounges, a table and four chairs on the aft deck and it was absolutely charming.

'Oh I love it!' said Danni.

'Me too,' agreed Bel then Tim and Rama chimed in with 'Me three' and 'Me four.' They all stood around grinning happily at each other as the small harbour receded behind them.

Isy seemed pleased with their reactions and took them on a quick tour of the boat beginning with a small, open roofed cabin on the lower aft deck which turned out to be the bathroom. He explained that the shower pumped water direct from the river so it was cold water only, which in the tropical heat was unlikely to be a problem and the toilet flushed straight into the river so they were to dispose of toilet paper only in the bin provided. From the aft deck they followed Isy through a small doorway into the galley, a small space with low headroom so that they had to crouch down. The walls were adorned with hanging pots, woks, plastic tubs and utensils, one corner contained a large cooler, a big wooden chopping block and a charcoal brazier sitting on the middle of the floor and squatting among them working away was their cook. She looked up and gave the group a friendly smile as they passed through then turned her attention back to the job at hand.

From the galley they entered the central cabin, a much larger space with ample headroom and big open windows. It was unfurnished but for a well-stocked bookshelf at one end which Isy told them to feel free to use and a pile of foam mattresses and bedding neatly stacked under the stairs which Danni guessed was what they would be sleeping on. They peered through another small doorway at the front of the cabin into the wheelhouse, a tiny space with just enough room for the captain behind the wheel.

'Please feel free to use the *klotok* at your pleasure,' Isy said at the conclusion of the tour. 'Also, when the engine is running we have power available for charging your camera batteries and so on.'

'Isy, this is great mate,' said Tim giving him a friend slap on the back.

Isy smiled. 'Okay, so please relax and enjoy the cruising and soon we will serve afternoon tea.'

'Dibs on the hammock,' said Bel, kicking off her sandals and climbing in. Tim lounged beside her on the cushions leaving the sun lounges up front free for Danni and Rama.

Danni lay back and propped her feet on the side rail. 'This is really good,' she said. 'The view from up here on the upper deck is excellent.'

Rama grinned, looking supremely happy with the set-up. 'Damn fine way to travel.'

The captain steered a course down river passing the occasional fishing boat and carefully navigating around their long nets. Afternoon tea was brought to the table about half an hour into the journey; *pisang goreng* and sliced fresh fruit washed down with cold lemonade. The trip was off to a very good start and the mood as they ate and watched the passing scenery was light-hearted and happy.

Away from Kumai, jungle grew right to the river's edge so thickly it looked like an impenetrable green wall but as they finished lunch, the boat slowed and turned towards a smaller river mouth flanked by a dense mass of low palms. Not wanting to miss anything, everyone returned to the foredeck, Danni and Rama claiming the sun lounges again, Bel and Tim sitting on the upper deck with their legs dangling over the front. Isy appeared on the lower foredeck and scanned ahead.

'This is the nipas palm forest,' he told them. 'It marks the entrance to Tanjung Puting and the Sekonyer River.' Danni snapped off some photos, determined to capture the start of their adventure. They chugged onwards, waving happily to a passing boat heading upriver.

'What's he doing Isy?' Danni asked when they passed a lone man loading palm leaves into a canoe.

'The locals use the nipas palms to make roof thatching, mats, baskets and other goods.'

'Are they allowed to do that? I thought this was a national park.'

Isy nodded, 'Without any other means to make a living, many local Dayaks rely on the natural resources within the park for their livelihood.'

'So are there Dayaks living in the park?'

'Yes, at Tanjung Harapan village. We will go past there today. If you like on the way home we can stop in so you can tour the village.'

'I'd like that,' Danni confirmed.

As they travelled further upriver, the vegetation changed again; the nipas palms giving way to low jungle growth and pandanas palms, forming a tangled mass of tree roots and vegetation at the water's edge. Suddenly Isy straightened and hurriedly tapped on the wheelhouse roof signalling the captain to slow. 'Look, look, there,' he said urgently, pointing into a stand of pandanas palms. Everyone one sprang to their feet just in time to see the unmistakable orange fur of an orangutan before the startled creature made a hasty retreat into the thick undergrowth and was quickly lost from sight. It was only a fleeting glimpse but the excitement among the friends was palpable and even Isy looked pleased.

'Oh my God, our first orangutan already!' said Bel excitedly, almost dancing around on the spot. 'I didn't think we'd see one so soon.'

Isy was smiling broadly. 'You're very lucky to see a wild orangutan already.'

'So that was definitely a wild orangutan and not a rehabilitated one?' asked Danni.

Isy nodded emphatically. 'Yes for sure. On this side of the river, always wild orangutans. Rehabilitated orangutans were only released on the other side of the river.'

'And they haven't swum across?'

'No, no. Orangutans don't swim.' Isy explained.

The friends grinned at each other. 'Well it looks like Pieter and Jon were spot on with their advice to come here,' said Tim. 'Isy, what are our chances of seeing more today?'

'Later when we get into the taller jungle we might see one or two in their nests,' said Isy. 'By late afternoon they climb into a tree to make a nest for the night. Sometimes we can see them from the river.'

From then on everyone kept their eyes peeled on the river banks. They passed by Tanjung Harapan village, a small settlement set back from the water's edge which was crowded with canoes and longboats. It looked interesting but Danni was content to visit on the way home, for now she was more interested in Tanjung Puting's natural attractions. About two hours into the journey the jungle got noticeably thicker and the trees taller, some giants soaring well above the surrounding canopy. It was in one of those that Isy pointed out an old orangutan nest which looked like a crude oversized birds nest. 'Will it get used again Isy?' Danni asked.

He shook his head. 'No, they make a new one each night.'

Within a few minutes Isy spotted another one, this time occupied, the matted orange fur of a sleeping orangutan clearly visible. Isy produced a small pair of binoculars and passed them around for the group to use. Even with the binoculars it was impossible to make out the orangutans features but it was interesting just the same. Once again everyone settled back down to scan the river bank and then about two hundred metres ahead Danni noticed some tall trees bending and swaying in a cascade along the river bank. She stood, eyes fixed ahead. Isy followed her gaze, 'Proboscis monkeys,' he announced.

'What, where?' said Bel and once again everyone was back on their feet. As the *klotok* chugged closer the monkeys came into view, a whole troop of two dozen or more individuals clinging to the trees. The captain brought the *klotok* to a stop right alongside, giving them a great view and so close they could make out the monkey's pale faces and long noses. Danni was surprised how big the adult monkeys were, especially compared to the macaques she was used to seeing around Bali. The troop seemed quite unperturbed by their audience; in fact several individuals seemed as interested in the *klotok* passengers as they were in them, peering intently down at them from their lofty perches. Others in the troop put on a show for them, swinging through the branches and taking giant leaps between trees, long limbs spread wide and tail in the air to stabilise their flight.

'Despite those noses, I think they're kind of cute,' announced Danni to her friends.

'So do I,' agreed Bel. 'Look at that little one staring at us through the branches.'

'They look like they've been drinking too much beer,' laughed Tim referring to their pot-bellies.

Danni glanced across at Rama and looked away quickly when she caught him looking at her. With all the excitement, her feelings for him had been pushed aside and now suddenly they were back in her mind. Silently she cursed, determined not to let it ruin what was shaping up to be an amazing few days. She glanced at him again, relieved that his attention was once more on the monkey's. Following his lead she turned back to the monkeys, snapping off lots of photographs as she tried to capture their antics.

Finally, when Isy was sure they'd seen enough he called to the captain who got the *klotok* underway again. As it turned out, they saw a lot more proboscis monkeys and even a few long-tailed macaques. Isy explained that both species were most active in the early morning and late afternoon which was why cruising the river at that time of day was so rewarding. The four friends quickly became adept at spotting them in the trees; their loud honking calls, the swaying branches and loud rustling of the leaves as they crashed through the trees was a dead giveaway. Now they knew what to look for, they even spotted a few more orangutan nests although only one was actually occupied.

As the sun was getting low, the captain nudged up to some branches sticking out into the river and tied off the *klotok*. This was where they were spending the night. With the engine off and the monkeys in the trees around them having settled down for the night all was quiet. Whilst Isy and the crew busied themselves around the boat, the four passengers enjoyed some downtime, reading or dozing and just soaking up the ambience. Just as darkness fell Isy and the cook brought dinner to the table, a tasty meal of stir-fried vegetables, noodles and chicken washed down with sweet tea and consumed in the flickering candlelight as cicadas sung in the night around them.

Whilst the friends enjoyed their meal, Isy and the crewman dragged mattresses onto the deck and made up their beds within the confines of a protective mosquito net they dropped down from the rafters. After inquiring if they had everything they needed, Isy pointed to a lights switch then retired below deck, presumably to have his dinner with the rest of the crew.

'This is magic,' said Bel. 'Absolute magic!'

'I'll say,' agreed Danni. 'Never in a million years did I imagine myself doing something like this. This is the sort of thing you usually only see on TV documentaries. It never occurred to me if film-makers can do this sort of thing so can ordinary people like us.'

'Judging by all the posters at the airport and the number of *klotoks* in the port, there must be quite a few people doing it,' comment Tim.

'Isy told me he guides people all year round, even during the monsoon when the low-lying park becomes quite inundated. If you can put up with the heat and the rain, the advantage of travelling at that time of year is they can get the *klotok* into areas that are inaccessible the rest of the year,' said Rama.

'Well so far, I'm fast becoming a *klotok* devotee,' laughed Bel. 'It's a fabulous way to travel, especially when we've got such a good crew looking after us. Rama, do you think there'd be any opportunity for Tim and I do some river trips where we'll be going?'

'Yes definitely, *klotoks* are in use all over Borneo. Most of them are working boats carrying cargo and passengers so they won't be quite as comfortable as this, but the owners will never turn down an opportunity to earn a few extra rupiah from a special charter and you'll always be well looked after.'

Bel and Tim looked at each other and nodded. 'It's certainly worth looking into,' said Tim.

Danni put her hands over her ears. 'Stop talking, I'm getting jealous!' she laughed.

The four friends lingered around the dinner table, chatting quietly amongst themselves, until Isy and the cook returned to collect their dirty dishes. 'Thank you, that was a lovely meal,' Danni complemented the cook, earning her a shy smile when Isy translated for her.

'Okay, so we will leave you to yourselves now,' said Isy. 'But if you need anything just call me. Tomorrow we will visit the orangutans at Pondok Tanggui and take a short trek through the jungle and later we will travel on the black water river to Camp Leakey.'

'Sounds excellent,' Tim told him as they all bid him goodnight.

'You know what?' said Danni stifling a yawn. 'That bed looks pretty good to me so I'm going to call it a night if no one has any objections?'

Bel pushed back in her chair. 'I'm with you Danni. I've got no idea what time it is but I'm knackered too.' The two men obviously agreed because after they'd given the girls a few minutes to get changed and sort themselves out for bed, they slipped in under the mosquito net and settled themselves into bed. The mattresses were arranged side by side across the deck, Danni having chosen the foremost one, then Bel, Tim and Rama, an arrangement that suited Danni as given how she felt about Rama the thought of lying beside him, no matter how innocent, made her feel rather uncomfortable. Unbeknown to Danni, Rama was also quite happy with the arrangement but for an entirely different reason; he simply didn't trust himself not to reach for her in the night.

Danni slept soundly right through the night, lulled to sleep by the sounds of the jungle. There was a light mist hanging over the river when she woke. The cicadas' song had long since faded and it was still and quiet but for the deep breathing of her companions and the occasional plop-plop of fish feeding at the surface. As quietly as she could, Danni rose and stepped over her sleeping companions as she made her way to the *mandi* where she used the toilet and splashed some water on her face. Returning to the upper deck she quietly located a hair band among her luggage and caught her hair up in a loose bun, totally unaware the Rama was watching her through the netting. The short cotton sleeping shirt she was wearing wasn't meant to be sexy but he could tell she wasn't wearing any bras underneath it and when she raised her arms to fix her hair, the hem lifted high on her thighs. Rama's breath caught in his throat and he felt his blood rushing to his loins. He willed himself to close his eyes or look away but he simply couldn't. He watched her for a few minutes more as she leaned against a pillar and gazed out over the river and only when he was sure he wouldn't embarrass himself did he rise and go across to join her.

Danni turned and smiled at him as he stood beside her. 'Beautiful isn't it? And peaceful.'

'There are worse things to wake up to in the morning that's for sure,' Rama agreed.

'I wonder what that noise is?' said Danni, cocking her head at the haunting whoop-whoop call ringing out across the jungle. 'I've been hearing it since before dawn.'

'I think its gibbons.'

Danni grinned delightedly, 'Really! I can't believe I'm on a boat on a river in the middle of a jungle in Borneo being woken by gibbons. Pinch me, this can't be real!'

Rama grinned at her. Danni's enthusiasm was contagious and he thought not for the first time, how much he loved her lack of pretence. 'It is kind of surreal isn't it?'

'Rama, can I ask you something?'

'Sure.'

'How do you reconcile your two worlds? I mean, life here in Borneo, even Bali to an extent, is so different to Australia. How do manage to move between the two without suffering some kind of culture shock every time?'

Rama looked thoughtful. 'To tell you the truth, these days I spend very little time in Australia. Mostly I only go back for business trips and they're usually far apart. But yeah, I do find it a shock when I walk out of the airport into the madness of Sydney or Melbourne. It takes me a few days to get used to the pace and to be honest I usually can't wait to leave, although I always make a point of catching up with friends and family.' He shrugged. 'I guess the truth of it is that my life is primarily in Indonesia now.'

'So you don't ever see yourself living back in Australia?'

Rama shook his head. 'No not really, at least not permanently. I would like to get married and have a family one day and then I'd have to think about kid's education and their opportunities and whether they would be best served in Australia. It's the same issue my parents faced with me.'

'I can see that would be a bit of a dilemma.'

Rama shrugged a little self-consciously, 'Well it's not something I have to worry about for a while yet since I have neither a wife nor kids. What about you Danni? Are you planning on having kids one day?'

Danni looked out across the water. 'Maybe, we haven't really decided. Rob's fairly indifferent about it and I guess I…' she trailed off with a shrug. 'I don't know.' The truth was she did want to have children one day but she wanted Rob to be as committed to it as she was. It was definitely another aspect of their marriage that needed to be addressed, but in the meantime she wasn't about to discuss any of that with Rama.

For his part Rama found her answer a little surprising. The Danni he knew was warm and nurturing and it was hard to imagine her going through life childless. He understood that she had a career, but he didn't get a sense from her that it was an all-encompassing at the expense of everything else deal. And these days having a baby didn't necessarily mean having to put a career on hold, especially not if one had a supporting partner. Perhaps the indifferent husband was the issue? But he reminded himself, it was none of his business so instead he just said, 'Well for what it's worth, I think you'd make a great mum.' And if you were my wife, I'd love to make babies with you, he added silently.

Danni let Rama's observation pass without comment and continued to stare across the water, apparently lost in thought. Rama waited, sensing she had more to say and eventually she stirred, murmuring quietly, 'You know, since I've been here in Borneo and seen the hardships that so many people face here day to day, I can't help but feel as if my life is a bit self-indulgent. Back home we have so much stuff in our lives that is just superfluous to our needs. We think all that stuff will make us happy but it doesn't, not for long anyway. The people I've met here in Borneo are among the happiest people I've ever come across yet they have so little. That doesn't mean they don't strive for more, dream of an easier life, but it won't make them any happier because they already have true inner happiness.'

Without looking his way, Danni could feel Rama staring at her intently. Finally he said, 'Danni, as far as what is really important in life I think you're starting to get it. The day I arrived in Banjarmasin, I remember saying that spending time here in Borneo would develop your cultural competency. I think you've come a long way already because you're starting to look beyond the accepted western ideologies that you were raised with and are opening your mind to other possibilities. In my experience, being able to transcend accepted cultural ideologies is something very few people ever achieve.'

'Well in that sense I'm an accidental traveller,' said Danni. 'It's not something I've consciously set out to do. It's just happenstance. Meeting Bel and Tim and Rob having his accident which ultimately brought me to Borneo, meeting people such as yourself and Maya, finding Sweetie-pie and just seeing some of the things I've seen here. It's made me question things about myself and life in general. To be perfectly honest part of me is a little bit scared that I won't be able to go back to my normal life and find the happiness and contentment I used to have.'

'Some would say that's fate Danni. That all these things are part of your journey to meet whatever it is fate has in store for you. Perhaps fate doesn't intend for you to go back to that life. Have you really been happy and content in your normal life?' Rama asked quietly.

Danni bit her lip. 'I think so, at least I was once. Lately I don't know.'

'Things have a way of creeping up on you. Maybe you've been feeling a little discontent for a while without even realizing it.'

'Yes or maybe it's just a reaction to the here and now. Maybe once I get home and back to what's familiar I'll realize that my life is perfectly fine after all. Right now I just don't know.'

'Or maybe this trip is the catalyst that has brought feelings that were already lurking below the surface to a head. There are lots of possibilities but ultimately does it really matter when you started feeling this way? Doesn't it just come down to how you feel know and what you're prepared to do about it?'

'You make it sound so simple Rama,' said Danni wistfully.

'You might be surprised Danni. Sometimes the hardest part about doing something is making the decision to do it,' said Rama lightly.

Danni was saved from answering when Tim called out, 'Hey you two, where's our coffee? Bel and I've been waiting patiently.'

'This isn't a P&O cruise you know,' retorted Danni.

'Lucky or you'd be out of a job with an attitude like that missy,' Tim replied quick as flash, earning chuckles all round. 'Good thing I've got Bel here to get me a coffee,' he continued. There was a muffled noise from behind the netting which sounded a lot like someone being hit with a pillow. 'Ouch, damn what's a man gotta do…' Rama and Danni were still laughing when Tim stumbled out from the netting rubbing his head and trying, but failing, to look mildly affronted.

Isy opened the hatch covering the narrow staircase to the lower deck and popped his head through. 'Good morning everyone. I trust you slept well?'

'Very well thanks Isy,' Danni answered for them.

'Okay, we will have breakfast shortly,' he replied, then disappeared below deck again.

One by one, they all used the bathroom to change and wash and as promised, breakfast arrived on the table soon after; delicious banana pancakes and an omelette each and Tim finally got his coffee, mumbling 'At least someone cares,' which earned him a playful slap from Bel. As they ate, Isy and the crewman dismantled their bedroom, returning all the bedding back under the stairs on the lower deck. The mist had lifted from the water and activity on the riverbank increased so they ate breakfast surrounded by proboscis monkeys moving and leaping about in the adjacent trees.

'I feel like I'm on a movie set,' commented Bel. 'Like a scene out of the African Queen.'

They were still lingering over breakfast when the *klotok* got underway. Isy came by again to tell them they had about forty-five minutes cruising time to Pondok Tanggui where the first of the orangutan feeding stations was located. Since they would be there early he planned to lead them on a short trek through the jungle and advised them to wear sturdy shoes. Not wanting to miss anything Danni took herself off to the sun lounge on the foredeck as soon as she finished her tea and was joined shortly afterwards by Rama; Bel and Tim content to remain at the table.

Isy took up his usual spot on the bow propped against the wheelhouse. 'Isy, you mentioned a feeding station at Pondok Tanggui. How often are the orangutans fed?'

'Actually the park has three feeding stations, one at each of the original release sites. Feedings occur morning and afternoon at each site, only enough to supplement the orangutan's daily requirements so must still forage for themselves.'

'So are these rehabilitated orangutans being fed?'

'Yes some, but in fact the last orangutan was released into the park in 1995 so now we see also the second and third generation coming in. Sometimes, especially if the season is bad we see wild orangutans also. But sometimes if the season is good even the rehabilitated orangutans don't come in.'

'Is this a good season?' Danni asked.

Isy smiled. 'Don't worry, you will see them,' he assured her.

'Why did they stop releasing orangutans into the park?' Rama asked.

'So as not to put too much pressure on the wild orangutan population. Now under the law, it is possible to release orangutans only where there is not already a large wild population.'

Rama nodded. 'Makes sense.'

Along the way to Pondok Tanggui they passed some locals heading upriver in a wooden speed boat and a fisherman's tiny, thatched hut, as crudely built as anything Danni had seen in her travels so far, but as he was climbing into his narrow canoe the man raised his arm above his head and waved happily.

Bel and Tim joined them on the foredeck as the sturdy timber jetty of Pondok Tanggui came into sight. Excitedly, Bel pointed, 'Look there!' Casually lounging in the branches hanging over the jetty was a mature orangutan, quite unperturbed by the *klotoks* arrival and the excited passengers. 'That's Daisy,' Isy told them. 'One of the rehabilitated orangutans. She likes to be around people.' As soon as the *klotok* was tied alongside the jetty, Isy and the four friends clamoured ashore and peering up at Daisy who looked back nonchalantly and pursed her lips at them. Once the group pulled their attention away from Daisy, Isy led them along a timber boardwalk through the freshwater mangroves and lumbering slowly towards them on all four limbs, came another orangutan. The group hesitated as they drew closer but the orangutan kept coming, then stopped and stood up when she reached them.

Danni giggled, 'Looks like she came to welcome us. Another rehabilitated orangutan I take it Isy?'

'This is Princess. She likes to meet the *klotoks* in the hope of scoring something to eat.'

'Will she?' Bel asked.

'No it's not allowed but it doesn't stop some of them trying.'

They took some photos and said goodbye to Princess and continued on their way, as Princess headed on towards the jetty. After a couple of hundred metres they stepped onto dry land and entered a small settlement of timber huts. They spotted another two orangutans hanging around the buildings but Isy urged them on. 'Soon there will be more *klotoks* arriving for the morning feeding but often the orangutans come in early so if we get there first you may have some time alone with them before other people arrive.'

'Good plan Isy,' said Tim. 'Lead the way mate.'

Isy took led them off along a narrow jungle track into a dark, dank world of giant buttress roots, moss covered logs, ferns and creeper vines. Isy demonstrated his extensive knowledge of the jungle, pointing out and naming different trees and brightly coloured fungi. He broke open logs to show them the termites and grubs at work and found a large clutch of gorgeous pitcher plants which Danni found fascinating and spend some time trying to photograph them from several angles until she felt a sudden, excruciating pain in her leg.

'Ouch! Ouch, ouch, ouch,' she shrieked stomping around on the spot. Isy reacted quickly, moving everyone along the track at the same time as lending Danni a hand.

'Fire ants,' he told them. 'Very painful bite, just like touching fire.'

'Geez no kidding,' breathed Danni, still catching her breath and rubbing her leg. Noticing the consternation on Isy's face, she forced a laugh. 'Don't worry Isy, it's not your fault. Besides now I've got another story to tell my friends back home.' He seemed relieved that Danni was taking the incident in her stride and truthfully the pain from the bite was easing quickly so in a couple of minutes Danni was ready to walk on, although from then on she kept a wary eye on the ground wherever she stood.

'You alright?' Rama asked falling into step beside her when the track widened five minutes later.

Danni flashed him a smile. 'Fine now. My leg is a little sore but not so much that it's bothering me. Hey look up ahead; looks like we've arrived.'

Isy had brought them to a rough clearing containing a two metre high wooden platform and a single strand of rope to cordon it off from a viewing area several metres away. 'Is that where the orangutans get fed?' Bel asked.

Isy nodded. 'Yes, soon they will come in. If you listen you will hear them coming before you see them.' Right on cue, came the sound of breaking branches and rustling foliage. Everyone searched the surrounding trees intently but it was Isy's experienced eyes that spotted the big female orangutan first.

'There,' he said quietly, pointing beyond the edge of the clearing. 'She will have a look first before she comes in.' Sure enough the big primate stayed among the trees for several more minutes until she was satisfied all was well. The group held their collective breaths, waiting for her to move.

'Here she comes,' whispered Danni excitedly.

'Come on girl, we won't hurt you,' Bel coaxed. And then finally the orangutan lowered herself to the ground and stepped into the clearing. She paused again, looking at the small group then moved in behind the feeding platform, presumably for security. The friends were so focused on this first orangutan they almost missed the arrival of the next one, who came in around their flank.

'They are coming now,' Isy told them unnecessarily as several more orangutans entered the clearing over the next few minutes.

There was little chatter among the friends; being so close to the precious creatures in their natural habitat was absolutely enthralling and they were thrilled to have this opportunity to be alone with them before they were joined by half a dozen more tourists. Bringing up the rear was the ranger carrying a big basketful of bananas. Recognizing him, the orangutans converged on the feeding platform where the ranger tossed the bananas then backed up a respectable distance. The orangutans perched themselves around the platform and began to feed. Although they stuffed their mouths and cheeks amazingly full it was quite an unhurried affair. They were even joined by a pair of opportunistic squirrels who flittered among the big primates snatching what they could.

'This is fabulous,' said Danni, smiling across at Rama.

'Yes it is. I'm really pleased I came with you guys; this isn't something I would want to have missed.'

'I'm surprised you haven't been before,' Danni commented.

Rama shrugged. 'All work and no play.'

'You're not the only one guilty of that Rama. I definitely need to look at my work life balance and make some changes when I get home.'

'Me too. Spending this last week with you guys has made me realize I need a little work life balance too.'

'What do you think guys?' said Bel coming to join them. 'This is so much more than I'd hoped for. I've taken so many photos; thank God for digital cameras eh?'

'I've done the same,' agreed Danni. 'It's a good thing we can recharge the batteries back on the *klotok*.'

The assembled audience watched the orangutans until all the bananas were gone and most had drifted back into the surrounding jungle. 'Ready to go?' Isy asked. 'We will see more this afternoon.' Receiving general agreement from the four friends, he led them away from the clearing along a different track to the one they'd arrived by. 'This way we will complete a loop back to the *klotok*,' he explained. 'Plus I want to show you something else.'

Intrigued, the friends followed Isy along the jungle path until unexpectedly they emerged from the forest into a wide open field. There were no trees, not a single one, only a carpet of bracken fern so thick it looked impenetrable. The contrast to the lush jungle was startling.

'Fire?' Tim surmised.

Isy nodded. 'Yes fire, a big one in 1997. There were many fires throughout Kalimantan, Sulawesi, Java and other parts of Indonesia, Malaysia and the Philippines also. For many months the air was full of smoke.'

'Was it deliberately lit?' Bel asked.

Isy shrugged. 'Who is to say? There are many fires in Kalimantan, some from nature and some not. Either way it is very bad. Many animals died here and the forest is lost forever.'

'It's awful,' said Danni looking at the devastated landscape around her. 'We're no strangers to bushfires in Australia but our eucalyptus forests are far more resilient. It only takes a few weeks after a bushfire to see new regrowth coming through.'

'Then you are more fortunate than us. Our forests will not regrow,' Isy repeated sadly. 'Come, let's walk on. There is an old fire watch tower up ahead you may climb if you wish.'

At the tower, the girls took one look at the steep, narrow ladder leading to the viewing platform some twenty metres above the ground and decided to keep their feet firmly on the ground. Boys being boys, the three men scrambled to the top without hesitation.

'What can you see?' Bel called up, worried about what she was missing.

'Not much to be honest. We can see the edge of the jungle in the distance but around here it's just more of the same devastated landscape I'm afraid,' Tim told them and a few minutes later he, Rama and Isy climbed back down.

They slowly made their way back to the boat, ambling along chatting and enjoying the scenery once they re-entered the undamaged jungle. Back at the boat landing, Daisy was still lazing about in the overhead tree watching the comings and goings with interest but Princess was nowhere to be seen. Not unexpectedly, there were several other *klotoks* moored nearby and Danni noticed most of the passengers were enjoying a meal on deck or just relaxing whilst the crew lounged around.

'We'll get moving then eat,' Isy told them. 'It is better to be the first boat along the river; more chance of seeing some wildlife.' Once again Jon and Maya's recommendation of Isy's skill as a guide was paying off.

As promised, morning tea was brought up on deck shortly after they got underway, then the foursome settled back in their customary spots to enjoy the two and half hour cruise to Camp Leakey, the birthplace of Tanjung Puting and the legend of Galdikas. Isy propped himself on the foredeck about an hour into the journey, telling them they would soon enter the black water river. They felt the boat slow before they saw the entrance to the river and the four of them stared eagerly ahead as the captain turned the *klotok* into the smaller river. The vegetation was much closer and thicker than before with many overhanging branches and submerged logs in the narrow waterway. A hundred metres from the river mouth the muddy brown water met the shadowy black waters that gave the river its name. Black it may be but it was also clear and clean, like a strong cup of tea.

'The colour comes from the peat swamp forest,' Isy explained. 'The peat has built up over thousands of years and is over two metres deep in places. Tomorrow when we walk through the peat forest you will feel how spongy it is underfoot. When it rains the tannins in the peat wash into the river and turn the water black.'

As he finished his explanation, Danni noticed a brightly coloured bird perched on a branch overhanging the river. Whipping out her camera, she zoomed in and managed to get a close up shot before it flew off, its brilliant red beak and blue and yellow body flashing through the trees. 'A stork-billed kingfisher,' Isy told her. 'There are many lovely birds in the park.'

For the remainder of the cruise Isy stayed on the foredeck scanning ahead and tapping on the wheelhouse cabin to signal the captain to slow whenever he spotted something of interest; each time causing a flurry of excitement on board. Somehow he managed to pick out a well concealed estuarine crocodile floating among the gnarled and twisted tree roots near the river bank. They struggled to see it at first since its leathery skin was almost as black as the river water but as they honed in on it, the long thin snout and bulging head was unmistakable. Suddenly aware that he was the centre of attention, the shy creature quickly disappeared from view beneath the surface.

As the travellers tuned into the watery jungle, they also became more adept at wildlife spotting; picking out large water monitors, macaques, birds such as darters and herons, even a proboscis monkey feeding on young Pandanus fronds right at the water's edge. At one stage they came to a dense patch of river reeds, where the river channel was so narrow the broad, green leaves brushed against the side of the *klotok* as it pushed its way through.

They came upon Camp Leakey quite suddenly, a couple of brightly painted *klotoks* visible before the faded timber jetty. Just like Pondok Tanggui, there was a delightful welcoming committee; several long-tailed macaques and best of all a female orangutan with a small infant perched on the railing watching them with interest.

'Oh my God, she's so cute,' exclaimed Danni referring to the infant that she guessed, based on what she'd learned from their recent visit to the rehabilitation centre, was about six months old. Tucked securely under her mother's arm, the infant peered out at them with big, brown eyes. A tuft of orange fur topped a face more pale that her mothers, with creamy rings around her eyes that would fade as she grew into youth.

'A healthy happy version of Sweetie-pie,' commented Rama giving Danni's a hand a squeeze.

'Here at Camp Leakey we will see many babies,' Isy assured them. 'But first we will tie up to the opposite river bank and have some lunch and relax a little, then later we will go ashore for feeding time. We cannot stay tied to the dock because the monkeys and the orangutans will try to come aboard looking for food.'

'Cheeky beggars,' Tim joked.

Sure enough as they ate lunch on the deck watching other *klotoks* arriving, they were well entertained watching mother orangutan, infant clinging to her back, hanging and stretching from the pylons trying to reach the boats which dropped their passengers and backed away from the dock as quickly as possible in a well-rehearsed manoeuvre. 'I wonder how often the orangutans win,' Bel laughed.

After lunch it was their turn to run the gauntlet of the welcoming party and once they were safely ashore, Isy led them along the boardwalk through the mangroves to the small Camp Leakey settlement. They paused to take their photos beneath the 'Welcome to Camp Leakey' sign and read the information board but when they were inclined to poke around the settlement Isy urged them on and for the second time that day set off through the jungle to the feeding station. Once again thanks to Isy's careful planning, they enjoyed half an hour alone watching the orangutans arrive without the distraction of other tourists and just as he had promised there were several nursing mothers among the group, much to everyone's delight. One tiny infant in particular caught their eye; a baby boy only a few weeks old Isy told them. As well as nursing mothers, there were several juvenile orangutans who were on the verge of, or had just recently, left their mother's side.

As other tourists and their guides began to trickle in, there were some other arrivals to the feeding station; two not-so-wild boars who Danni thought were rather intimidating due to their large size, protruding tusks and wiry hair. As they snuffled around the trees and beneath the feeding platform, the foursome were intrigued to see one of nursing mothers lift a large stick to hit the boar with when they got too close. As Isy explained, native boars were natural predators of orangutan and although they appeared quite tame around the feeding station, they were opportunistic feeders who would take advantage of an unwary orangutan given half a chance.

When the ranger appeared with a basket of banana's there was a flurry of activity on the platform as the orangutan moved in. There was obviously a hierarchy of sorts as several orangutans clutched fistfuls of the sweet treat then moved into the trees to eat whilst several other older orangutan squatted around the platform hoarding feasting on the lion share of the bananas.

'Look what she's doing,' Danni whispered to Bel as a mother orangutan disgorged a handful of chewed banana and fed it to her infant. 'That's what Maya told us mothers do as they start to wean their babies and introduce solid foods. That's why Sweetie-pie was starving; she just couldn't handle the raw fruit she was being given. It's sad to realize what she's missing out on.'

'They're just so darling aren't they?' Bel replied. 'Look at that little one nursing.'

A little while later there was an excited murmur through the crowd. 'Look there,' Isy pointed. 'That's Big Tom, boss male.'

At the edge of the clearing, standing on all fours was the biggest orangutan Danni had ever seen. He was absolutely enormous, probably 120kg, with a long shaggy coat, massive cheek pads, great sagging jowls and altogether intimidating. He paused, surveying the scene before him whilst the onlookers held their collective breath and waited for him to move. Finally he lumbered forward, bypassing the feeding platform and cutting a path straight through the startled onlookers who hurriedly scrambled out of his way. There was a tense silence as he paused in their midst, eyes fixed firmly on a young female orangutan who had been enjoying a fistful of bananas adjacent to the crowd.

Isy stepped in front of the four friends, placing himself between them and Big Tom. 'If Big Tom moves, we move and fast! That way,' he said in a low voice, jerking his head over his shoulder. Nobody moved as the standoff continued, Big Tom sizing up the young female whilst she eyed him warily. After what seemed an interminable amount of time, Big Tom finally turned and lumbered back to the feeding platform, apparently deciding not to push the matter.

'Oh my God,' breathed Danni. 'That was amazing.'

Isy looked relieved as he faced the group. 'That was serious, very dangerous. If Big Tom decided to take her and she ran, we do not want to be anywhere near the tussle.'

'So he would he force himself on her?' Rama asked.

'Yes if he wished. He is very powerful and despite his size very fast. He will take what he wants.' For all the familiarity between man and beast, the incident was a timely reminder that the orangutans of Tanjung Puting were essentially very much wild animals.

Once Big Tom was a safe distance away on the platform enjoying the banana picnic, the mood lightened once more and then Camp Leakey delivered another surprise when a lone gibbon dropped in to share in the spoils. Moving with incredible speed and agility he leapt through the trees, pausing for only a moment before launching himself onto the platform to snatch a clutch of bananas from right under the orangutan's noses, then retreating to the safety of a nearby tree to eat his prize.

'Now that's a snatch a grab raid if ever I saw one,' laughed Tim.

'By a genuine masked bandit too,' added Rama referring to the white fur around the gibbons eyes, a stark contrast to his otherwise dark grey colouring. Not quite done, the gibbon made another raid before disappearing back into the jungle as quickly as he had come.

'Did you notice how the orangutans were glaring at him?' Bel laughed. 'They were genuinely annoyed I think.'

The group waited until the last of the orangutans retreated into the jungle before returning the *klotok* where their cook had afternoon tea waiting for them and brought it onto the deck just as they pulled away from the jetty. It was a moment too soon as the friends became the victims of their own snatch and grab raid by a cheeky macaque who leap aboard, grabbed a handful of the *pisang goreng* off their plate and was gone before anyone could react but left them all laughing in its wake.

Everyone was in high spirits after their amazing day but their excited chatted soon turned to weariness as they chugged back down the river. At the reed bank, their captain tied up for the night and the five men on board positioned themselves around the boat fishing whilst Danni and Bel raided the bookshelf in the main cabin and spent the remainder of the afternoon reading until the sun dropped and the light faded. Between them the men caught a few fish, enough to supplement the rice and vegetables cook made for dinner. It was an idyllic end to a wonderful day, made even more so when a swarm of fireflies danced around the reed beds putting on a dazzling light show before they were once again lulled to sleep by cicadas and frog song.

Danni was the first one up again the next morning and before the others woke, entertained herself watching a beautiful black and white songbird building a nest in the fork of a Pandanus. After breakfast they returned to Camp Leakey to visit the information centre and museum which was housed in one of the wooden cottages in the small settlement then Isy led them on another short hike through the peat jungle, once again displaying his extensive knowledge of the flora and fauna. It was dank and dark under the dense canopy, the ground thick with leaf litter and other debris. They scrambled over and under logs, negotiated giant buttress roots and bounced on the spongy peat beneath their feet and then Isy pointed to a thumbnail size hole in the ground. 'That's a tarantula hole.'

'What! Where,' shrieked Bel leaping behind Tim who seemed highly amused by her reaction.

'Would you like to see?' Isy asked.

Clearly Bel didn't and Danni was unsure but both Rama and Tim nodded enthusiastically and moved in close to watch as Isy poked a long twig into the hole in an effort to entice the spider from its lair. When there was no reaction Isy scanned around and found another hole and tried again. Danni glanced around nervously, realizing now she knew what to look for that there were tarantula holes everywhere; thank god she was wearing closed in shoes. There was a murmur from the men as Isy successfully teased the spider out. About the size of a man's hand, black and hairy it looked every bit as terrifying as Danni had expected and no amount of coaxing from the men could get her and Bel within a couple of metres of it. They both breathed a sigh of relief when it retreated back into its hole which they gave a very wide berth as they moved on.

They left Camp Leakey without seeing anymore orangutans and returned to the *klotok* to begin their homeward journey. Eagle-eyed as always, Isy found them another crocodile and they got a fleeting glimpse of a wild orangutan among the twisted tree roots at the river's edge before it beat a hasty retreat into the safety of the jungle. Before they left the black water river the bright blue sky clouded ominously and before long a torrential downpour had everyone hurrying to drop the clear rain covers down both sides of the *klotok*. Confined indoors, they foursome hunkered down on the floor cushions reading and chatting until as suddenly as it had begun the rain stopped, leaving the countryside cleansed and glistening in the sunshine.

They had a third and final feeding station to visit at Tanjung Harapan, the closest one to Kumai but since the schedule feeding wasn't until mid-afternoon they docked opposite at the village they'd passed on their first day out and Isy took them on a guided tour. It was a small village of only twenty or thirty dwellings, small wooden huts on raised stilts, a riverfront store, a mosque and pleasingly, a school. Everything was arranged alongside a single raised footpath running parallel to the river and it was evident that the village spent much of the year inundated. Not surprisingly, Rama was interested in the village economy and questioned Isy about it.

'It is difficult for the villagers,' Isy told them. 'There are not so many jobs here. The village floods most rainy seasons so there are many challenges to deal with. They try to take advantage of the tourists to Tanjung Putting by offering overnight hikes through the surrounding area and they make handcrafts to sell to the tourists. Also they operate an eco-lodge but most visitors prefer to stay on the *klotoks*. Some are employed on re-forestation projects in fire damaged regions of the park. So they make a little money but it is not enough and they are forced to use the natural resources in the park; harvesting the nipas palms, fishing and hunting. They know it's not good for the park but they do what they must,' he finished despondently.

'I would have thought there were lots of opportunities to take advantage of the tourist trade,' Tim commented.

'Most people come to Tanjung Puting to see the orangutans. The *klotoks* bring them in and take them out. The villagers benefit only a little.'

Bel, Tim and Danni looked expectantly at Rama. 'This sounds like a challenge for Helping Hands,' Danni ventured.

'Possibly,' he agreed thoughtfully, then seeing their hopeful faces he shrugged. 'I can't promise you anything other than I will look into it.' And it was all they could ask of him.

Before they left the village Danni and Bel made a point of dropping into the little shop and buying some handmade souvenirs; in Danni's case a carved image of a male orangutan and an intricately woven rattan shoulder bag.

Their visit to the Tanjung Harapan feeding station was bittersweet; their delight in the orangutans was tinged with sadness knowing this was the last of their close encounters with the wonderful creatures. Danni watched the last of the orangutans wander away from the feeding station with tears in her eyes. Self-consciously she brushed them aside and when Rama squeezed her hand sympathetically, she ignored the pang of envy she felt for Bel who was in Tim's arms being comforted and mustered a grateful smile instead.

It was a quiet group that followed Isy back the *klotok* but as it happened Tanjung Puting wasn't quite done with them. Not long after they left the camp the *klotoks* engine spluttered and died. Tim and Rama went below decks to investigate and reported back that the captain up to his elbows in grease and they could be there awhile which didn't concern them in the least since there were far worse places to be stuck. It was another hour before the captain had them underway again so by the time they left the park and turned into the Kumai River the sun was dropping fast and they chugged into the port under a brilliant crimson sunset; a most fitting way to end what Danni considered the most amazing experience of her life.

***

Danni checked her hotel room in Pangkalanbun one last time to ensure she hadn't forgotten anything before zipping her bag closed. She was staring out of the fifth floor window across the town wishing she had time to explore when there was a light tap on the door and she swung it open to find Rama standing there. 'Hi, what's up?'

'I've come to say goodbye,' he said quietly, then when Danni gave him a puzzled look he added, 'I can't make it to the airport I'm afraid. I'm going to meet someone to discuss the Tanjung Harapan situation to see if there's anything Healing Hands can do for them.'

He watched the emotions play across Danni's face, first surprise, then confusion, then understanding and that was when he knew Danni finally understood the depth of his feelings for her. He saw her catch her breath and struggle to keep her expression neutral and then finally she nodded. 'I understand,' she said quietly and she did; he was in love with her. It was easier to say goodbye this way, in private.

Rama handed her a small brown paper wrapped parcel. 'Here, this is for you.' Danni reached for it but when Rama didn't relinquish his hold on the parcel she lifted she lifted questioning eyes to his and their gazes locked. Slowly Rama ran his forefinger across hers; a small caress spoke volumes and confirmed what she already knew. Then finally he let go, dropping his hand to his side and stepping back. 'Travel safe Danni,' he said softly then turned and walked away. If he'd looked back he would have seen Danni wrap her arms around herself and slump against the wall as the pain of separation coursed through her.

If Bel and Tim thought Rama's absence from the airport was strange they kept their thoughts to themselves. 'He came by my room earlier and said his goodbyes,' Danni said lightly, forcing a nonchalance into her voice she didn't feel. Since non-ticket holders weren't permitted into the departure lounge, Danni check-in for the flight then rejoined Bel and Tim at a small café outside the terminal building.

'I can't thank you guys enough for inviting me along,' Danni told them. 'I've had the best time.'

Bel grinned at her. 'We're glad you came, actually you and Rama both. We couldn't have asked for better travelling companions. It won't feel right flying back to Banjarmasin without you.'

'Tell me about it. Apart from seeing Rob and my family I can't say I'm looking forward to going home, back to the hustle and bustle of city life, work and the usual pressures. I can only imagine how hard you guys will find it after another twelve months over here.'

'It will be an adjustment that's for sure, but we'll be ready to be home by then.' They fell silent as an announcement came over the loudspeaker.

'I think that's your flight Danni,' confirmed Tim. The three friends stood and embraced and made their goodbyes. Bel and Tim lingered whilst Danni headed through the metal detector then she turned and gave her two dear friends a final wave before heading to the departure gate to begin the long journey home.

As the plane lifted off, Danni stared out the window watching the Kumai River and Tanjung Puting recede from view with a heavy heart. Only when they were well out over the Java Sea and the coastline was completely out of sight did she allow the tears to fall.

Her homeward journey was a reversal of the outbound trip, requiring a connection via the Javanese city of Surabaya to Denpasar, Bali. It was on this leg that Danni finally opened the package Rama had given her, finding a small thin leather bound book. The cover was worn and the pages well-thumbed and instinctively Danni knew that it was something that Rama had treasured. Curiously she opened the cover and read the title 'Ramayana' retold by C. Rajagopalachari. Rama's namesake! He'd once told her he would tell her the story of his namesake. Then she noticed the inscription on the inside cover. *Danni, my Sita.* Intrigued, she started to read...

CHAPTER FOURTEEN

Perth, Australia, 2 weeks later

Rob was standing at the kitchen bench making himself a toasted sandwich when Danni came through the door from the garage. 'Hey babe. Another long day at work huh? Thought you would have caught up by now.'

Danni dropped her laptop bag on the bench, followed by her scarf and gloves. 'I have but I stayed back to do a bit of work on the Helping Hands campaign.'

Rob frowned. 'You haven't bitten off more than you can chew have you? You've hardly relaxed since you got home. Maybe you need to tell this Rama fellow that you can't help him after all. I mean, it's not like you're getting paid for it.'

'No, I made a promise and I intend to see it through,' said Danni firmly, 'and it's not about money; it's about doing something worthwhile and helping people who desperately need it.'

Rob held up his hands, palms out. 'Hey it's your choice. I'm just concerned about you. You've just seemed a bit pre-occupied since you got home, not quite yourself.'

Danni sighed and gave him a wry smile, realizing she'd been a bit quick to jump down his throat. 'Sorry hon. You're right, I have been pushing pretty hard since I got back and I guess it's caught up with me. What I need is something to eat, a long hot shower and an early night.'

Rob handed her half his toasted sandwich. 'Here, start on this and I'll make us some more.'

'Thanks hon.' Danni gave him a quick kiss on the cheek and taking the morsel with her, headed off to the bedroom to shower and change, emerging ten minutes later wearing her favourite terry towelling bathrobe, hair wrapped in a towel and flush faced from the hot shower. Rob was just plating up their sandwiches so Danni poured them a glass of juice each and followed him to the dining room. 'Hmm these are good,' she said taking a bite. 'Sorry I wasn't home to cook dinner. I'll make us something nice tomorrow night.'

'I'll have to take a rain check; it's pub night tomorrow,' Rob reminded her.

'Oh right, I forgot,' she mumbled. To be honest, Danni didn't really mind pub night but it did remind her that she and Rob really needed to talk about the amount of time he spent with his mates. She'd raised the issue in Bali and during that awful argument they'd had over the telephone when she was in Banjarmasin, but since returning Danni hadn't felt like tackling the issue and Rob seemed to have shrugged it off and was happily continuing with what had been the status quo throughout their marriage and frankly, their entire relationship.

Besides all that Danni another bigger issue to deal with - Rama. After two weeks at home, any hope she'd had that her feelings for him would begin to fade with distance were proving forlorn. That was one of the reasons she working long hours; to try and keep her mind off the aching desolation that had become her constant companion since boarding the airplane in Pangkalanbun.

After dinner, Danni tidied up the kitchen and then joined Rob in the lounge to watch a little TV, curling up on the sofa beside him. Casually Rob reached across to caress her leg. They hadn't made love since Danni's return, due entirely to her avoiding it. At first she'd pleaded tiredness and lately she'd made a point of staying up late at night working so Rob was already asleep when she finally went to bed. It troubled her greatly as she and Rob had always had a good sex life but now Danni just couldn't seem to work up any enthusiasm for it and she didn't have to be Einstein figure out what the problem was. But abstaining from lovemaking wasn't fair on Rob and maybe a little intimacy with him was just what she needed to help her get past this thing with Rama. With those thoughts in mind, she uncurled her legs and gave Rob a small smile. He grinned back and leaned across to claim her lips and when he slid his hand higher and Danni felt a familiar tightening in the pit of her stomach she groaned, half from relief, and let her eyelids flutter closed.

Several hours later Danni lay in bed staring into the darkness. The lovemaking with Rob had been nice but afterwards she'd been overwhelmed with guilt. It had taken all her willpower not to turn away from him and draw her robe around her. Instead, she'd stayed in his arms and fought back an overwhelming urge to cry. God, what a mess!

Quietly Danni slipped from the bed, retrieved her robe and padded out of the bedroom. In the kitchen she poured herself a glass of milk then took her laptop through to the study and flipped it on. She was browsing the news on the internet when the incoming mail box popped up. She clicked it open and felt a tiny flutter in her chest when she realised it was from Rama.

Hi Danni,

Hope you are well. Just a quick note to say thanks for the fundraising proposal you sent through. I wasn't expecting anything from you so soon; thought you'd be busy settling back in at home and catching up on work.

The proposal looks great and in principle I agree with the strategy you have proposed. I've made a few comments on the proposal and attached it for your review. Nothing major. You've obviously put a lot of work into it and I want you to know how much I appreciate it.

All the best,

Rama

Danni re-read the email a couple of times. It was succinct but friendly and gave nothing away about his feelings for her. Regardless, she was overjoyed to hear from him and felt compelled to reply straight away.

Hi Rama,

I'm well thanks. I hope everything is good with you too.

Thanks for getting back to me about the proposal. Once I've had a chance to go over your comments I'll get moving on the next stage.

Regards,

Danni

Rama's reply was almost instant.

Hey, you're up late.

So are you, she replied.

Can't sleep, he wrote back.

Me neither. Haven't been able to settle since I got home.

There was a brief pause before Rama's next response, as if he had to think about what to say next.

Danni, if working on the Helping Hands campaign is awkward for you, I'll fully respect your decision to drop it.

They both knew that he was referring to his feelings for her and for the first time Danni wondered if she should drop out of the campaign. Cutting off all contact with Rama would be the smart thing to do. She thought of Rob, sleeping in the next room and felt the familiar tinge of guilt return. But the thought of cutting all ties with Rama was unbearable. Besides she loved him and this campaign was the one gift she could give him. If it worked as well as she hoped, it would be a lasting legacy she could leave him with before she stepped back and handed it over to someone else the carry forward into the future.

It's not. I want to do this for you Rama.

Okay, if you're sure.

I am. Now tell me, how are things going up there?

Things are going well. I'm back in Bali at the moment, catching up on office work. Bel and Tim have started their assignment. I plan to call in and check their progress in a few weeks.

They chatted back and forth for another hour or so, mainly Rama bringing her up to date with Helping Hand's activities in Borneo. With the awkwardness of their initial emails forgotten, Danni was happy to discover Rama was as easy to talk to over an email chat as he was in person. It made her realize how much she valued his friendship. If only they could overcome their deeper feelings for each other!

Glancing at the clock on her laptop, Danni was surprised to see it was well past midnight. Since Bali and Perth were on the same time zone, Rama was burning the midnight oil too.

Hey look at the time. You've kept me up, she wrote whilst stifling a yawn.

You going to bed? he wrote back.

I'd better or I'll be asleep at my desk tomorrow. Not a good look!

No I suppose not. I've enjoyed our chat.

Me too. Night.

Sweet dreams.

Danni was smiling as she shut down her computer and padded back to bed. Carefully, so as not to disturb her sleeping husband, she slipped under the covers and was asleep almost as soon as her head hit the pillow.

Over the next couple of weeks there were more email exchanges, usually instigated on the pretext of business; even minor issues and queries warranted an email from one or the other, followed by casual chat. However, Danni had been careful to avoid a repeat of their late night discussion for two reasons; the first being that in the harsh light of day it seemed a bit intimate and for both their sakes she felt it best to discourage it. Secondly, the last thing she wanted was to raise Rob's suspicions. As much as she tried to convince herself there was nothing wrong with emailing a friend, she knew she was treading a very fine and somewhat blurry line between what was and wasn't appropriate behaviour for a married woman.

If Rama had noticed the new boundary, he hadn't commented. Instead he seemed to accept the unspoken ground rules and kept his messages light and friendly.

Unfortunately, things between Danni and Rob hadn't improved. Although Rob had tried to initiate intimacy on several occasions, Danni just hadn't been able to face it. When her excuses began sounding trite, even to her own ears, she found herself avoiding him and when Rob took off with his mates she was torn between relief and despair. The strain was beginning to take its toll on her and finally came to a head one evening after dinner when she not-so subtly rebuffed another of Rob's passes.

'Jesus Danni! What is going on with you lately?'

Danni couldn't blame him for being annoyed and she had no excuse to offer other than a totally inadequate 'I'm sorry Rob. I just don't feel like it.'

'Gee no kidding,' he replied sarcastically causing Danni to flinch. But she deserved it she supposed. 'You haven't been the same since you got back from Borneo. Are you still mad at me for not going with you? Is this your way of getting back at me?'

Danni shook her head. 'No Rob, I'm not still made at you. But since you brought it up, don't you think it's time we sat down and had a talk about it? About all the time you spend with your mates. About the fact we hardly ever do anything together. When was the last time we just sat and had a conversation? Can you even remember because I sure can't?'

Rob stared at her as if he suddenly had no idea who she was. 'Where the hell is all this coming from?'

'Maybe it's been building up over the last few years Rob. I don't know and frankly it's irrelevant. Why don't you just answer the question? When was the last time we just sat and talked?'

Rob opened his mouth to answer then clamped it shut when the answer eluded him. 'We talk all the time,' he pointed out weakly, 'like over dinner.' But he was clutching at straws and they both knew it.

'I'm not talking about the niceties like how was your day or could you pick up my suit from the drycleaners,' Danni clarified. 'I'm sure you find plenty to chat about with your mates. Am I asking too much to expect the same from you?'

'It's hardly the same thing Danni. The boys and I do a lot of stuff together so there's always something to talk about.' The words were already out when the penny dropped.

'I rest my case,' said Danni quietly.

Rob slumped onto the lounge and ran a hand through his hair. 'Ah crap! So what do you want from me Danni? You want me to stop hanging out with the boys?'

He looked so forlorn Danni felt a rush of affection for him. She sat down beside him and reached across to brush the lock of hair out of his eyes. 'No hon, I don't expect you to do that. All I'm asking for is a little balance. I just feel like we're stuck in a rut and I'm sick of spending my weekends alone. Honestly, sometimes I just feel plain lonely.'

'I've never stopped you hanging out with your friends Danni,' Rob pointed out.

'I'm aware of that but to be honest, most of them are usually busy doing things with their partners and I often end up feeling like a third wheel. And you know some of them have kids now so they're doing the family thing.'

'Is it kids? Is that what you want? A baby?'

Danni shook her head. The last thing they needed to bring into their relationship right now was a baby. 'No that's not it. What I want is more of you Rob. But just for the record, I do want kids. I've never made a secret of that. I'll be thirty-one next birthday and sooner rather than later it's something we're going to have to address, but not right now.'

Rob grunted. Like her he seemed happy to let that particular issue drop for the time being, so Danni continued, 'I'm just trying to point out that things have changed Rob; we're not part of the singles scene anymore. Most of our friends have other demands on their time. You're the only one of your mates who's consistently at every outing. Haven't you noticed that? '

Perhaps Rob saw some truth in Danni's comments because he didn't argue. 'So where do we go from here Danni? I'm prepared to make some changes but it goes both ways you know. You say you want to spend more time with me yet I've had the distinct impression you've been avoiding me lately.'

It was Danni's turn to shrug. 'Not intentionally,' she lied. 'I think spending time away from you made me realise how disconnected our lives have become and I guess I've just found it a little hard to re-connect since I got home. On its own making love isn't enough for me anymore. I need more from you.' I need to know that you value me, she thought but didn't add. I need you to make me feel the way Rama makes me feel. Like he wants to be with me and enjoys being with me.

Rob put his arm around Danni and pulled her into his side. 'You know babe, I don't like this distance between us any more than you do. What's say we make a pact to work on closing it together? I'll be more mindful of the time I'm spending with my mates but you're going to have to help me with the other stuff. You know I'm a bit of a numpty when it comes to the hearts and flowers stuff so you might need to give me a few pointers whilst I'm getting the hang of it. Deal?' he asked holding out his hand.

Danni grinned as they shook on it. 'Deal.' Rob could really be very sweet when he wanted to be.

They cuddled on the couch for a while and then Rob surprised her by suggesting a game of scrabble, an offer she readily accepted. Whilst he went off in search of the long abandoned game, Danni made them both a hot chocolate and put some cookies on a plate for them and for the first time in a very long time they had fun together, just the two of them.

Rob surprised Danni the next day by calling her at work and inviting her to lunch. It was predictably rushed since they both had to get back to work, but it was the thought that counted and she had to give Rob the kudos for it. They played scrabble again that evening and when Rob tentatively offered to take a pass on pub night the following evening she insisted he should go. It was never her intention to curtail Rob's outings with his friend's altogether, all she wanted was a little moderation.

On Friday night they caught up with friends for drinks after work which extended into dinner, and although Rob was up early the following morning to go surfing with a mate, he was home by mid-morning so they went out for a long lunch and spent what was left of the afternoon working in the backyard together. Rob was being true to his word and really making an effort to be more mindful of Danni's needs and she loved him for it. And it was working; she actually felt like they were on the same wavelength and starting to re-connect. It helped that the emails from Rama had dried up for the time being whilst he was back on the move in Borneo.

She had however, received her first email from Bel and Tim.

Hi Danni,

Glad to hear you got home safely. Tim and I are now settled in at a little village on the Kedang Kepala River, a full day's boat ride from Samarinda. As planned Rama came in with us and spent a few days introducing us around and getting us started on the project, then he left us to it. After travelling with the two of you it was very strange to be on our so suddenly. We do miss you guys.

Now let me tell you about the project. Helping Hands is sponsoring a village co-operative to produce and sell pre-fabricated timber huts. The timber is sourced from plantations upriver from here and for years the villagers have watched the timber barges pass by on their way to Samarinda. The project is a way for them to make use of a readily available resource and hopefully develop a viable income for the villagers. It's still in its very early stages but the villagers are extremely motivated and all the signs are looking good.

Tim's working with the villagers to help them convert their design concepts into building plans that meet building standards and can be easily replicated in bulk. This involves building and setting up the workshop, making up jigs and pro-forma models so that it's easy for unskilled workers to complete and replicate every building component. He's even working with a few of the bright young lads teaching them to read and understand building plans.

It won't be any surprise to you to know I'm working in the local school teaching the kids English and basic computer skills using a few computers that Helping Hands has provided. There are several teenagers here that have the potential to go onto to university so I'm giving them extra tuition to try to bring them up to the necessary standard.

We're both loving it here. The villagers have made us feel very welcome and are doing their best to teach Tim and I Bahasa Indonesia. So when we meet again we may well have better than passable Indonesian.

Say hello to Rob for us and remember us to Emily and Dave. I'll be in touch again when I can. We have no email or internet service in the village so we have to wait until we come up to Muara Kaman town to pick up our messages. Tim says hi.

Love ya,

Bel

It was great to finally hear from her friends. Of course, Rama had filled her in on the details of where they were and what they were doing but it was nice get a firsthand account. She responded immediately with her own email.

Hi Bel,

Lovely to finally hear from you. I'm glad you're all settled in and enjoying your new assignment. It certainly sounds like an interesting project.

It sounds like you're probably more settled than me. I've been home for over a month now and still having trouble adjusting. Still wishing I was back in Borneo with you guys and Sweetie-pie.

Speaking of Sweetie-pie, Mia emailed me the attached photos. Apparently Jon was at the rehab centre a few days ago dropping off yet another poor unfortunate infant and he made a point of checking up on her for us. How nice is he?! As you can see from the photos Sweetie is doing very well, has been released from quarantine and is enjoying the company of her new mums and the other orangutans in the nursery. Such a change from the poor little mite we rescued from the market.

As promised, I'm pulling together a marketing campaign for Rama to help with fundraising. I've asked him to send some photographs of the work that Helping Hands has undertaken over the years. Any contributions from yourself and Tim would be greatly appreciated.

Danni

The following Saturday, Danni finally had her first chance to catch up with Emily and Dave in person since her return from Borneo as she and Rob had been invited over for dinner. Their friends lived in Attadale, an old suburb adjacent to the Swan River about twenty minute's drive from the city. Unlike Danni and Rob who'd opted for a new house in a new estate, Em and Dave had bought an old three bedroom brick and tile house on a big block and had been extending and renovating it on and off for the last five years or so. There'd been a lot of blood, sweat and tears shed on the old place but they both claimed it was a labour of love and gradually they'd transformed the ordinary, rundown bungalow into a spacious, modern family home filled with lots of love and laughter and thus far two adorable children.

It was the older of the two that burst through the front door before they had a chance to knock and threw himself at Danni. 'Aunty Danni, I've been waiting for you for ages,' he said accusingly, dragging out the ages as if she and Rob were an hour late instead of right on time.

Danni laughed and bent down to give the fair-headed five year old an affectionate hug. 'Well I've been just as anxious to see you too Mace,' she assured him, adopting the shortened version of his name. 'But if I'd known I was going to get such a lovely greeting I would have come sooner. Where's your brother?' she asked as Mason led her by the hand towards the kitchen.

'He was having dinner in the highchair but mum said he had to have his hands cleaned before she set him loose on you and Uncle Rob.'

Mason had just finished his explanation when a smaller, plumper version of himself trotted into the hallway. A little less confident than his older brother, Jamie paused when he spotted the visitors, overcome by a sudden bout of shyness. Coming up behind him, Emily scooped him into her arms and brought him the rest of the way. Danni gave her best friend a warm hug then turned her attention to her offspring, giving his round tummy a gentle tickle.

'Hey Jamie, how're you doing?' she asked lightly, earning an endearing smile from the toddler. He considered her for a moment longer then held his arms out so Danni could take him. 'That's better,' she said dropping a gentle kiss on his baby soft curls as she settled him onto her hip.

Reaching down, she reclaimed Mason's hand and gave it a squeeze. 'Well you two certainly know how to make a lady feel welcome.'

Mason was practically bouncing along beside her as she followed Em and Rob to the big kitchen at the back of the house. 'That's 'cause we missed you Aunty Danni. We haven't seen you for ages,' he squeaked dragging out the ages again so Danni had to stifle a giggle.

'That's because I've been away on holidays,' Danni explained.

'That's what my mum said. She said you got to see a whole lotta monkeys and or...oranna...'

'Orangutans,' Danni supplied for him.

'Yeah those,' Mason confirmed with enthusiastic nodding of his head. 'Did you get to play with them?'

'Well not exactly, but I did get real close and I got to watch them play in the trees. I even got to look after a baby orangutan for a while.'

Mason was looking suitably impressed and about to launch into his next question when Dave came across the room to greet them. 'Mace, why don't you give Aunty Danni a chance to say a proper hello to me and mum whilst you go and clean your teeth and get ready for bed.'

'Bed already! But mum said I could visit with Aunty Danni and Uncle Rob awhile.'

'You can,' promised Dave patiently, 'but you can at least get ready for bed whilst I get our guests something to drink.'

'Aww dad...' Mason grumbled, but he went off to do what he was told leaving Danni grinning after him.

'Sorry about that. He can be pretty full-on at times. Glass of wine?'

'Thanks Dave. I can't believe how much the boys have grown in just a couple of months.'

'Tell me about,' said Dave grinning. 'Em and I were looking at baby photos the other day and couldn't believe the change in them. It seems like only yesterday when we brought Mason home from the hospital. Now he's at kindy.'

'You'll be out the back kicking a football around with them soon,' Rob commented.

Dave grinned. 'I already am. Mason is determined to play Nippers football next season.'

Jamie wriggled in Danni's arm and reached for the glass of wine Dave had handed her, 'Oh no you don't,' Danni smiled at him as she placed it on the sideboard out of his reach. 'Why don't we go find your mum?'

She found Emily in Mason's bedroom, picking up toys and trying to encourage Mason to do the same, a task he quickly abandoned when Danni entered the room.

'Sorry.'

Emily looked up and grinned. 'Don't be. Mason's been looking forward to seeing you. Sorry about the chaos Danni; I truly had planned to be a bit more organized than this. Dinner's in the oven so I just need to make the gravy and get the boys into bed so we can sit down for a nice quiet adults only dinner. I can't wait to hear all about your trip. It sounds like you had a marvellous time.'

'Em, go and do what you need to do in the kitchen and leave these two to me. We've got a bit of catching up to do don't we Mace?' Danni said giving Mason a squeeze.

'Thanks Danni. You're a doll,' said Emily giving her friend a quick, grateful hug as she left the room.

Danni spent the next twenty minutes entertaining the boys and when Emily returned she found the three of them curled up on Mason's bed together as Danni read them a story book. Jamie was already very nearly asleep when his mum lifted him from the bed and took him through to his own bedroom. She returned a minute later and roused Mason just enough to get him to the toilet and back to bed. Danni leaned over and kissed his sweet little cheek and stepped out of the room, leaving Emily to say goodnight to her son.

She found Dave in the kitchen carving a roast and Rob propped up on a kitchen stool chatting about football. 'All tucked up in bed?' Dave asked, looking up from his task.

'Yep, probably asleep already too.'

'Thanks for doing that Danni,' Emily said coming back into the kitchen. 'I had hoped to have everything done before you got here but best laid plans…Anyway, grab yourself a fresh glass of wine and relax. Dave and I will have dinner on the table in a few minutes.'

'No problem. I enjoyed catching up with them,' said Danni sincerely. She really did adore the two little boys.

'Now tell us all about your trip. Have you heard from Bel and Tim?'

'I have actually and they sent their regards to you all.' Danni proceeded to fill them in on the details Bel had provided which led them all into a deeper conversation over dinner about Rama and his work with Helping Hands and the projects they sponsored.

'I must say, I'm impressed with the whole concept; helping people to help each other,' commented Dave. 'It's no wonder they're getting results.'

'It is clever, I'll grant the guy that,' Rob agreed. 'He's basically working on the economic multiplier principle. For every dollar you put in, you get multiple times that original amount back in terms of overall benefit. Sort of like the gift that keeps on giving.'

'I hadn't thought of it like that,' said Danni. 'Unfortunately though, like most NGO's, Helping Hands relies on donations and sponsorship to fund its work and there's never enough. Rama told me he has quite a few viable projects on hold waiting for funding so I've offered to put together a marketing and fundraising campaign for them. It's not the same as being on the ground helping but it's something at least,' said Danni finishing with a shrug.

'Oh Danni, that's marvellous,' exclaimed Emily. 'If there's anything I can do to help just let me know.'

Danni grinned at her friend. 'Well…'

'Uh oh, looks like you walked into that one Em,' laughed Rob, earning him a playful elbow in the ribs from Danni.

'Okay, I'll admit I was hoping you'd offer,' Danni conceded graciously. 'The thing is, Helping Hands could do with a bit of a face lift. Nothing fancy or over the top, just a fresher more professional look. One of the young guys at work has volunteered to update their website but I could with some help from someone with your graphic design expertise to develop the overall look and come up with a new logo.'

Emily didn't hesitate. 'Actually I love to do it. It's sounds like a very worthwhile project and now that I'm no longer working, I'm sure I can find some time to do it.'

'Are you sure Em? I don't want you taking it on if it's going to be too much of a burden.'

Emily shook her head emphatically. 'It won't be. My heads filling with idea's already. What so funny?'

Danni was biting her lip to stop herself from laughing but her amusement was obvious. 'I was just thinking how much I sound like Rama. He's always worrying that I've bitten off more than I can chew and I'm always reassuring him that I haven't. Yet here I am doing exactly the same thing with you.'

'Well I'm not so sure you haven't taken on more than you can chew,' said Rob frowning, then to the others, 'Danni's been burning the midnight oil working on this campaign ever since she got home.'

'Well I think it's commendable,' said Emily leaping to her friends' defence. 'Obviously whatever you saw over there in Borneo has got you highly motivated.'

'It definitely has. The Bornese are such lovely people I can't begrudge them a little bit of my time. The whole place made a big impact on me.'

'I have to admit, after hearing about your adventures, I'd love to see the place for myself,' said Dave. 'We'll have to add it to our bucket list hey Em?'

'Definitely, when the kids are a bit older. It would be lovely to take them to see the orangutans. In the meantime Danni, when are we going to see some photos?'

'I'm afraid I've been so focused on the Helping Hands campaign I haven't had time to sort through my photos. Even Rob hasn't seen them yet. But I did promise everyone a slideshow night so how about a fortnight today at our place. Bring the kids if you like; you can put them down in Rob and my bed.'

Em looked to her husband for confirmation then tilted her glass in Danni's direction, 'You've got yourself a date.'

***

Despite her heavy workload over the next fortnight, Danni was conscious of setting time aside each evening to spend with Rob, including ensuring she was home from work in time to prepare their dinner.

Consequently Danni found herself engaged in a fine balancing act of trying to spend quality time with Rob, progressing the Helping Hands campaign and preparing for the slideshow. Often she went to bed with Rob then woke early to spend a couple of hours before breakfast working at her laptop as well as working through her lunch break. Far from finding some of the work life balance she'd promised herself during the Borneo trip, she was now busier than ever.

For his part, Rob seemed to be making a genuine effort to mend some bridges between himself and Danni. His outings with his mates had been curtailed to a large degree and although he didn't complain he was restless and distracted at times and Danni got the distinct impression that whilst he was with her in body, his mind was elsewhere. She told herself not to take it personally; he was simply going through an adjustment period. But what really bothered her most was that after only a few weeks of togetherness, they seemed to have run out of things to talk about. Since Rob was already sensitive about Danni's work for Helping Hands and her solo trip to Borneo she felt those subjects were best avoided and Rob seemed to have taken a similar stance regarding his exploits with the boys. It didn't leave much else to talk about which was rather confronting in itself; did they really have so little in common? It was a question Danni was forced to ponder again when Rob tentatively mentioned an upcoming morning of windsurfing with the boys and she encouraged him to go; in fact she was rather relieved that it gave her time to focus on her own activities.

Focusing proved difficult though. Turning on her laptop, her heart skipped a beat as it usually did, to find an email waiting for her from Rama; the first in several weeks.

Hi Danni,

I hope this email finds you well. As you've probably gathered I'm back from Borneo where I spent a very busy three weeks checking up on several of our Helping Hands projects and laying the groundwork for a new project we're hoping to commence later this year.

I called in to see Bel and Tim, taking some equipment with me. They are both well and doing an extremely good job as I knew they would. They've settled in very well and are not-surprisingly popular with the villagers. I also caught up with Jon and Maya who both send their regards. Things were a bit crazy at their place as Jon and his team had just brought in a mixed bunch of gibbons, orangutan, a sun bear and some loris; all confiscated from an illegal wildlife trafficking ring that they'd been tracking for some time. Unfortunately the poor creatures were all very stressed and some not as lucky as Sweetie-pie I'm afraid.

On a happier note, Ahmed is the same as always; big-hearted, effusive and happy. He spent my entire visit asking me when I was bringing you back and chastising me for letting you go. Of course I insisted we were just friends but he simply won't have it. Anyway he asked me to say hello, to remind you to keep up your cooking and not to forget what he taught you.

Now to business, I've had a look over the final plan you sent me and I'm both impressed and appreciative of all the effort you're putting in. Your proposed date for the fundraising gala suits me fine so go ahead and lock it in. I've blocked out my calendar so I'll have several days in Perth. I'm back in Bali for at least the next month so if there's anything you need from me, just holler. Take care.

Your friend,

Rama

Danni read it over several times; it was friendly, newsy and brought a smile to her face. Quite aside from her feelings for Rama, it was incredible how much she missed her new friends and how much she longed to be back in Borneo. Right then and there, she vowed to go back again one day even if it meant going alone. However unlikely it seemed, she would love for Rob to come with her; but even as she thought it she had to concede he probably wouldn't 'get' Borneo or her new friends anyway. Which brought her thoughts right back to the issue that had been troubling her; just how much did she and Rob have in common?

***

The slideshow evening rolled around very quickly. Somehow in between work, spending time with Rob and progressing the Helping Hands campaign, Danni had managed to squeeze in time to sort through her photographs and stitch them together into what she hoped was an interesting presentation for her family and friends. To add a bit of flavour to the night, she'd put together an Indonesian feast that she hoped would do Ahmed's cooking lessons some justice; grilled prawns and chicken with an accompanying array of dipping sauces, coconut flavoured rice, a fresh mango, cucumber and bean sprout salad and in lieu of *kangkung*, baby bok choy and onion sautéed in garlic butter and topped with chopped peanuts. For dessert she'd prepared banana pancakes with sweet coconut milk custard. Without the benefit of a smoky charcoal brazier and genuine Indonesian ingredients, the meal was definitely an Australian take on these classic Indonesian dishes but as Danni laid out the buffet, she was nevertheless quite pleased with her efforts.

Danni's folks, her brother and sister-in-law, Emily and Dave were all present, sans children who had been farmed out to their respective grandparents for the evening so it was a nice casual group that gathered around the table to eat.

'Wow, this is quite a spread Danni,' her brother Chris commented appreciatively as he piled his plate high.

'She's been cooking all day,' said Rob. 'I suggested pizza instead but I have to admit, I'm glad she didn't listen to me. I didn't even know Danni knew how to cook Indonesian.'

'I did tell you I had some cooking lessons with Ahmed,' Danni pointed out.

'That's the guy you told me about who used to be a cart vendor and now has a successful restaurant isn't it?' Emily asked. 'I'd love to meet him; he sounds such a character.'

'He is,' confirmed Danni smiling fondly. 'I hope I can get back to Borneo sometime to see him, Jon and Maya and Sweetie-pie again. I've just got to talk Rob into it.'

'Well I'll wait until I see your photos babe,' said Rob noncommittally.

'I can't wait to see them Danni. The few that you showed me in relation to the Helping Hands campaign looked intriguing,' said Emily.

'This tastes a delicious as it looks,' complemented her father between mouthfuls. 'Remember when your mum tried to replicate the chicken satay sticks you get in Bali? She managed the chicken okay but God knows what she did to the peanut sauce but it was awful,' he said grinning.

'Oh yeah, I remember that,' said Chris with a laugh. 'The three of us were practically gagging but mum had put so much effort into it you were looking at us daggers lest we complained so we sat there and forced ourselves to eat it.'

Danni was laughing at the memory too. 'In the end it was mum who finally got up and emptied the contents of her plate into the bin, much to everyone's relief. We ended up ringing out for pizza,' she said, drawing a laugh from everyone else.

'It wasn't one of my finer moments in the kitchen,' Catherine conceded, laughing along with the rest of them.

Later after everyone had eaten and was comfortably settled in the lounge room, Danni turned on her laptop and commenced the slideshow, running it through the widescreen TV thanks to Rob's technical know-how. She began with some photos of downtown Banjarmasin, the market and the old riverside quarter, then a journey of the waterways; the dilapidated canals, the riverside warehouses and the colourful floating markets. There were plenty of gasps of amazement, questions and comments from her audience, all of whom seemed quite enthralled. The next set of slides took the audience to Loksado, the Dayak villages of the Meratus Mountains, bamboo rafting along the pretty Amandit River, the swimming buffalo of Negara and the Cempaka gem fields which drew plenty of interest.

The series of slides on Sweetie-pie were both sobering and uplifting. Danni had included some photos Bel had taken of her feeding Sweetie-pie as well as shots of Jon and Maya and the children and a beaming Ahmed outside his restaurant. And last but not least, photos of Danni's amazing journey to Tanjung Puting National Park which predictably sparked a lot of interest among the audience.

It had been a difficult task for Danni to cull her collection of photos down to the handful that she presented but judging by the appreciative reactions from her audience she'd managed to share her memories without boring everyone to tears.

'That was fabulous Danni,' Emily enthused as the slideshow ended.

Bill agreed. 'I'll say luv. You certainly had quite an adventure. I'm rather interested in seeing something of the place myself.'

'Me too,' echoed Emily. 'I'd love to take the kids to Tanjung Puting. They'd love to see the orangutans and monkeys, not to mention staying on a *klotok*. What do you think Dave? Maybe in a couple of years when they're a little older we should go.'

Dave grinned indulgently at his wife. 'It certainly looks doable; with or without the kids I'd love to go.'

'I'm thinking the same thing,' said Jenny, Danni's sister-in-law. 'Maybe we could all go together; our kids are similar ages so they'd have a lot of fun together.'

Emily was nodding enthusiastically. 'That's a great idea.'

As the Emily and Jenny pursued the idea, Chris draped an affectionate arm across Danni's shoulders. 'I'm a bit envious sis; it looks like you had a great time. I can certainly understand how the place got under your skin. It's amazing to think Borneo is so close to us here in Australia yet so vastly different.'

'I must admit, it was a bit of a culture shock for me,' Danni admitted. 'But the locals were so friendly and nice I got over that very quickly. Plus being with Bel and Tim and Rama was a bonus; they were such good travelling companions.'

'Well I'm proud of you honey,' said Catherine adding her two cents worth. 'It took guts to take yourself off without Rob and it certainly paid off.'

'Thanks mum.' Danni glanced over at her husband who seemed strangely quiet and had a tight smile plastered on his face. Figuring he'd overheard her mother's comment and didn't like to be reminded of his wife's show of independence, Danni chose to ignore his sombre mood turned her attention back to her guests. By the time everyone had left and she'd finished clearing away and headed to bed, Rob was already asleep and Danni had forgotten about his sombre mood altogether.

She was reminded of it the very next morning; Rob was withdrawn the entire day and kept himself busy working in the yard and cleaning cars, leaving Danni with the decided impression he was avoiding her. He made a show of upholding their recent routine of spending the evenings together by joining Danni in the lounge after dinner to watch TV but he sat apart from her and after an hour took himself off to bed early, leaving Danni quite bewildered. He was definitely peeved about something and she had had no idea about what or why.

It all became very clear the following day when Danni arrived home from work to find Rob waiting for her with the copy of Ramayana that Rama had given her in his hand and a filthy look on his face.

He barely waited for her to put her bag down before attacking. 'Have you got something to tell me Danni?' he snarled waving the book in front of her.

'Rob, what are you doing with my book? Did you go poking in my drawers? You have no right to do that.' Danni asked incredulously.

'I have every right! I'm your husband just in case you've forgotten that you are actually married,' he ground out.

'What's that supposed to mean?'

'It means maybe you forgot that little fact when you were in Borneo hanging around with this Rama guy.'

'Don't be ridiculous Rob,' Danni said indignantly.

'Oh I don't think I'm being ridiculous and I'm not blind either. I saw the photos last night Danni; of the two of you together. You looked like you could barely keep your hands of each other. That's when I knew something was up. And then I found this,' he said waving Rama's book around again. 'How the fuck do you explain this?'

'Did you read it?'

'Enough to know it's a story about two eternal lovers. Enough to know that it's not the sort of gift a man gives a woman unless there's something going on between them. So tell me Danni, what has been going on? Did you fuck him?' he ground out, eyes blazing. 'Is that why you've been so fucking frigid with me since you got back from Borneo? Saving it all for your Asian boyfriend or did he just wear you out?'

Danni flinched under the force of Rob's fury. 'Jesus Rob, do you have to be so crude?'

'Just answer the fucking question!' he yelled.

'No I didn't,' she yelled back indignantly. 'I never fucked him as you so crudely put it. I never kissed him, I never hugged him, nothing, nada, zilch!'

Rob glared at her as if he wasn't sure whether to believe her or not. Roughly he opened the front cover of Ramayana and read Rama's inscription aloud. 'Danni, my *Sita*. The guy's obviously in love with you. I may have been a bit slow to catch on Danni but I'm not entirely fucking stupid. Something's gone on and I want to know what it is.'

'Rob, we're just friends,' Danni said, but even to her own ears it sounded weak.

'Jesus Danni, even you can't be that bloody naïve,' Rob spat out.

Despite her best effort to remain calm, Danni bristled. 'Is it my fault he fell in love with me Rob? It's not like I set out to seduce him or anything. It just happened and frankly I was absolutely astounded when I realized.'

'So you thought you'd just have a bit of fun, string him along a little?'

'No of course not!' Danni denied hotly. 'I didn't even realize until I was practically heading to the airport. I figured it had nothing to do with us, with our marriage.'

'And yet knowing how he feels, you've continued to communicate with him,' Rob ground out. 'I just don't get that Danni and don't tell me it's all about fundraising for the good folks of Borneo.'

'It is—'

'—Bullshit Danni. I know you; at least I thought I did. I never took you for the cheating kind.'

'I've already told you, I did not sleep with Rama,' she ground out.

'Maybe you did, maybe you didn't. How am I supposed to know? All I know is that you're still communicating with this guy. Well that stops right now! Get your laptop started up and send him an email telling him you're done with the campaign.' Rob folded his arms across his chest and stood there expectantly.

'What, right now?'

'Yes right fucking now, whilst I'm watching.'

Danni shook her head, 'I'm not doing it Rob,' she said firmly, even though she was trembling all over.

Rob's eyes narrowed on her, 'Don't toy with me Danni.'

'I'm not toying with you, but I won't do it. I promised Rama a marketing campaign and I intend to deliver.'

Rob shook his head in disbelief. 'So you expect me to believe you never slept with this guy, that there's nothing going on between you and yet you'll put him before me, before our marriage? I just don't get it unless…unless…' Rob looked her confounded, then gave a self-mocking laugh. 'Jesus, you're in love with him aren't you?'

Danni opened her mouth to deny it, but all that came out was an anguished cry.

'Oh Jesus,' muttered Rob to himself. Danni saw the fight go out him; the anger that had twisted his features just moments ago was replaced by a look of absolute despair. He sunk onto the lounge and covered his face with his hands looking like a broken man.

Watching him and knowing that she was responsible, Danni felt almost physically ill. More than anything she wanted to take Rob's pain away, to comfort him. She reached out and put her hand on his shoulder but he flinched away and held a hand up to ward off her touch. 'Don't. Just don't.'

Danni stared at her husband's bowed head until the silence grew unbearable. She wanted to tell him how sorry she was, how much she still loved him and remained committed to their marriage; but it was obvious Rob wasn't ready to hear it. Quietly she left the room, heading for the back patio where she sucked great gulping mouthfuls of the cool night air then sank into a chair and stared into the darkness, trembling with shock but too numb to cry. God what a mess.

Danni wasn't sure how long she'd been outside when the damp chill eventually drove her back indoors. The house was ominously quiet and she had to steal herself to peak into the lounge room to see if Rob was still there. He wasn't. Nor was he in the kitchen, the study or their bedroom; but the dawning realization that he wasn't in the house didn't stop her checking every room. His car keys weren't on their usual hook inside the kitchen and when she looked in the garage and saw his car gone, the tears that had eluded her thus far finally fell. Blindly she stumbled to her bedroom, sank onto the empty bed and wept herself to sleep.

Sunlight was streaming in through the curtains Danni had forgotten to close the night before when she woke the next morning. For a brief moment, she stared blankly at the empty space beside her before everything came rushing back with hideous acridity. Quickly she pushed up off the bed and headed through to the lounge room hoping that Rob had come home sometime through the night, even if he'd chosen to sleep on the couch rather than with her. But there was no sign of him. She reached for her mobile phone to call him but her finger hesitated over the call button and after wavering for a minute she finally decided to have a shower and head to work and give Rob the opportunity to come home when he was ready.

It never occurred to Danni that Rob wouldn't come home eventually but when she arrived home from work that evening and discovered a note on the kitchen bench her heart sank. I'm staying at a hotel, Rob. Disbelievingly she read the note over but there was no way to make the words sound anything other than what they were; cool and foreboding. A quick check of their wardrobe confirmed that Rob had taken some clothing and personal items with him, a sure indication that he was planning to stay away for several days at least. Danni was upset, no question, but she was also annoyed. They needed to talk and staying away wasn't going to resolve anything.

Before she had second thoughts, Danni dialed Rob's mobile phone. It rang four times before going to message bank. It was extremely rare for Rob not to answer his phone; in fact she'd often teased him that his phone was virtually another appendage, so Danni suspected he was deliberately ignoring her. She dialed again and this time when her call went to message bank she left a message, 'Rob I understand you're hurt and angry with me but please call. We can't resolve anything if you won't at least talk to me.'

Rob didn't call and continued to ignore Danni's attempts to get in touch until she eventually gave up. In fact, she didn't hear from him for over a week until he turned up unannounced early one Saturday morning when Danni was still drinking her morning coffee, sitting at the small dining room table in her robe. At the sound of a key in the lock her heart skipped a beat as she watched her husband come through the front door.

'Uh you're up,' he said coming to a halt when he spotted Danni in the room.

'Hi Rob,' she said, giving him a hesitant smile. 'It's good to see you.'

'Ah yeah,' he said awkwardly shifting from foot to foot. 'I um…I just came to get my golf clubs. I'm playing around with one of the guys.' He may not have come to talk but at least he had the good grace to look guilty at Danni's crestfallen expression. 'The golf clubs are in the spare room,' he mumbled as he disappeared down the hallway.

By the time he emerged a few minutes later, clubs in hand, Danni had had time to gather her wits and was waiting for him. 'Listen Rob, this is ridiculous. Can't we at least talk? This silence is getting us nowhere.'

Whether it was because he was cornered or he agreed with Danni, she couldn't say but Rob gave her a rueful look, then dropped his golf clubs on the floor with a heavy sigh and sank his hands into his pockets. 'Yeah I guess.'

'Can I get you a cup of coffee?' Danni asked. 'Fresh pot; I just made it.'

'Thanks.'

When Danni returned to the table a minute later with coffee for both of them, Rob had plonked himself down on the furthermost chair to hers with his legs stretched out and arms crossed over his chest in a show of disinterest. 'So how have you been?' she asked to break the ice.

'Okay given the circumstances.'

Danni chose to ignore the accusatory tone. 'Rob, I'm sorry I hurt you. It was the last thing I ever wanted to do.'

'Yeah well that's big of you, but it doesn't change the facts does it?' he said sarcastically.

'Look Rob, I'm trying to be reasonable here. The least you could do is give me a fair hearing.'

'That's rich coming from you Danni. What you did wasn't exactly reasonable or fair.'

'Rob you make it sound like I deliberately set out to…to…to…'

'To fall in love with someone else? Isn't that what you're trying to say Danni. You know, what I don't understand is how one minute you're supposedly in love with me and then the next you're in love with someone else. How do you manage to turn your emotions on and off just like that?' Rob said snapping his fingers.

Danni shook her head. 'It wasn't like that Rob; my feelings for Rama just crept up on me. But I've never stopped loving you, not for a single minute.'

For the first time since the whole mess had blown up, Danni sensed some of Rob's anger dissipating. 'So what are you saying? You're in love with both of us?'

Danni nodded miserably. 'Yes.'

'So you thought you'd just come back from Borneo and continue on with our marriage as if it didn't matter?'

'Yes,' she admitted quietly. 'It just turned out to be a bit harder than I expected. But I was working through it Rob; I just needed some time.'

Rob shook his head at the ceiling and snickered disbelievingly. 'And where did I figure in all of this Danni? Did you even give a thought to how it would make me feel? For weeks I made excuses for you not wanting to be intimate with me until it got to a point where I couldn't make excuses any longer and it just became plain bloody hurtful to me. Then you had the hide to make out that it was my fault because I was neglecting you and like a poor, dumb bastard I actually bought into it and was trying to change my ways. Talk about being played for a fool.'

'I didn't play you for a fool Rob. The issues we discussed were very real issue to me and had been for quite some time; long before Rama came along. And I really felt like we were making some progress.'

'You mean you were getting over your boyfriend?' Rob's sarcasm was back in full force.

'Rob, that's not helpful. You know what I meant. Surely you're not going to sit there and tell me that you didn't feel it too; that we were reconnecting?'

Rob's silence was an admission in itself but he wasn't ready for reconciliation yet. 'So what do you plan to do now Danni? How do you suggest we go forward?'

'Why don't we just take it one day at a time?' Danni suggested. 'But you need to come home Rob. We'll never work through things if you're not here.'

'Are you still communicating with him Danni?'

Danni licked her lips, knowing Rob wasn't going to like her answer. 'Yes but only in a professional capacity; the campaign...'

Rob pulled his mouth into a tight line and his nostrils flared in barely contained anger. 'No more Danni. That's an absolute no brainer for me.'

'Rob, I just need to see things through to the launch then I'll step back, hand it all over. Another few months then that's it I promise. It's not just Rama and the beneficiaries any more. I've had a lot of help and support from friends and colleagues here in Perth now, Emily for example. It just wouldn't be fair on them to simply dump it and walk away.'

Suddenly Rob stood up, came around the table and held his hand out to Danni. Hesitantly she took it, allowing Rob to draw her to her feet. He reached out to cup her cheek, stroking his thumb across her chin as he leaned closer and claimed her mouth. Despite her confusion at his sudden attention, Danni responded to Rob's kiss. He deepened the kiss, forcing her lips apart and plundering her mouth with his tongue. There was no softness in his touch, it was hard and invasive and confusing but it wasn't until Rob shoved a hand inside her robe and roughly grabbed her breast whilst attempting to force her panties down with the other hand that she wrenched herself away, pulling her robe protectively around her. 'Jesus Rob, what's got into you?'

'Still don't want me touching you?' he snarled.

'Not like that no!' she replied indignantly. 'Oh my God, were you testing me? Is that what that was about?'

'Did you sleep with him Danni?'

'I've already told you I didn't.'

'But you wanted to didn't you?' he accused. 'Didn't you?'

Suddenly Danni's thin grip on her emotions snapped. Rob's assault had been the final straw. 'Yes I wanted to! Is that what you want to hear? Does that make you happy?' But as quickly as it had come, the anger was gone as Danni crumpled to the floor sobbing. 'Jesus Rob.'

She felt a movement beside her. 'I'm sorry Danni,' Rob whispered close to her ear. Tentatively he rubbed her back. 'I'm really sorry,' he repeated, 'I just wanted to hurt you,' he confessed, drawing more sobs from Danni. He pulled her into his arms and she sagged against him, burying herself deep into the warm cocoon of his arms. They stayed there on the floor, holding each other until Danni's sobs subsided.

Finally Rob spoke. 'Danni, I love you but I can't do this.' She wasn't quite sure what he was referring to but waited for him to continue. 'I can't play the third wheel.' When Danni started to protest he stopped her. 'Please let me finish. I just can't be with you knowing there's another man in your heart. I'll always be wondering if it's me you want or him or wondering how I compare to him. I just can't do it.'

'What are you saying?' Danni whispered although she already knew the answer.

'It's over Danni. I'm really, truly sorry but I just can't do it,' he said rising to his feet and bringing Danni with him. Gently he reached out and brushed her hair away from her face then gave her a gentle kiss on the cheek. 'I love you but I just can't. Do you understand?'

Numbly Danni nodded. As much as her mind and heart railed against it, Danni did understand where he was coming from. Worse, this was a mess of her making; she had no right to beg Rob to stay with her. This is what she had done to them.

Rob gave Danni one last long look then stepped away from her. 'I'll come by in a day or two to sort some stuff out with you.' Once again Danni just nodded. She didn't turn to watch him leave, didn't even hear the door close behind him.

CHAPTER FIFTEEN

Hi Danni,

Well things are going great guns here. Hard to believe we've been here six weeks already.

The project is coming along very nicely. Rama sent up a whole bunch of equipment several weeks ago which Tim and the villagers now have set-up and running in the new workshop they built to house it. The next challenge is to get some prototypes built. Once they've done that and tested and refined their designs, it will be onto making up the jigs and guides.

My kids are doing very well and learning lots. They pick up English surprisingly quickly, far more quickly than I'm picking up Bahasa Indonesian which they've all taken upon themselves to teach me!

I've attached some photos for you as requested. I'm not the best photographer in the world but hopefully there's one or two amongst them you can use. I'll forward more as the project progresses.

I was thrilled to get the photos of Sweetie-pie. Maya, Jon and the kids are a lovely family. We're hoping to catch up with them again before we head home.

I hope you've settled back in by now. I'm not surprised you've had trouble adjusting; probably a little reverse culture shock after our amazing trip. Imagine how Tim and I will feel after a year here!

Take care my friend. Our regards to Rob.

Luv ya,

Bel

***

Hi Bel,

Hope everything is good with you guys. Sorry it's taken me awhile to reply to your last email. Things have been a little hectic around here lately.

Working on Rama's campaign and long hours at work are keeping me very busy. Not that I mind at all, it keeps me occupied. I do so want the campaign for Helping Hands to be a success so that Rama and people like you and Tim can continue to help the lovely folks in Kalimantan. I only have to think of Ahmed's success to remind me how effective the organization is. By the way, the photos you sent are great! I will certainly make use of them. Keep them coming please.

Emily put her hand up to do some graphic artwork for Helping Hands which has been a fabulous help. Actually I've been lucky to have received some help from various colleagues so I'm going to owe quite a few favours around the place by the time this is done.

Anyway Em and Dave both say hi. Take care and give my love to Tim. I'm missing you both.

Luv Danni

***

Hi Danni,

Sounds like you're working too hard. Tell Rob he needs to take you away for a romantic weekend so that you forget about work for a while. We had a visit from Rama last week and I know he's concerned about you working too hard; I think he feels a little guilty about all the effort you're putting in for Helping Hands.

Speaking of Rama, he was thrilled with the progress we've been making up here, especially Tim and the workshop. They have now built, tested and approved three different designs for the prefabricated huts so they're moving steadily towards the production phase now. Meanwhile, Rama and his team are busy trying to secure a buyer. If all goes well we hope to have the first order of huts complete in just a few month's time.

After that, Tim and I are planning to have a week off and take a boat trip further up the Mahakam River. There's a riverboat captain who brings supplies to the village regularly who can set the trip up for us. It won't be the same without you and Rama travelling with us though!

Well that's all our news. More photos attached for your viewing pleasure. And remember, all work and no play makes Danni a very dull girl!

Luv ya,

Bel

***

Hi Bel,

Sounds like you guys are making some real progress up there, not that I ever doubted you would. Loved the latest batch of photos you sent. You're both looking well.

So listen, I have something to tell you. I've been procrastinating for weeks but its time you knew so here goes...Rob and I have separated. Wow, just five little words to describe such a big event; seems inadequate somehow. Anyway, that's the state of play here. I'm not really sure what the future holds but there's no chance of reconciliation so divorce seems inevitable. At the moment I'm just trying to find my feet.

Please don't think badly of Rob. I bear much of the responsibility for what has happened and suffice to say he is hurting as much as I am.

I'd appreciate it if you didn't mention this to Rama. I don't want him to think the pressure of building the Helping Hands campaign contributed in any way to the separation. If he was to get that idea into his head he'd likely pull the campaign and all my work will have been for nothing. The culmination of the campaign is a gala fundraising dinner event in just eight weeks' time. It would be a shame to jeopardize it when we're so close. And from an entirely selfish point of view, I'm happy to have the distraction.

My apologies for dropping such a bombshell on you. Telling my family and friends has been extremely difficult as you can imagine. Of course I feel pretty raw but I'm doing okay so I don't want you worrying about me.

Luv to you both,

Danni

***

Hi Danni,

I'm so, so sorry to hear about the separation. Although we haven't actually known each other for long, I do consider you one of my dearest friends so I feel your pain. Please know that if there is anything Tim and I can do to help, we will in a heartbeat. I just wish we weren't so far away at the moment. Come to us if want to. It might sound like a ridiculous idea but you'd love it here and a change a scene might be just what you need.

Rest assured your secret is safe with us. We wouldn't dream of telling Rama; it's your business and yours alone.

Danni, I know you're strong and will come through this okay. You have a good heart; I'm confident you will find happiness in the not too distant future. Take care dear friend.

Luv Bel and Tim

***

Hi Bel,

Thanks for your words of support. I'd love to return to Borneo and have a spell with you guys but as difficult as things are, I really need to stay here and face them. Things are getting a little easier although my future is still very much up in the air. I guess I need to start making some decisions soon.

I won't complain about working hard; to tell you the truth it's been a godsend to have something else to occupy my mind other than the pitiful state of my personal life.

The Helping Hands gala is now only a few weeks away and is coming together very nicely. I'm grateful to have had some much needed help from Emily and some of my colleagues who have really gotten behind the event and the Helping Hands agenda. Even without meeting him, Rama has the ability to inspire people.

Now enough about me and my life. How are things going with you guys? You must be looking forward to some time off and the riverboat trip.

Luv to you both,

Danni

***

Hi Danni,

We only have a short time in town before we head back to the village so just a quick email to wish you the best of luck with the fundraising gala this coming weekend. Tim and I are both confident it will be a big success.

Glad you sounded a bit chirpier in your last email. Hang in there girl.

Luv Bel and Tim

PS: Things are going well with the project. I'll send a big, newsy email next time around.

CHAPTER SIXTEEN

Danni stood near the podium and surveyed the function room one last time ahead of the evenings gala event which not only marked the launch of the marketing campaign for Rama's organization, it was also the first of what she hoped would become an annual fundraising event. Danni couldn't remember having ever been so nervous at a campaign launch, but then she'd never been so personally or emotionally involved before. She'd worked hard, put everything she had into pulling it together and she knew it was some of her best work. But it would all be for naught if the invitees, some of Perth's most influential business people, didn't respond and open their wallets as she hoped they would.

'It'll be fine,' said Emily, standing beside her. 'You've done a fantastic job Danni.'

'God I hope so Em, and not just for Rama but for all the people his organization can help. The Bornese are some of the friendliest, warmest people you could ever meet, despite having so little. Even small things can make such a difference in their lives. This is for them more than anything and I'd hate to let them down.'

The intensity of Danni's emotions was almost palpable and it was only then that Emily truly understood how much the Borneo trip had impacted on her friend. She threaded her arm through Danni's and gave it a reassuring squeeze. 'Borneo changed you didn't it?'

'Yes it did,' said Danni truthfully. 'I guess you could say I had an awakening of sorts,' Danni said, laughing softly at Emily's puzzled look. 'Sounds cliché I know but being there made me question things about my life and how I was living it.' She shrugged self-consciously. 'I guess that's obvious since Rob and I split up.'

Emily glanced at her friend with surprise. To the outside world, Rob and Danni appeared to have a happy, loving marriage so the split had come as a major shock to everyone. Neither Rob nor Danni had elaborated on the reasons behind it; in fact apart from quietly announcing their separation, they'd said very little and out of respect for both of them during what was obviously a painful time, their friends had refrained from prying.

'Danni, I haven't had a chance to tell you how sorry Dave and I were to see you guys separate,' Emily began cautiously, 'but I want you to know that we're here for you. If there's anything we can do...'

Danni patted her friends arm and smiled softly. 'Thanks Em. I know you've probably got a million questions but I just haven't been able to talk about it, probably because I was still trying to figure it all out myself. And to be honest I'm not particularly proud of myself Em. It's taken a lot of soul searching to get to a point where I can feel good about myself again.' Danni took a deep breath, 'You see Em, the whole thing was my fault because I fell in love with another man.'

Danni almost laughed at the shocked expression on Emily's face, only it wasn't funny at all. She knew she'd dropped a bombshell but Danni felt she owed her best friend an explanation. To Emily's credit, she recovered quickly and Danni could pick the precise moment the penny dropped. 'Rama?' Danni confirmed it with a nod. 'Does he know?' Emily asked.

'Does he know that I love him or that Rob and I have split?' Danni shook her head. 'No, I haven't told him either. I'm not sure I'm going to.'

'Why not? Surely he deserves to know?' Emily paused when a thought struck her. 'He does he love you doesn't he?'

'I think so,' Danni said slowly. 'I believe he does, but we've never spoken about.' Suddenly it was important that Emily understood. 'Em, I didn't go to Borneo and have a torrid affair with Rama. It wasn't like that. Our feelings just crept up on us and to be honest, it took me awhile to even recognize what was happening, what had already happened by then.

But I was married so we just tried to ignore it and pretend it wasn't happening. The thing is, I still loved Rob too. I honestly thought I could lock my feelings for Rama away and come home and continue be married to Rob.'

'But you couldn't?'

Danni shook her head. 'No. I tried but Rob soon figured out something was wrong. Eventually he put two and two together.'

'So he knows about Rama?'

'The night of the slideshow when he saw a picture of us together he figured it out. I assured him I hadn't been unfaithful, at least not physically, but he was crushed just the same.' Danni trailed off, thinking of that awful moment when Rob realized the truth. 'We tried to move past it but it turns out it's not so easy to be with one man without feeling like I was cheating on the other. Eventually, it became obvious to both of us that I was short changing Rob and our marriage.'

'Oh Danni, I'm so sorry,' Emily sympathized. 'But I don't understand why you haven't told Rama about any of this?'

'There are a lot of reasons Em. For starters, I've never met a man with more integrity than Rama. Despite our feelings he never behaved any way towards me other than honourably and I'm sure that was out of respect to me and my marriage to Rob. He'd hate to think he was to blame for our separation. Secondly, Rama's life is very different to mine, to everything I've ever known. Being with him would mean taking on a life I've never contemplated. I don't think it's fair to involve Rama or get his hopes up until I've worked through everything myself and I'm not quite there yet.'

'But he's going to be here tonight Danni,' Emily pointed out. 'Surely whilst he's here in Perth is the perfect time to talk to him about everything.'

'Logically. But I'm just so nervous Em. Part of me can't wait to see him and part of me is dreading it,' Danni confessed.

'You'll feel better once you've talked to him Danni,' said Emily confidently.

Danni breathed a sigh of relief when the first of the guests arrived right on time, the start of a steady stream. It was looking good for a full house. In between greeting and circulating among the guests, she kept an eye on the caterers making sure there were plenty of hors d'oeuvres and drinks being offered around. Thankfully, Emily and a couple of Danni's colleagues from the agency had volunteered their time to help. Her brother Chris and his wife Jenny were there, having left the kids with a babysitter and Danni's parents, both looking very smart in their formal attire.

'Hi luv, looks like it's going to be quite a shin ding,' her dad said as gave her a peck on the cheek.

'I certainly hope so dad. I can't thank you enough for getting your rotary mates interested enough to come along.' Danni turned and gave her mum a hug. 'I'm so glad you could make it. I can do with all the moral support I can get.'

'We wouldn't have missed it for the world sweetheart. We know how hard you've worked and how much it means to you,' said Catherine looking passed her shoulder. 'Now dear, I can see a young man trying to get your attention so we better let you get back to your other guests. We'll catch up later.'

Danni turned and caught her breath when she found herself looking straight at Rama. He smiled and stepped towards her to place a chaste kiss on her cheek.

'Hi Danni, it's good to see you,' he said softly as he stepped back.

'You too Rama,' said Danni, smiling back and hoping she didn't sound as sappy as she felt. Just seeing him again was like elixir to her soul.

'You look stunning. I almost didn't recognize you,' he lied. He would have recognized Danni anywhere and he hadn't had to search the room for her; his eyes had zeroed in on her the moment he stepped through the door and she'd taken his breath away. Her dress was a slim fitting number with a plunging back and skirt that finished just above the knees. He couldn't place the fabric, but as she moved it shimmered somewhere between silver and black depending on the light, accentuating her curves. Her long blonde hair was unrestrained, hanging freely around her shoulders, something he'd only seen the morning he found her brushing her hair on the veranda of the lodge in Loksado. Unconsciously she tossed her hair over her shoulder and he caught a glimpse of silver hoop earrings in her ears. He liked the way the chunky bangles on her arms accentuated her slim wrists but what appealed to him most was the black onyx pendant hanging from a silver chain at her neck; he recognized that as the piece she'd bought at the Cempaka gem fields.

'Thank you. You look rather handsome yourself,' she smiled back then laughed when Rama grimaced and pulled at the tie around his neck.

'Thanks. I had to buy the suit this afternoon especially for tonight. Not much call for suits in Indonesia.'

'You'll survive,' Danni sympathized. 'If tonight goes well you can hang it back in the wardrobe until next year.'

Rama surveyed the room with interest. 'This is pretty fancy Danni. Big crowd too.'

'Don't worry, I haven't blown your budget. I called in a few favours and roped in some volunteers. Plus once I told my boss at work what I was doing he gave me carte blanche to use whatever resources I needed, including access to our client list so I could send out invitations. If tonight goes well I'm hoping we'll see some big dividends.'

'I wasn't worried about the budget Danni; I knew you wouldn't be wasteful. But listen, however it goes tonight I want you to know how grateful I am for the effort you've put in. I hope it hasn't been too much of a burden.'

'Thanks Rama, I appreciate your confidence in me,' Danni said. 'So you know what you have to do tonight?'

Rama nodded. 'Yep, make my presentation and schmooze with potential donors afterwards. Do you want me to go mingle now?'

Danni reached out and snagged his wrist to check the time on his watch and shook her head. 'No, we'll be seating everyone for dinner in a few minutes so you can hang with me if you like.' I'd like that very much, thought Rama.

Now the initial awkwardness had passed, it was amazing how quickly they fell back into the same easy relationship they'd shared almost from the start. Danni asked after his parents and Maya and Jon and laughed when Rama told her Ahmed was still singing her praises to him every time Rama stopped by for a visit, but all too soon the caterer signalled Danni that it was time to get everyone seated.

Danni left Rama just long enough to step up to the podium and asked everyone to take their assigned seats, then took him over to the table they would be sharing with her family and Emily and Dave. After making the introductions, she made a quick circuit of the room to ensure everyone had found their seats. By the time she returned to the table Rama was chatting comfortably with everyone, leaving her free to relax and simply enjoy watching him interact with her family and friends. Danni wasn't the only one watching; although she and Rama were completely unaware they were doing it, the stolen glances, the soft smiles and easy familiarity was a dead giveaway that there was something more than friendship between them. Danni's parents exchanged pointed looks and seeing them together, Emily had no doubts everything would work out for them.

After the main meal, Danni stepped up to the podium to thank everyone for coming and began the presentation, starting with a moving speech about the living standards in Indonesia and Borneo in particular. As she spoke about the grinding poverty and the battle the Dayaks were facing as they transitioned between traditional village life and the modern era, a photographic slide show filled the big screen behind her; photos from her own collection depicting the dilapidated canal homes in Banjarmasin, women squatting beside the floating outhouses to wash, children playing in the dirt outside tiny thatched huts, smiling locals clad in little more than rags and the burnt out remains of once pristine forests. The effect was thought provoking and confronting and there were more than a few gasps from the audience. That's when Danni pressed the point that this was the reality of life for many in a country that was Australia's nearest neighbour, only a few thousand kilometres away. Pressing on she outlined the work of Helping Hands and after running through Rama's credentials, invited him to the podium.

Rama took the microphone and after thanking Danni for her introduction, he began to speak in his even, confident manner taking the audience on a journey through the history of his organization, focusing on several projects including the elevation of Ahmed from simple cart vendor to successful restaurateur. Danni had asked Rama to provide as many photos as possible and from somewhere amongst them she'd found an old photo of Ahmed standing barefoot beside his dirty cart, another one of he and his family squatting on the floor of their little home. As Rama spoke about the genesis of the restaurant and how the Helping Hands network was used to get it off the ground, there were more photos of various workers, locals and volunteers, involved in the fit-out, Ahmed inspecting fresh produce at a market garden, a restaurant full of patrons, smiling trainees working in the kitchen and finally a beaming Ahmed with his daughters proudly wearing their school uniforms. Although she'd put the presentation together and seen a draft of Rama's speech, it still brought a tear to her eye. And by the time Rama had gone through a couple of other projects; the Dayak fish farm and the pre-fabricated hut project that Bel and Tim were currently involved in, the entire audience was visibly moved. Rama's passion and commitment was obvious to everyone.

At the end of his speech Danni stepped back onto the stage to join Rama. Taking the microphone from him she spoke about the indelible spirit of the Bornese, their resourcefulness, their friendliness and love for family. Then she reminded the audience that the work of Helping Hands could only continue with the ongoing support and sponsorship of generous donors and asked them to dig deep and open their hearts and their wallets. There was a thunderous applause as she and Rama left the stage and Danni prayed that it translated into the donations that Helping Hands so needed.

The rest of the evening passed in a blur. Rama was swamped by people eager to talk to him and find out more about Helping Hands. Danni was kept busy keeping track of pledges that were made there and then and other would be donors who asked her to contact them in the following days. Her boss came by to congratulate her on a successful event and to compliment her on what he thought was her best work to date. He even hinted that the company may be able to run to a suitable donation. Her father let her know that the men from the rotary club were so impressed by what they'd seen they were considering adopting Helping Hands, which would mean ongoing sponsorship. But somehow amidst the chaos, Rama found time to seek out Danni to introduce him to everyone who had assisted in the event so that he could personally thank them.

Danni lost track of her brother and his wife, but Emily came and gave her a congratulatory hug as she and Dave were leaving and offered a whispered observation that Rama was 'quite a man'. When her mum made a similar observation, adding that she and Rama made a good team, Danni was left wondering just how transparent her feelings for Rama were.

It was late when the last of the guests left and Danni was finally able to plonk down into a chair. She unclipped her stilettos, wiggled her toes and groaned appreciatively. Rama sat on the chair beside her, stretching out his long legs and loosening his tie. Seeing the funny side of it, they looked at each other and laughed. Then Rama reached across and took her hand. 'Danni, I don't know how to thank you. Tonight was just amazing. You were amazing; the way you pulled this whole thing together, the concept, the presentation, everything.'

Danni smiled at him. 'I was happy to do it for you Rama and I'm glad it went so well. I was so worried I'd let you down.'

'You couldn't,' he said emphatically. He paused for moment, as if he was considering what to say next. 'Danni, I met your entire family tonight, except your husband. Where is he?'

During the course of the busy evening Danni hadn't given Rob a thought, and perhaps naively, it hadn't even occurred to her that Rama would notice his absence, so his question took her by surprise. But she wouldn't lie to him.

'We've separated,' she admitted quietly.

Rama's heart thumped in his chest, but he forced himself be calm. 'Why?'

Taking a deep breath Danni looked him squarely in the face. 'Because I'm in love with you.'

Rama felt like he'd been hit in the solar plexus as the air was sucked from his lungs. He hadn't come here tonight expecting this. He'd expected to meet Danni's husband and have to pretend it wasn't killing him to think of her with him. Instead, Danni had spoken the words he never thought he would hear. He reached out, curling his fingers into her hair and gently pulling her towards him until their lips were so close he could feel her breath on his skin. 'Does this mean I can finally kiss you?' he whispered.

In answer, Danni tilted her head slightly, closing the last few millimetres between them and suddenly they were kissing, gently at first, as if they couldn't quite believe it, and then the kissed deepened as they poured all their pent-up emotions into it. Finally Rama broke away, gasping for air. 'Danni, I have a room upstairs. Will you come up with me?' he asked.

'I'd like that,' she said honestly. She reached down to replace her stilettos then took the hand Rama held out to her and walked with him.

He didn't bother turning the light on in the room. There was enough light streaming in through the open curtains and that was how he wanted to see Danni in his bed; naked in the moonlight. Taking her hand, he led her to the bedside. 'You're trembling.'

Danni nodded, 'It's just I haven't...haven't been with anyone but Rob for so long.'

Rama put his arms around her and silenced her with his lips. He didn't want to think about her with anyone else. 'Ssh, it's okay. We can go slow until you're comfortable with me.'

But in the end they didn't go slow. When Rama kissed her again and placed his hands on her body for the first time, Danni forgot all about her nervousness and simply lost herself in his arms. Afterwards, when they lay facing each other in a tangle of sheets and limbs, Rama told her he loved her.

'When did you know?' Danni asked softly.

'Maybe Loksado, definitely by Negara,' he confessed.

He saw Danni smile in the dimness. 'You hid it well,' she said. 'I had no idea.'

'I did my best to hide it but there were a few times I nearly gave myself away. I spent hours watching you sleep whilst we were caring for Sweetie-pie. But in the end you knew didn't you?'

'Yes, although I was a bit slow on the uptake,' Danni admitted. 'Once it actually dawned on me that you found me attractive, it wasn't long before I began to suspect your feelings ran a bit deeper.'

'What about you?' Rama asked as he played with a lock of her hair. 'When did you know?'

'That day at Ahmed's when I made you *Bingka Barandam*. It came as a very big shock I can tell you. I had a minor meltdown in the bathroom,' Danni said, then laughed when a funny thought struck her. 'Oh my, if Ahmed could see us now he'd be having kittens.'

Rama chuckled but Danni had shifted slightly and he was distracted by a shaft of light streaming across her breast. He reached out and touched her nipple and when it hardened beneath his finger, he leaned across to suckle her and then everything receded but the two of them.

Danni stayed with Rama through the night and well into the next day.

The made love and slept and made love again. When hunger got the better of them they ordered room service and ate off the tray, sitting naked on the bed. The real world only encroached for a few minutes when Danni suddenly sat up in bed with a panicked look on her face. 'Oh my God, I need to call mum and dad.'

Rama looked at her like she'd gone stark raving mad. 'I temporarily moved in with them after Rob and I split. They're probably worried sick that I haven't come home,' she explained, reaching across the bed for the phone.

Admitting to either parent that she was with Rama was always going to be awkward but Catherine surprised her by saying, 'We knew where you were luv. We'll see you when you get home.'

When Danni hung up the phone, Rama was lying with his chin propped in his hand smirking at her. 'Finished checking in with the folks?'

Danni threw a pillow at him. 'Okay I'll admit it's not ideal but they have a big house and it seemed like the logical thing to do until I figure out what I'm going to do with my future.'

Rama pulled her down on top of him. 'What you could do is marry me and live happily ever after.' Danni's laughter stilled on her lips and he felt her stiffen. He hadn't intended to propose, well not like that, but it was out there now and more than anything he wanted Danni for his wife.

Danni pushed herself up off his chest. She'd never imagined Rama would propose to her. So much had happened in the last six months she'd barely given the future beyond Rob any thought. She was just treading water trying to come to terms with everything that had happened. 'Rama I can't marry you. It's too soon. For starters, legally I'm still married to Rob and secondly I just don't know if marriage is the right thing for us.'

Rama stroked her arms and looked at her earnestly. 'I know it seems sudden Danni, it is for me too, but I love you and you love me. Why wouldn't marriage be the right option for us once your divorce is through?'

Danni rolled away from Rama and sat up. 'Rama, your life is in Indonesia. As your wife, that's where my life would be too and I'm just not sure how I feel about that. I've never considered living anywhere but Australia.'

Rama propped himself up against the bed head. 'Danni, I know it would be a big change for you but we could have a good life together over there. And it's not like you'd be cutting ties with Australia altogether. You could come back as often as you like. My parents managed it and I know we could too.'

Danni shook her head in frustration. 'Rama, it's not just that. Six months ago I was happily married to Rob. Okay it wasn't perfect but I loved him; I still love him,' she admitted. 'I never envisioned not being with him, not growing old with him. Then I met you and everything changed almost overnight, and now this…us' Danni gestured to Rama and herself and the bed. 'I just never saw any of this coming and to be honest I'm still grappling with it. I've hurt Rob, badly, and I feel a lot of guilt about it. I can't carry that into another marriage or it will just fester and destroy any chance of happiness in the future. I need to be able to forgive myself first and until then I'm just not in a position to make a commitment. I need some time.'

Rama studied her for a moment and then held out his arms to her. Danni crawled up beside him and lay her head on his chest. Rama looked down at the woman in his arms and thought about how badly he wanted her to be his wife. But he understood that she needed time and as much as it pained him to do so, he schooled himself to be patient. 'You still love Rob?' he asked, absently stoking her back.

He felt her sigh. 'I do,' she admitted. 'Rob was my first love Rama and that's something that will never change. Even after I admitted my love for you I thought I could still save my marriage and be with him. But I couldn't stop thinking about you, missing you…and then when I saw you again last night and this happened I've realized what you and I have is different. I love Rob, but I'm in love with you. Maybe I'm not making any sense but that's how it is.'

Rama hugged her tightly. 'It makes perfect sense Danni. Your whole world has been turned upside down. Despite the selfish part of me that just wants to put a ring on your finger as quickly as possible, if you need some time that's okay with me. Just try not to take too long,' he said kissing the top of her head.

By the following day they were ready to venture out but Danni only had the cocktail dress she wore to the reception and there was no other option but to drive to her parent's house for a change of clothes. They found her folks in the back yard raking up leaves and sweeping the patio and after a quick hello Danni scurried up to her room to change, leaving the three of them making small talk. Desperate to spare both them all any embarrassment, Danni quickly threw a few toiletries and another outfit into an overnight bag, changed into a simple summer dress and sandals and was back downstairs within ten minutes. But she need not have worried, Rama and her folks were sitting on the back patio chatting easily.

Rama smiled up at her. 'Ready to go?'

'Yes all set,' then turning to her folks. 'I'll be back tomorrow. Dad, is it okay if Rama and I use your office for the follow-ups?' Knowing that a successful fundraising gala would involve quite a bit of follow-up work to finalise the pledges, send out more information to those that had requested it and personal thank you letters from Rama to the donors, Danni had already arranged a couple of days off work to get through it all.

'That's fine luv. You're welcome to it,' said Bill. He stood up and shook Rama's hand. 'I'll see you tomorrow then son.'

'Lovely to see you again Rama,' Catherine added warmly, leaving Danni rather surprised as how readily her parents seemed to have accepted the new man in her life.

Since Rama wasn't very familiar with Perth, he left it to Danni to choose a lunch spot. She drove them to up to Kings Park, Perth's most iconic attraction. In a rare example of political foresight, the four hundred hectare reserve was set aside for public purposes just two years after the settlement of the Swan River Colony in 1829 and in the years since had become a much loved and admired landmark by both city residents and visitors alike. Situated on Mount Eliza adjacent to Perth's central business district, the park comprised sprawling parklands and botanical gardens and afforded spectacular views over the city and the Swan River. Danni drove them up the tree-lined avenue and parked, then she and Rama walked hand in hand to the State War Memorial where they stood in the shadow of the towering granite obelisk admiring the view from the Mount Eliza bluff. They paused at the Flame of Remembrance and read the names of the fallen from the memorial wall, but even the sombre reflections couldn't dent their happiness. They revelled in the freedom of openly being a couple, of being able to walk hand in hand and steal quick kisses when nobody was watching. They ate lunch at a café overlooking a lake then strolled along the Federation Walkway, stopping to admire the native flora and Aboriginal artwork; but mostly they just enjoyed the sunshine, the fresh eucalypt scented air and each other. On an elevated glass bridge, they walked through the treetops and stood at the highest point to kiss and hold each other. When another couple came along, Rama handed them his phone and asked them to take of photo of them together and when they finished walking they lay down on the grass in the shade, talking and laughing and just enjoying being together. When Danni rolled onto her stomach and propped herself across Rama's chest he smoothed the hair away from her face and looked at her with such adoration, she impulsively leaned forward and brushed a feather light kiss across his lips. Rama groaned and put a hand to the back of her head, forcing her lips back to his and claiming her mouth in a crushing, bruising kiss that left them both panting with need.

'Time to go,' said Rama, standing and holding out his hand to help Danni to her feet.

They barely made it three feet inside Rama's hotel room before they were naked and he scooped her up and marched over to the bed where they finished what was started with that kiss in the park.

Monday morning rolled around far too soon; neither of them wanted to leave their weekend cocoon. On the pretext of waiting for the peak hour traffic to pass, they milked the most out of the morning, until reluctantly driving south to her parent's house to work.

'It's just me and Rama,' Danni called as she let them into the house with her key. But the house was silent and going through to the kitchen she found a note from her mum saying they'd gone out to run some errands and would be back later, so Danni took Rama through to the well-equipped home office and they set to work. They worked together as well as they did everything else, with Danni working the phone doing follow-up calls and Rama sorting through the pledges already received. Catherine popped her head in around lunchtime to say hello and offered to make them some lunch which she brought to them on a tray shortly afterwards so they could eat at the desk as they worked. It was after four before Danni stretched in her chair and announced she'd had enough.

Rama tossed his pen down and grinned at her. 'I thought you'd never stop. You're a slave driver you know.'

Danni looked mortified. 'Oh geez, I'm really sorry Rama. I can get a bit single-minded when I work,' she apologized.

'Hey, I was only teasing,' he laughed. 'Actually I loved watching you work. It's a side to you I haven't seen before. We make a good team you know.'

'Funny, that's exactly what mum said to me after the gala on Friday night,'

'Then she's an astute woman. Now if you were even half as astute you'd realize how badly in need of a kiss I am right now and do something about it,' said Rama grinning at her.

'Is that right?' Danni drawled, lips twitching. 'How badly in need are you?'

Rama's eyes gleamed. 'Why do you come over here and find out for yourself?' he challenged.

Taking her time, Danni stood up and covered the few steps towards him then sank down onto his lap. Deliberately she wiggled her backside until her thigh came into contact with the hard lump at his crutch. 'Hmm, do you think a kiss will help or just make it worse?' she asked with mock seriousness.

'Danni,' Rama bit out hoarsely, something between a warning and a plea.

But she just wriggled some more and laughed, determined to make him wait. Feigning shock, she shook her head, 'Rama, I never would have guessed behind that gentlemanly exterior you displayed in Borneo was such an insatiable man.'

'The same could be said for you woman and if you don't kiss me right now I might just have to go back to being a gentleman because this is torture. How would you like that?' he asked, squarely turning the tables on his tormentor.

Danni grinned and lowered her head. 'Well now that you've put it like that...' she whispered just before she claimed his lips. Rama groaned, deepening the kiss and thrusting his hand up under her dress to rub her thigh. When he slipped his thumb under the elastic of her panties Danni reached down to stop him. 'No not here Rama. Mum or dad could walk in any time,' she reminded him.

'Then stop wriggling,' Rama whispered back, placing both hands on her hips to still her. He tilted his back to suck in some deep breaths, then looked ruefully at Danni. 'You're killing me Danni. I can't seem to get enough of you. I don't know how I'm going to function without you. It was bad enough the last time when you left to come home. I know I said I'd give you whatever time you needed but I'd be a very happy man if you'd change your mind and come back to Indonesia with me on Wednesday.'

Danni looked stricken. 'Wednesday? It's too soon Rama. Can't you stay longer?'

Rama shook his head. 'I wish I could. More than anything in this world I wish I could. But I've got an important meeting with a government minister lined up for later this week. It took me months to get an audience with him so there's just no way I can cancel it.'

Danni laid her head on Rama's shoulder. 'Rama, I wish I could just throw caution to the wind and come with you but I just can't, not until I've sorted a few things out.'

Rama stroked her hair. 'I know sweetheart. I've waited for you this long, I can wait a bit longer. When you come to me I want you to do so wholeheartedly, without any doubts, without reservations, without guilt and for the rest of our lives. Do you think you can do that?'

Danni nestled deeper into the crook of his neck. 'I hope so Rama. I love you.'

'I love you too Danni,' he whispered back as they held each other and tried not to think about the long separation ahead of them. Danni wasn't sure how long they stayed like that but it was some time later when her father knocked on the door and popped his head inside. If he had any thoughts about finding his daughter on Rama's lap he kept them to himself.

'You two staying for dinner? I can pop some steaks on the BBQ,' he asked as Danni extricated herself from Rama's lap.

Danni looked at Rama who nodded his agreement. 'Sure, especially if there's a cold beer to go with it?'

'I'm sure I can rustle one up,' Bill grinned. 'You finished for the day?'

'We have,' Danni confirmed, reaching across to shut down the computer and together they all left the office and headed to the back patio. 'I'm sorry we haven't been much company today dad.'

Bill waved her apology aside. 'That's fine luv. You guys had work to do; your mum and I weren't expecting a social visit. Now let me get this barbeque warmed up. Rama, have a hunt around in that fridge over there for some beers. I think there's a bottle of wine in there for the girls too.'

'I'll go see if mum needs any help in the kitchen,' said Danni. She found her mum pulling salad makings out of the fridge and automatically reached for the knife to start slicing and dicing. Catherine came and stood beside her at the sink whilst she washed the lettuce. They could see the two men through the kitchen window as they worked.

'Well I guess I know now what prompted you to leave Rob,' said Catherine quietly.

'Mum!'

'What? You're obviously both smitten with each other and that didn't just happen over the last couple of days.'

There was no point denying the obvious but Danni did feel the need to set the record straight on another score. 'For the record mum, I didn't leave Rob, he left me.'

Catherine stopped what she was doing and fixed her daughter with an indulgent look. 'Sweetheart, whether you realize it or not, you've been leaving Rob for years.' When Danni opened her mouth to protest, Catherine held up a hand to silence her. 'Rob was a fool. I've no doubt he loved you but he took you for granted. Left you to your own devices far too often. I'm not surprised you ended up in another man's arms.'

'Mum!' Danni exclaimed, mortified to think her mother might think she'd had an extra-marital affair. 'I didn't leave Rob for Rama and I certainly didn't cheat on him.'

'I never thought for a moment you did honey. But I'm guessing meeting Rama made you give your marriage a long hard look.'

Danni squirmed under her mother's gaze. As close as they were she wasn't particularly comfortable discussing her marriage or her relationship with Rama. Thankfully she was saved from having to answer when Rama came in carrying a glass of wine each for them.

'Here you go ladies,' he said proffering the glasses. 'Can I do anything to help?'

'Thank you Rama. Here, can you take these out to Bill please,' Catherine said handing him a tray of steaks. 'We're just about done here.'

Danni followed him to the patio door. 'Thanks for agreeing to stay for dinner,' she said quietly so her mum wouldn't overhear. 'I know this is probably a bit awkward for you...'

But Rama just grinned and leaned forward to snatch a kiss. 'Hey it's no big deal. I like your folks and I like seeing you in your own setting, doing your day to day stuff. Maybe later you can show me your bedroom.' He was laughing as he went back to the patio, leaving Danni shaking her head and a smiling behind him. When she and her mother joined the men a few minutes later Rama and her father were deep in discussion about the family business but he acknowledged her with a smile and reached for her hand when she sat down beside him.

It was a typical balmy summers evening, pleasantly cooled by the Fremantle Doctor, the locally named sea breeze that blew its way up the Swam River estuary most summer afternoons. These were the times that Danni loved best, that were at the very heart of her fondest childhood memories; relaxing on the patio overlooking the big, shady yard where she and her brother had climbed the jacaranda trees, played totem tennis or hung out with their friends, the smell of meat grilling on the barbeque wafting across the yard or big slabs of sweet watermelon gulped greedily down. Sitting there with Rama, Danni experienced a bone deep sense of contentment. She shut her eyes and sighed deeply, determined to imprint it on her mind, something to fortify herself with when Rama left.

***

They returned to work in her father's office again the next day and by lunchtime were grinning delightedly at the number on the bottom of the spreadsheet. 'That's unbelievable,' said Rama giving Danni a big noisy kiss. 'Thanks to you Helping Hands has now got more than enough money to fund our current program and take on some additional projects that have been on hold for a while. And not only that, this will free up so much of my time to be more hands on and involved in the projects.'

Rama's delight was infectious. 'And the pledges are still coming in Rama,' she reminded him. 'I expect the final number will be higher still.'

Rama was pinching himself. Since establishing Helping Hands, he'd spent so much of his time scratching around trying to secure funding, to suddenly have the money he needed sitting there in the bank was astounding. 'I told you we're a good team Danni. With me overseeing the projects and you looking after the marketing and fundraising side of things we're formidable. Come and work with me Danni. I can't pay you much but there'd be some fringe benefits,' he said grinning.

Danni laughed. She loved this playful side of him. 'Hmm, maybe we could come to some arrangement but my charge out rate is quite high you know. The fringe benefits would have to be substantial.'

Rama's eyes narrowed on her. 'Maybe we should head back to the hotel and open negotiations.'

'It could take a while to thrash out the details,' Danni warned, trying to keep a straight face.

'Then the sooner we get started the better, wouldn't you agree?' And with that Rama jumped to his feet and planted his hands on either side of Danni's chair, effectively pinning her to the seat whilst he very thoroughly kissed her. They were both panting for breath when he finally broke away. 'Just to show you I'm committed to negotiating in good faith,' he said smugly.

They spent most of the afternoon negotiating until Rama called a stay in proceedings so he could take Danni out to dinner, determined to make their last evening memorable. Rama pulled on the suit he'd worn to the fundraising gala and having been forewarned, Danni dressed in a dark blue, figure hugging cocktail dress that she'd bought on impulse over a year ago and had so far not had the opportunity to wear.

Rama waited patiently for her whilst she fastened her hair up loosely with a silver clasp and applied her make-up and let out a long whistle of appreciation when she emerged from the bathroom.

'God, you're beautiful Danni,' he said sincerely, taking her hand and stepping back to admire her. 'It was worth getting back into this monkey suit just to see you dressed up.'

Danni gave Rama a once over. 'You do look very handsome in a suit Rama but I think I prefer you shirtless in a sarong.'

Rama grinned delightedly. 'Come back to Indonesia with me Danni and I'll promise to wear a sarong for you every day,' he challenged.

'Rama, I can't. I do love you but it's just too soon,' she said softly, shaking her head.

Rama took her in his arms. 'I know honey. I just can't bear the thought of leaving you tomorrow. It just about killed me when you left Borneo. Back then I didn't think you could ever mine, that we could ever have a future together. I told myself I just had to get over you. But it's different this time. I know how good we are together.'

Danni ran her hand through his hair and kissed his neck. 'I'm sorry Rama. Please be patient with me,' she implored him.

'However long it takes Danni, I'll be waiting for you.' Rama continued to hold her until a tear slipped from Danni's eye and she stepped back to wipe it away before it ruined her make-up.

Rama gave her hand a squeeze. 'Come on, let's get going.'

They got a taxi to the restaurant so Danni didn't have to worry about drinking and driving but when Rama gave the taxi driver the name of one of the city's finest restaurants, she put a cautionary hand on his. 'Umm Rama, I don't think we'll get in without a booking.'

'I have a booking,' he said smugly earning him a surprised look from Danni. The restaurant was well known for being booked up months in advance. 'I asked your dad to recommend the best place in town,' Rama explained, 'and he pulled a few strings to get me a booking. Apparently the owner is one of his Rotary mates.'

'Ah, how very secretive of you two,' said Danni relaxing back in her seat.

Their dinner was everything you'd expect of a top restaurant and although Danni was initially concerned about the cost, Rama assured her he could afford it. 'I don't pull much of an income out of my organization but my living expenses in Indonesia are very modest,' he explained. 'Over the years I've managed to sock a bit away.'

So in the end Danni stopped worrying about the prices on the menu and relaxed. The restaurant was lovely; the décor striking the perfect balance between modern elegance and warmth, enhanced by dim lighting and soft background music. The wait staff were attentive without being intrusive and meal was simply divine. The both ordered an entrée and main course, exchanging tastings of each other's meals. Rama ordered a bottle of champagne for them to share but when he later admitted to not being too fond of it, Danni insisted on swapping to a full bodied red wine that was more to his tastes.

Neither was particularly hungry when the waiter offered them dessert but in the end they shared a chef's tasting plate and lingered over coffee. 'This has been really nice Rama. Thank you for bringing me here.'

Rama grasped her hand across the table. 'My pleasure. I wish I could do more of it for you.'

But Danni shook her head. 'No, I don't need all this fancy stuff Rama. I mean this has been really nice because it's a special treat but I'd be just as happy at Ahmed's or a little warung on the beach, just as long as I'm with you.'

'Me too,' agreed Rama, trying not to think about how much time would pass before that could happen. Suddenly he wanted to get out of there, to be alone with Danni, to take her in his arms and make love to her in a way she'd never forget. 'You ready to go?' he asked in a tight voice.

Danni nodded quickly as if she could read his thoughts and was just as anxious to be alone with him.

Twenty minutes later they were back in their hotel room. There was no waiting, no foreplay as they tumbled onto the bed and coupled within seconds, still almost fully clothed, but it didn't matter; Danni was ready for him and lifted her hips to meet his every thrust. Within minutes they shattered around each other and lay panting together, almost shell-shocked by the urgent intensity of their lovemaking.

Finally Rama lifted his head and grinned apologetically. 'Sorry that was a bit quick. I had planned to make love to you all night long.'

Danni laughed softly against him. 'No need to apologise. I wasn't exactly complaining.'

'I noticed. We're a good match Danni, in everything we do,' said Rama emphasizing 'everything'.

They lay together quietly until Rama sat up and swung his legs off the bed. 'I think it's time I got into something a little more comfortable,' he said pulling off the remainder of his clothes and coming back to the bed naked, where Danni was lying on her side with her head propped in her hand watching him. Rama bent over her and ran a hand along her thigh and up under her skirt. 'Aren't you a little over dressed?' he commented.

Danni grinned. 'I was just admiring the view. Besides, I need help with my zip.' She saw Rama's eyes narrow before he moved over her and slowly drew her zipper down, dropping feather light kisses on her back as each inch of skin was revealed. Danni shuddered and groaned and lost herself to the sensual onslaught that Rama unleashed.

***

The mood was sombre as Danni drove Rama to the airport the following morning. He'd offered to take a taxi but she insisted in seeing him off, even though she knew she was just prolonging the agony. They found a corner table in one of the airport coffee lounges and sat holding hands as they sipped on their coffee and tried to make small talk but they were too sad and eventually Rama dragged his chair around beside Danni's and pulled her into his arms and they just held each other until it was time for him to join the queue through immigration.

'Come as soon as you can Danni,' Rama implored her as they finished a lingering kiss. 'I'll be waiting for you.'

More than anything Danni wanted to tell him she would but it was a promise she couldn't make so instead she tucked her head under his chin and hugged him tight. 'I love you Rama,' she loved him and hoped that would be enough for him to keep the faith.

Rama stroked her hair as he held her against him. 'I love you too,' he told her as he kissed the top of her head and then he turned and walked through the door to immigration and was lost from sight. Danni bit her lip tightly as she retraced her steps back to her car and only then did she let the tears fall.

CHAPTER SEVENTEEN

Hi Danni,

Congratulations on the success of the fundraising gala. Rama has just been up for a visit and was full of it and how great you were. I'm not surprised; I knew you'd pull it off.

Rama mentioned you'd spent some time together and he obviously knew about your separation from Rob so I guess the cat is out of the bag now. But he also assured us you seemed happy which Tim and I were very pleased to hear.

Now to bring you up to date with things at our end…Tim and I are both well. Our Bahasa Indonesia skills have developed to a point I'd call conversational, although we're still some way off being fluent. But the good thing about it is we're now able to engage with the non-English speakers in the village, which is most of them, so we're really starting to feel like part of the community. Even when we go into town now people recognize us and want to stop and talk which is lovely.

The first shipment of the pre-fab huts went out on a barge earlier this week which was cause for much celebration. Rama and his team had arranged a buyer who came up to the village and inspected everything before accepting the shipment. By all accounts he was very impressed and has promised a new order in the next week or two.

With that milestone under our belt we've decided it's time for a break so we're now on our way to catch our boat for a week cruising up the Mahakam River. Captain Husni who services our village has arranged for another captain friend of his to take us up the river, stopping off at points of interest along the way. He knows the river and the settlements along the way well so we're assured of seeing some places well off the tourist map. Apparently there are still Dayaks living in traditional longhouse villages a couple of days cruising from here and naturally Tim and I are keen to call in and have a look.

I must go now. Tim's giving me a hurry-up look as we still have to pick up some supplies. Wish you were coming with us.

Luv from both of us,

Bel

***

Hi Bel,

I hope you guys enjoyed your well-earned break up the river. I must say I was quite envious of you! With your new found language skills I imagine it was very satisfying to be able to converse directly with the locals. I can't wait to hear all about it.

Yes the fundraising gala went wonderfully well, exceeding all my expectations. Rama has agreed to make this an annual event so it's officially been adopted as the main fundraising strategy for Helping Hands. Of course, there's still work to be done throughout the year keeping in touch with the donors and making sure they know how their money is being spent.

It was lovely to see Rama again. He was good company as always.

I'm pleased to hear the project is going so well. It must have been immensely satisfying for you both to see off that first shipment of huts.

Hard to believe you've now passed the six month mark and are on the downhill side of your assignment. Rama has been trying to talk me into coming back to Indo. I'm sure I will one day but I'm not sure when. As much as I'm looking forward to catching up with you guys it probably won't be before you get home to Perth.

Luv to you both,

Danni

***

Hi Danni,

The trip was fabulous! Our captain and crew looked after us very well and the weather was perfect. Best of all we got to visit a couple of Dayak villages where they are still living very traditional lives. We were invited to stay a couple of days in one village which we did, sleeping in the longhouse with everyone else.

Tim even went out on a pig hunting trip with some of the men. I would like to have gone too but it was a men only trip. However, I did enjoy hanging out with the women and children. They were very interested in my life back in Australia but thought it very strange that Tim and I haven't got any children yet. They were convinced we must have problem and insisted on dragging me off to see their shaman to see if he could help. Too funny!

Anyway, the men did actually get a pig so the whole village got involved cooking it up and preparing a big feast in honour of our visit. As you can image, we felt very privileged. It still brings a tear to my eye thinking about it. I've attached some photos for you.

The other good news is that we arrived back at the village to learn that they have received another order for more huts so everyone is busy in the workshop. I also have a new assignment; as well as continuing my work with the kids I'm training several villagers in basic book keeping skills. Speaking of the kids, Rama has made arrangements for two of our older students to go to Jakarta to take courses in design and drafting. The whole village is very excited about that because they're the first kids from the village to have a chance to go away to study. The bonus of course is that they'll be able to come back to the village to live and work and put those skills to good use.

Now enough about us. I have a feeling you've been holding out on me! Rama has been up for another visit and couldn't stop talking about you. He didn't say anything of course, too much of a gentleman, but do I detect something romantic between the two of you??? You don't have to tell me if you don't want to but I'm absolutely dying of curiosity. But if, hypothetically speaking, there was something developing between you and Rama, Tim and I both think it's fabulous. Two of our dearest friends together; what could be better?

Take care my friend.

Luv from us,

Bel & Tim

***

Hi Bel,

What a wonderful experience the river trip must have been. I loved the photos and I can't wait to see and hear more some time.

I'm also pleased to hear the hut project is going so well. Not that I'm surprised; the Dayaks are hardworking, motivated people and with you and Tim and Rama behind them, it was bound to be successful.

In answer to your not-so-subtle inquiry about Rama and me, yes I have to confess that we have developed strong feelings for each other. What this means for us going forward I'm still trying to figure out. It's an understatement to say my life has been completely turned on its head over the last eight months so it's taking me awhile to sort through things. I feel that I need to let the dust settle before I can make any decisions about the future. Thankfully Rama is being very understanding and patient with me.

Luv to you both,

Danni

***

Hi Danni,

I want to be mad at you for holding out on me but I can't because I'm just so thrilled that you and Rama are an item. Tim and I detected a spark between the two of you when we were all together over here so we're not surprised at all that things have developed. You guys are perfect for each other. Tim and I both have our fingers crossed that you can find a way to be together.

Now I have some BIG news of my own. Remember I told you the Dayak villagers up the Mahakam River took me off to see their shaman to rectify mine and Tim's childless status? Well the shaman's mumbo-jumbo must have been stronger than my contraception because I'm pregnant! Tim and I can't believe it but we're both absolutely thrilled.

I expect the baby will arrive sometime in August. So far no morning sickness but maybe it's too soon for that? Anyway, I'm feeling really fit and healthy so there's no reason we can't stay here and finish our assignment. I'll be back in Perth early on in my second trimester so perfect timing really.

Luv from mamma and papa in waiting,

Bel and Tim

***

Hi Bel,

OMG, what fabulous news! I'm so thrilled for you both. You'll make awesome parents. Whatever it is the shaman is doing, he should bottle it; he'd make a fortune. I hope you're still feeling well and Tim is looking after you.

I've already been out baby shopping for you so expect lots of lovely presents when you get home. In the meantime, let me know if you need anything sent to you. Rama told me he's heading your way in the next month so I could send something to him and get him to bring it with him.

Not much to report at my end. I still haven't figured out what I want to do. Of course Rama is continues to be very patient with me but having a long distance relationship is awfully frustrating and we miss each other terribly. I feel like I'm being rather unfair to him but I just can't seem to make a decision. I just hope he doesn't decide it's all too hard.

Give Tim a big congratulatory hug from me. Look after yourself.

Luv,

Danni

***

Hi Danni,

I'm jealous! You got to go baby shopping. I must be in an early nesting phase because that's the one thing I'm really missing not being able to do. Other than that, I'm feeling great. Still no morning sickness or baby bump to report.

The villagers here are all very happy for us and I've got all the women here giving me helpful advice on everything to do with the pregnancy, determining the sex of the baby, safe sex positions whilst pregnant (OMG!), remedies for morning sickness, breastfeeding, childbirth, motherhood and lots of other stuff I can't even comprehend. All I know is that Indonesian's can be quite forward and frank in their conversations so there have been a few rather embarrassing discussions. But they do mean well and I feel well cared for.

Tim is also doing his bit to look after me. One minute he's strutting around like a peacock, the next he's being a big doting teddy bear. It's so funny.

Rama came up as planned, bringing with him the care package you sent. The Tim Tams were devoured within a couple of days, the massage oil has been put to good use and we're still working our way through the book of baby names.

As for Rama getting impatient with you and changing his mind, rest assured you have absolutely nothing to worry about in that regard. He's completely head over heels in love with you. But I have to say girl, he's such a honey I don't know how you can bear to be away from him. So with the best of intentions, I'm giving your butt a big kick into gear all the way from Borneo!

Luv from both of us,

Bel

CHAPTER EIGHTEEN

Danni stepped through the revolving doors into the busy city street and blinked in the bright sunshine. It was one of those perfect, clear autumn days that Perth often strings together before the chilly bite of winter sets in. She backed up against the building wall out of the flow of the pedestrian traffic to retrieve her sunglasses from her bag.

'Hi Danni.' The quietly spoken greeting brought her head up with a jerk.

'Hello Rob.' She gave him a hesitant smile. Apart from a few brief phone calls to arrange the collection of her personal items from the house and the division of assets, Danni hadn't seen Rob since that fateful day they called their marriage quits. 'How are you?'

Rob shrugged. 'Okay considering. Hell of a lot of changes.' It was a mammoth understatement.

'Yes,' agreed Danni carefully, unable to think of any other way to respond.

There was a brief awkward silence, until Rob cleared his throat, 'Um, do you have time to grab a coffee?' The invitation took Danni by surprise but she recognized it as an olive branch of sorts and was happy to take it.

'Sure,' she said, falling into step beside Rob as they crossed the street to the nearby cafe. They found a table on the sidewalk and sat, Rob choosing the seat in the sun, Danni sitting in the shade, just as they had always done. It was the kind of automatic, unspoken decision that was unique to long term couples who knew each other's preferences well and the irony was not lost on either of them. It was the same when the waitress came and took their order. 'Flat white with skinny?' Rob confirmed expectantly, without having to wait for Danni to make her choice.

'You look tired,' he commented once they were alone.

Danni shrugged. 'Things have been pretty hectic at work.' It was partly true; work was busy but no more than usual. The extra hours she was putting in were her way of fighting off the loneliness that swamped her when she was alone in bed at night.

'I thought you'd have started a new life in Indonesia by now,' Rob said lightly, although Danni could see it took him some effort.

Danni looked away. 'I just...I'm not...' She struggled to find the right words, 'I just haven't been ready to make a commitment,' she said shrugging. She could tell Rob all sorts of reasons why she wasn't with Rama but even to her own ears they would sound trite. Rob eyed her speculatively but remained silent. 'Rob, I know this probably sounds inadequate but I want you to know I'm really sorry for everything that's happened. I know I hurt you and believe me that was the last thing I ever wanted to do. I don't expect you to forgive me but I hope one day you can find it in your heart to a least stop hating me.'

Rob sighed and shook his head. 'Danni I don't hate you. Okay, maybe at the time I thought I did,' he admitted ruefully, 'but as much as I wished I could, I just couldn't stop loving you.' He held up his hand at Danni's surprised expression. 'Don't worry, I'm not telling you this in an attempt to win you back but I have come to accept what happened and even to accept that I have some responsibility to bear in it.'

Danni opened her mouth to protest but Rob stopped her again. 'Danni, please let me say this whilst I have the courage. I told you there was no room in our marriage for three people; well I've come to realize that there was always three parties in our marriage; you, me and my mates. After you left and I had a lot of time on my own, I started to realize what it must have been like for you trying to fill the evenings and weekends on your own when I was off with the boys. Even after my accident in Bali you were right, there was no good reason for me to come home but once surfing with the guys was off the agenda, well there just didn't seem to be any point hanging around. I could have stayed and spent the time with you like you wanted but I chose not to. It was stupid and selfish of me and it took you leaving for me to realize how hurtful that must have been for you.'

Rob paused but sensing he had more to say, Danni stayed silent, giving him time to compose his thoughts. 'I've spent a lot of time regretting that decision to leave Bali; a lot of time beating myself up about it. In the beginning I even convinced myself that if you'd never gone to Borneo and met this Rama fellow we'd still be together. But later I realized that Borneo or not, eventually you would have found someone else who would give you what I was too self-absorbed to.'

Danni's eyes were glistening. 'Oh Rob, it sounds like we've both spent the last six months blaming ourselves. Please don't think even for a moment that I went looking for love elsewhere. It just happened.' She reached across the table to squeeze his hand, pleased when he returned the gesture. They stared sadly at each other for a few moments, both realizing they'd taken the first important steps towards forgiveness and healing. Finally Rob sat back in his chair and took a sip of his now cold coffee. He grimaced and put it down, then regarded Danni thoughtfully.

'So why aren't you in Indonesia with Rama right now Danni? You still want to be with him?'

'Yes, more than anything,' she whispered.

'So what's stopping you?'

Tears filled Danni's eyes. 'I don't know Rob,' she admitted. 'I just haven't been able to go to him.'

'You feel like you need to do some penance before you deserve some happiness?'

Rob's insight was surprising, but in that moment Danni finally understood that was exactly what she was doing. In an instant her face crumpled and mortified, she put her hand to her mouth to stifle a sob. 'Yes'.

Rob stood and hauled her to her feet, wrapping her in his arms and holding her until the last of her sobs subsided. When he was sure she was done crying, he snagged a serviette off the table and passed it to her. 'Hey Danni?'

'What?'

'Consider your penance done okay. It's time to move on. For both of us.' He was right; it was time to move on. Suddenly Danni felt her heart swell with happiness. Who would have thought after everything that had happened it would be her soon-to-be ex-husband who would clear the way for her to be with Rama? Impulsively, Danni stood on tip-toe to kiss his cheek. 'Thank you Rob, you're a remarkable man,' she said smiling. 'Does this mean we can be friends?'

Tenderly Rob tacked a stray tendril of hair behind her ear and grinned. 'You know, I think it does.'

Danni returned to the office just long enough to hand in her notice, effective immediately, and clear out her desk as shocked colleagues watched on. Considering how important her career had been to her, it was shocking how easy it was to walk away from it. Danni's only thought was being with Rama. After months of procrastinating, suddenly all she could think about was getting to him as quickly as possible.

At her parents' home she deposited the box of personal items from her office on the sideboard inside the door.

'Hi dad,' she said breezing past her startled father on her way to the office to email Rama. 'I'll explain later.'

'No need,' he called after her. 'About time you came to your senses. You've kept that fella waiting long enough already.'

Danni waited impatiently for the computer to boot up then opened an email to Rama. Quoting lines from Ramayana, she wrote:

'What message am I to carry to Rama?'

'I am eager to be in his presence. That is all.'

There was no hesitation when she hit the send button. Danni was in the process of booking her flight to Bali for the very next day when Rama's reply popped up on the screen.

'Were they not Eternal Lovers reunited? And so they rejoiced like lovers come together after separation'

Come quickly my love. I've been waiting for you.

Danni's eyes were glistening as she finished booking her flight. She attached the flight confirmation to an email back to Rama and typed, *I'll be there tomorrow. I love you.*

Rama was obviously waiting by his computer because his reply came straight back.

This is going to be the longest night of my life. I love you too.

Danni was still grinning stupidly at the computer screen when another email popped up from him.

So does this mean you're going to marry me?

Yes, I think it does. If the offer still stands? she wrote back.

Never doubt it. I plan to make you my wife as soon as humanly possible.

I look forward to it. I'm afraid we might have to live in sin for a while though. Danni replied, trying not to think about how long it could take for her divorce to come through.

Oh I intend to be very sinful around you my love. Rama replied instantly, causing Danni to laugh delightedly.

Well then I look forward to that too! she wrote back.

You're killing me Danni. Did I say tonight was going to be the longest night of my life? You've just doubled it. There'll be punishment you realize?'

You started it! she reminded him.

Good point. You'll have to punish me too, he shot back.

You're incorrigible. But I'm completely crazy about you anyway. Now enough of this. I have packing to do, not to mention breaking the news to mum and dad.

I'm completely crazy about you too. See you tomorrow.

Danni waited a few minutes to make sure there were no more emails from Rama before she shut down the computer and went to find her parents.

'Well I haven't seen you smiling like that since I don't know when,' her mum said by way of greeting when she found them together in the kitchen. 'Except when Rama was here.'

Danni stood on tiptoe to give her a kiss on the cheek. 'Right now I feel happier than I have since I don't know when.' Danni propped herself on a stool at the breakfast counter next to her father and watched her mum chopping vegetables. She didn't offer to help knowing her mum would waive the offer away, citing Danni's long day at work.

'Listen, I have something to tell you.' She paused to take a deep breath. 'I'm going to join Rama in Bali.'

'Well we've been expecting it honey,' Bill told her matter-of-factly. 'Your mum and I knew as soon we saw you two together at the big fundraiser there was something between the two of you that was more than a passing fancy. It's time you got on with your life.'

'You've procrastinated long enough,' agreed Catherine. 'I know you feel bad about Rob but you can let that hold you back. He was never the right husband for you.'

'Well it might surprise you to know that it was Rob who convinced me it was time to put the past behind me and get on with my future with Rama,' said Danni feeling the need to defend her not-yet-former husband. 'We ran into each other in the city today so we had a coffee and cleared the air. You're right mum, I have been feeling terribly guilty about falling in love with Rama, wrecking our marriage and hurting Rob. But it turns out Rob has been doing some soul searching of his own and has pretty much came to the same conclusion as you. He took me for granted and put his own interests ahead of mine. Anyway, he told me it was time I stopped shouldering all the blame and time we both moved on. I guess it's what I needed to hear,' she finished with a shrug.

'Well, well, sounds like the boy has finally done some growing up,' her father commented.

'I'll never regret the years I spent with Rob but considering how things have turned out, I guess marriage wasn't the right option for us. But I do wonder where we'd be right now if I hadn't met Rama,' Danni pondered.

Catherine shook her head. 'Don't waste your time thinking about what might have been sweetheart; what's done is done. You've got a brighter, happier future with a man who adores you to look forward to.'

Danni reached across the bench to squeeze her mother's hand. 'You're right; no regrets and no what-might-have-beens.'

'That's my girl,' said Bill. 'No point kicking your heals around here when you've got a life with Rama waiting for you.'

'So you don't mind that I'll be living in Indonesia?'

'I'd be lying if I said I wouldn't prefer you to be living closer but sometimes fate makes decisions for us and we just have to accept them,' Catherine said. Danni noticed a look pass between her parents then her father delivered a bombshell of his own.

'Listen luv, don't worry about what we think. As I said before, we've been expecting this so we've been making a few plans of our own. Been thinking I might head on up to Indonesia myself and give Rama a bit of hand,' he said casually then laughed at his daughter's open-mouthed surprise. 'Actually it was Rama's idea; we talked about it a bit when he was here. Said he could use someone with my business skills and importing and exporting expertise. To be honest now your mum and I have had the big trip away, I'm struggling a bit with boredom—'

'—He's been driving me nuts,' her mother chimed in.

Bill grinned at his wife then continued, 'Anyway we reckon we could split our time between here, helping Rama wherever he needs me and catching a bit of downtime in Bali, especially if our daughter and the grand kiddies we're hoping for are going to be based there.'

'Dad that's a fantastic idea,' Danni enthused. 'I can't believe neither of you mentioned it until now.'

'Well, we didn't think it was appropriate to mention it until you'd made your move. Didn't want you thinking we were trying pressure you into anything with Rama; that was something you had to come to in your own good time. But you know after watching your dedication to fundraising for Helping Hands, meeting Rama and learning all about the organization, I'd made up my mind to volunteer my services to Helping Hands regardless of what happened with the two of you; it was just a matter of when. Tell you the truth I'm really looking forward to it. I've even started an online Indonesian language course.'

'My suggestion,' Catherine clarified. 'Gives your father something to do until we can get ourselves sorted out. Now tell me, when are you leaving?'

Danni squirmed uncomfortably on her stool. 'Um tomorrow actually,' she admitted then rushed on, 'I know it's sudden but now that I've made up my mind I can't wait to be with Rama. I'll have to come back soon to sort out all my stuff. After that I'll be back and forth fairly regularly; there's the divorce to deal with and I'll continue to run the fundraising side of things for Helping Hands of course.'

Catherine smiled lovingly at her daughter, 'Well honey, I expect you've got a lot of packing to do. Go and make a start and I'll call you when dinner's ready.'

Danni looked at both parents and felt a groundswell of love for them. Impulsively she hopped off the stool and caught first her mum and then her father in tight hugs. 'I love you guys,' she declared then practically bounced out of the kitchen on a tide of happiness.

EPILOGUE

1 year later

Leaving her high heeled shoes under the table, Danni left the shaded protection of the palm trees and wandered barefoot across the lush lawn and down to the water's edge, sighing contentedly as she sank her feet into the damp sand. In the late afternoon sunlight, the beach glowed golden beneath the pale blue sky and the dark silhouette of Mt Agung. Shielding her eyes against the glistening sea, Danni watched an outrigger sailing parallel to the beach, sail billowing in the light sea breeze. Nearby, several children swam and played around another outrigger moored inside the safety of the reef, climbing and jumping from the jutting prow.

Danni felt an overwhelming sense of contentment. This last year with Rama had been the happiest of her life in every sense. With Rama by her side, adapting to life in Indonesia had been easy. His parents Ngurah and Glen had welcomed her into the family without reservation and she had become extremely fond of them both. As well as mastering the language, she was learning about the Balinese culture and in this Ngurah had proven a generous and patient tutor. For the time being Danni and Rama shared the little flat above the Helping Hands office but she had a feeling they might soon be moving into the family compound and she didn't mind at all.

On a professional level, Danni had no regrets about walking away from her corporate marketing career. As well as her ongoing fundraising work for Helping Hands she was now helping out in other areas of the organization and finding immense satisfaction in the achievements of Helping Hands and the beneficiaries.

Her father had also followed through on his plans to volunteer his services to Helping Hands and was proving an invaluable addition to the team. Over the last twelve months Danni's parents had split their time between Australia, Bali and Borneo and Bill seemed to be thriving on the challenges that Helping Hands presented. Outside that, her parents had adapted to the ex-pat lifestyle with relative ease, establishing a growing network of friends among the local Balinese and ex-pat community and a firm friendship with Rama parents; so much so they had fast become a fixture around the Thom family compound.

There'd been more changes over the last year. Bel and Tim had finished their assignment and after spending a week with Danni and Rama in Bali, had returned to Australia to prepare for the birth of their first child. It was ironic thought Danni, that it was now she living and working overseas whilst they were adapting to normal life back in Perth; circumstances conspiring to keep the friends geographically separated, as was the case with Chris and Jenny, Emily and Dave and her other friends. But with modern communications it was easy to stay in touch and of course, Bali remained ever popular with Australians and if the past twelve months had been any indication, she and Rama would have no shortage of visitors.

Since joining Rama in Bali, Danni had accompanied him on several trips to Borneo. That first reunion with Ahmed, her and Rama's coming out as a couple, had been met with much jubilation by the big man who was convinced he played an integral part in their romance. He was here now, in Bali for the wedding and enjoying his first ever family holiday with the exception of his eldest daughter who was now at university in Jakarta, much to his immense pride.

Jon and Maya hadn't seemed surprised by her return and in the intervening months their early friendship had been firmly cemented. Recently, Jon had organized for Rama and Danni to return to the BOS rehabilitation centre to visit Sweetie-pie where Pieter had greeted them with the happy news that Sweetie had been transferred to the forest school where she was learning to fend for herself. He'd taken Rama and Danni into the protected forest to watch Sweetie and her fellow classmates climbing and foraging in the trees. It was almost impossible to reconcile the healthy, contented orangutan with the sickly baby they'd rescued a year and a half before.

Afterwards when they'd returned to Banjarmasin, Danni had asked Rama to take her back to the bird market from where they'd rescued Sweetie. They found her ex-captors still manning their stall and when Rama and Danni approached, the woman's eyes had flashed with recognition and wariness until Danni produced some photos of Sweetie-pie to show her. She looked at them carefully, smiling as she passed them to her husband, then clasped Danni's hands and with Rama acting as interpreter, told her that God had smiled on her family since they had given up Sweetie to them; they'd recently become proud grandparents of twin boys.

Hearing soft footfalls in the sand behind her, she smiled over her shoulder at Rama.

'Happy?' he asked hugging her to him.

'Very. You?'

'Ecstatic.'

Danni grinned, still not quite believing this wonderful man was now her husband. She snuggled back into his embrace, 'Danni Thom,' she said trying out her new name. 'I like it, actually I love it. It just sounds right.'

'That's because it is; this is what fate had in store for us Danni Thom,' he said looking down at her. 'We were meant to be.'

'Well I'm still pinching myself. I can't believe how much my life as changed over the last eighteen months.'

A shriek of childish laughter drew their attention to a group of children running down the sand towards the water. It was a large group, at least a dozen of whom belonged to Rama's extended family. Among the brown skinned Balinese children were Maya and Jon's children Dian and Bejo , Emily and Dave's two boys Mason and Jamie, and Danni's niece Nicola with her younger sister trailing behind, her little toddler legs pumping for all she was worth. Bringing up the rear at a far more relaxed pace, her sister-in-law Jenny, a heavily pregnant Emily and Bel with Danni's godson perched on her hip.

'Maybe we should start thinking about making one of our own,' Rama whispered in her ear as he planted a kiss on her neck.

'Hmm…It might be a little late for that,' said Danni smiling up at her soul mate. It took half a second for the penny to drop and the look on Rama's face when it did was priceless.

'What? You mean…you're pregnant!'

Danni nodded and laughed out loud, unable to contain her joy. It became a full throated laugh when Rama whooped excitedly and lifted her off the sand to swing her around in his arms. 'I take it you're happy with the news?' she asked when he finally put her down.

Rama placed a protective hand on her belly and kissed her firmly on the lips. 'Thrilled beyond words,' he said, giving Danni a look that was so chuffed and sappy at the same time that she couldn't help but laugh.

Watching the newlyweds from the cover of the palm trees, Catherine and Bill Lewis shared delighted smiles. 'Looks like we might have something else to celebrate,' Catherine observed.

'Looks like,' Bill agreed, thinking how pleased he'd been when he placed his daughters hand in Rama's a few hours ago, reciting from Ramayana as he did so.

Here is my daughter Sita, who will ever tread with you the path of dharma. Take her hand in yours. Blessed and devoted, she will ever walk with you like your own shadow.

Then Rama had surprised them all when he had taken Danni's hand and responded with his own version of the great Hindu epic:

Here am I Ramayana, who will ever tread with you the path of dharma. Take my hand in yours. Blessed and devoted, we will walk together side by side, united by fate and love for all eternity.

THE END

I hope you enjoyed this book as much as I enjoyed bringing the story and characters to life. I also write genre romance under the penname **Tess McCallum**. *If you're interested in checking it out, please take a look on the following pages…*

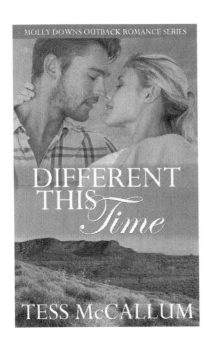

Different This Time

BOOK 1

Molly Downs Outback Romance Series

Ten years after fleeing her outback home, international model Jenny Hynes was back to settle her father's estate and close the book on their fractured relationship. She had no intention of sticking around any longer than absolutely necessary and certainly no intention of rekindling her relationship with the man who had shattered her tender, eighteen year old heart. If only he didn't still make her body sizzle with desire…

The moment Scott Armstrong set eyes on Jenny Hynes again, he was determined to win her back. But a decade is a long time and she was no longer the shy, impressionable girl who had won his heart. The new Jenny was confident, worldly and very, very guarded. It would take all his patience, persistence and a healthy dose of chemistry to convince her they were meant to be together.

One Time Thing

BOOK 2

Molly Downs Outback Romance Series

A year after her divorce, photographer Jess McAllister was ready to dip a toe back in the water. So when she found herself alone in the outback with a seriously hot chopper pilot it seemed like a perfect opportunity to have a little 'no strings attached' fun. Or so she thought…

For Teague Quinn, a little bit of Jess McAllister was never going to be enough. Maybe he was old fashioned but he firmly believed when two people connected the way they did it was worth pursuing. So when fate stepped in and brought them together again, it was an opportunity not to be squandered.

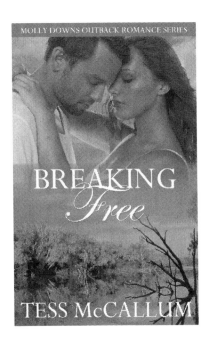

Breaking Free

BOOK 3

Molly Downs
Outback Romance
Series

Heiress Katrina Redmond was heartily sick of living the life her father had mapped out for her. Six months ago she'd finally made a stand and had been engaged in a battle of wills with her father ever since. His latest attempt to draw her back into the family business involved blackmailing her into attending a corporate wilderness fishing camp. She didn't do wilderness, she didn't fish and she didn't want to be there so it was always was going to be a disaster. But she hadn't expected to get her heart broken as well.

Dillon Armstrong never mixed business with pleasure but where Katrina Redmond was concerned he just couldn't seem to help himself. The chemistry between them was sizzling hot but the more time they spend together, the more she intrigued him in other ways. And that wasn't good for a guy who had sworn off serious relationships years ago and had no intention of changing his mind.

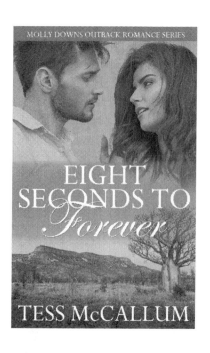

Eight Seconds To Forever

BOOK 4

Molly Downs Outback Romance Series

Anthropologist Taylor Armstrong was smart, dedicated and hard working. As a born and raised country girl, she had nothing against cowboys. But when a certain footloose fancy free cowboy with a love-them-and-leave-them reputation wandered into her life, she wasn't about to invest time or energy in a relationship that was going nowhere. No matter how tempting he was.

When Mac Dawson's old boarding school mate offered him a place to hole up whilst he figured out what to do with the rest of his life now that his professional rodeo career was over, he gladly accepted. Messing with his friend's sister wasn't exactly the ideal way to say thank you but Taylor Armstrong PhD was just too darn irresistible. Besides, no one had ever accused him of being a gentleman.

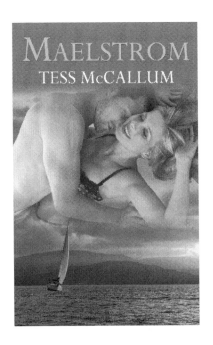

Maelstrom

- A powerful whirlpool often hazardous to approach.

- Any state of affairs signified by turmoil, disorder, confusion, chaos or upheaval.

- The romance between Erin Johnson and Drew Bradley.

After years focusing on her career, Erin Johnson surprised everyone including herself when she turned her back on Sydney and headed north to start a new life. Everything was going great with the exception of her prickly new boss who was determined to think the worst of her one minute and was kissing her senseless the next.

Drew Bradley recognized trouble when he saw it and his sexy new Marketing Manager was trouble with a capital T. As far as he was concerned, the sooner she got sick of small town living and headed back to the city the better. In the meantime, all he has to do is keep her away from his best friend and keep a lid on his desire.

25534674R00190

Printed in Poland
by Amazon Fulfillment
Poland Sp. z o.o., Wrocław